MW00606530

Strangers in the Night

*Law and Medicine in
the Managed Care Era*

Strangers in the Night

*Law and Medicine in
the Managed Care Era*

PETER D. JACOBSON

OXFORD
UNIVERSITY PRESS
2002

OXFORD

UNIVERSITY PRESS

Oxford   New York

Auckland   Bangkok   Buenos Aires   Cape Town   Chennai
Dar es Salaam   Delhi   Hong Kong   Istanbul   Karachi   Kolkata
Kuala Lumpur   Madrid   Melbourne   Mexico City   Mumbai   Nairobi
São Paulo   Shanghai   Singapore   Taipei   Tokyo   Toronto

and an associated company in Berlin

Copyright © 2002 by Oxford University Press, Inc.

Published by Oxford University Press, Inc.
198 Madison Avenue, New York, New York 10016

www.oup.com

Oxford is a registered trademark of Oxford University Press

All rights reserved. No part of this publication may be reproduced,
stored in a retrieval system, or transmitted, in any form or by any means,
electronic, mechanical, photocopying, recording, or otherwise,
without the prior permission of Oxford University Press.

Library of Congress Cataloging-in-Publication Data

Jacobson, Peter D.
Strangers in the night : law and medicine in the managed care era /
Peter D. Jacobson.
p. cm.
Includes bibliographical references and index.
ISBN 0-19-515271-9 (cloth : alk. paper)
1. Managed care plans (Medical care)—Law and legislation—United States.
2. Medical care—Law and legislation—United States.
3. Medical laws and legislation—United States.
4. Medical policy—United States.   I. Title.
KF1183 .J33 2002
344.73'032104258—dc21   2002022908

2 4 6 8 9 7 5 3 1

Printed in the United States of America
Since this page cannot legibly accommodate all the copyright notes,
the page following constitutes an extension of the copyright page.

Excerpts and adaptations from the following articles are used in this book with permission from the respective publishers:

M.T. Cahill and P.D. Jacobson, "Pegram's Regress: A Missed Chance for Sensible Judicial Review of Managed Care Decisions," *American Journal of Law & Medicine*, vol. 27:4 (Winter 2001): 421–38 (© 2001, reprinted with permission of the American Society of Law, Medicine & Ethics. May not be reproduced without express written consent).

P.D. Jacobson and M.T. Cahill, "Applying Fiduciary Responsibilities in the Managed Care Context," *American Journal of Law & Medicine*, vol. 26:2&3 (Summer/Fall 2000): 155–74 (© 2000, reprinted with permission of the American Society of Law, Medicine & Ethics. May not be reproduced without express written consent).

P.D. Jacobson, "Legal Challenges to Managed Care Cost Containment Programs: An Initial Assessment," *Health Affairs* 1999; 18 (4):69–85.

P.D. Jacobson and Matthew L. Kanna, "Cost-Effectiveness Analysis in the Courts: Recent Trends and Future Prospects," *Journal of Health Politics, Policy and Law* 2001; 26:291–326.

P.D. Jacobson, "Regulating Health Care: From Self-Regulation to Self-Regulation," *Journal of Health Politics, Policy and Law*, 2001; 26:1095–1107.

P.D. Jacobson and K.E. Warner, "Litigation and Public Health Policy: The Case of Tobacco Control," *Journal of Health Politics, Policy and Law* 1999; 24:769–804.

P.D. Jacobson, E. Selvin, and S.D. Pomfret, "The Role of Courts in Shaping Health Policy: An Empirical Analysis," *Journal of Law, Medicine & Ethics*, 29:3&4 (2001): 278–89 (© 2001, reprinted with permission of the American Society of Law, Medicine & Ethics. May not be reproduced without express written consent).

P.D. Jacobson and S.D. Pomfret, "ERISA Litigation and Physician Autonomy," *Journal of the American Medical Association* 2000; 283:921–26 (© 2000, American Medical Association).

M.G. Bloche and P.D. Jacobson, "The Supreme Court and Bedside Rationing," *Journal of the American Medical Association* 2000; 284:2776–79 (© 2000, American Medical Association).

P.D. Jacobson and N.M. Patil, "Managed Care Litigation: Legal Doctrine at the Boundary of Contract and Tort," *Medical Care Research and Review* 2000; 57:440–463 (© 2000 by Sage Publications, reprinted by Permission of Sage Publications, Inc).

For Linda, Alexander, and Hannah—
with much love and gratitude

PREFACE

IF law seems omnipresent in American culture, there is a good reason for that impression. In recent years, the public has experienced a veritable civics lesson in how the legal system operates. Whether it is the role of the courts in deciding presidential elections, the spectacle of the O. J. Simpson murder trial (with its celebrity fixation), or the drama of the Clinton impeachment (with its mix of perjury allegations and salacious details of sexual misconduct), the law has provided some of the country's most riveting and shared cultural experiences.

In some ways, the public's fascination with the law is nothing new. Think back to other events that have shaped our cultural history and shared experiences: many times those events involved the legal system, especially criminal trials. The Lindberg kidnapping case, the Rosenberg espionage trials, the "Impeach Earl Warren" signs so prevalent in the South to protest the judicial assault on segregation and the famous Miranda warnings, all revolved around the role the legal system plays in shaping our public consciousness. Some of the most highly-rated television shows, such as *LA Law* and *The Practice*, reflect the human drama played out in the courts on a daily basis.

We are, after all, a nation of laws, and the rule of law is what binds us together as a society. So it should not be surprising that the law is integral to and shapes many of our social institutions. But it does so in ways more enduring and much less obvious than the high-profile legal cases that absorb our short-term attention. The role of the legal system in shaping our health-care delivery system is a perfect example.

Most people probably think of law and medicine as being two separate, though prestigious, professions that occupy independent realms. It seems doubtful that the average patient stops to think about how the legal system might influence the physician–patient relationship, or how legislation might shape the organization and financing of health care. Nor are patients likely to ponder the role courts might play in permitting or rejecting managed care's cost-containment programs.

In fact, the legal system plays a far more substantial role in health-care delivery than most people might suspect. It does so through regulatory oversight of medical practice, legislation mandating that certain benefits must be provided, and judicial rulings imposing liability for substandard medical care. The legal system also determines who may obtain a license to practice medicine and the scope of medical practice. More than ever before, the legal system is an integral part of virtually every aspect of the modern health-care system, from its organization to how it is financed and delivered. Patients thus have a large stake in how the legal system oversees medical care. This book explains how the legal system helps shape health-care delivery and policy, offers new ways of looking at and understanding the relationship between law and medicine, and reflects on why it all matters.

Every day (or so it seems) some aspect of the connection between law and medicine is in the news, even if the public does not always make the connection. For example, the congressional debate over patients' rights legislation is not just about whether patients should be able to sue their managed care organization (MCO) for delayed or denied health care. It is also about appropriate legal oversight of the managed care industry. Discussions about whether MCOs should have external review processes to reconsider the denial of health care involve questions of legal process.

Protecting the right to sue is not the only aspect of law and medicine that gets our attention. News articles detail threats to privacy from the availability of sensitive information, such as the results of genetic tests, and the need to develop appropriate legal protections. And the transformation of health care into a large business enterprise unavoidably involves legal rules and regulations.

In the not-too-distant past, patients did not need to be as aware of the legal system's involvement in health care as they do today. All that has changed with the arrival of managed care. Patients raised on the fee-for-service system, with its much simpler structure, may well be confused by the bewildering array of health-care terms, and options, acronyms, including PPOs (Preferred Provider Organizations), POSs (Point of Service plans), and IPAs (Independent Practice Associations). At one time, physicians had almost complete control over health-care delivery, and patients could look to physicians to secure their health-care needs. That control changed with the advent of managed care as the prevailing health-care delivery system. Managed care, which arose largely out of dissatisfaction with unlimited cost increases in the fee-for-service system, imposes limits on physicians autonomy that were not present in fee-for-service medical care. Patients may well feel overwhelmed and insecure about the transition to the new system.

After a period of optimism that managed care might solve the problem of rising health-care costs, there is now a widespread public perception that it compromises patients' ability to receive high-quality medical treatment. Not surprisingly, patients are expressing increased discontent with managed care. Naturally, dissatisfied patients take their complaints to the legal system—either to request legislation to protect individual access to health-care services or to challenge in court the denial of health-care benefits.

An important question for patients, physicians, health-care administrators, and policy makers is how the legal system will respond to managed care's perceived shortcomings. In managed care, the need to preserve the plan's resources for the patient population can take priority over the individual patient's needs. In a world where cost matters much more than it once did, and where access to health care remains a critical policy objective, one goal cannot be abandoned for the other—the two goals must be balanced. Will the courts be able to balance the two goals in resolving patients' litigation against managed care plans? Will the legal system put limits on the operation of cost-containment strategies, or will the law largely defer to the marketplace to determine how health care is delivered? Under any circumstances, the legal system will play an important role in deciding how the trade-offs between conflicting policy objectives will be resolved.

The rapidly changing health-care delivery system and the legal system's role in overseeing how the managed care system operates provide a perfect opportunity for a broad discussion about law and medicine. As the book's title implies, attorneys and physicians are not exactly partners in resolving problems in the health-care delivery system. The level of mistrust between the legal and medical professions is deep and has adverse implications for patient care that must be addressed. Despite this mistrust, law and medicine are in fact closely connected and interact visibly on many levels. How they interact—namely, their ability to cooperate and accommodate professional differences—has important implications for health-care delivery.

The managed care system and the legal system's response to it are still evolving. Already, the managed care system shows signs of significant change from what it was just ten years ago, having moved away from health maintenance organizations (HMOs) toward more flexible health plans. To a certain extent, therefore, the book tells a story before its ending is clear. It explains how the legal system is responding to a new and radically transformed social institution while the transformation and legal response are still under way. Telling the story now will help readers make sense of the remarkable changes taking place in health care.

The scope of this book grew from an attempt to address a relatively straightforward question: what role does the judicial system play in shaping health policy? The answer is by no means obvious. Addressing the question requires equal consideration of the legislature's role and of the relationship between attorneys and physicians. The book explains the development of legal doctrine in response to managed care and describes the interchange between the courts and the legislative branch, as each struggles to reconcile difficult policy choices. Some readers may reject the notion that the courts should have any role whatsoever in setting health policy, while others will accept that role only reluctantly. But there is no denying the reality that courts are an integral part of the nation's policy-making process, whether for health-care delivery, tele-communications, or the environment. If so, we must assess the implications of judicial involvement in contested areas of social policy, examine how different legal rules might affect policy, and suggest how courts might improve their decision-making process.

The book is divided into three parts. Part I describes the historical context of the relationship between law and medicine. Chapter 1 provides an overview of how law and medicine interact. Chapters 2 and 3 ask how that relationship has developed and why it matters, focusing on current policy debates. Chapter 2 examines the beginning of the relationship, from its antecedents in the early 1800s until World War II. Then, Chapter 3 traces the momentous changes in the relationship after World War II to the present, focusing on the transition to managed care as the dominant health-care system. These chapters show how the law has moved from the periphery of health care to the center of managed care as a business enterprise.

Part II considers how the judicial system has responded to managed care. The courts are in the midst of developing legal doctrine (rules) in managed care, and the guiding principles are still in dispute. It may be instructive to examine how courts struggled to understand and deal with similar social and economic upheavals in the past. To provide a historical context for litigation in the managed care era, Chapter 4 explores how courts responded to previous industrial transformations, examining the introduction of railroads and the distribution of mass-produced goods.

Since readers may not be entirely familiar with the legal system and its specific relationship to health care, Chapters 5 through 7 will include sections outlining basic legal issues in nontechnical language. Without some background on the interplay between legislation and common law doctrine, the explanation of how and why the courts have decided managed care cases will be incomplete.

Chapter 5 examines the scholarly debate over whether legal doctrine in managed care should be determined by contract or by tort remedies. The discussion is not simply an abstract academic exercise. To the contrary, the outcome of this debate will have important practical implications for patients who believe that their medical care has been improperly delayed or denied.

Tort law has traditionally been available to correct harms to individuals. A strict contract approach would considerably limit an individual's ability to challenge an MCO's delay or denial of care.

In Chapters 6 and 7, we will explore the trends to date in litigation challenging various managed care practices. By following judicial decision making as courts grapple with the policy conflicts created by managed care, we can come to a better understanding of how difficult it is for courts to respond to dramatic changes in social institutions. We will also consider what the appropriate policy response should be, in view of the developing legal trends. Chapter 8 concludes this part by examining the meaning of the judicial cases for the physician–patient relationship and how the judicial and legislative branches of government interact to influence health-care delivery and policy.

The last part of the book, Part III, deals with the health policy and health-care delivery implications of judicial decisions. This part describes ways to accommodate and reconcile the relationship between law and medicine (attorneys and physicians) in the managed care era and ways to restore the physician–patient relationship to the center of health-care delivery. Part III offers an approach that might help reconcile the differences between the two professions and deal more effectively with the managed care environment.

Chapter 9 sets forth the underlying causes of the mutual antagonism between physicians and attorneys. It then outlines why it is that scholars and commentators have focused on the differences between the two professions rather than their similarities. Unfortunately, shared experiences and values between attorneys and physicians have been overlooked and are actually more important in the managed care era than the differences. There is nothing inevitable about the antagonism between physicians and attorneys.

Chapter 10 presents an approach to address patient and physician discontent with the managed care system. The approach is based on the concept of fiduciary duty, which is the duty of loyalty a physician owes to a patient or an attorney owes to a client. For judges and health-care administrators, a fiduciary-duty framework will be a useful mechanism in balancing the conflicting policy objectives of cost containment and access to health-care services. The fiduciary duty principle also offers an alternative way for physicians and attorneys to focus on their shared values and experiences rather than on their differences.

Chapter 11 discusses the practical and policy implications of the interaction between the legal and health-care systems. This chapter also reflects on how judicial decision making affects health-care delivery, and considers how physicians, administrators, and attorneys can better communicate to minimize the disruptions occasioned by the emergence of managed care and potential intervention by the courts. I ask and answer several questions raised by the overlapping stories presented throughout the book: Why should we care about the relationship between law and medicine? Can the law be an effective instrument for returning the physician–patient relationship to the center of the health-care enterprise? How do judicial decisions fit within the broader health policy environment? Is there too much law in health care? Chapter 11 concludes with final thoughts about law, medicine, and legal accountability.

Ann Arbor, Michigan   P.D.J.

ACKNOWLEDGMENTS

THROUGHOUT the research and writing of this book, I have benefited from the help of extraordinary research assistants. At the University of Michigan, former students Scott Pomfret, Michael Cahill, Neena Patil, Rosemary Quigley, Elizabeth Selvin and Soheil Soliman provided both expert research and outstanding analysis. Pomfret's and Cahill's imprint on my thinking is reflected in the articles we have co-authored and in my approach to judicial decision making.

I have also benefited from the advice and suggestions of outstanding colleagues at the University of Michigan and at RAND, where the research was originally conceived. Two University of Michigan colleagues—Ed Goldman, the Medical Center's attorney, and Peter Hammer at the Law School—have generously spent many hours responding to various theories and approaches. My colleagues at the School of Public Health have encouraged and supported my work and have created an environment where scholarship is integral to the teaching mission.

At the formative stages of this work, my former RAND colleagues Deborah Hensler (now at Stanford Law School) and Jeffrey Wasserman provided intellectual guidance and support in shaping the research. Jeffrey read the entire manuscript and provided indispensable advice. My gratitude is enormous for his invaluable insight into health policy, and his many suggestions of language to clarify the narrative. Jon Merz (now at the University of Pennsylvania) provided excellent suggestions on which types of cases to review. Julie Martinez, then a UCLA law student, and Brigitte Sheehan-Watanabe, then a Loyola of Los Angeles law student, assisted ably during the project's early stages. Stanley Siegelman provided expert editorial review. And I owe special gratitude to my secretary, Susan Corner, for her expert and painstaking work on the manuscript.

I am grateful for the funding and support of the Robert Wood Johnson Foundation's Investigator Award in Health Policy Research Program. Early in the project, Robin Osborn and the late Sol Levine were instrumental in helping me think about how best to organize my research. During subsequent phases, Al Tarlov and Barbara Krimgold provided support and encouragement for expanding the research into new and fruitful directions. At the editing stage, David Mechanic and Lynn Rogut provided additional funding.

Several health law colleagues have read and critiqued various aspects of this book. David Hyman at the University of Maryland Law School, Haavi Morreim at the University of Tennessee at Memphis, Marc Rodwin at Suffolk University Law School, Gregg Bloche at Georgetown Law Center, and Gail Agrawal at the University of North Carolina Law School have provided valuable insight into the issues discussed. Daniel Lang, M.D., and Sally J. Rubenstone, M.D., provided key advice from their perspective as physicians. I am also indebted to the journal editors and anonymous peer reviewers whose comments on articles helped improve various aspects of the book. The comments from three anonymous peer reviewers helped shape the final manuscript, and I received expert advice from Jeffrey House at Oxford University Press in preparing the book for publication.

Last, but certainly not least, my wife and children have been incredibly supportive of my work, often at their own expense. I owe them everything and dedicate the book to them. I, of course, take full responsibility for the contents of this book. Any remaining errors are mine alone.

CONTENTS

PART I

Historical Perspectives on Law and Medicine

1

Law and Medicine—An Overview

WE live in a very litigious age. For some, litigation is a means to change public policy; for others, it is a cudgel to deter future careless behavior. But most people resort to litigation to recover damages from injury or to protect a contractual or property interest.[1] Patients, for instance, may seek to recover damages after they fail to receive expected health-care benefits or after medical intervention goes awry.

Not too long ago, a patient's individual case against a health-care provider was important for that patient but had few broad social or political implications. Now a single case can potentially attack the heart of the health-care delivery system by directly challenging the cost-control concepts and financial incentives that propel the managed care revolution. True, it is unlikely that any one case will so dramatically undermine the health-care system. Yet the mere possibility that a lawsuit would terrify an industry says a great deal about the role of courts in health care and raises some fundamental questions: What is it about managed care that makes it so vulnerable to litigation? How can the courts resolve the difficult policy choices presented by managed care's cost-containment programs? More to the point, why are the courts involved in social and political questions anyway?

The conventional wisdom is that it is easy to win large verdicts against businesses with "deep pockets" (i.e., considerable financial assets), especially industries that are unpopular. Commentators who argue that the tort system is a lottery promoting frivolous litigation to extort settlements from innocent but wealthy corporations further encourage this perception. (*Torts* are civil wrongs where an injured person seeks monetary damages for the harm suf-

3

fered.) Medical malpractice litigation is an area often cited by critics of the tort system for just these types of abuses. So it may come as a surprise that people suing a managed care organization (MCO) often do not win their case.

Take, for example, what happened to Diane Andrews-Clarke.[2] Ms. Andrews-Clarke maintained a health insurance plan through her employer for herself; her husband, Richard Clarke; and their four children. In 1994, Mr. Clarke was admitted to the hospital for alcohol detoxification and medical evaluation. He was diagnosed with alcohol dependence and related physical symptoms. Under the insurance plan, any treatment needed preauthorization from a utilization review (UR) firm. (Utilization review is a process designed to evaluate the appropriateness of the proposed medical treatment based on established medical criteria.) Although the insurance plan provided for one 30-day inpatient rehabilitation stay per year, the utilization review firm authorized only five days. Less than one month after the discharge, he resumed drinking and voluntarily admitted himself to a different hospital. This time, the UR firm approved eight additional inpatient days. After only one day following the second discharge, another drinking binge led to a failed suicide attempt and then involuntary commitment to a 30-day inpatient detoxification program. The UR firm refused to pay for this private placement, despite the terms of the insurance contract, and Mr. Clarke was sent to a public institution. As the court then put it, "Clarke's life now spiraled inexorably down and out of control." Episodes of heavy drinking were followed by hospitalization. At age 41, Richard Clarke committed suicide.

After his death, Ms. Andrews-Clarke sued Travelers Insurance and the UR firm in the Massachusetts state court system. She asserted ". . . that her husband's death was the direct and foreseeable result of the improper refusal of Travelers and its agent Greenspring [the UR firm] to authorize appropriate medical and psychiatric treatment. . . ." The primary legal bases for the lawsuit were breach of contract, medical malpractice, and wrongful death. In the conventional wisdom, this should have been an easy case for Ms. Andrews-Clarke (the plaintiff) to win—so easy that one might have expected Travelers (the defendant) to settle the case quickly for a large sum of money. In reality, the case was just the opposite. Ms. Andrews-Clarke's lawsuit was dismissed in federal court without a trial, even though the judge in the case, William Young, said that "the tragic events set forth in Diane Andrews-Clarke's complaint cry out for relief."

Not too long after Ms. Andrews-Clarke lost her case, Teresa Goodrich was awarded a $120.5 million verdict against Aetna U.S. Healthcare in a case remarkably similar to the Andrews-Clarke situation. In the Goodrich case,[3] 41-year-old David Goodrich was diagnosed with leiomyosarcoma, a rare form of cancer classified as a soft tissue sarcoma. Goodrich was advised to have the cancer treated with high-dose chemotherapy and a bone marrow transplant.

These procedures are very expensive and are considered by many to be experimental. Even with Aetna's initial willingness to cover the treatment, it took four months to begin the procedure because of delays in referrals and arranging to see out-of-plan specialists. During the interim, the cancer metastasized to his liver, forcing physicians to abandon the planned treatment in favor of standard-dose chemotherapy.

After some improvement following the treatment, the cancer returned. Aetna physicians then approved a cryosurgical resection, and proceeded without financial approval from the health plan. Even though Aetna subsequently paid for the resection, the plan initially denied payment because Mr. Goodrich sought care without prior approval. Aetna defended its process by saying that the payment decisions had no effect on the outcome and that all of the requested treatment was provided. Following Mr. Goodrich's death, Ms. Goodrich sued and was awarded $116 million in punitive damages because the jury felt that Aetna was guilty of bad faith in delaying Goodrich's treatment. (Bad faith met the California standard of fraud, malice, and oppression, for awarding punitive damages.) According to one juror, "We wanted to send a message that everybody deserves to be treated fairly, especially when they are sick."[4]

Here we have two comparable cases, at least in general outline, but with dramatically different results. From a distance, it would seem that the stronger case lost while the weaker case won. If either should have benefited from a jury's anger, the Andrews-Clarke situation appears to be more compelling, though it produced nothing. Some observers might be tempted to argue that the two cases reflect the random and capricious nature of litigation. Instead, the results can be explained by the interaction between legislatures and courts in setting health-care policy. Far from being erratic and arbitrary, these judicial decisions follow from policy choices made by legislatures, from the unintended consequences of ambiguous legislative language, and from the difficulties courts face in responding to a rapidly changing industry. In many cases, legislative policies leave judges little choice but to confirm results they believe are unjust.

The facts leading up to the Andrews-Clarke and Goodrich litigation, along with the reasoning behind the courts' contrasting responses, help us set the context for some of the central premises and tensions underlying the legal system's response to managed care and to conflicting public policy objectives. Each case is indicative of what any patient may face in navigating through both the health-care and legal systems. Whatever one thinks about the ultimate results, the reasons why the cases were resolved differently offer a revealing glimpse into the major challenges now roiling the health-care industry. Periodically I will return to these cases to explore and reexamine several facets of the relationship between law and medicine. One facet is how the courts have responded to managed care's cost-containment initiatives and the inevitable questions about conflicts of interest regarding the allocation of resources under managed care. An equally important part of the story is how physicians and attorneys deal with one another and how their mutual antagonism affects patient care. In the end, the lessons from the two stories will coalesce in an approach that can improve judicial decision making and provide the basis for accommodating the disparate interests of physicians and attorneys.[5]

That approach is anchored in the concept of *fiduciary* duty. Briefly, a *fiduciary* is someone who is entrusted to act for the benefit of another person. Physicians and attorneys, for example, owe fiduciary duties to their patients and clients, respectively.[6] In the fiduciary-duty framework, health plans would use procedures to reach impartial health-care decisions based on the best available medical and scientific evidence. A health plan fiduciary would be required to objectively balance the merits of an individual health plan member's care with the financial effects of that care on the entire health plan.

The fiduciary-duty framework provides a way for health plans to ensure that individual medical decisions are not compromised by cost-containment objectives. Implementing the fiduciary duty framework is important for patients because it directly addresses their concerns that an MCO may arbitrarily deny or delay needed health care without adequate explanation. As we will see, it also protects the primacy of the physician–patient relationship.

Strengthened judicial oversight is a key component of the fiduciary-duty approach. Judicial review allows the courts to support the viability of managed care's cost-containment objectives while still protecting the individual's legitimate medical needs. In this way, the law can be instrument for restoring a proper balance between individual patients and the MCO's patient population.

Applying the fiduciary-duty framework to the world of managed care is not necessarily a simple solution to the problems it addresses; but simple solutions have not been very effective so far. Even if initially complex, attorneys, physicians, and health care administrators already apply fiduciary-duty principles in their everyday work. Since they are likely to be comfortable with a method that puts fiduciary duty at the core of clinical decisions, it may also provide an opportunity to mitigate the antagonism between physicians and attorneys. Combining the concept of fiduciary duty with an enhanced oversight role for the courts can inject new fairness and clarity into managed care decisions. A decision-making process rooted in fairness would begin to restore Americans' trust in their health-care system.

At the end of his opinion in the Andrews-Clarke case, Judge Young asked provocatively: "Does anyone care? Do you?" Or, to reframe Judge Young's questions somewhat, why should we care? This book addresses a range of issues that will help us understand how and why Judge Young felt compelled to rule against Ms. Andrews-Clarke, how he came to ask such despairing questions, why Ms. Andrews-Clarke lost while Ms. Goodrich won her case, and why these cases matter to us.

The Health Policy Context

During the past two decades, the health-care system has undergone a radical transformation in how health care is organized, financed, and delivered. Health care has shifted away from a system in which individual physicians provide care for individual patients and toward a system characterized by large patient populations within integrated delivery systems. The generic name for the new health-care delivery system is *managed care.* Perhaps the most dominant social force behind this transformation has been the need to contain the rising cost of delivering health-care services.

The concept of managed care poses a direct challenge to many long-held assumptions and how we think about health-care delivery. For many Americans, managed care is a forbidding world of new concepts and acronyms that barely existed in the public consciousness 10–20 years ago. Consider just a few of the health-care terms, acronyms, or concepts that have entered the public vernacular and policy debate within the past decade or so: managed care, managed care organizations (MCOs), capitation, independent practice associations (IPAs), health maintenance organizations (HMOs), preferred provider organizations (PPOs), point-of-service (POSs) plans, utilization review, drive-through deliveries, and the Employee Retirement Income Security Act (ERISA). This partial list represents not just a new language of health-care delivery, but an imposing, formidable, and sometimes impenetrable environment to navigate. Patients' complaints about managed care may stem as much from confusion as from dissatisfaction. Before discussing where the courts fit in, it might be useful to say a few words about managed care, how and why it emerged, how it differs from the traditional fee-for-service system, and what the important health-care policy and delivery implications are.[7]

Prior to the advent of managed care, fee-for-service medicine dominated the delivery of medical care. In the fee-for-service system, which has not been entirely displaced by managed care, patients pay a fee for each visit and service provided. The patient either pays for the care out-of-pocket, or more typically after World War II, the employer provides it through a third-party commercial indemnity insurer. In this system, the financing and health-care delivery aspects are arranged by separate organizations. The insurer pays for what the physician orders (assuming the benefit is covered by the insurance premium) with minimal interference or oversight by the insurer. Any contractual problems with the insurance carrier are resolved by bringing a breach of contract case. Problems with medical treatment are resolved exclusively with the medical care provider, perhaps by suing for medical malpractice.

From the rise of modern medicine to prominence after World War II until the early 1990s, health-care delivery and health policy were largely dominated by physicians.[8] When fee-for-service medicine was dominant, there was very little interference with physician autonomy (i.e., full control over medical decisions) from insurers, hospital administrators, or patients. At the time, prepaid care—the upfront payment of a fixed premium in return for a range of health-care services that has come to be called managed care—was limited in scope and isolated from the dominant fee-for-service sector. As an industry, fee-for-service medicine was hostile to the idea of prepaid health care; physicians encouraged and supported laws impeding the expansion of prepaid care.[9] Most important, the costs of care mattered little to either patients or physicians. To physicians, the only issue was the care a patient needed—cost was not generally a consideration. Except for the premium charge, the entire health-care bill was paid by a third party insurer. No one in the system had much of an incentive to control costs (what economists term "moral hazard," which means that people change their behavior when insurance protects them from the consequences of their actions).[10]

Managed care revolutionized health-care delivery by combining the financing and medical (clinical) aspects into one package.[11] Instead of paying a fee for each service, the patient subscribes to a managed care plan for a monthly fee that covers and provides a defined set of benefits. For each visit or service, patients may be required to make an additional co-payment of $5 to $20. At the heart of managed care is the promise that a new approach could lower costs by imposing restraints on the amount of care provided without sacrificing quality of care. To achieve these goals, managed care initiated the widespread use of cost-containment practices and financial incentives to encourage physicians to limit medical treatment. These practices range from aggressive utilization review to *capitated funding arrangements* (i.e., paying physicians a set monthly fee for each managed care member to provide needed health-care services). Other cost controls include limitations on choice of providers, limitations on benefits (e.g., ten physical therapy visits), exclusive contracting arrangements with a single physician group, and financial incentives such as bonuses and withholds (i.e., end-of-year payments based on controlling health-care resources). While these techniques are now also used by commercial insurers, managed care providers have been much more aggressive in using them.

From a public policy perspective, there are significant differences in the two approaches. In the fee-for-service era, the primary regulatory questions dealt with curbing incentives for overutilizing health-care services and monitoring the quality of medical practice. Quality concerns remain in the managed care environment, but new uncertainties appear. In managed care, the pressure is to underutilize health-care services, just the inverse of the fee-for-service incentives. The regulatory structure must therefore develop new tools to ensure that the public has access to needed services.

Another difference, important to both policy makers and patients, is who controls health-care resources. In the fee-for-service system, the physician was dominant, and his or her autonomy was preserved. For the insured patient, this meant almost unlimited access to health-care services. But the shift to managed care reduces the physician's autonomy and emphasizes cost-containment initiatives at the expense of both physician autonomy and the physician–patient relationship. For the patient, this means potentially less access to health-care services and greater difficulties in maneuvering through the system. For physicians, the central dilemma in the new health-care environment is being caught between their moral and professional obligations to provide individual patients with appropriate care and the health plans' desire to control costs. The conflict faced by physicians and health plan administrators between the health-care needs of individual patients and the need to preserve scarce resources for other patients in the health plan shapes both the political and legal setting for managed care. Physicians must now weigh the patient's best welfare against the financial and professional cost of being overly generous in ordering tests and medical interventions.[12]

Adding to the complexity of the problem, administrators and physicians potentially infuse their own economic interests in making individual clinical decisions. Every health plan administrator must consider how individual medical decisions will affect the availability of the health plan's financial resources for all other plan members. Health policy scholars use the phrase *resource allocation* to describe the trade-offs between spending health-care dollars on individual patients or on an MCO's entire patient population. Administrators operating a for-profit health plan also need to satisfy shareholders' expectations.

Physicians, too, are rightly concerned that reconciling patient expectations for fee-for-service levels of care with the economic constraints of a managed care environment places them in a vulnerable position. They cannot simultaneously satisfy both interests without sacrificing either their own economic interests or their professional obligation to the patient. The omnipresent threat of malpractice liability exposure for inadequate care acts as a reminder that current legal doctrine (i.e., the development of judicial rules that guide subsequent behavior) still demands adherence to levels of care more appropriate to a fee-for-service system. This is a difficult, if not untenable, situation for doctors.

Traditional medical ethics placed the physician–patient relationship at the center of the clinical encounter, not at the periphery. Managed care moves the physician–patient relationship to the periphery of health care through financial incentives designed to reduce health-care use, with less concern for continuity of care.[13] A physician's responsibility to the MCO's patient population puts additional strain on that relationship. As an ethical transformation, this represents a fundamental philosophical shift away from the prevailing medical ethos that the needs of the individual patient always come before other values, including reducing health-care costs. It also represents a profound social and economic challenge to the physician's control over health-care resource allocation decisions.

Whatever the benefits of a patient-centered health-care system, it had one obvious flaw that was exposed with the increasing availability of high-technology medicine—it did a poor job of controlling costs. The inexorable rise in health-care costs that began in the late 1960s was not sustainable. It still took until the early 1980s before policy makers seriously addressed cost containment, and until the late 1980s before the health-care industry began to attack rising costs. As one scholar has observed: "Perhaps the most profound change spawned by the current economic upheaval is the introduction of competing goals into health care. Cost is now highly relevant and patients' benefit is no longer the sole objective."[14] Managed care became the primary vehicle for cost containment in the 1990s.

The concept of prepaid health care had its origins in the late 1800s, and its operational beginnings in the late 1920s and early 1930s. It became part of the public policy agenda in the early 1970s under the name of *health maintenance organizations* (HMOs). In 1970, prepaid care enrolled about three million people within 33 months.[15] *Managed care* as a term arose in the late 1980s.[16] Media reports often refer to "HMOs" as the generic term for all types of managed care organizations. Because managed care has moved beyond HMOs to encompass a wide variety of organizational types, this book will use the term *managed care organizations* (MCOs) as the generic term.

In March 1970, the Nixon administration decided to offer an HMO option under Medicare and Medicaid. After various stops and starts, Congress passed the Health Maintenance Organization Act of 1973.[17] "The Act was designed to provide financial assistance, to preempt restrictive state laws, and to mandate employers who are covered by the Fair Labor Standards Act to offer an HMO option to their employees."[18] Despite the Nixon administration's ambitious plans for the new health-care financing option, the bill initially hobbled the HMOs with regulation.[19] In return for federal qualification, an HMO was required to offer a generous benefit package, which raised premiums and discouraged enrollment.[20] Consequently, HMO growth was slow, while political pressure to reduce the rising costs of health care (particularly Medicare) continued to mount.[21] In 1978, Congress amended the laws to increase federal aid to HMOs. In this climate, managed care began to flourish—first in particular geographical sections of the country, including California, the upper Midwest, and certain cities in the Northeast, and then in a more widespread fashion. Managed care's growth accelerated throughout the 1990s, and clearly dominates the current health-care delivery system.

In the past two years, though, managed care's growth has slowed considerably. Even now, managed care does not operate uniformly across the country. It varies from region to region in the type of MCO available, the extent to which health care is managed, and the percentage of the population MCOs cover. Not only is there a wide variety of MCOs, they also vary as to how actively they manage clinical care. Some aggressively review clinical decisions and require physicians to follow clinical practice guidelines. Others act more as traditional insurers, often delegating substantial responsibility (and risk) to physicians.[22]

Another reason why managed care expanded was the 1974 enactment of the Employee Retirement Income Security Act, commonly known as ERISA. As we will see, ERISA is a complex law that dominates the judicial and political health-care environment. For now it is sufficient to note that ERISA preempts (i.e., supersedes) state laws regulating MCOs. Through its preemption provision, ERISA operates to prevent states from regulating managed care plans and blocks patients' state court challenges to delayed or denied health care. Managed care became the ideal employee health-care benefit once large employers recognized that under ERISA they could save money and avoid state regulation by contracting with MCOs. Without ERISA, managed care might not have achieved its current market dominance, at least not this quickly. A major result of managed care's rise has been a nearly complete shift of power within health care from doctors to corporate MCOs.

Before the 1980s, health-care delivery was largely a local cottage industry dominated by medical professionals and charitable institutions (hospitals). By the mid- to late-1980s, it was rapidly becoming a national industry increasingly guided by traditional marketplace rules and consisting of large, integrated health-care systems. Health care now accounts for nearly 14% of the gross domestic product, generating considerable debate about how much money ought to be spent on it and how those dollars should be allocated.[23]

The expansion of managed care coincided with a political and intellectual push for less regulation and a "market-based" approach to health policy and health-care delivery. With the elections of Ronald Reagan and George H. W. Bush, the public also signaled a willingness to entertain market-based solutions to reduce health-care costs. At the same time, proponents of market-based approaches were developing alternative approaches to health-care delivery. For example, scholars devised what they termed *managed competition*, an attempt to introduce competition into health-care delivery.[24] Employers, who play a critical role in health care because most Americans receive health insurance through employee benefits, began insisting that the health-care system contain its costs. To lower their ever-increasing cost of providing health-care benefits, businesses formed health-purchasing coalitions to negotiate lower prices with large insurers and managed care plans.

The market revolution was confirmed with the defeat of President Clinton's proposed Health Security Act in 1994.[25] President Clinton's proposal was based largely on the theory of managed competition, and the construction of governmental health-purchasing structures that would use their bargaining power to simultaneously reduce costs and expand coverage for medically uninsured persons. By a resounding margin, Congress rejected the Clinton administration's expansive system. Responsibility for containing health-care costs thus shifted to the private sector, primarily through the cost-containment programs introduced by managed care organizations. When this shift occurred, the health insurance and managed care industries became the dominant forces in health care delivery and policy.

In retrospect, it seems clear that the country, in the 1994 policy debate, decided to rely on market mechanisms to shape our health-care delivery system as opposed to relying on the government to redress the health-care system's perceived deficiencies. The market has indeed achieved, at least until the past year, what competitive markets are best at doing: relentlessly reducing the cost excesses of the old health-care order. But reliance on the market has had other consequences that the public is finding troublesome, such as the lack of direct access to specialty care, inadequate patient protections, limitations on health care, and larger numbers of people without health insurance coverage. In fact, there is a backlash from the public and much of the medical community against the perceived deficiencies in the managed care approach.[26]

Despite a decade of radical transformation, it is unlikely that the health-care delivery system has reached a point of equilibrium. We can be reasonably certain that health care will remain a dynamic and constantly changing institution. One commentator argued in 1999 that managed care was shifting toward what he termed "multiproduct, multimarket health plans," amounting to diversified national organizations. Two years later, he wrote about the death of managed care.[27] Reports of managed care's demise seem a bit premature, and more permutations and changes will no doubt alter how managed care operates. Even if managed care disappears tomorrow, the health policy dilemma will remain what it was at the start of the managed care era: how to contain the high cost of health care without unduly limiting individual access to needed health-care services.

To that dilemma, we might add the continuing problem of rising numbers of uninsured Americans. Any proposed solution to deal with the contentious resource-allocation issues in managed care must take into account the potential effects on the number of Americans without health insurance coverage. Policy makers are wary of taking action that might cause employers to drop health insurance benefits, which would further reduce the insured population.

An additional complication in the health policy environment is the increasing tendency of attorneys and physicians to view each other as antagonists, making it difficult to formulate policies to resolve the conflicts presented by managed care.[28] The two professions have not always been antagonists.[29] In the early nineteenth century, they cooperated on matters of mutual interest, but expectations for an enduring, cooperative relationship did not last long. Especially during the past thirty years, there has been considerable conflict between physicians and attorneys over the perceived intrusiveness of the legal system into medical practice. The conflict between the two professions has been exacerbated by the decline of physician dominance and authority over health-care delivery and the rise of managed care.

A consequence of this ongoing battle is that too much attention is devoted to what divides the two professions, and too little reflection is dedicated to what the professions have in common, which might serve to revive better communication and cooperation. While some tension between law and medicine is both inevitable and useful, the current level of antagonism is not helpful to patients and contributes to gridlock in forming public policy.

Establishing better lines of communication and cooperation between attorneys and physicians is important for patients. Without it, patient care may suffer if disagreement between the two professions compromises sound clinical judgment. Public policy suffers when they publicly fight over how to resolve contentious issues such as the appropriate response to medical errors. One way to stimulate cooperation is for those not trained in the law to have a comprehensive and accurate guide to how law adapts to changing social and economic circumstances. Physicians need to understand not only *what* courts decide but *why*. Judges and attorneys need to understand the values that motivate medical and health-care policies and practices and the ethical dilemmas physicians face in the managed care environment. As this book's title implies, the level of mistrust between the legal and medical professions results in a dialogue that is more adversarial than cooperative. Both professions need to understand the ways they are inevitably intertwined, why they argue, and how they might cooperate to improve patient care.

The surge in managed care and the negative public reaction to its cost-control policies have engendered a legislative and regulatory response at both the state and federal levels. Whether and how to regulate managed care is one of the most divisive public policy debates now on the political agenda.

State and federal legislators and regulators play an integral role in overseeing the entire health-care enterprise. For purposes of this book, the most important aspect of that role is how legislatures and regulators interact with the courts to comprise the health-care regulatory structure. So far, a coherent regulatory framework for monitoring managed care has yet to emerge.[30] In part, this is because many state laws are preempted by ERISA (that is, blocked from going into effect). Much of the congressional health-care debate since the demise of the Clinton administration's Health Security Act in 1994 has been dominated by the questions of whether to allow patients to sue MCOs in state courts and allow states to regulate managed care. Understanding ERISA and the judicial response to it will be central to the story told in subsequent chapters.

Before World War II, Congress played a minor role in health-care delivery. Since health care was considered a matter for states to handle, there was no federal legislative involvement. Aside from delegating responsibility to state regulators to oversee professional and hospital licensure, most states enacted little legislation. The era of federal legislative detachment ended after World War II. At first, federal involvement remained limited. By the mid-1960s, with the steady accretion of low-income people without insurance and an aging population unable to afford health insurance, Congress responded by enacting the Medicare and Medicaid programs. From that point forward, Congress has played a major role in health policy and is now engaged in every facet of health-care delivery. One of the criticisms of federal health-care regulation is that Congress is legislating by "body part," or piecemeal, in response to powerful political pressures, rather than developing a more coherent approach.[31] An example is the pressure for laws designed to mandate 48-hour hospital maternity stays after delivering a baby.

Legislative oversight of health care has also increased steadily at the state level. All indications are that many states would go even further were it not for ERISA preemption. In many ways, the managed care backlash has been most evident in state-level attempts to control MCOs. States have attempted to impose external grievance processes, which would allow patients to contest delayed or denied care or to require the disclosure of financial incentives. Early laws governing MCOs focused on the right of physicians to participate in MCO networks (so-called "any willing provider" laws), and on the right of physicians to discuss any aspect of care with their patients that related directly to managed care's financial incentives (so-called "anti-gag" rules). More recently, some states have imposed requirements mandating direct access to specialists. Many states have imposed limits on managed care's financial incentives by prohibiting incentives that would lead to the denial of medically necessary care.[32] Some of these laws have gone into effect, but others have been preempted by ERISA.

An important market-based response to public concerns about the lack of accountability for managed care has been the rise of two independent, nonprofit accrediting bodies for hospitals and managed care plans. Through industry-based efforts at self-regulation, these entities operate to establish and monitor standards for quality of care. While their functions are not traditionally regulatory, since they have no official governmental sanctioning authority, they play a role that is tantamount to regulation through the accreditation process. Failure to obtain full accreditation because of deviations from the accreditation standards can put a health-care institution at a severe competitive disadvantage in the marketplace. As a practical matter, the accrediting bodies possess considerable authority in overseeing quality of care.

Law and Health Care: Framing the Issues

As difficult as the health-care delivery and health policy problems are to solve on their own terms, the prospect of extensive legal intervention in health care further complicates their resolution. Law and health care intersect at various points. At both the state and federal levels, all three branches of the legal system—the legislatures, regulatory agencies, and courts—have been persistently involved in setting health-care policy and monitoring health-care delivery since the mid-1960s. With the increasing size of MCOs and the shift to managed care as the predominant method of providing health care, legal oversight has intensified. One reason is that the popular backlash against managed care generates demands for the legal system to respond to managed care's perceived inequities and shortcomings. The relationship between law and health care has never been more visible, intertwined, or manifest than it is today.

It should not be surprising that two of America's most important institutions, the legal and health-care systems, are so intertwined. Since the early 1800s, medical jurisprudence, where physicians are called as expert witnesses and where the courts act to regulate the quality of medical care, has been an integral part of the growth of the health-care enterprise.[33] As one scholar has noted, ". . . medical jurisprudence . . . figured prominently in early American medical history . . . ; neither subject can be fully understood in its modern context without taking the history of legal medicine into account."[34] To put it mildly, the involvement of the courts in health-care delivery is not new.

For many years, courts have actively monitored the quality of care through determining the standard of care for medical liability[35] and interpreting contractual definitions of medical necessity.[36] Courts have also been called upon to interpret the vast array of state and federal legislation regulating health-care delivery.

By tradition, health-care litigation, such as patients suing physicians or hospitals to recover monetary damages for medical injuries, is resolved in state courts. Before the rise of managed care, health insurance cases were litigated in state courts, often to decide whether an insurer should pay for care already provided. Managed care changes the policy and litigation context in two respects. With the integration of financing and care delivery under managed care, refusing coverage means denying care altogether. Then, if a plan subscriber challenges the denial, the MCO can invoke protection from liability under ERISA's preemption provision. ERISA preemption allows health plans to avoid going to trial in state courts.

Regardless of the inevitable ebbs and flows of the links between law and medicine, their relationship was essentially stable from the mid-nineteenth century until the mid-1960s.[37] As recently as the late 1960s and early 1970s, health-care attorneys and health-care executives had a relatively easy set of liability rules to live with. That relative stability was largely shattered by the growth of managed care. The framing of the legal issues in the managed care era reflects the dramatic changes engulfing the health-care system since the mid-1980s and the resulting policy conflicts that have arisen.

In responding to litigation challenging managed care's cost-containment practices, judges must address a threshold question of what role courts should play in monitoring the managed care environment, as compared with legislatures. Courts face the challenge of either applying common law liability principles to new situations or deferring to elected representatives to set public policy. (*Common law* is the ". . . body of law that develops . . . through judicial decisions, as distinguished from legislative enactments.")[38] In the new health-care environment, courts will be asked to distinguish the economic aspects of managed care that order relationships between health plans, physicians, and patients, from the incentives that contribute to below-standard care. The former are usually legislative prerogatives, while the latter are normally within the judicial purview. The evolution of both common law and constitutional law is replete with examples of this tension. In some instances, courts have expanded liability principles, such as imposing strict liability for mass-produced goods (i.e., liability for an accident regardless of fault). In others, as with physician-assisted suicide, courts have deferred to the legislatures.

As critics of judicial intervention have noted, litigation is reactive and generally focused on individual situations. This is why many observers think that courts favor individual litigants in their challenges to policies that limit goods and services. Yet there are many reasons why the courts are likely to become even more deeply involved in health-care issues with the expansion of managed care. What is new in the managed care environment is the types of issues likely to emerge, particularly the conflict between population-based cost containment and health-care services for individual subscribers, the multiplicity of actors in a given case,[39] and the evolving nature of the new organizational structures. Conflicts may arise when patients' desires for unlimited health care clash with managed care's cost-containment initiatives. For example, an on-cologist in an MCO may debate whether to use an experimental procedure, such as autologous bone marrow transplant, for a patient with an advanced stage of cancer. If treatment is provided, the individual patient may benefit, but at the cost of depleting resources available to serve others in the health plan's patient population. Limiting care to the individual patient frees re-sources to be shared among plan members, but to the patient's potential detriment.

To take another example, suppose a health plan limits mammograms to women over 50 to reduce plan costs and to allocate the resources elsewhere. Then a 40-year-old patient requests a mammogram. If the mammogram is ordered, the physician may be at risk of plan-imposed sanctions, perhaps the loss of bonus income, or the plan sets a precedent by allowing it. But if refusing to order the mammogram leads to a failure to detect cancer at an early stage, the physician may be at risk of malpractice liability. Either way, the physician is in a morally conflicted situation that has important implications for the physician–patient relationship.[40] And patients who feel that health care has been denied or delayed may seek redress in the courts.

Many health-care stakeholders, including physicians, may also resort to the courts to protect their own interests. Physicians who are adversely affected by MCOs' cost-containment initiatives may sue to protect their economic inter-ests and professional autonomy. For instance, physicians may attempt to use antitrust challenges to block selective contracting (where a plan contracts with a limited number of physicians or a single physician group) and the practice of economic credentialing (where staff privileges depend on controlling re-source utilization).

Without doubt, conflicts over control of resource-allocation decisions will raise questions about the restrictions on physician autonomy that affect patient treatment and are likely to generate litigation. Already the backlash against managed care is generating wide-ranging state legislation to protect patients' rights. Since judges routinely interpret legislation and regulations, attempts to regulate MCOs will generate considerable litigation.

Courts have often served as a venue for balancing conflicting social policy goals, such as weighing public safety protections against individual privacy rights, and remain institutions of considerable power, authority, and legitimacy. That power includes the potential for judicial doctrine to influence health policy and medical practice. A 1989 editorial in the *Journal of the American Medical Association* predicted that "For better or worse, health policy of the future will be decided in the courts. . . ."[41] This prediction presumes that courts will be actively engaged in the policy-making process.

Consider the Andrews-Clarke situation. Suppose, for the time being, that no statute governs this case, leaving the issue to be decided by the common law in Massachusetts. Suppose further that the legal issues present a "case of first impression," meaning that the court will set a precedent that might guide other courts in deciding similar cases. In this instance, the court must confront an entirely new set of circumstances that were not present in a fee-for-service health-care environment, especially the health plan's responsibility to provide cost-effective care to the plan's patient population without compromising the individual's health-care needs. These new issues raise fundamental social policy conflicts that have not yet been resolved by the medical profession or by policy makers (including legislators). Asking the courts to resolve such questions is a peculiarly American phenomenon with a rich history that stretches the limits of the courts' legitimacy and capability.

Reconciling how courts and policy makers approach these and other potential clinical conflicts poses an enormous policy and legal challenge. Health policy makers and courts frame the inquiry in conceptually different ways. The driving force in contemporary health policy is how to allocate finite resources to serve society at large. In economic terms, this is most often framed as a problem of containing aggregate (or total) health-care costs. By contrast, the courts are traditionally concerned with protecting individual liberties and rights, with features designed to protect individual litigants.

This fundamental difference in perspective is not merely academic. The success of the recent changes in health-care delivery depends largely on whether cost-containment efforts and other managed care innovations can lower health-care expenditures without reducing the quality of care. To a substantial degree, the ability to sustain and expand those innovations also depends on how courts decide the emerging litigation. How the legal system responds to changes in health-care delivery will influence the extent and direction of those changes. Managed care's cost-containment initiatives are likely to be challenged in court if they result in delaying or denying an individual's health care. If courts consistently rule in favor of individual patients' service delivery needs, it may be difficult to sustain cost-control mechanisms. If, instead, courts consistently rule in favor of cost-containment programs, individuals will have little recourse when medical care is denied and institutions will feel less constrained in introducing cost-containment programs. A large jury verdict in *Fox v. HealthNet*[42] for HealthNet's failure to justify its criteria in refusing to provide an autologous bone marrow transplant is indicative of the courts' potential to curtail cost-containment policies. After that verdict, many MCOs decided not to challenge similar bone-marrow transplant requests. Judicial decisions will also influence the expansion of the new organizational forms and whether physician autonomy will be safeguarded.

Whether and how the courts should respond to managed care's cost-containment initiatives has been the subject of intense scholarly debate. Many previous commentators expected that the courts would most likely frustrate managed care's cost-containment initiatives. They surmised that judges would either endorse physician dominance or refuse to hold patients to their signed contracts (or both). One study assessed legal challenges to cost control initiatives adopted by hospitals in the 1980s, largely in a fee-for-service context. After finding that courts did not embrace prior authorization, physician payment incentives, and physician selection restrictions, the study concluded that serious cost-containment innovations would not survive judicial scrutiny.[43] Another scholar argued that courts have expanded their influence over health policy by overturning insurers' coverage decisions and favoring hospitals, as opposed to states, in Medicaid rate-setting cases.[44] Other analysts have argued that courts tend to side with individual patients against insurers in deciding whether expensive technologies are covered benefits.[45]

Scholars also generally discuss the strengths and weaknesses of resolving health policy disputes in the courts,[46] usually accentuating the weaknesses. Some commentators have argued that there are no compelling reasons for courts to be deciding the substance of health-care disputes.[47] They propose limiting the courts' role to ensuring that fair processes have been followed and argue that the parties' contractual arrangements should determine how the court rules in the case. By far, the dominant scholarly approach favors reliance on negotiated contracts between patients and MCOs to determine the level and type of services to be provided.[48]

Few legal scholars argue outright for greater judicial involvement in resolving health-care disputes, either through tort law or for an alternative that does not rely on contract principles. About the only opposition to this view is one scholar's argument that courts should establish individual entitlements for health-care services.[49] Even a few of the legal scholars who acknowledge the need for tort law oversight still argue that courts should make radical changes in how medical liability doctrine is developed.[50]

An interesting debate over how the legal system should respond to managed care cost-containment initiatives anticipated the struggle judges would have with cost-containment programs.[51] One side argued that the traditional liability standards, deferring to customary medical practice to establish the applicable standard of care, were no longer adequate to reflect the realities of a resource-constrained environment and needed to be changed. In response, the other side asserted that common law is capable of incorporating cost-conscious medical decisions within the conventional standard of care framework, albeit on a more incremental basis than others might prefer. As we will see, the incrementalist argument proved closer to how the courts have actually ruled, though both sides can claim some vindication.

The scholarly debate as to the judiciary's proper resolution of health policy disputes, while interesting and useful, offers limited assistance to judges in balancing conflicting policy objectives. Courts are as unlikely to impose a general entitlement to health care as they are to defer exclusively to market arrangements. At a minimum, judges will play an important interpretive role, since neither contracts nor legislation can specify or anticipate all the situations likely to occur.

Judges are aware of the need for a new approach. Several years ago, a prominent jurist with experience in handling complex litigation proposed that judges apply a framework based on communitarian theory in deciding the social policy issues now confronting the courts.[52] A communitarian approach would require a judge to consider the effects of a decision on what would be good for the community, and not just reflect the preferences of the individual litigants.[53] Without detailing how to apply the communitarian theory in deciding cases, he argued that judges currently lack an adequate conceptual framework for balancing complex policy trade-offs between individual litigants and the collective interests of other affected groups. Regardless of the merits of the communitarian framework, the article demonstrated that judges are striving to devise and apply innovative approaches to problems that the courts have had difficulty resolving.

Many influences converge to shape the health-care delivery system and health policy, including legislation, regulation, stakeholder policies, and judicial decisions. At times, these influences may be contradictory. In the 1970s and 1980s, health-care providers received signals from legislatures to reduce costs, while courts were simultaneously requiring expanded services.[54] Similar inconsistencies exist today throughout the system. Both directly and indirectly, these contradictory policy signals and the tensions created by managed care leave patients in an unenviable position. It is hard enough for patients to decipher managed care's complexity without having to worry about how the legal system influences their care or coverage.

The critics of judicial intervention in health-care disputes are perhaps correct in maintaining that the narrow prism of legal analysis is not the best mechanism for analyzing and resolving complex social policy questions. But the courts are already deeply involved in health-care issues and are likely to remain so, at least as long as many stakeholders, including physicians, resort to the courts to protect their individual interests. While courts play an important role in shaping health-care delivery and policy, the dominant influence on policy formation remains the interchange between legislatures, regulators, and stakeholders. Courts largely respond to the policies of the political system and the decisions made by health-care providers and insurers. In the process, courts provide a public forum for addressing the conflicting policy objectives inherent in the managed care environment.

Once again, this is not a new challenge for the courts. When the railroads arrived as a dominant economic force and when mass-produced goods became available, courts had to consider the new legal ramifications based on a framework that was designed to resolve different types of problems. When hospitals became central to health-care delivery, the courts had to adapt medical liability principles that were developed to resolve a patient's lawsuit against a physician and apply them to hospitals. Just as the shift to hospital care raised different issues than those found in a patient's lawsuit against a physician, the same process is now underway with regard to the emerging organizational forms comprising managed care. The process is not straightforward; nor are trends easy to predict. At the beginning, courts lack an understanding of the social and economic changes when judges begin to adopt principles derived from a different era to the new situations. Over time, judges learn more about the changes and apply more sophisticated thinking in developing legal doctrine. Sorting out which party is legally responsible for delayed or denied care and the acceptable level of care resulting from cost-containment strategies remains, as we will see, a work in progress.

Health-care policy involves important questions about our society, including the responsibilities we as a community owe to those less able to thrive because of illness. The judicial approach to these challenges will play a significant role in shaping society's response. At its best, the judiciary provides an unbiased tribunal for the careful articulation and balancing of conflicting values and goals. Managed care is rife with conflicts and potential conflicts. The legal system's success in balancing these conflicts and resolving competing health-care policy objectives would go a long way toward reconciling the public to managed care and reconciling physicians to attorneys.

Notes

1. For a more detailed exploration of the various uses of litigation, see Jacobson and Warner (1999).

2. The following description is taken directly from *Andrews-Clarke v. Travelers Insurance Co.*, 984 F. Supp. 49 (D. Mass. 1997). The case was decided on a motion for summary judgment. When a motion for summary judgment is made, the court must take the facts alleged by the plaintiff (Ms. Andrews-Clarke in this case) as true for the purposes of ruling on the motion. Thus, the facts discussed here are only those as stated by Ms. Andrews-Clarke. No doubt Travelers' version would be very different.

3. The following account is taken from Klein (1999).

4. Cited in Klein (1999), p. 31.

5. A note about my research methods. For the most part, the book will focus on trends and directions that might suggest how courts have responded to litigation challenging managed care programs and policies. Trying to trace trends in how courts have shaped legal doctrine is an exercise in analysis, nuance, and judgment rather than being

able to exclusively use quantitative techniques. To address these issues, I have incorporated both qualitative and quantitative methods in my research, with the emphasis on the qualitative. First, I conducted a comprehensive search and synthesis of the health services and law review literature dealing with the relationship between law and health care. Second, I conducted a quantitative (case content) analysis of trends in health-care litigation.

The qualitative analysis includes extensive reading and analysis of judicial decisions in health care, focusing on cases involving managed care organizations. In social science research, a random sample of cases would be the preferable methodology. That methodology has only sporadically been used in legal research. In traditional legal scholarship, commentators analyze a large number of cases for trends or focus on a few leading cases to suggest both the doctrinal implications of the decisions or ways in which the decision could be improved. In litigation, not all cases are created equal. Some cases, by virtue of the reputation of the particular court or judge, because they may set precedent, are the subject of extensive scholarly commentary, or are cited by other courts, become more important than other cases. Thus, legal scholars focus on prominent cases, as will much of this book.

For the quantitative analysis, I used standard legal research tools, Westlaw and Lexis/Nexis, to review and code a targeted sample of nearly 500 cases from a total universe of at least 3,750 cases. The search included the terms "health maintenance organization," "HMO," "preferred provider," "utilization review," "managed care," and "IPA" (independent practice association), and elicited a wide variety of cases, including antitrust disputes.

The purpose of the case content analysis was to provide insight into: how courts have resolved the inherent conflicts presented by managed care (i.e., between cost containment and access to health-care services); what analytical approaches judges use to resolve cases; whether there are different approaches across case types, such as utilization management, medical necessity, or antitrust; and the role policy considerations play in case outcomes. Each case was coded for the following indicators: whether the opinion discussed health-care policy considerations; which policies were at issue; case outcome; procedural considerations, such as setting the burden of proof or the standard of review; reliance on the facts of the case; reliance on precedent; and deference to legislation or contractual obligations.

The case content analysis established the information base to categorize and explain trends and differences in the development of legal doctrine in managed care. For more details on the results, see Jacobson, Selvin, and Pomfret (2001).

6. Southwick (1988), p. 123. Another example is that a trustee of an estate owes a fiduciary duty to invest money wisely and distribute the assets according to the donor's wishes.

7. For a description of managed care, see Kominski and Melnick (2001). For a critique of the language and rhetoric of managed care, see Hacker and Marmor (1999) and Annas (1995).

8. For an excellent and thorough history, see Starr (1982).

9. Friedman (1996). These laws prohibited the corporate practice of medicine, a concept that would have permitted organizations to hire physicians. Although corporate practice acts were not originally aimed at MCOs, they were used to discourage their operation. (See Chapter 2.)

10. An example of moral hazard is that some people will drive recklessly if they think that safety devices, such as anti-lock brakes, will protect them.

11. This is a far more transforming departure than the shift from in-office physician care to hospitals because it changes all aspects of the health-care enterprise. See, e.g., *Darling v. Charleston Memorial Hospital*, 211 N.E. 2d 253 (Ill. 1965).

12. Morreim (1994a, 1994b, 2001); Rodwin (1993). Morreim frames the problem with financial incentives very nicely. "Ideally, a well-designed incentive should create just enough hesitation for the physician to consider carefully whether a proposed intervention is genuinely desirable for the patient, but not enough to override good judgment." Morreim (2001), p. 98. Furrow (2001), p. 384, agrees. While that is a very difficult balance to maintain, the fiduciary-duty framework described in Chapter 10 is designed to achieve such a balance.

13. Emanuel and Dubler (1995) provide an overview of managed care's improvements and problems. Among the problems are shorter offices visits, lack of continuity of care, and other access barriers. Improvements include expanded choice of preventive care, quality measurement strategies, and increased numbers of primary care providers. For general critiques of managed care, in that it manages costs, not care, see Anders (1996) and Kleinke (2001). For a general overview of managed care, see Millenson (1997), Robinson (1999b).

14. Morreim (2001), p. 29.

15. Millenson (1997), p. 290.

16. For a useful summary of the history of prepaid care, see Block (1997).

17. 42 U.S.C.A. Art. 300E(b)(1)A-V.

18. In particular, the Act provided capital for development and preempted state laws prohibiting the corporate practice of medicine (Brennan, 1998).

19. Starr (1982) p. 407.

20. Millenson (1997), p. 290.

21. Starr (1982) pp. 411–17.

22. See, e.g., Noble and Brennan (2001); Robinson (1999a); Morreim (2001).

23. Current aggregate health care spending hovers around 14% of GDP.

24. Enthoven and Kronick (1989a, b).

25. The American Health Security Act of 1993, H.R. 1200, 103rd Congress, 1st session (1993). See also, Skocpol (1996).

26. For an extensive consideration of the managed care backlash, see the articles collected in the *Journal of Health Politics, Policy and Law*, October, 1999, 24(5):873–1244.

27. Robinson (1999); Robinson (2001).

28. Fox (1987).

29. Mohr (1993).

30. Brennan (1998); Miller (1997).

31. Hyman (1999a).

32. Miller (1997).

33. Mohr (1993).

34. Mohr (1993), p. 251.

35. Jacobson (1989); Furrow (1997).

36. Hall and Anderson (1992); Eddy (1996).

37. Mohr (1993); Stryker (1932).

38. *Black's Law Dictionary* (1991). Common law principles vary across states because each state court system develops its own common law rules. In the late twentieth century, state legislatures have increasingly acted to usurp what was previously in the judicial domain of developing common law precepts. Even though health care is an

area where legislatures have been increasingly active, the courts continue to play an important common law role through private litigation.

39. Instead of the simpler fee-for-service-era model of litigation involving one physician and one patient, managed care litigation may include the patient, the physician, the health plan, the utilization review firm, and the administrator of an ERISA-covered plan.

40. Rodwin (1993).

41. Cole (1989).

42. No. 219692, Superior Court of California (1993).

43. Hall (1988).

44. Anderson (1992).

45. Ferguson, Dubinsky, and Kirsch (1993).

46. Capron (1990); Stone (1985); Anderson (1992).

47. Havighurst (1995); Hall and Anderson (1992).

48. *Ibid.*

49. Rosenblatt (1993).

50. Havighurst (1995) argues that the standard of care should be determined contractually, essentially allowing providers to bargain with patients over the level of care to be provided. Abraham and Weiler (1994a, b), along with others, argue that courts should shift medical liability from physicians to the enterprise providing the care, such as an IPA or another MCO. This standard, known as *enterprise liability*, would provide the enterprise with greater incentives for monitoring the quality of care.

51. Hall (1989); Morreim (1989).

52. Weinstein (1994).

53. Selznick (1987), p. 460.

54. Stone (1985); Hall and Anderson (1992).

2

From Cooperation to Contention

THE rivalry and tension between physicians and attorneys is easy enough to observe. From disputes over the regulation of health care and medical liability standards to contentious courtroom confrontations, the two esteemed professions have been engaged in a rather acrimonious dialogue. Even calling it a "dialogue" overstates the way the exchanges take place. For the most part, the two groups are discordantly talking at or past one another. Supreme Court Justice Benjamin Cardozo described the tension between the professions when he virtually warned of a medical profession burgeoning in brilliance and broadening in scope:

> We must keep a sharp lookout, or you will supplant us altogether. . . . How it will work out, whether we shall sit beside you or above you, or perhaps even below you, I am not wise enough to say. The physician may be merely the ally of the judge in the business of admeasuring the sentence, or, as to that branch of work, may even drive the judge away.[1]

Physicians resent being sued and having their clinical practices and motivations impugned by laypersons. Unsurprisingly, they are not at all appreciative of an attorney's withering cross-examination during a trial. Nor do they readily accept the role of courts and juries in setting medical standards of care. In their view, medical professionals should set clinical practice standards—without second-guessing from the legal system. Physicians also resent the continuing intrusion of legislation and regulation into the clinical practice setting. They remain protective of their rigorously developed expertise and mistrustful of attorneys' methods and motivations for challenging that expertise.

The relationship between law and medicine has not always been this contentious. Historically, law and medicine have been interdependent professions,[2] with mutual engagement on a range of issues. These include the role of law in monitoring medical practice, the importance of medical evidence in legal issues, and the importance of retaining their status as preeminent professions. They are also competitors for professional and social stature. In the early nineteenth century, the two professions cooperated on matters of mutual interest, and there was hope that they could jointly develop a field of legal medicine. That hope has never been realized, largely because of continuing disputes over medical malpractice cases. According to one observer, ". . . the conflict between physicians and lawyers, though it is rooted in the modern history of the two professions, has become more intense in recent years as the authority most people accord to physicians has diminished."[3]

Attorneys and physicians routinely clash during malpractice trials. Aside from the searing emotional consequences of being in court as a defendant in a medical liability trial, physicians resent being forced to settle a medical malpractice claim that appears not to be supported by scientific evidence. Settlements for reasons of expediency are unpalatable to physicians because they are a retreat from principle.[4]

To many physicians, the legal system does not value or understand medical practice, resulting in actions that undermine public confidence in medicine and lead to the practice of defensive medicine (conducting tests and clinical procedures solely to avoid liability).[5] In contrast, lawyers have an aversion to the imperious physician who defies honestly offered counsel on compliance with laws and policies. Some attorneys believe that physicians resent and reject even reasonable regulations, with an above-the-law attitude.[6]

Physicians, who once dominated the provision of patient care, no longer have the ability to exercise the same level of control over health-care delivery and the politics of health care that they once could. Physicians must now contend with patient autonomy (i.e., informed consent), utilization review, and credentialing requirements, all concepts that are in no small part governed by the law. Writing in 1986 about physicians' disillusionment with medical practice, one scholar argued that a ". . . general explanation is the pervasive, unwelcome, crushing embrace of medicine by law. Every participant in the health care system . . . is beset by an onslaught of new laws and regulations affecting every phase of medicine. . . ."[7] Perhaps paradoxically, physicians must rely on the reviled legal "standard of care" to insulate their professional autonomy from increasing control by MCOs.

This chapter and the one that follows put in historical context the professional animosity between attorneys and physicians and the current debate on the law's role in regulating medicine. We will look first at the simultaneous evolution of both attorney and physician professional engagement and the fledgling efforts to regulate the practice of medicine, from the early 1800s until the 1965 enactment of Medicare and Medicaid. The chapter then concludes with a discussion of how the legal system came to support the physicians' dominance over the health-care enterprise, in spite of their mutual antagonism. Because the relationship between law and medicine changed dramatically after 1965, we will look at the post-1965 developments in the next chapter.

Early Interaction Between Physicians and Attorneys

During the middle of the nineteenth century, the prognosis for a cooperative and interdependent arrangement between attorneys and physicians seemed promising. One reason for optimism was a common interest in preserving their mutual professional status during the rising anti-elitist sentiment in Jacksonian America. People were distrustful of the professional classes as a whole. Another reason was the fact that doctors and lawyers often came from the same background and class. Unfortunately, cooperation soon turned to contention; contention then turned to antagonism.

Initially, there was little conflict between physicians and attorneys; in fact, they had much in common. In the early 1800s (roughly between 1820 and 1850), physicians and attorneys collaborated in developing medical jurisprudence, defined as "... the interaction between those who possess medical knowledge and those who exercise legal authority."[8] Medical jurisprudence was conceived as a separate, but collegial and cooperative professional field mediating between law and medicine. In 1825, a participant "envisioned medical jurisprudence serving as a link to unite physicians and lawyers in the detection of error, the vindication of accused innocence, and the conviction of guilt."[9] The training of subspecialists in medical jurisprudence took off, largely under the initiative of the nation's preeminent medical education institutions in Philadelphia and New York.[10]

Starting in the mid-1800s, the development of and demand for medico-legal expertise made physicians' knowledge a crucial tool of legal practice. Lawyers were much in need of the expertise physicians had to offer, first in the area of forensic medicine (using the science of medicine to solve legal questions), in interpreting the circumstances of injury, rape, or death (mostly in criminal cases), and then in mental health and medical malpractice cases. The physician's opinion on these matters was either advisory to the judge or was expert testimony introduced in court for the jury's consideration. Either way, the influence of the medical testimony was considerable and vital to a case. Physicians brought logic and science to the courtroom in an effort to dispel previous myths and outdated assumptions. The interdependence of medicine and law in this period is self-evident. Lawyers needed physicians to make their arguments in court persuasive and "true."

A major facet of medico-legal intervention dealt with the social treatment of the insane and the state's assumption of this responsibility, as well as questions of competence in disposing of material wealth. Medical testimony and expertise were essential to determining mental incompetence and commitment to institutions. Without the justifications offered by medical professionals, public policy and legal rules surrounding mental health would not have been legitimate.[11]

Physicians, too, needed this niche to develop their professional reputation and legitimacy.[12,13] Medico-legal cases received considerable public attention, and a physician could quickly gain status by proving a case in court with medical evidence. The fact that a murder conviction and the validity of a will could be decided by a physician's testimony was of great importance to the law and to the public. A physician could be called a hero and hailed in public for his (and, on rare occasions, her) insights in court. Subsequent publicity could easily translate to an appointment to a medical faculty, a more lucrative practice, and added prestige.

Thus the burgeoning field of medical jurisprudence proved to be a popular avenue for gaining wide recognition in medicine, and even stimulated research and advances in medical knowledge. But legislative efforts to provide financial support for the field were thwarted at the state level, and physicians were left mostly uncompensated for their time and effort. Physicians were compelled by subpoena to testify in court for the same fee of fifty cents per day afforded to other witnesses, even though their costs could be quite considerable.[14]

The reasons why legislative efforts to enhance cooperation between law and medicine were blocked are only beginning to be explored by historians, but the social and political anti-professional sentiments of the day no doubt played a part.[15] In turn, the failure to sustain this field had a broader effect than simply blocking state-funded medical jurisprudence. The focus of the field shifted away from forensic examination of evidence to investigations into the practice of physicians themselves, and to direct confrontation over alleged medical malpractice.

Malpractice litigation became a serious breach between the two professions in the 1840s, as legal practitioners identified lawsuits against physicians as a potential growth area. The mid–nineteenth-century surge of malpractice litigation doomed the promise of a separate field of medical jurisprudence,[16] and opened permanent fissures between doctors and lawyers.

With the failure of medico-legal jurisprudence to take hold as a joint endeavor, the relationship between attorneys and physicians changed. In the 1840s, a number of developments occurred that resulted in an almost overnight rise in medical malpractice cases in the American legal system. Changes in the public's outlook on health, advances occurring in medicine, and alterations in tort law contributed to the rise in medical malpractice litigation. When patients' increasing expectations for improved medical care were not met, they expressed their displeasure by filing lawsuits. Instead of mutual support and trust, the camaraderie between doctors and lawyers began to fray with the increasing tension over expert medical witnesses and medical malpractice cases.

The only recourse for patients after suffering an adverse medical outcome was to ask a court to hold individual physicians accountable.[17] Before the 1840s, litigation against physicians was rare, though the concept of medical malpractice had already been adopted from English legal theory.[18] In 1768, Sir William Blackstone, in his *Commentaries on the Laws of England*, defined what he called *mala praxis* (literally "wrongful or bad practice," particularly applied to unskillful medical management).[19] The *Commentaries* was widely read in the colonies, but there were few cases that called for malpractice actions before 1840.

Most physicians resented and feared court appearances.[20] The initial cause of the professional rupture between doctors and lawyers was the confrontation over conflicting medical testimony that was virtually unavoidable in the context of a medical malpractice trial.

> Expert witnesses as often as not made professional knowledge look shaky rather than strong; . . . the insanity issue had evoked a popular backlash rather than continued public support; and suits against shabby medical treatments, which might have helped drive quacks from the field, had instead ignited a continuing, even growing, firestorm of malpractice indictments against the regulars themselves.[21]

The nature of the adversarial legal system exposed expert witnesses to withering cross-examination, which was especially effective in an era of limited scientific support for clinical theories. As a result, physicians in the mid–nineteenth century were offended by the role of the attorneys and the court in questioning their medical judgment.[22]

Malpractice suits often pitted physicians against each other and were sometimes used as a ploy by one physician to discredit a rival. Physicians who differed in the style of medicine practiced often played out their disputes over the standards of care in the courtroom. It was not uncommon to see generational differences, with older physicians supporting more traditional viewpoints, lamenting that younger physicians were more aggressive and entrepreneurial.[23]

> Medical witnesses seemed to confuse as much as they clarified, and revealed flagrantly obvious geographical and ethnic divisions within the medical establish-

ment. Baltimore physicians fought Philadelphia physicians; German doctors fought Anglo-American doctors; organized experts in medical jurisprudence fought everyday healers and local practitioners.[24]

Lawyers commonly seized on these disputes for their own advantage, choosing whatever standards of care fit their particular needs and finding physicians to support their claims. Doctors refused to appear in court unless they were paid. The increasingly lucrative fees expert medical witnesses could command from private litigants led to complaints that they were willing to tailor their testimony to be favorable to the party paying for it.[25] Along with the dubious scientific base for medical opinions, witness fees undermined medical authority. The various forces driving the testimony of physicians further eroded public confidence.

Doctors soon felt that lawyers were encouraging and even inciting the general public to sue. Physicians' concerns over malpractice suits grew in the face of the ever-increasing number of lawsuits. Medical journals of the day called for physician solidarity and urged doctors to protect each other from these invidious forces. Medical societies inaugurated legal defense funds, collected pledges of mutual defense, and launched the first use of malpractice insurance as a way of helping doctors defend themselves against the surge in malpractice suits. Doctors would thus defend other physicians in court, even when they did not necessarily agree with them, because of their frustration with medical malpractice lawsuits.

Medical historians have observed that the battle for control over medical practice in the 1800s was not the sole province of physicians. Many types of medicine were practiced in the mid-1800s, and the skill of practitioners varied widely. The profession was open to anyone who could persuade citizens to use their services—no quality assurances were in place, no licensure laws, and no commonly agreed-upon standards of care. Competitors included adherents of botanic medicine (using herbs and other natural remedies), homeopaths, and others who disdained the scientific basis of medicine.[26] At this point, it was not clear which group would eventually dominate medical care, especially since a prevalent public attitude was that everyone could be his or her own physician and, in any event, most care was provided by the family. Formal medical education was not well-established until the twentieth century, and the practice of medicine was widely regarded as an inferior occupation well into the nineteenth century. It was not until the beginning of the twentieth century that physicians were able to consolidate their professional authority.[27]

Fueled by increasing public demand for perfect health, medicine made great strides during this period toward developing more effective scientific treatments. Medical advances for the first time allowed physicians and health departments to provide demonstrably beneficial services, particularly in disease prevention. In 1854, for instance, Louis Pasteur first identified viruses under his microscope, but it would take about 25 years for the medical community to embrace the theory that disease is spread by microorganisms. Along with the 1843 introduction of ether as an anaesthetic and Florence Nightingale's work in 1854 to improve the quality of nursing and the cleanliness of hospitals, these discoveries greatly increased patients' survivability and led to an upsurge of public confidence in hospitals for emergency care.[28]

The end of the Civil War and the Reconstruction era witnessed a rapid expansion of health care, largely driven by advances in science. Take, for example, the changing role of hospitals. Before the Civil War, hospitals were essentially almshouses for the poor, "serving general welfare functions and only incidentally caring for the sick."[29] But between 1870 and 1910, hospitals evolved into physicians' workshops. Scientific advances permitted doctors to provide treatment rather than just caretaking, as "medical and surgical treatment supplanted religious . . . objectives."[30] Reflecting their origin as almshouses for the poor, community hospitals were organized as charitable institutions. Today, most hospitals are still organized as charitable institutions, with tax-exempt status and a requirement to provide care to the community.

To attract patients, health practitioners in the mid-to-late nineteenth century were making hyperbolic claims about what they could perform, without scrutiny from any governmental entity. The fissure between physicians and attorneys came about in part as a response to the growing entrepreneurial nature of medical practice, amid a "surge of aggressive and flamboyant medical advertising."[31] In the 1840s, both the federal and state governments were hesitant to regulate professionals, reflecting the pervasive anti-government sentiment of the Jacksonian era. A *laissez-faire* attitude pervaded medical practice and governmental oversight.

Although technical advances in medical care would seem to increase positive patient outcomes and satisfaction, to a certain extent the advances made matters worse for physicians. With advances came added risk. In their attempts to be entrepreneurial and aggressive, physicians often experimented with new procedures. Innovative and sometimes radical techniques raised expectations of cures but were often not understood by the general public.[32]

New techniques and medical advances allowed better physicians to take on more difficult cases. In the case of a compound fracture, for example, an educated physician would attempt to save the limb rather than amputate. Often the result was that the limb was shorter, with some loss of functioning. Patients unhappy with the results looked to the courts for compensation. A less qualified practitioner might decline to treat such a case altogether. In large part, medical advances came to delineate the standards of care for the "better" practitioners. These standards became the basis of a lawsuit when the result was not what the patient anticipated. Educated physicians could have the body of texts they relied on used against them as standards from which they were deviating. Physicians became "ironic victims of their own medical advancement."[33] As physician training and capabilities expanded:

> Rather than pay their doctors for doing as well as they could under the conditions at hand, an increasing number of patients instead sued their doctors for failing to prevent or for apparently inflicting permanent disabilities and deformities; for failing to deliver on an implied contract of full recovery or restoration.[34]

Innovation in the areas of radiography and orthopedics was particularly susceptible to a lawsuit.[35]

Physicians wishing to try experimental treatments refrained from alerting their patients to the potential outcomes for fear of losing their business altogether. One observer warned physicians to "See that some responsible party understands what operation you intend to do, and what may be reasonably expected from it."[36] Physicians would later be held accountable for not informing the patient and their family of the potential risks; such disputes were precursors to the concept of informed consent.

Accompanying the mid-1800s medical advances, peoples' attitudes changed in ways that directly affected physicians. There was a decrease in the passive acceptance of bodily suffering, and people were no longer willing to accept disease and disability as divinely preordained. Beyond that, a health movement swept the nation in which people were concerned with attaining perfect physical health and fitness.[37] New public expectations, combined with physicians' aggressive advertising for medical services and changes in medical practice, set the stage for the expansion of medical malpractice lawsuits.

Coinciding with the changing public attitudes and advances in medical practice, there were significant changes in legal practice and rules of court that facilitated malpractice litigation. Courts eased the once rigid standards for initiating civil tort proceedings, encouraging this trend. The advent of contingency fee arrangements further encouraged and aided the rise of medical malpractice suits by freeing patients from the financial constraint of paying lawyers upon retaining their services. Under the contingency fee system, patients would pay their attorneys a portion of the damages awarded if they won the case, and nothing if they lost. The monetary awards became a strong incentive and encouraged lawyers to be aggressive and select cases they felt they could win. With the development of contingency fee arrangements and the increasing use of the American jury system to set common-law liability standards, the legal world was poised to sanction physicians for any departure from prevailing practice norms.[38]

Initially, physicians welcomed the malpractice suits, thinking that this would rid the profession of "quacks" and "charlatans." In reality, it was the well-educated and successful physicians who took the brunt of the lawsuits. The wave of malpractice litigation in the 1840s and 1850s was directed against successful practicing physicians, rather than medical charlatans and amateurs (i.e., quacks).

Quacks, rarely attempted anything beyond oils, ointments, and herbal treatments, and therefore could not easily be sued for their results. As amateur healers, they often claimed to treat each case individually, providing tailored "remedies" for what the patient required. They followed no prescribed clinical protocols. Also, there was no financial incentive to sue amateur healers, because they had paltry assets. Established and educated physicians, on the other hand, often had considerable means, and the payoffs in court, for both lawyers and patients, could be substantial.[39]

Some physicians were happy to have "bad" practitioners exposed, but many recognized that the courts were not the best venue for settling medical controversy. They believed that medical societies and journals should decide on matters dealing with standards of care. The questionable value of expert testimony led to recommendations for use of court-appointed medical experts to circumvent the problem of bought testimony. Another recommendation was to replace the traditional jury with juries composed of experts in the specific medical area involved.[40] Physicians complained that juries could not understand the complexities of the arguments and were easily swayed by nonmedical factors. But there was strong public support for trial by a jury of one's peers. The public felt that the jury system protected them from the federal government and from the upper classes. Jury sympathies often lay with the plaintiffs; here again the anti-professional sentiments of the day were on display. The tendency for juries to favor patients helped drive the increases in malpractice suits as lawyers felt they now had better chances of winning.

The press had a powerful role in swaying the opinions of citizens. Complex matters of medical treatment were not only being debated in the courts, but in the public arena as well. Physicians' acceptance of the press reports varied depending upon the facts, the outcome of the case, the particular physician involved, and the newspaper's stance in relation to a given physician's opinion.

All of these trends came together at the end of the nineteenth century in a trial that generated considerable press attention and concern within the medical profession. The case of Mary Dixon Jones exemplifies a situation in which the medical profession, as well as an individual physician, was on trial.[41] In 1889, the Brooklyn *Daily Eagle* ran a series of articles accusing Dr. Dixon Jones, a well-known gynecological surgeon in Brooklyn, of committing financial and medical improprieties that resulted in loss of life. After the stories were published, Dr. Dixon Jones faced eight malpractice cases and was indicted for two manslaughter charges. Over the next two years, she was exonerated of all criminal and civil charges. In 1892, Dr. Dixon Jones sued the newspaper for libel, but the jury returned a verdict against her.

Dr. Dixon Jones was not well liked by the medical community, partly because she was a woman (female physicians were rare at that time), and partly because she failed to display the feminine reserve typical of the era. Some physicians also criticized her medical skills. One physician reported that he no longer consulted with her and that she had operated on two of his patients against his wishes. Despite his concerns, he testified on her behalf at the manslaughter trial, and was satisfied when she was acquitted. Other reputable physicians traveled from Manhattan to Brooklyn (at some personal inconvenience) to defend Dr. Dixon Jones in court, even though they were not in the habit of consulting with her regularly.

The Dixon-Jones case highlights the solidarity that was forming among physicians to defend the profession against what they viewed as excessive intrusion from the press and especially from the legal profession. In sum, the reasons underlying the split between attorneys and physicians are not hard to discern.

Regulating Health Care

Along with the evolving relationship between attorneys and physicians, the country struggled in the nineteenth century with questions about how to regulate the practice of medicine. Before describing the historical development of regulation, let us take a brief look at its background and purposes. Since so much about the contemporary health-care system and relations between the legal and medical professions hinges on their interaction with the regulatory system, it is useful to say a few general words about regulation.

Debates over the role of government in the private economy date back to the emergence of the American market economy in the early nineteenth century. At that time, the Federalists, led by Alexander Hamilton, argued that a governmental presence was needed to guarantee property, enforce contracts, and to encourage the nascent entrepreneurial ethos.[42] In contrast, the Jeffersonians argued against intrusive government and in favor of self-reliance. That dynamic continues today over the proper regulatory oversight of health-care delivery.

An enduring debate is over which level of government should have primary responsibility for domestic social policy. Our governmental system is based on the concept of dual sovereignty between the states and the federal government—known generally by the term *federalism*. In a federalist system, states and the federal government share sovereignty over domestic policy.[43] One of the permanent features of American political history is the shift in dominance between the two for policy control. Before the New Deal era of the 1930s, states rights dominated public policy. From the 1930s through the 1970s, the federal government was in control. Now the pendulum has shifted again, with states dominating the policy arena.

Under the Constitution, certain rights and responsibilities, such as preparing for national defense and conducting international affairs, are reserved to the federal government. Other activities, including responsibility for public education, are traditionally within the states' authority. Health-care regulation was an area almost exclusively left to the states. Using the police powers (that is, the right of a sovereign government to protect the health and welfare of the state's citizens), states have taken lead responsibility for licensing medical professionals, determining standards of medical care, and regulating how health care should be organized and delivered.

An important aspect of the balance between federal and state authority is the concept of *preemption*. Preemption means that the superior governmental unit (the federal government) can block the inferior governmental entity (the states) from regulating a particular area. The rationale is to permit national uniformity in certain areas. When Congress legislates in a certain area and reserves power to the federal government, states may not regulate. For example, the federal government has exclusive authority for regulating nuclear power, which precludes state or local attempts to regulate this area. Sometimes the extent of federal preemption is unclear, requiring judicial interpretation of how much flexibility states have in regulating. A prime example is the extent to which Congress intended to preempt state regulations under ERISA, a subject that will be considered in detail in Part II.

It may seem that health care has always been a heavily regulated endeavor. Not so. Most health-care regulation has occurred since the enactment of Medicare and Medicaid in 1965. Before then, health care was largely a private sector enterprise dominated by physicians. States were primarily concerned with controlling infectious diseases, and secondarily with professional licensing requirements. Until the enactment of Medicare and Medicaid, the federal government played a decidedly secondary role in regulating health-care delivery. Since then, the federal government's role in health care has expanded tremendously, in both legislation and regulation.

For our purposes, the term *regulation* encompasses both legislative and regulatory oversight of the health-care system. For health care, regulation encompasses two fields—health professionals and the health-care system. Historically, physicians have been regulated differently than health care as a system. Physicians have been largely self-regulated, while government has played a more traditional regulatory role in monitoring the health-care system.[44]

Overall, government regulation is designed to ensure competition, reduce cost, provide information, improve quality, and impose sanctions on providers who do not meet appropriate standards. The general justification for regulation is to redress market failure, that is, where market competition is not working. Markets work best when consumers have access to information and where competitors can easily enter the market. If there is no competitive market, barriers to competition can be eliminated only by government or other non-market institutions.[45] Health-care delivery is generally not considered to be a competitive market because consumers lack the necessary information to judge quality. Patients have difficulty understanding complex medical information and must rely on a physician's judgment. Also, the availability of health insurance means that patients are somewhat insulated from the true costs of their health care.

Health-care regulation comes in a variety of forms. Licensing of health-care practitioners, including physicians, non-physician practitioners, hospitals, and MCOs, is one important form. Health facility licensing, analogous to physician licensing, is another important state responsibility. For the most part, state licensing of health-care facilities focuses on financial solvency requirements, safety of the facility and equipment, proper sanitation and disposal policies, and personnel staffing ratios.[46] While the ultimate goal of regulation is to improve the quality of health care, quality is not, in reality, extensively regulated by the government.[47] Instead, quality of care in hospitals and MCOs (to the extent that it can be defined and measured) is regulated by independent, non-governmental accreditation entities. In the 1950s, the Joint Commission on Accreditation of Hospitals (now known as the Joint Commission on Accreditation of Healthcare Organizations) was formed as a voluntary organization to establish quality of care standards for hospitals and to accredit the facilities adhering to the standards. In the 1980s, the National Commission on Quality Assurance was formed to accredit MCOs. Neither government licensing nor private accreditation has made a major difference in improving quality of care;[48] nor has either entity used its sanctioning powers very often.

During the period before the Civil War, health care was viewed as a private sector activity and subject to very little state intervention. At this time, there was little federal involvement in health care, and most states were concerned with regulating public health rather than with licensing physicians. State legislatures were primarily concerned with stopping the spread of infectious diseases and with improving sanitation. Early state regulations to combat smallpox and yellow fever involved quarantines and smallpox inoculations, actions that were very controversial.[49] (Childhood vaccinations remain controversial today, and many states now have laws exempting religious objectors from childhood vaccination requirements.) States also retained jurisdiction to provide care for the mentally ill.

After the Civil War, the states became more active in regulating public health, especially in establishing a systematic public health infrastructure and creating mental health hospitals. In 1856, Louisiana created a statewide board of health. By 1873, the states of Massachusetts, California, and Michigan had also formed state boards of health, and 19 states followed that model by 1879. A National Health Board was formed in 1879, and for four years struggled to establish itself by aiding the states in their quarantine regulations. But state resistance to federal intrusion was strong and the Board disintegrated by 1883.[50]

State and municipal health-care regulation proliferated during the early decades of the twentieth century. Advances in the understanding of medicine forced a more rigid academic study of medicine, and states started to aggressively regulate educational programs from 1905 to 1927. Formal medical specialties emerged in the 1930s, beginning with the training of surgeons and diagnosticians. The promise of higher wages attracted better students, so that by the end of the second world war, doctors and hospitals experienced a dramatic gain in public trust.

At the federal level, most regulation between the Civil War and the beginning of the twentieth century dealt with public health concerns. Before the New Deal era in the 1930s, the federal government's primary regulatory involvement was limited to either military personnel or seamen—especially quarantines to limit the spread of contagious diseases.[51] Courts narrowly interpreted the federal grant of authority in health care, thereby limiting the federal government's involvement in health-related legislation.

The New Deal generated the initial social welfare legislation that supported federal aid to the states for health and welfare services. Through the Social Security Act of 1935, Congress established the Old Age, Survivors' and Disability Insurance programs that provided the philosophical basis for the enactment of Medicare and Medicaid in 1965 and established the principle of federal aid to the states for health and welfare programs. For the first time, the federal government took financial responsibility for a segment of the population that was unable to take care of itself. Yet direct federal aid for health care remained limited to active military personnel, veterans, and Native Americans until the 1960s.[52]

During the New Deal, the federal government began to regulate aspects of the marketplace, including health care, that had previously been controlled by the private sector. For example, the death of several children from elixir of sulfonamide led to the enactment of the Food, Drug, and Cosmetic Act in 1938, requiring manufacturers to demonstrate product safety (subsequently expanded to include efficacy) before marketing to the public.[53]

Also during the 1930s, the federal government responded to the increasingly scientific nature of medical practice by expanding the National Institutes of Health (NIH). Recognizing the need for disease-specific research and the need to provide research training, Congress expanded NIH by establishing a series of disease-specific institutes such as the National Cancer Institute. After World War II, NIH became the primary sponsor of biomedical research and research training: ". . . in the period after World War II until the 1960s, federal support for biomedical research was one of the few areas of health policy in which the federal government was active."[54]

Another area of federal activity during and after World War II was in stimulating the construction of new hospitals. With the expansion of scientific knowledge and the rising importance of hospital-based care, it became apparent that hospital physical plants and equipment were inadequate to meet the increased demand. In response, Congress enacted the *Hospital Survey and Construction Act of 1947*[55] (popularly known as the Hill-Burton Act, named after its primary congressional sponsors) to construct and modernize hospitals. Under this program, the federal government provided funds for states to assess and plan their hospital capital development needs, and provided matching funds for hospital construction and modernization programs according to that plan. From 1946 to 1976, the Hill-Burton program supported the construction of 40 percent of the hospital bed capacity in the United States.[56]

The Hill-Burton program underwrote the postwar hospital construction boom and was "remarkably successful."[57] Well into the 1970s, this program was a major source of funding for the hospital industry, with only limited regulatory constraints. Recipients of Hill-Burton funds were required to provide a certain level of uncompensated care to the poor (proportionate to the amount of money provided by the government) and to provide community service.[58] Each facility's uncompensated care responsibility lasted no more than 20 years, but the community service requirement, remains for the life of the facility. The "community service obligation" and the "reasonable volume" (or "uncompensated care") assurance were not well defined and initially not widely enforced. They were largely ignored by hospitals receiving Hill-Burton funds until the late 1970s, when federally funded poverty lawyers persuaded the federal courts to enforce the Hill-Burton requirements.[59] In 1979, the Department of Health and Human Services issued regulations that set forth the expectations for meeting both obligations.

Some supporters of Hill-Burton hoped that the program would be used as a mechanism for planning how health care should be delivered. But states and the hospital industry clearly viewed Hill-Burton as a construction program, not as a planning apparatus. For any number of reasons, the planning process was quickly overtaken by the imperative to construct inpatient beds. Hill-Burton contributed to the oversupply of beds rather than encouraging a rational planning process for hospital construction and modernization.[60]

Legal Support of Physician Dominance

During the first part of the twentieth century, the medical profession gained in scientific prowess and came to dominate the health-care delivery system.[61] The existing regulatory structure did little to impede physician dominance. To the contrary, the medical profession was considerably aided by the legal system in establishing its primacy. Even though medical malpractice litigation continued to vex relations between doctors and lawyers, in other ways the legal system was very accommodating to the medical profession. The state licensing of medical practice was largely controlled by the medical profession, virtually ensuring physician predominance. And legal doctrine developed in ways that actually supported physicians control over health-care delivery, largely affirming the prevailing model of physician autonomy. For the most part, quality of care monitoring was ceded to physicians in the fee-for-service system.

Until the emergence of large, integrated health systems (i.e., managed care organizations) in the 1980s and 1990s, licensing and general oversight of medical practitioners were arguably the most important aspects of state-level health-care regulation. Licensing medical professionals serves several purposes. The process defines who is capable of practicing medicine and specifies the scope of practice and of professional autonomy. An important function is to ensure minimum levels of competence in an area that is difficult for laymen to monitor on their own. Licensing agencies develop and monitor ongoing education requirements and impose sanctions on behavior that falls below acceptable standards. Each state maintains its own licensing system, though most states have similar requirements. For example, most states require doctors to graduate from an accredited medical school and pass a state entrance examination designed to evaluate the applicants' training and fitness.

Although licensing of medical professions dates back to the early seventeenth century,[62] most licensing laws had been repealed by the middle of the nineteenth century. The primary reasons for their repeal were the inadequate scientific basis for medical practice and the populist approach of the Jacksonian era. By the end of the nineteenth century, however, all states required medical practitioners to be licensed, and those laws were strengthened during the first part of the twentieth century.[63]

Physicians led the restoration of medical licensing in the late nineteenth century, largely to secure control over the practice of medicine by ". . . protecting themselves against competition from untrained practitioners."[64] Physicians anticipated that strict state licensing requirements would provide them with a dominant voice in setting standards of practice and in controlling the licensing process. Over time, this is exactly what happened. State licensure laws delegated control to agencies dominated by physicians.[65] To be sure, these agencies have always retained the power to sanction practitioners or revoke their license, but this rarely happens. Except under egregious circumstances, state licensing agencies have been reluctant to revoke a physician's license over quality-of-care concerns. In recent years, state licensing agencies have been more aggressive in removing licenses for related issues, such as drug use. Overall, the agencies have insulated physicians from competition by restricting the scope of clinical practice for nurses, nurse practitioners, physician assistants, and other potential competitors. All potential competitors are also licensed to practice by the state, but usually under more restrictive circumstances than apply to physicians.

In addition to excluding competitors from practicing medicine, state licensing laws give almost complete control over who can practice medicine to the medical profession, thereby preserving physicians' economic and professional status. The medical profession controls the number of applicants admitted to medical school, the medical curriculum, and the boards of medical examiners who set state admissions and education requirements, essentially controlling the licensing process. In turn, this virtually assured physician control over medical practice throughout the first six decades of the twentieth century. Since physicians could either exclude competitors or restrict their scope of practice, they had no serious challengers to their primacy.

It did not take long before excluded practitioners challenged the legitimacy of medical licensing laws. In 1882, the West Virginia State Board of Health rejected Frank M. Dent's application for a medical license. Even though Dent was already practicing medicine in the state, he was denied a medical license because he had not graduated from a reputable school (he had graduated from the American Medical Eclectic College). After being fined and convicted for the unlicensed practice of medicine, Dent challenged the authority of the state's licensing system all the way to the United States Supreme Court. A unanimous Supreme Court rejected Dent's challenge, holding that the regulation was a reasonable measure to ensure professional competence and to protect the public.[66] Most important, the Court said that a license provided the public with the assurance that the physician possessed the necessary qualifications to practice medicine as determined by those able to judge the physician's qualifications, skill, and learning. The Court endorsed the argument that lay people lacked the expertise to judge medical competence and need regulatory intervention to protect them.[67]

The Court also showed considerable deference to the medical profession's expertise, a deference that would recur throughout most of the twentieth century. As a matter of separation of powers, courts generally defer to the police powers inherent in governmental sovereignty and the state's regulatory authority. The *Dent* case assured that states would be granted wide-ranging authority to regulate medical care. After *Dent*, reasonable state regulations would be upheld against most challenges.

The *Dent* case is a valuable demonstration of the interaction between the courts and regulators. Courts retain the authority to strike down regulations when a legislature or regulatory agency has acted beyond its authority, but tend to use this authority only in extreme cases.[68] For instance, the Environmental Protection Agency was blocked from banning asbestos because the agency did not consider the harms from potential substitutes in its cost-benefit calculations.[69] In the latter half of the twentieth century, virtually every major health-care statute and regulation has been subjected to judicial challenge, and most have survived judicial scrutiny. As long as the regulatory record, when viewed as a whole, supports the regulatory agency's decisions, courts will defer to the agency's technical expertise and delegated authority.

Controlling the licensing process was a necessary aspect of securing clinical autonomy and dominance over health-care delivery, but was not sufficient by itself. Legal doctrine (common-law rules to define professional liability) could undermine the physicians' dominance if liability rules permitted social control by non-physicians (such as prepaid health plans, employers, or hospital administrators) over medical practice. Allowing employers to hire doctors and control clinical decisions could also compromise physicians' autonomy and professional dominance.

During the first half of the twentieth century, the development of legal doctrine regarding health-care delivery centered on defining the extent and conditions of physicians' professional liability. The fee-for-service system, where most people received their health care, defined both the nature of medical practice and the legal response to it. In the fee-for-service system, the primary relationship was between the physician and the patient, with the patient or the insurer paying for whatever the physician ordered. Until the mid-1960s, hospitals had little control over clinical care and no independent responsibility for the patient's well-being. Most physicians were engaged in the solo practice of medicine; physician specialty groups were rare at that time. The legal rules developed to adjudicate liability claims were based on the nature of the fee-for-service system and rested on the assumption that physicians controlled most health-care resources. Prior to the mid-1960s, the legal system enhanced physicians' dominance over the health-care system rather than supporting external controls over medical practice.[70]

Another set of assumptions was that the standard of care was to be defined by customary care offered by one of ordinary skill, and that other physicians were best able to define the professional standard of care. The liability rules that developed did not require a physician to guarantee success, merely to practice medicine in the same way as would a practitioner of similar skill. (See Chapter 5.) From the late nineteenth century onward, the courts deferred to the medical profession to set its own standard of care rather than imposing community standards of reasonableness determined by judges and juries. Reliance on physicians to set the standard of care reinforced physician autonomy.[71]

Until the late 1980s and early 1990s, there was a symbiotic relationship between law and medicine, with the courts actually upholding physicians' dominance over health-care delivery[72] and acting as a conduit for the expansion of the medical industry.[73] In this sense, the courts reinforced what has been termed the *professional dominance model* where physicians controlled the health-care delivery system. Throughout this period, courts generally deferred to the treating physician's judgment in deciding what services should be provided and how the clinical encounter should be conducted.

Despite the complaints doctors raised about malpractice litigation, the courts developed "implementing rules" (that is, rules of how to interpret the legal standard) to apply the standard of care that were highly favorable to physicians. These rules had the effect of guaranteeing the individual physician autonomy over medical decisions. Until the 1960s, for instance, "customary practice" was defined by using the locality rule.[74] Under this rule, the standard of care was defined as customary practice within the same community. Often, this made it difficult for an injured patient to recover because of trouble obtaining testimony from another physician in the same community. The locality rule did not begin to erode until the mid-1960s and became largely obsolete by the mid-1980s.

Another rule, the "captain of the ship" doctrine, actually exposed physicians to greater liability, but further secured their autonomy. As "captains," courts presumed, physicians were in charge of medical procedures and were thus accountable for the actions of staff working under their direction, such as nurses or other hospital personnel. Courts imposed liability on the physician as the party responsible for quality of care. Perhaps paradoxically, ". . . the legal responsibility [physicians] bore both reflected and enhanced their status in hospitals."[75] In the first part of the twentieth century, this distinction made sense. Most hospitals were immune from tort liability before the mid-1960s as charitable institutions, and physicians largely controlled how resources were allocated. It was not until the 1960s that hospitals became central to health-care delivery. At that point, courts began to reject claims of charitable immunity and held hospitals accountable for their quality of care.

An equally important set of judicial rulings constrained the institutional control over medical practice in the first half of the twentieth century. Courts reinforced the gains physicians made through licensing laws in several ways.[76] The courts broadly interpreted physician licensing laws to restrict entry by competing practitioners, such as chiropractors. Most of the time, judges also upheld physicians' challenges to the unauthorized practice of medicine based on the licensing provisions.

Legislatures generally, and courts specifically, supported doctors' resistance to institutional control over their clinical autonomy. Many states enacted laws, at the behest of physicians, prohibiting corporations from employing physicians to deliver health care. Known as the "corporate practice of medicine doctrine," these laws stated that only licensed medical practitioners can practice medicine, not corporate entities. The corporate practice of medicine doctrine sharply reduced the ability of alternative health-care delivery systems, such as prepaid health care (i.e., HMOs and MCOs), to expand.[77] This doctrine was repeatedly upheld by the courts to prevent institutional or lay control over medical decisions; even hospitals were blocked from employing specialists in response to changing technological needs in the 1950s.[78]

In supporting the doctrine, the American Medical Association (AMA) admonished physicians not to provide services under conditions that might prevent doctors from exercising medical judgment with complete freedom, or under conditions that might result in lower quality of medical care. The medical profession has been persistently opposed to corporate sponsorship of health care or other alternative health-care coverage and delivery structures, e.g., prepaid group health plans, deeming such arrangements a threat to their professional autonomy, income and prestige, not to mention to the quality of care.[79]

A similar approach by the courts in early hospital liability cases resulted in legal doctrine insulating hospitals from any liability for medical decisions. Before the mid-1960s, hospitals could be held liable only for their administrative decisions, not for how medical care was delivered.[80] The reasoning underlying both of these developments was that ". . . a licensed physician may not accept directions in diagnosing and treating ailments from . . . an individual who is not a licensed practitioner."[81] A corporation headed by a non-physician, which cannot qualify for a medical license but can employ physicians, would therefore be practicing medicine without a license.

Another area of legal doctrine provided further support for the treating physician's exercise of clinical autonomy. Many commercial insurers (and then Medicare and Medicaid as well) began to include provisions in their contracts with patients to provide only care that was "medically necessary."[82] In a trend that would accelerate during the 1970s and 1980s, many courts basically disregarded the medical necessity limitation by deferring to the treating physician to determine the patient's needs. In a typical case, a court required reimbursement for an obese patient who was hospitalized for observation because ". . . only the treating physician can determine what the appropriate treatment should be for any given condition."[83]

At the midpoint of the 1960s, then, the courts supported the sanctity of the physician–patient relationship. In effect, the law erected formidable barriers to institutional interference with a physician's clinical judgment. The courts provided consistent support for physician autonomy and control over medical practice decisions. As one observer noted: "The courts have often shown themselves willing to defend the rights of patients to receive, and doctors to prescribe whatever medical services might be of some help—without regard to cost."[84]

By the mid-1960s, the federal and state governments had only established a minimal presence in health care, which was largely peripheral to the private sector's control over the health-care system. Health care was not heavily regulated, except perhaps for professional and institutional licensing, and was still viewed as a private sector activity. Indeed, health care was an important, but relatively small aspect of the American economy and social structure, which was controlled by physicians. The legislative and judicial environment was very supportive of the physician-dominated model of health-care delivery.

To this point in time, most of the contact between doctors and lawyers, and between the legal and medical systems, took place in courtroom battles over medical malpractice and the use of physicians as expert witnesses. Nevertheless, there was a certain stability in the health-care order. All that would change with the enactment of Medicare and Medicaid in 1965 and the expansion of managed care in the 1990s.

Notes

1. Quoted in Stryker (1932), p. xxi.
2. Mohr (1993).
3. Fox (1987).
4. Naitove (1982); Fox (1987); Gibson and Schwartz (1980).
5. Fox (1987).
6. Gold (1981). Gold argues that the essential tension between law and medicine is the tension between the principle of technical knowledge and democratic control and accountability.
7. Yale Medical School Dean L.E. Rosenberg, as cited in Dickens (1987).
8. Mohr (1993). Mohr defines medical jurisprudence as a separate professional field "facilitating or mediating" between law and medicine (p. xiii).
9. *Ibid.*, p. 47.
10. *Ibid.*, p. 77.
11. *Ibid.*, pp. 58, 74–75.
12. *Ibid.*, pp. 51–52.
13. Hall (1988) pp. 445–446.
14. Mohr (1993) p. 91.
15. *Ibid.*, p. 112.
16. At least as understood in the nineteenth century as a collegial, cooperative enterprise. Medical jurisprudence survives today as the use of medical expertise in court.
17. Mohr (2000).

18. Mohr (1993) implies that most previous malpractice litigation was directed toward medical charlatans, and hence was supported by trained physicians.

19. *Black's Law Dictionary* (1991).

20. Mohr (1993); Morantz-Sanchez (1999).

21. Mohr (1993), p. 236.

22. *Ibid.* pp. 100–101.

23. Morantz-Sanchez (1999).

24. Mohr (1993), p. 186.

25. *Ibid.*, p. 198.

26. Starr (1982).

27. *Ibid.*, p. 77.

28. Ayers (1996), pp. 8–15.

29. Starr (1982), p. 149. For more detail about the origin of hospital care, see Starr (1982) and Stevens (1989).

30. Starr (1982), p. 158.

31. *Ibid.*, p. 112.

32. Morantz-Sanchez (1999).

33. Mohr (1993), p. 114.

34. *Ibid.*, p. 112. Mohr goes on to note that rising expectations for health and physician intervention fueled such attitudes. This is similar to what occurred during the medical malpractice crises in the 1970s and 1980s (Jacobson, 1989).

35. Mohr (1993).

36. Morantz-Sanchez (1999), p. 201.

37. *Ibid.*

38. Mohr (2000), p. 1735.

39. *Ibid.*

40. Morantz-Sanchez (1999).

41. This account is taken from Morantz-Sanchez (1999).

42. Sellers (1991).

43. The Tenth Amendment reads, "The powers not delegated to the United States by the Constitution, nor prohibited by it to the states, are reserved to the states respectively, or to the people." This was intended both to ensure that the federal government would not encroach too greatly upon the autonomy of the state governments and to maintain a federalist structure of government.

44. Regulation in general may also be viewed along a continuum, from rules that facilitate market-based arrangements (e.g., private accreditation or professional ethical codes) to rules that substitute for or displace market strategies (e.g., health planning or national health insurance).

45. Arrow (1963). There is an extensive academic literature on the theory of regulation that goes beyond the basic market-failure explanation. For example, a competing explanation—the capture theory of regulation—maintains that regulations are adopted in response to the demands of various interest groups. In a different analysis, public choice theorists assume that regulators attempt to maximize their own power and that altruistic, public interest goals are insignificant factors. Perhaps the most complete theory of the political process is Wilson's (1980) classification in terms of the distribution of perceived benefits and costs to the public and to affected industries.

46. Jost (1995). According to Wing (1999, p. 128) ". . . licensing generally has been regarded as setting minimum standards for safe facilities, not normative standards for the delivery of care."

47. Brennan (1998).

48. *Ibid.*

49. See, e.g., *Jacobson v. Massachusetts,* 197 U.S. 11 (1904), rejecting an individual's challenge to a Cambridge, Massachusetts, law mandating smallpox inoculations.

50. Smillie (1976), pp. 331–39.

51. Smillie (1976), pp. 258–68. The federal government passed its first law requiring that ships provide passengers certain minimum accommodations in 1790. This code was later amended to require minimum berth space, hospital space, and ventilation. The limit of government's human concern is evidenced by an 1848 law explicitly exempting slave ships from the minimum space requirements (Federal Statutes at Large, Vol. 1, p. 135, and Vol.9, p. 210).

52. Lee and Benjamin (1999), p. 451.

53. *Ibid.*

54. *Ibid.*, p. 452.

55. 42 U.S.C. §§291–291(0) 2C.F.R. §124.508.

56. Rosenblatt et al. (1997).

57. Wing (1999), p. 132.

58. Sadly, Hill-Burton also permitted facilities to remain segregated under provisions that allowed for separate but equal hospital admissions. The "separate but equal" provision was overturned in *Simpkins v. Moses H. Cone Memorial Hospital,* 323 F.2d 959 (4th Cir. 1963). For an excellent history of Hill-Burton within the broader context of racial discrimination in health care, see Smith (1999).

59. Rosenblatt et al. (1997): Blumstein (1984). In *Newsom v. Vanderbilt University,* 453 F. Supp. 401 (M.D. Tenn. 1978), the court declared that indigent patients had a "constitutionally protected right . . . to needed uncompensated services under the Hill-Burton Act."

60. Wing (1999), pp. 132–33.

61. Starr (1982).

62. For example, Virginia enacted a law to regulate medical practitioners in 1639, followed by Massachusetts in 1649. Smillie (1976).

63. Wing (1999).

64. Starr (1982) p. 102.

65. Economists and political scientists use the term *capture* to indicate that the regulated industry exercises a great deal of control over how the regulations are developed and implemented. See, e.g., Weissert and Weissert (1996) and Wilson (1980).

66. *Dent v. West Virginia,* 129 U.S. 114 (1889). For additional detail, see Starr (1982) p. 106; and Jost (1997), pp. 1–2.

67. Jost (1997), p. 2.

68. For an example, see *Boreali v. Axelrod,* 517 N.E.2d 1350 (N.Y. 1987).

69. *Corrosion Proof Fittings v. EPA,* 947 F.2d 1201 (5th Cir. 1991); Sunstein (1996).

70. While the legal system played an important role in securing physician dominance, it was not the only influence. Hall (1988) notes, for example, that the indemnity insurance model that developed in the 1930s was based on physician autonomy for medical practice. Also, the medical profession had the ability to block national health insurance or other prepaid insurance mechanisms that threatened their professional sovereignty (Hall [1988], p. 446; Starr [1982], p. 306). For additional detail, see Starr (1982), pp. 295–310.

71. Hall (1988), p. 448; Silver (1992). See other sources noted in Silver at footnote 59, p. 1213. Silver argues that the courts in the late nineteenth century departed from

earlier cases that required showing ordinary care, as determined by reasonableness principles, as opposed to customary care among physicians.

72. Hall (1988).

73. Kapp (1985).

74. *Brune v. Belinkoff*, 235 N.E.2d 793 (Mass. 1968).

75. Havighurst (1997), p. 595.

76. Hall (1988).

77. "During the 1930s, when prepaid group practices (now known as HMOs) were being developed in response to severe gaps in insurance coverage, the corporate practice of medicine doctrine was a major obstacle that took decades to remove." Hall (1988), p. 510. The corporate practice of medicine doctrine has been widely and severely criticized by legal scholars. See, e.g., Hall (1988), pp. 511–21. The doctrine is rapidly eroding. One court declared the doctrine to be obsolete and refused to uphold it, and many states have enacted laws providing numerous exceptions or overturning it altogether.

78. *Ibid.*

79. Chase-Lubitz (1987), pp. 458, 478.

80. Hall (1988); Havighurst (1997).

81. *Iterman v. Baker*, 15 N.E.2d 365, 370 (1938)—cited in Hall (1988).

82. *Medical necessity* is a notoriously difficult term to define and implement effectively. See, e.g., Jacobson, Asch, Glassman, Model, and Hernandez (1997).

83. *Mount Sinai Hospital v. Zorek*, 271 N.Y.S.2d 1012, 1016 (N.Y. Civ. Ct. 1966)—cited in Hall (1988).

84. Relman (1985), p. 109—cited in Hall (1988).

3

From Liability to Business

PHYSICIANS and health-care executives routinely and legitimately complain that the legal system is more intrusive than ever before. Over the past 30 years, the regulatory structure overseeing health care has exploded, and the perceived intrusiveness of the courts has only increased. In the managed care era, courts are deciding challenges to cost-containment innovations while legislatures are considering numerous patient protection provisions and other laws regulating health-care delivery. Insurers' attempts to limit the amount of health-care resources used leads to litigation to determine what constitutes medical necessity.[1] There is constant litigation to interpret the large volume of state and federal legislation now regulating health-care delivery. And successive medical malpractice insurance crises have resulted from increasing liability litigation.[2]

When Professor Arthur Southwick of the University of Michigan published his seminal treatise *The Law of Hospital and Health Care Administration*[3] in 1978, the health law world looked very different than it does today. In may ways, it more resembled the world described in Chapter 2, with the exception of greater regulatory requirements. By the second edition in 1988, Professor Southwick added only two new chapters, on antitrust law and quality assurance, that represented a substantial departure from the first version. If he had lived to revise his text for a third edition, he would have had to completely rewrite major portions of it. Considerable changes in legal doctrine and substantially increased regulation during the past decade would necessitate revising the otherwise unchanged chapters from the first to the second edition. Professor Southwick would also need to account for the stunning rise of managed care and the concomitant legal implications.

48

Consider just two items from the Southwick text to illustrate the changes. Note, first, the prominence of the word *hospital* in the title. In all likelihood, a revised edition would delete that word from the title, focusing instead on *health care institutions* as the more applicable term. Perhaps even more striking, Professor Southwick said the following in the preface to the second edition (at page xiii):

> It is the belief of the authors that a discussion of the legal aspects of governmental regulation of the health-care industry . . . [is] best reserved for separate books and courses of instruction. Moreover, some instructors believe that regulation should only be taught after a student has studied the law of contracts and tort.[4]

That statement is unimaginable today.

During the past three decades, we have witnessed the rise of the federal regulatory presence in health care, the erosion of physician control over the health-care system, the shift in public policy from the federal government back to the states, and the emergence of managed care. Health law has developed as a separate legal specialty in response to these events.

Health Law in 1965

As recently as the late 1960s and early 1970s, health-care attorneys and health-care executives had a relatively easy set of legal rules to follow. The liability rules and the elements required to prove a departure from the standard of care remained stable and predictable until the arrival of managed care.[5] Both sides could predict the nature and scope of litigation since the fundamental rules establishing the standard of care and the types of lawsuits initiated varied little during this period. A typical court case involved one patient suing one physician, guided by liability rules that reflected judicial deference to physicians in setting the standard of care. After the mid-1960s, a hospital might also be sued. Although there were constant complaints from physicians about the intrusiveness of medical malpractice law and an incipient rise in medical liability claims, litigation was confined to a few areas affecting the delivery of health care.

At this time, there were no health law professional associations: they were not formed until 1968 (the American Academy of Hospital Attorneys) and 1971 (the National Health Lawyers Association).[6] If one were to consider health law courses offered in the late 1960s and early 1970s, it would be apparent how limited they were. The courses consisted primarily of one on law and medicine and another on law and psychiatry. Both dealt almost exclusively with court decisions on medical liability and medical forensics,[7] the same types of cases that dominated law and medicine from the beginning. Legislation and regulation were simply not discussed, in large part because they did not exist. A commonly held perception was that the legal system's primary health-care role was to monitor quality of care through highly contested medical liability determinations.[8] Even the Medicare and Medicaid rules were at first limited to reimbursement concerns, rather than addressing regulatory concerns.

In the late 1960s, most professional contact between physicians and attorneys was through malpractice litigation, primarily with the lawyer seeking information on a patient during discovery, or cross-examining the physician as an expert witness. Since then, with the expansion of medical care into a national enterprise, physicians have become intimately familiar with attorneys in many formal contexts. Increasingly, attorneys serve as counselor to physicians and to health-care executives in negotiating some complex medico-legal issue, such as the acquisition or organization of a physician group or the development of a joint venture.

The initial change in health law came in response to the rising importance of hospital care. By the mid-1960s, as hospitals became increasingly central to health-care delivery, the need to hold them legally accountable for care within their facilities was apparent to the courts. But that was no small task, since hospitals were immune from liability as charitable institutions. In any event, physicians, not hospital administrators, treated patients. How could liability be imposed under these circumstances?

Hospitals developed as charitable institutions from almshouses for the poor. As the charitable form of hospital organization took hold, the law responded by immunizing hospitals from liability for the medical care provided within the hospital. In most states, charitable immunity prevented the patient from suing the hospital for medical injuries occurring there.[9] Beyond this, the corporate practice of medicine doctrine made it difficult to sue hospitals directly for negligence committed by its professional employees (i.e., a nurse or physician). The patient was forced to sue the treating physician under the theory that only licensed practitioners, not corporate entities, were responsible for medical care.

In the mid-1960s, courts began to apply certain liability principles (known as agency law) to hospitals. Under these principles, a hospital could be indirectly (or vicariously) responsible for an employee's conduct. The availability of indirect liability allowed patients to sue the hospital for any negligence committed by its employees. Courts still did not impose legal responsibility for quality of care on hospitals, so they could not be sued directly for a patient's injury. Since most physicians were independent contractors, with staff privileges to admit and treat patients in the hospital, rather than employees, hospitals were not held legally responsible for their actions. To the patient, the nuance of the physician's status as an independent contractor or a hospital employee was usually lost during treatment. Even if the patient were informed of the distinction, it seemed appropriate to hold the institution responsible for care managed in its facility. From a policy perspective, liability should be assessed against hospitals to encourage them to develop and impose quality of care measures.[10]

The courts responded first by imposing direct institutional liability for substandard quality of care by employees, and then by expanding vicarious liability to hospitals for the actions of their independent contractors. Courts accepted the argument that hospitals could bear liability for professional employees whom it hired or fired, and that hospitals "... could ensure that the tasks assigned to them were within their demonstrated competence."[11] From there, it was but a small step toward holding hospitals vicariously liable for actions taken by the independent contractors, such as radiologists, anesthesiologists, and pathologists, over whom the hospital exercised control.

Beginning with the precedent-setting cases of *Bing v. Thunig*,[12] and *Darling v. Charleston Memorial Hospital*,[13] courts applied agency law principles to the hospital setting. In the 1966 *Darling* case, the plaintiff was treated for a leg injury at the hospital's emergency room. Ignoring evidence of serious postoperative complications, neither the treating physician nor the nurses took adequate steps to prevent subsequent harm. As a result, the leg had to be amputated. The court ruled that the hospital could be held directly liable for failing to monitor the physician's performance. Although the physician was an independent contractor, the court also ruled that the patient reasonably believed that the physician was the hospital's agent. Reflecting changes in health care delivery—namely, hospitals' increasing importance at the center of health care—other state courts followed *Darling* and applied vicarious liability principles to hospitals for actions that were previously the physician's exclusive responsibility. As we will see, this same process is occurring with the judicial response to managed care.

The addition of hospital liability was a boon to patients, risk managers, and malpractice attorneys, but it did little to change the nature of the dynamic or of the dialogue between physicians and attorneys. Most of that dialogue remained about liability and, from the physicians' perspective, how to make it go away. Most hospital grand rounds (lectures) involving legal issues were discussions of narrow liability questions. Since staff privileges were rarely denied, and were certainly not based on economic performance (as is now customary in managed care) there was little discussion of litigation over their denial.

Besides hospital immunity from litigation, the health law world of the late 1960s and early 1970s offered no barriers in the form of antitrust restrictions.

At that time, the antitrust laws did not apply to the learned professions, including law and medicine, and were considered irrelevant to health care. Sustained antitrust activity lay dormant until the mid-1980s as a factor leading toward a more competitive health care market.

During the late 1960s and early 1970s, health-care business transactions were limited and relatively straightforward, rarely requiring intensive legal advice or participation. For example, hospitals were required to meet state laws concerning financial solvency and corporate governance. The corporate practice of medicine doctrine meant that physicians, not hospitals, were the moving agents of change, and physicians were not interested in any changes. There was little, if any, federal regulation concerning hospitals, and state law was largely concerned with licensing physicians and hospitals, not with the business of health-care delivery. What might surprise a newly hired health care executive in the twenty-first century is that complex business decisions were the exception in the late 1960s. Contracting as an issue for hospital executives was limited to affiliation agreements allowing students to train at the facility. The use of contracts as flexible mechanisms to develop an endless array of joint ventures and other creative organizational forms lay many years in the future.

The period between 1965 and 1975 thus involved significant changes in liability rules and legal responsibility, roughly reflecting changes in how health care was organized and delivered. But the relationship between attorneys and physicians still revolved largely around medical liability principles, with hospital liability adding somewhat more complexity to a typical lawsuit. Nonetheless, the basic principles and relationships remained reasonably settled.

The era of relative stability lasted until the mid-1970s, when the nature of the cases and the direction of judicial decisions began to change. In three areas, courts clearly stimulated changes in health-care delivery: informed consent, bioethics, and antitrust law. What we see represented in these areas is not just a shift in the types of health-care cases reaching the courts, but a shift in judicial attitude as well. With these cases, courts indicated that they were less likely to treat the health-care industry as sacrosanct. In turn, physicians no longer viewed courts as agents assisting the medical profession but as adversaries usurping the medical profession's role in shaping health-care delivery, and interfering with patient care. As one scholar has noted,

> Although the legal system originally bolstered the old medical regime and embodied many of its tenets, changes in legal rules and doctrine eventually contributed to the old system's demise and its replacement by a more chaotic, partly market-driven system.[14]

The first judicial incursion into clinical practice beyond medical malpractice standards was the judicially imposed concept of *informed consent*. Consistent with the professional dominance model, physicians were often accused of paternalism—making decisions on behalf of their patients without explaining the risks and alternatives and without obtaining the patients' consent. With *Canterbury v. Spence*[15] in 1972, the courts started holding physicians accountable for seeking their patients' consent as part of the therapeutic encounter. In *Canterbury*, the plaintiff submitted to back surgery without being informed about the risk of paralysis. In a precedent-setting opinion, the court held that physicians have a duty to disclose such risks and to seek the patient's knowing consent to the medical intervention. The informed consent doctrine requires physicians to explain the risks of, and alternatives to, clinical interventions and to obtain a patient's written consent for a given medical procedure. A more rigorous professional informed consent requirement came in 1980 with the case of *Truman v. Thomas,*[16] holding a physician liable for not telling a patient about the potentially fatal consequences of refusing a suggested Pap test.

Many have questioned the extent to which informed consent has truly altered the physician–patient relationship.[17] Yet there seems little doubt that the development of this doctrine has been a contributing factor in shifting the nature of the relationship away from paternalism and toward one with greater patient involvement in medical treatment decisions. By compelling physicians to take account of patient autonomy and self-determination, the courts facilitated the move toward the patient's involvement in health-care decisions, including the development of patient satisfaction measures.[18] No doubt this has contributed to the erosion of physician dominance.

The second major foray the courts made into the clinical realm was to intervene in end-of-life situations. Indeed, the broader involvement of courts in health-care policy is most evident in bioethics. Interestingly, the field of bioethics, which was a dominant source of health policy and health-care delivery debates during the 1970s and 1980s, did not even exist in the 1960s.[19] Long before courts became involved, the bioethical questions were debated and quietly resolved in private between physicians, patients, and family members. Starting with the Karen Ann Quinlan[20] right-to-die case in 1976, courts became the central forum for resolving these issues. The resolution of bioethical dilemmas shifted from private bedside decision-making to very public litigation over issues ranging from termination of life-sustaining treatment and substituted judgment, to physician-assisted suicide. The ever-evolving constitutional doctrines of privacy and due process were stretched to encompass these medico-legal questions. That the courts were not necessarily prepared for this role is entirely beside the point.

The most obvious reason for judicial intervention in bioethics was the absence of consensus among health-care practitioners or legislators for resolving contentious issues created by technology's ability to keep greater numbers of people alive, but in a suspended state of consciousness. A second reason was the physicians' search for immunity from prosecution by applying for a court order about how to proceed in individual cases. More often than not, legislators and practitioners abdicated final decision-making authority to the courts. Many cases have been litigated because families and the medical profession could not agree on the appropriate clinical treatment. The burden on the courts has been recently alleviated by internal institutional mechanisms, such as ethics committees or bioethical consultants, that provide case-specific judgments and establish policy guidelines. But litigation continues because new issues constantly arise, including reproductive technology, genetics technology, and physician-assisted suicide, indicating a prominent ongoing role for the courts.

The bioethics revolution is closely tied to changes in the informed consent doctrine. Once courts started using principles of choice and autonomy to guide the physician–patient encounter, it became an incremental extension to apply these concepts to end-of-life decisions. The individual's right to develop advance directives or appoint health-care proxies to determine how his or her end-of-life care would be managed was codified in the federal Patient Self-Determination Act of 1987. Soon enough, the right to know about and opt for, or out of, certain treatments, even lifesaving experimental ones, would become the next cutting edge issue to litigate.

The third area in which the courts changed doctrine during the 1970s and 1980s was in applying antitrust principles to the learned professions (i.e., law and medicine). Antitrust laws seek to protect competition by prohibiting anti-competitive behavior. For example, antitrust laws prohibit competitors from colluding to fix prices or agreeing not to compete in certain geographical areas. Before the precedent-setting cases of *Goldfarb v. Virginia State Bar*,[21] and *Arizona v. Maricopa County Medical Society*,[22] the courts took the position that the learned professions were not subject to antitrust scrutiny. Without the incentive of antitrust liability, there was no meaningful role for competition in the health-care industry. At the same time, the courts showed considerable tolerance for restrictions on private health care market arrangements.[23] In 1975, however, the United States Supreme Court ruled that these professions were not immune from the antitrust laws.[24] The change in antitrust oversight opened health care to competition by preventing physicians from setting prices, controlling entry into the profession, and collectively organizing to forestall prepaid health care.

The involvement of courts in driving changes in the health-care delivery system toward a more competitive environment is perhaps most pronounced in the antitrust cases. Antitrust decisions influence the structure and organization of health-care delivery systems, in some instances dictating who can be a member of a medical staff. Changes in antitrust doctrine did not cause industry restructuring and organizational change, but they did help remove professional barriers to market reforms.[25] In the intervening two decades, antitrust law has played a pivotal role in the transition of health care from a professional dominance model to a more competitive industry. Changes in antitrust law, by inhibiting physicians' ability to set prices, have allowed MCOs to bargain over reimbursement rates and have forced physicians to compete over prices charged to health insurers.

Antitrust decisions have also undermined physicians' efforts to block entry for competing professionals. In *Wilk v. American Medical Association*,[26] the court ruled that the AMA restrained trade in violation of the antitrust laws by conducting an illegal boycott against chiropractors. Similar judicial opinions limit the power of organized medicine to control who its competitors will be, to inhibit individual physicians from contracting with managed care organizations, and to foster agreements among competing physicians to set maximum fees.[27] Yet courts have also refused to declare peer review activities anticompetitive under the antitrust laws. These decisions established the foundation for economic credentialing (the ability to base staff privileges on resource use patterns) and exclusive contracting arrangements (the ability to contract with one group of physicians as opposed to numerous individual practitioners).

The Shift to Business

In the mid- to late 1980s, health-care delivery rapidly changed from a local industry dominated by medical professionals and non–market-based (charitable) considerations into an industry increasingly guided by traditional market rules and arrangements. Now that health care is a big business, it is subject to a wider array of legislative and regulatory concerns. Not surprisingly, lawyers are directly and integrally involved in the business of health care.

Twenty to thirty years ago, the attorney's primary contact with the health-care system was with the physician, and secondarily with a hospital administrator, both contacts occurring through medical liability litigation. Most hospitals obtained their legal advice *gratis* from an attorney on the board of directors. Today, hospitals and health-care systems are run as business enterprises, requiring a wide array of legal services to support the various business arrangements. The hospital lawyer's primary responsibilities are to the health-care administrator and financial officers on business transactions, and lawyers are hired as employees or retained from private law firms specializing in health-care law. Except for those lawyers specializing in medical liability law, an attorney's role in the new environment has shifted from dealing with questions regarding patient care to focussing on business arrangements and relationships. Medical liability remains a point of contention between the professions, but it is no longer the center of their contact.

Right now, the most dominant transaction in health care is the increasing need to create joint ventures, which are arrangements between physicians and hospitals or health systems to own and operate separate businesses, such as ambulatory surgical centers. Joint ventures are based on complex contractual negotiations over how they should be organized, governed, funded, and operated. The competitive health-care environment requires flexible arrangements between physicians and hospitals or health systems to offer services that neither is willing (or perhaps able) to fund alone. Attorneys are intimately involved in facilitating those negotiations because the parties must take into account antitrust law, fraud and abuse regulations, reimbursement law, tax issues, and general corporate law principles. A typical deal could involve lawyers for the institutions, the physicians, and the government, and would be closely observed by attorneys representing competing institutions.

One clear consequence of the changes in health law is that lawyers and the legal system are now integral to all phases of the health-care delivery enterprise. The attorney has become an indispensable part of the management team, both to interpret law and to suggest legally appropriate initiatives. Physicians and health-care administrators must be conversant with the law and must spend an increasing amount of time with their lawyers on all sorts of matters that are important for, but peripheral to, providing health care to patients.

A question that arises from this brief overview is what role the legal system has played in the development of health care as a business. Has the legal system responded to the changes in ways that simply provide rules of the road, or has the legal system played a more facilitating role in the process? In some areas, that question is relatively easy to answer. The bioethics revolution started with the *Quinlan* case and was propelled throughout by judicial decisions. The courts also drove the informed consent revolution, though one might debate how revolutionary it is in reality. And the courts played an important role in antitrust decisions to eliminate certain barriers to competition, thereby providing a catalyst for further change. At a minimum, the courts have at least facilitated (and, in some aspects, supported) the shift to health care as a business. On a more restrained note, one observer concludes that "Despite its successes, the antitrust initiative has clearly failed to create a true, consumer-driven market for health services in the United States."[28]

The Expansion of Regulatory Oversight

Simultaneously with the developments in common law and the role of attorneys in business transactions, the 1970s, 1980s, and 1990s saw an inexorable expansion of federal and state regulations governing health-care delivery. The great divide in health-care regulation is the 1965 enactment of Medicare and Medicaid (Medicare is the federal insurance program that provides health insurance coverage for persons beginning at age 65. Medicaid is a state-federal program that offers health-care benefits to low-income and disabled individuals who meet established qualifications.) From that point forward, the federal government established a growing presence in health care as provider, insurer, purchaser, and regulator. The structure of regulation changed from mostly monitoring professional self-regulation to increasing governmental oversight, and also shifted from professional licensing to regulating health systems.[29]

Medicaid and Medicare changed the regulatory environment in many ways. By stimulating the development of health care as a national industry, these programs helped move control over health care away from physicians. Federal reimbursement, primarily Medicare, constitutes nearly 40% of a hospital's revenues. Hospitals have little choice but to follow federal regulations throughout the facility, which has the effect of subordinating state regulations to federal concerns. Within a few years after enactment, the costs of the Medicare and Medicaid programs began their steep ascent. One of the major regulatory battlegrounds after 1965 has been over whether and how to control the spiraling costs of medical technological advances. Among other cost-control mechanisms, the federal government initiated the process of technology assessment in determining whether to reimburse certain procedures and new technologies under Medicare and Medicaid. If reimbursement is denied, the cost of expensive technologies and interventions (such as transplants) is beyond what most people can afford to pay on their own.

One way to think about the federal government's post-1965 regulatory role is to look at three specific areas that tend to dominate health-care policy: access, costs, and quality. Before 1965, the government played a minimal role in guaranteeing access, limiting costs, and monitoring quality. The government's growing investment in Medicare and Medicaid and the ongoing concern about the number of people without health insurance virtually required the government to become more involved.

From the 1960s until the late 1970s, the dominant federal regulatory focus was on ensuring access to health care. During this time, Medicare and Medicaid were enacted and the leading policy debates were about the need for national health insurance. True, some commentators expressed concerns about controlling rising costs stemming from Medicare's generous reimbursement policies, but the regulatory battles were largely over the need for improved access to health-care coverage. For example, the first sentence of the State Health Planning and Resource Development Act of 1974 states that "access to health care shall be a priority of this statute."[30]

With one exception, lawmakers' concern for access declined almost completely after the mid-1970s, until a renewed focus on Medicaid coverage for children surfaced in the 1990s. To ensure emergency room access for low-income persons, Congress enacted the *Emergency Medical Treatment and Labor Act* (EMTALA) in 1986.[31] EMTALA requires emergency departments to screen and stabilize any patient presenting at the emergency department, regardless of their ability to pay.

In the late 1970s and, especially following the election of President Ronald Reagan in 1980, the regulatory emphasis changed dramatically away from access and toward controlling costs. Starting with the development of Medicare reimbursement limits in the mid-1980s (using the Prospective Payment System, or PPS), and continuing to the present, the main federal regulatory focus has been on cost containment.[32] Under PPS, the government projects hospital costs for specific medical categories (called Diagnosis Related Groups, or DRGs) and provides funding prior to treatment. If the cost of care is less than the projected amount, the hospital keeps the difference; but if the cost of care is higher, the facility loses money. With PPS, hospitals have an incentive to provide cost-effective care and curtail excessive institutional spending.

Concerns about the cost of health-care have dominated debates involving proposed federal health care legislation since the late 1980s. Proposed legislation to expand access for the medically under- or uninsured has continually been diverted because there is no obvious way to pay for it. Take, for example, congressional consideration of whether to eliminate disparities in insurance coverage between mental and physical health benefits—often called mental health parity. At the close of the 2001 congressional session, mental health parity failed because opponents argued that it would increase employer costs and lead to higher numbers of employees without any health insurance coverage.[33] The contours of the debate, between those who favor expanded benefits based on equity and those opposed because of costs, is a familiar refrain across a range of health-care issues. Even though the demise of the Clinton Administration's Health Security Act meant that the private sector would bear primary responsibility for cost controls, Congress continues to scrutinize proposed legislation for its potential cost implications. Legislation designed to protect patients' rights is scrutinized in the same way.

Growing concerns about the overall quality of health care and about medical errors set the stage for the trends that now shape the regulatory environment: controlling quality-of-care and shifting regulatory responsibility to the private sector. The government's primary quality of care oversight mechanism has been Medicare's Conditions of Participation. The Conditions set out certain minimum quality standards that facilities must meet to be eligible for Medicare and Medicaid participation. Congress also enacted the Health care Quality Information Act in 1986, providing protection for a hospital's internal peer review (i.e., quality control) processes.[34]

Each of the major public and private regulatory or accrediting bodies, the Medicare Conditions of Participation, the Joint Commission on Accreditation of Healthcare Organizations (JCAHO), and the National Commission on Quality Assurance (NCQA), relies largely on process indicators to measure quality. Except for medical malpractice litigation, there has been little oversight of the quality of medical professional services. Not only is quality notoriously difficult to measure and monitor, but "[t]he quality of care is not heavily regulated."[35] Some individual physicians, for example, have been barred from Medicare, but very few (if any) institutions have lost their Medicare certification because of low quality health care.

At least since the mid-1980s, Congress has considered a variety of market-based reforms to extend the market revolution in health care delivery. To stimulate patient choice of health care and encourage competition among health care providers, Congress enacted in 1998 a pilot test of Medical Savings Accounts (MSAs) in the Medicare program.[36] MSAs allow individuals to spend tax-free dollars to purchase health care and to retain any savings. The goal is to expand patients' choice of health-care providers through market-based competition. MSAs have not yet generated widespread acceptance in the marketplace, but the concept is a key aspect of market-based health-care reform strategies.

It seems undeniable that the scope of regulation has increased tremendously during the past ten years at both the state and federal levels. The larger the health-care enterprise, the more it resembles a business as opposed to a not-for-profit industry based on charitable principles; the more money at stake, the more the regulators are going to be involved. Perhaps the most evident governmental response to the growth of market-based health care has been the extensive and growing enforcement of laws prohibiting fraud and abuse in health care, such as regulations designed to limit financial kickbacks in return for referrals.[37] Billing and reimbursement procedures in institutions ranging from academic health centers to home health agencies have also been vigorously scrutinized.

Many of the new rules attempt to regulate the financial aspects of health-care delivery while preserving its charitable attributes. For example, EMTALA was enacted in response to concerns that patients without insurance were being "dumped" to public hospitals without being stabilized prior to the transfer. Likewise, the Internal Revenue Service closely monitors transactions involving for-profit and not-for-profit entities to ensure that the transaction furthers the charitable mission of the not-for-profit facility.

Even antitrust doctrine comprises aspects of a regulatory approach. During the 1990s, most recently in 1996, the Federal Trade Commission and the Department of Justice issued guidelines to define what types of market arrangements would be protected from antitrust scrutiny.[38] For example, the guidelines define practices that the regulators argue should constitute a "safe harbor" and be protected from an antitrust challenge. Activities outside the safe harbor might be antitrust violations. The guidelines have been most important in antitrust challenges to mergers and joint ventures where courts must balance the efficiencies of the activity with any anticompetitive effects, such as reduced access to services or the potential use of market power to raise prices.[39,40] Judges have relied on the guidelines to determine whether a proposed merger violates antitrust laws.

Along with federal legislation, states have been very active in health-care legislation and regulation. Recall from Chapter 2 that states have historically had primary responsibility for health-care regulation. Current state laws encompass a wide array of efforts to respond to the most prominent public complaints, although there is little uniformity in states' attempts to hold MCOs accountable.[41] Such laws include mandating access to specialists, requiring external review of health coverage denials, and determining which providers are eligible to contract with MCOs. Were it not for concerns about ERISA preemption, it seems likely that states would be even more aggressive in regulating managed care. If one views this environment in its best light, myriad state experiments are underway that, with the proper evaluation and analysis, will provide insight into the best mechanisms for monitoring managed care. In a less flattering light, it resembles a wish to do something regardless of whether the legislation is an effective approach.

Health System Regulation

Many health-care providers, especially physicians, still view the health-care delivery enterprise as a local industry. Against this view, its sheer size, scale, cost, and importance inevitably invite regulatory oversight and scrutiny from federal and state policy makers. Without question, as with fraud and abuse and data privacy regulations, that oversight can at times be most intrusive. What is lacking at this point is a consistent framework for a regulatory structure that responds to managed care's shortcomings while still permitting cost-containment initiatives to be implemented.

In deciding what type of regulatory system to develop, one might ask three questions. First, what is the specific justification for regulating? One justification is that neither the market nor the medical profession adequately protects the public. Another is that health care is not a competitive market. As we have seen, the causes of market failure include information disparities between physicians and patients, uncertainty in understanding the quality of medical care, the uncertainty of medical intervention, and the use of insurance to protect patients from the costs of health care.

Second, what is the regulatory structure (i.e., the source of regulatory authority) that should be devised? The possibilities include government regulation only—state or federal or both. An alternative would be industry or professional self-regulation (a voluntary market-based approach). A combined public-private approach can also be considered. An unlikely scenario is market self-correction requiring little or no regulatory oversight.

Third, what is the content (i.e., regulatory detail) of regulation? The possibilities include general guidance through broad standards, with specific process measures to be met. Accrediting body standards fit this approach. An alternative is prescriptive detail, such as top-down governmental regulation, where failure to meet the standards can be subjected to financial sanctions. Under either approach, compliance agreements between the government and the health-care facility provide considerable flexibility in how to meet the standards and are often used to settle antitrust or fraud and abuse allegations.

An aspect of health-care regulation that is problematic, but has not yet received much attention, is the potential conflict between the various legislative and regulatory mandates. In the mid-1980s, one scholar argued that court decisions mandating access to care conflicted with emerging public policy dictates to contain costs.[42] That disparity is now much greater, and the various regulations often seem to pursue contradictory social policies. Both physicians and health care administrators justly complain about pervasive and inconsistent regulations. The Federal Register, where federal regulations are initially published for public commentary, includes hundreds of pages on fraud and abuse and privacy, to name just two categories. It seems inconceivable that health plans and hospitals can comply with all of them, even with the best of intentions. One of the problems with the expansion of regulations during the past few decades is that it becomes difficult to devise a coherent regulatory scheme that does not overlap or contradict itself. In that regard, the regulatory system has not succeeded.

In fact, the post-1963 history of health-care regulation seems a study in contradictions and lack of coordination. The overall regulatory burden has expanded, but the very market failures that presumably justify the regulatory apparatus remain as intractable as ever. Some aspects—such as fraud and abuse—are heavily regulated, while other aspects, such as quality of care, lie seemingly beyond regulatory scrutiny. And the greater the number and type of regulations, the greater the likelihood that they will be inconsistent and perhaps contradictory.

One of the most egregious examples of this clash is that public policy specifically favors cost containment, yet the Inspector General of the Department of Health and Human Services has blocked a type of cost-saving agreement between hospitals and physicians known as "gainsharing" because it violates the fraud and abuse laws. In gainsharing, physicians share in cost savings resulting from reduced health-care utilization. The Inspector General ruled that this arrangement violates fraud and abuse laws because it may result in undertreatment. While that may be true in theory, it is hard to reconcile the attack on gainsharing with the underlying policy goals of reducing costs. Numerous other examples, especially centered around fraud and abuse, make it difficult to predict what practices will violate one set of regulations even as they conform to another.

Another example is the conflict between privacy and confidentiality expectations and improving quality assurance by reducing medical errors. It seems doubtful that we can have both simultaneously. Under private accreditation standards, as well as state and federal regulations, medical errors (or, in the language of the accrediting entities, "sentinel events") resulting in serious injury or death are to be disclosed voluntarily. Certainly this is a good idea in theory, but voluntary disclosure may expose the facility to medical liability actions. Unless the information being reported is protected from disclosure and use in a medical malpractice lawsuit, health plans and hospitals will be reluctant to report their mistakes. This reluctance undermines the ability to work with the accrediting agencies to develop effective systems to detect and prevent potential medical errors before they occur.

All of this regulatory activity has resulted in a great deal of confusion about what is required and how best to proceed. The salient question is not the appropriateness of the regulations themselves, which are likely to expand in any event, but where regulatory authority resides. Over the next few years, the issue will be whether the primary source of regulation will be the government or will inevitably move toward private sector entities such as NCQA and JCAHO. Private-sector, or industry self-regulation is likely to be less intrusive than governmentally imposed regulation.

It is unrealistic, however, for an industry that represents about 14% of the gross domestic product to expect anything other than comprehensive oversight, especially when the enterprise involves life-and-death matters and people's well-being. In either private or public regulation, the regulatory system needs to do a better job of responding to areas where the health-care market fails to protect patients.

To date, the primary market failures have largely remained beyond regulatory control. Not only is there little agreement on what aspects of health care should be regulated, there is no consensus on regulatory content even when agreement exists on what to regulate. In any event, ERISA preemption would be an important barrier to implementing regulation at the state level. Yet an interesting development is filling the void.

As an alternative to governmental regulatory control, there is an identifiable regulatory trajectory that is slowly but inexorably shifting back toward the self-regulation and market control that dominated the pre-Medicare health-care environment.[43] The demise of the proposed Clinton Health Security Act signaled that the primary source of regulation would be through the private sector. At least in the short term, the absence of serious consideration of national health insurance reinforces the shift of power to the private sector.

What has evolved, perhaps less by conscious design than by happenstance, is a mixed form of regulation that amounts to a public–private partnership (perhaps public-private competition is a more apt description),[44] distinct from the typical top-down model of governmental regulation. At key points, the political system has resisted a stronger regulatory structure in favor of competition between markets, government regulators, and private accrediting bodies for regulatory control. In the mixed-form system, the government's regulatory authority remains, but is becoming secondary to market-based control and professional self-regulation through accrediting entities. A contributing factor is congressional reluctance to modify ERISA preemption to permit greater state regulatory oversight. ERISA is responsible for what amounts to a regulatory vacuum because it preempts state regulation of managed-care plans without imposing a federal regulatory structure to replace state oversight. This limits governmental oversight of managed care and encourages self-regulation. Attempting to fill the vacuum, accrediting agencies are gaining recognition as key to the regulatory structure. As currently operating, the structure has three basic components.

The first component, government, continues to focus on a wide range of issues, especially costs and quality, but at the margins. Instead of considering universal access, Congress has taken incremental steps to increase access, such as mandating longer maternity stays. After largely unsuccessful efforts to expand health insurance to all residents in the early 1990s, states have taken their cue from Congress by attempting to implement incremental measures, such as mandating direct access of insured patients to specialists.[45]

The second leg of the triad is the managed care industry itself, exercising market-based controls. The major point of control is over physician behavior, both in restraining costs and regulating quality. Through utilization review and other cost-control initiatives (including bonuses and "withholds"), managed care organizations exert pressure to inhibit health-care costs and utilization. They also resort to selective contracting and economic credentialing to control physicians' resource use, and clinical practice guidelines to improve quality. The primary cost controls are now operated through the managed-care system, though federal reimbursement regulations continue to impose some limits on the amount to be paid for a given medical procedure.[46]

The third leg of the triad, accreditation, most resembles the self-regulatory structure for physicians. The accrediting bodies exert pressure on health systems to meet certain quality-of-care requirements. For MCOs, attaining NCQA's imprimatur is an important competitive necessity. Because employers are less likely to contract with MCOs that lack NCQA accreditation, meeting its standards is imperative.

One might add that employers play an important role in the shift to private sector regulation in dealing with MCOs. Certainly, large employers are more insistent on demanding that plans provide them with cost and quality data. At a minimum, employers exert some pressure to restrain costs and improve quality and certainly have the market clout to demand greater quality improvements. All the same, my reluctance to characterize them as a fourth pillar is based on skepticism about how much they will use their purchasing power beyond the immediate goal of controlling costs. In the mid-1990s, for instance, employer health purchasing coalitions were viewed as a major way of combining the employers' collective purchasing power to restrain cost increases. There is little evidence to suggest that these coalitions achieved their goals.[47]

A compelling indication of the mixed-form arrangement is the government's regulatory partnership with the private sector in the growing use of the negotiated regulation process (dubbed "neg-reg"). In the neg-reg process, the regulatory agency sits down with the affected industry to develop a regulatory approach that is acceptable to each side to avoid contentious and time-consuming litigation. It would be naïve to think that affected industries were ignored in regulatory policy before neg-reg, but the explicit inclusion of the industry in the regulatory process is substantially different.

So far, the managed care industry has successfully argued that the accreditation process and industry self-regulation can be more effective than command and control (i.e., governmental) regulations. Keep in mind that self-regulation in this context does not mean no regulation. On average, governmental regulation will be more intrusive, so the source of regulatory authority matters. Still, there is considerable pressure on the accrediting entities to be more aggressive in the accreditation requirements. If for no other reason, the managed care industry is well aware that the failure to implement adequate self-regulatory measures simply invites a more intrusive and Draconian governmental regulatory system.

The mixed-form result should not be surprising. Most commentators have rejected the one-dimensional notion of regulation versus competition in favor of a more sophisticated approach that tries to balance competition and regulation.[48] Except for libertarians, who eschew most governmental intervention in the market, the debate is over the level of regulatory oversight, not whether regulations *per se* are acceptable.[49] In many respects, this pragmatic approach is a typically American response to a problem—a little of this mixed with a little of that. Whether the amalgam is at all coherent is beside the point—it satisfies enough constituencies to be viable in the short run.

To understand why the mixed-form arrangement is gaining momentum, it is equally important to consider regulatory options that have not been adopted. Each of the following options has either been tried and abandoned or has been on the policy agenda for a long time without being pursued.

On and off for the past fifty years, Congress has debated issues related to health planning and national health insurance, with little to show for it. In 1974, Congress enacted a law that promised a much more extensive federal presence in overseeing state regulation of health-care delivery. The State Health Planning and Development Act of 1974 envisioned a significant federal role in promoting access to health care and a more active health-planning apparatus. But the Act engendered considerable state opposition and was repealed in the early 1980s. Two scholars succinctly summarize the fate of (and eviscerate) the health planning model by stating that:

> Health planning had to die a lingering death while policymakers came slowly, grudgingly to the realization that the problem with the health care system was not just access, fragmentation, and duplicate facilities. It was more fundamental: under the existing payment systems' incentives, nobody cared about costs and prices.[50]

In quick order, the short-lived era of health planning soon gave way to the cost-containment era that began in the 1980s.

At least health planning generated sufficient congressional support to be enacted. The same cannot be said for national health insurance. Since the Truman Administration, national health insurance has been on the policy agenda. Every time, it has been rejected. End of story. What is important about the rejection of these two options is what it says about the role of regulation as compared to competition. For all the complaints about the intrusiveness of the regulatory system into the delivery of health care, the reality is that serious governmental controls over health care have been consistently rejected. Beyond these two examples, voters in California soundly rejected a proposed initiative for a comprehensive statewide universal health insurance program, and the managed competition model at the heart of the Clinton Health Security Act went nowhere. As unhappy as the public may be with managed care, there is very little public support for universal national health insurance. At this point, governmental control over the health-care system is a political non-starter.

A less intrusive form of regulation than a government-controlled system would be a public utility model, perhaps along the lines of electricity companies or the former Ma Bell. Conceptually, the public utility model is similar to the Certificate of Need (CON) program, where requests for expensive new equipment or hospital construction require approval from a designated state health agency. The public utility model posits that because of the importance of the health-care industry to the general public, the body politic should have power to influence the industry's practices. The suggestion that health care should be regulated like a public utility arose in the 1970s but did not receive serious consideration,[51] in part because the fee-for-service system basically was a small, local industry.

Regulated public utilities in the United States have been characterized by four "duties" owed to customers and relating to the utility's status as a monopoly.[52] Only industries for which it is sensible to impose these four duties are appropriate candidates to be public utilities. The first two duties are that a utility must render "safe and adequate service" and must charge only a "just and reasonable" price for service (meaning a reasonable rate of return). The other two duties rest on the significance of the utility's product.

All regulated public utilities have a duty to serve all who apply, which amounts to a rule that forbids the utility from considering the profitability of expanding service or capacity to cover additional customers. Also, a utility may not discriminate in providing service.[53] Even if it is more expensive for the utility to serve some customers than others—or, conversely, even if some customers are clearly willing to pay more than others—the utility may not discriminate in price. A utility may divide customers into classes and charge distinct or graduated rates to each class so long as the classifications are reasonable, the rates are fair, and each member of a given class is treated equally with all other class members. Coupled with the duty to serve, the duty of nondiscrimination entails almost by necessity that the utility's revenue collection involves "widespread cross-subsidies, meaning that some customers pa[y] rates in excess of the fully allocated costs of service in order to allow other customers to be charged rates less than the fully allocated costs of service."[54]

Although a public utility model is more defensible now than it was in the fee-for-service system, regulation according to the traditional public utility model is no longer the norm for many traditional public utilities. Public and political support for this concept is unlikely, even if health care becomes controlled by a few large managed care firms.[55] A public utility model might be more appropriate if the managed care system consolidates into a few large providers. Note, in contrast, that CON programs have been abolished in many states and their effectiveness has been repeatedly questioned.

As someone who has generally supported universal health insurance coverage, it is tempting to argue that the roads not taken would have addressed the problems with the health-care system more adequately. National health insurance would reduce (if not eliminate) access disparities and inequalities, but it would do little to address cost and quality concerns. In truth, we can only speculate whether any of these discarded paths would have resulted in a better health-care system.

In the past 30 years, law has moved from a peripheral to a central force in the development of health care. The current range of health law topics and concerns is large and growing. With physicians and managed care patients chafing at the perceived limitations of the managed care system, we are likely to see continued policy debates over the need for, and proper role of, governmental regulation.

The paradox of the history of health-care regulation since 1965 is that the regulatory structure is moving back toward self-regulation, which should suggest fewer rules, even while the overall regulatory burden continues to increase. From a regulatory perspective, the fundamental concerns about the market for health care have not dissipated. Simply put, the government may perceive an obligation to scrutinize the industry closely. As a matter of social policy, individual laws, such as prohibiting drive-through deliveries, may not be a great idea for two reasons. One is that individual laws fail to deal with the serious problems in health care while giving the appearance of trying to respond to public concerns. In addition, these laws micromanage health care in ways that might not be medically appropriate.[56] But as a general proposition, the political system will respond to public complaints about such an important and highly visible industry as health care. In any event, the courts will have much to say about regulation and about patient challenges to cost-containment programs.

Notes

1. Hall and Anderson (1992); Eddy (1996).
2. Jacobson (1989).
3. Southwick (1978).
4. Southwick (1988), p. xiii.
5. Jacobson (1989).
6. Sage (2001).
7. Annas (1989b).
8. Furrow (1989).
9. Southwick (1988).
10. Havighurst (1997), p. 599.
11. *Ibid.*, p. 596.
12. 143 N.E.2d 3 (1957).
13. 211 N.E.2d 253 (Ill. 1965), *cert. Denied,* 383 U.S. 946 (1966).

14. Havighurst, Blumstein, and Brennan (1998), p. xii.

15. 464 F.2d 772 (D.C. Cir. 1972).

16. 611 P.2d 902 (Cal. 1980).

17. Jacobson and Rosenquist (1996). For an in-depth look at informed consent, see Schneider (1998).

18. Emanuel and Emanuel (1996).

19. Capron (1987).

20. *In the Matter of Karen Quinlan*, 355 A.2d 647 (N.J. 1976).

21. 421 U.S. 773 (1975).

22. 457 U.S. 3332 (1982).

23. Havighurst (2000a).

24. *Goldfarb v. Virginia State Bar*, 421 U.S. 773 (1975).

25. Stevens (1989); Havighurst (1986a); Costilo (1985). According to Havighurst (2001), p. 946, "antitrust law today leaves little leeway for professional competitors to agree not to compete or for organized provider groups to restrict the competitive freedom of their members or other market participants."

26. 895 F.2d 352 (7th Cir. 1990), *cert. denied*, 498 U.S. 982 (1990).

27. *Arizona v. Maricopa County Medical Society*, 457 U.S. 332 (1982).

28. Havighurst (2001b), p. 952.

29. This analysis is consistent with Krause's (1996) argument that the physicians' guild began to decline in power in the mid-1960s when government began to exert greater control over medical care.

30. See also the community service regulations issued by HHS in 1979 interpreting the Hill-Burton Act. 42 C.F.R. §§124.508.

31. 42 U.S.C.A. 1395dd (1994).

32. The primary exception to this was the congressional enactment in 1986 of the Emergency Medical Treatment and Labor Act (EMTALA).

33. Pear (2001).

34. 42 U.S.C.A. 11101–11150 (Supp. 1987).

35. Brennan (1998), p. 710.

36. Health Insurance Portability and Accountability Act of 1996, 42 U.S.C.A. 1320d-d8 (West Supp. 1998).

37. Social Security Act, Section 1877 (addressing whether a physician's referrals relating to certain designated health-care facilities are prohibited under the Medicare anti-kickback laws).

38. Revised Federal Trade Commission, Justice Department Policy Statements on Health Care Antritrust Enforcement, August, 26, 1996.

39. *Federal Trade Commission v. Butterworth*, 946 F. Supp. 1285 (W.D.Mich. 1996).

40. *United States v. Mercy Health Services*, 902 F. Supp. 968 (N.D.Iowa 1995).

41. Butler (2001).

42. Stone (1985).

43. To be sure, this is a contestable proposition. One might argue, as did an anonymous reviewer, that it is not "correct to say we're moving 'back' to self-regulation. We're not getting less regulation, nor more self-regulatory. Instead, the intensity of regulation is not building as rapidly. . . . A stalled trend is not the same as a reversal." Perhaps so. But the private accreditation system is gaining strength while opposition to governmental regulation grows.

44. Instead of a public–private partnership, others have termed this a competition between the three groups: "The government, the corporations (the market), and the

professions could be see as three competing forces. . . ." (Stevens [2001], p. 336; see also Krause, 1996).

45. Brennan (1998). It is not clear, however, whether these state laws will survive ERISA preemption challenges.

46. Note that the federal government has pulled back from imposing a cost-effectiveness criterion for making coverage decisions. See, Health Care Financing Administration, notice of intent to publish a proposed rule, Federal Register, Vol. 65, No. 95, Tuesday, 16 May 2000, pp. 31124–31129. For an argument that MCOs have not been aggressive in implementing cost-effectiveness criteria, see Jacobson and Kanna (2000).

47. See, e.g., Wicks and Hall (2000).

48. Peterson (1997); Health Care Study Group (1994).

49. It is certainly true excessive regulatory presence can stifle market solutions (such as the overbearing fraud and abuse regime now being imposed), yet an effective regulatory system provides certain protections that allow markets to flourish.

50. Weissert and Weissert (1996), p. 121.

51. Priest (1970).

52. Priest (1970); Rossi (1998).

53. In the context of health care, Priest (1970) argues that "[t]here plainly can be no discrimination between patients as to quality of care," p. 842.

54. Kearney and Merrill (1998), p. 1346.

55. Nor are the courts likely to view health care as a public utility. Most courts reject any broad comparison of health care services to public utilities. See, e.g., *Blue Cross & Blue Shield United of Wisconsin v. Marshfield Clinic*, 65 F.3d 1406, 1413; Sage (1997a).

56. For a thorough critique of drive-through delivery laws, see Hyman (1999b).

PART II

The Judicial Response to Managed Care

4

Historical Precursors

THE Andrews-Clarke and Goodrich cases did not arise in a legal vacuum. When the cases were filed, their attorneys relied on a century or more of common-law rules that would be used to determine if they would win. Common law is simply the body of law made through judicial decisions as opposed to legislation. The importance of common-law rules lies in establishing standards of acceptable behavior and determining whether and how injured people will be compensated for their losses.

It is tempting to think that every case in court is unique. In reality, how legal disputes are argued and decided depends on the shape and direction of common law. Judges must consider how to apply old common-law rules to new circumstances or whether to develop new rules to reflect the limits of prior common-law decisions. In the Andrews-Clarke and Goodrich cases, each claim raised difficult issues that courts were only beginning to confront in the context of the managed care revolution. Not only did this make their outcomes uncertain, it also meant the two cases would be among those that would help set judicial precedent for future challenges to managed care's cost-containment programs. The cases are all the more interesting for what they tell us about how courts will adjust common-law doctrine to new social and economic realities, and how legislation influences common law.

For the most part, the common law develops incrementally and slowly in response to changing social and economic circumstances.[1] The incremental approach to developing legal rules in a new or rapidly changing industry allows courts to adjust to changing market realities and to other judicial decisions before arriving at a consensus (if ever). Common-law decisions may not be the final word in any event; they can be altered by a legislature. For example, juries have discretion under common law to award damages for pain and suffering. Some states have legislatively placed a limit on how much a jury can award for pain and suffering in any given case. And as we will see in subsequent chapters, a congressional statute lies at the heart of why the Andrews-Clarke and Goodrich cases were decided differently.

Sometimes economic and social arrangements change so dramatically that the applicable legal rules are no longer very useful. The evolution of a familiar industry may be so sudden, pervasive, or extensive that it amounts to a revolution. The result of this revolution is a "new" or "nascent" industry (though radically new endeavors are rarely created without some dependence on ideas already being discussed).[2] When confronting a new industry, such as the Internet and related electronic issues, or a radically transformed industry, such as health care, courts must adapt the common law to changing circumstances. In these instances, there is an initial mismatch between existing legal doctrine and the reality of the newly developing industry. Courts must then adapt existing legal doctrine (rules) to industrial changes that have overtaken the context in which the original rules were developed.[3] In other situations, new technology appears to emerge from an industrial prototype that is not well-known or established, requiring courts to make analogies to other areas of law in devising new legal rules. An ongoing example of this is the appearance of the Internet and related technologies.

This chapter explores historical precursors to the upheaval in the health-care industry, focusing on how courts adjusted existing legal rules to the factual scenarios raised by new or radically transformed industries. In American legal history, two areas stand out as analogous to what the courts currently are confronting with managed care: the advent of the railroads and the development of mass produced goods. Like managed care, both of these industries transformed basically local activities into enterprises with national markets. The developments radically altered consumers' expectations of how goods and services would be delivered and raised new types of accident and injury claims that courts had not previously confronted.

A look at the history of how courts have responded to similar transformations seems particularly relevant in exploring how courts might think about ensuring accountability in managed care. Assessing the changes in the law that occurred with the development of railroads in the nineteenth century and mass production in the twentieth century will show that the courts' decisions in managed care litigation occur within a historical context. The railroad experience offers a lesson in how courts settled on the appropriate legal rules to maintain legal accountability for accidents as the railroads grew. The mass production experience provides insight because courts had to analyze mass production's combined product and service delivery aspects, much as courts must now analyze managed care's mixed financing and delivery aspects. Taken together, these case histories provide an introduction to the twists and turns in how legal doctrine is formed and an illustration of how common law has evolved.

Neither of the two industries is, of course, analogous in every respect to each other or to managed care. But the issues the courts confronted in these areas are remarkably similar to those they must face now in challenges to managed care's cost-containment programs. Looking at the historical examples will not provide easy or uncontroversial answers to the problems faced by managed care patients. Indeed, there is considerable controversy among scholars about how courts actually responded to previous industry transformations. Even so, assessing the historical analogies to understand how legal rules change may illuminate lessons judges can apply in confronting the challenging legal issues in managed care.[4]

How Legal Standards Develop

Before describing the railroad and mass production stories, let us briefly consider how courts develop legal standards. Defining a few legal concepts up front will help place the two stories in the proper context.

Common-law doctrine (that is, a rule, principle, or theory of the law that determines how cases will be decided) is not static. As industries and social organizations change, the common law responds by developing new rules. In most periods of change, legal principles will develop along four interrelated dimensions. The first, and perhaps most important, question for the courts is which legal area will be used to resolve litigation. Often, the primary battleground will be whether tort or contract law will predominate. One of the great battles in common law is the choice between *tort liability* and *contract* to set standards for personal and institutional behavior.

Torts are civil wrongs that involve injuries from a failure to maintain the appropriate standard of care—such as liability for negligence (unintended, but wrongful behavior)—and are brought after the fact to recover suitable damages. In contracts, parties negotiate among themselves over the price of a product and how to claim damages if the contract is breached. Tort law imposes standards of public accountability, while contract law endorses private choice of consequences if a contract is breached. The interplay between tort and contract law frames how the judicial system will hold an industry accountable for accidents and injuries (both avoidable and unavoidable). A crucial question is whether courts will monitor an industry closely by imposing tort liability, or defer to private contractual arrangements to determine responsibility.

Once the area of law is chosen, the second question is which liability standard will be used. Just choosing tort law over contract law does not mean that people who are injured will automatically recover damages. For example, if tort law predominates, courts must then choose between negligence and strict product liability as the tort law standard. *Negligence* is the failure to meet acceptable community standards of care and is based on showing that the defendant was at fault for the harm suffered. In strict product liability, the defendant is liable for exposing someone to injury from a dangerous activity without regard to who was at fault.[5,6] The classic case invoking strict liability is an exploding soda bottle. Each standard has different elements that must be proven to win the case. (See Chapter 5.)

The third decision occurs when courts address the rules that explain how judges will implement the chosen liability standard(s).[7] These rules are often termed *subsidiary rules*, which explain how a particular liability standard should be interpreted. Subsidiary rules are used by a court in applying a standard to a set of facts. Suppose, for instance, courts decide that the proper legal standard for assessing accidental wrongdoing is negligence. The elements of a negligence case include showing a duty of care and a breach of that duty. As an example, suppose that a surgeon leaves a sponge inside the patient's body after an operation. Ordinarily, the patient would have difficulty showing that the physician breached the standard of care, because the patient would have no knowledge of what actually happened. To redress what would otherwise be unjust results, courts developed the subsidiary rule of *res ipsa loquitur* (literally, "the thing speaks for itself"). When knowledge of what caused the injury is exclusively within the defendant's control, *res ipsa loquitur* can be used to shift the burden of proof to the physician. In essence, the rule presumes that the defendant was negligent. It is then up to the defendant to demonstrate that he or she was not at fault for the injury. Without being able to invoke *res ipsa loquitur*, the patient would often have no way of proving negligence.

The fourth factor is the interaction between the courts and the legislatures. Common-law rules can be nudged in a different direction by legislation or even directly altered. Congress, for instance, has debated whether to enact patients' rights legislation in response to ERISA's preemption provision, which has blocked patients' lawsuits against MCOs. Legislation did not play a prominent role in establishing the rules for railroad or mass production injuries, but it is quite important for managed care litigation.

Legal doctrine develops slowly over time, with a large number of cases needed before the stability and predictability of legal rules are achieved. The advantage of this is the ability to adjust to changing circumstances; the disadvantage is the initial lack of predictability. One might think about it as a distinction between the result in any individual case and the outcomes of a large number of similar cases. For the most part, any one case, while certainly important to the litigants, rarely defines what legal doctrine will emerge over time. At times though, one case is so powerfully reasoned and issued by a court with national prestige that it sets precedent and moves the law in one direction. Usually, we must look to a much larger number of cases before ascertaining the direction of legal doctrine.

Take, for example, the issue of whether a particular medical intervention is medically necessary. *Medical necessity* is a largely undefinable contractual term where an insurer is not required to pay for care unless the care is clinically appropriate. Patients often challenge denials to medical treatment based on how an insurer interprets the definition of what constitutes "necessary care." Looking at one case will tell us only whether the court ruled that the particular intervention was inappropriately denied, not how the courts will view other cases. But looking at hundreds of similar cases will tell us whether courts defer to the treating physician's judgment or uphold contractual limitations on the type and amount of clinical care to be provided.

In responding to rapid economic and technological changes, courts usually lag behind in reconsidering existing doctrine. Early case judgments often lack sophistication in understanding the substantive policy questions at stake, while later cases make adjustments based on better information. Medical necessity litigation illustrates this point. After courts initially favored patients who challenged insurance coverage denials, insurers responded by revising and tightening their medical necessity definitions to clarify exactly what was being excluded. Recent cases interpreting the revised definitions have been more favorable to insurers, though no conclusive judicial trend is evident.

While courts are bound by precedent and by general rules of statutory and contractual interpretation, judges have considerable discretion in developing decision-making principles and doctrine in common law. Judicial discretion is particularly important when courts are resolving disputes in a new industry. Broadly speaking, courts engage in a dialogue, particularly in unsettled or contentious areas, with other courts, legislators, policy makers, scholars, and stakeholders until a judicial consensus emerges. Often, a judicial consensus follows and affirms the underlying social trends. As the recent debate over health care reform demonstrates, however, political and social agreement on many aspects of health-care policy remain elusive. How courts and legislatures adjust previous doctrine—both tort and contract—will have important legal and policy ramifications. Legally, this adjustment will set the tone for how the courts will determine accountability in the managed care era. On the policy side, the outcome will influence the courts' receptivity to patients' challenges and the ability of MCOs to sustain their cost-containment objectives.

With this as the background, let us turn to the legal history of the railroads and mass production. Keep in mind that legal historians disagree about various aspects of the following accounts.

The Railroad Story

There is no single railroad story that accounts for changes in the law at the time of the rise of railroads, roughly 1830 to 1870. Historical distance and the fact that railroads tended to be creatures of the state in which they operated frustrate efforts to create an overarching theory. Not surprisingly, several competing stories have emerged.

All the stories share the fact that the railroad was revolutionary. It decreased travel time and cost and was the key to the nation's economic development, connecting farms to cities and seaports. The railroads' rise to dominance is reflected in the statistic that the miles of track laid rose from 3,000 in 1840 to 52,000 in 1870.[8] During the mid-nineteenth century, the railroad was in its relatively youthful stages and largely confined to specific geographic areas of economic importance. The first transcontinental railroad was completed in 1869, signaling perhaps the maturation of the industry. "The rail network completely transformed the West. It created cities where none existed, and businesses where none existed."[9] What is perhaps most interesting about the railroad's development is that it simultaneously offered enormous economic benefits and danger to people and property. The railroad

> . . . was the key to economic development. It cleared an iron path through the wilderness. It bound cities together, and tied farms to cities and the seaports. Yet trains were also wild beasts; they roared through the countryside, killing livestock, setting fires to houses and crops, smashing wagons at grade crossings, mangling passengers and freight. Boilers exploded; trains hurtled off the tracks; bridges collapsed; locomotives collided in a grinding scream of steel.[10]

Thus, aside from the industry's economic contributions, part of its revolutionary nature was the drastic increase in the number of personal injuries railroads produced, which courts were called upon to address. Accidents to innocent bystanders included fires started from sparks thrown off by locomotives that burned both fields and houses, as well as collisions with wandering cattle and inattentive human beings. Railroad accidents also included injuries to passengers and, perhaps most dramatically, terrible injuries to railroad workers. The fires and collisions were legally troublesome because they involved injury to innocent bystanders who generally lacked a direct link to the railroad company. The personal injuries—to workers especially—were troublesome because of their number and the severe types of injuries, which were unlike anything the courts had seen before. As an example of the carnage, consider that in a one-year period from 1888 to 1889, one worker died for every 357 employed, and one out of thirty-five was injured.[11]

Naturally, those who were injured wanted compensation for the harm and sued to recover damages. But lawsuits were seen as a threat to the health of a "precarious enterprise,"[12] as opposed to opportunities to compensate those who were injured. In facing the conflict between compensating injured persons and protecting the nascent industry, courts indisputably recognized the importance of railroads.

> Railroad associations have become of great and growing importance; they afford hi-ways of incalculable value to commerce, and the ever ready means of social intercourse between distant communities. They are, at this moment, welding together, link after link, the conservative chain, which is to hold in firm union, more than six and twenty States. . . . [13]

Judges were troubled by the potential for ruinous, unchecked liability that could inhibit economic initiative and threatened to clog the whole court system. Equally troublesome, the prevailing legal concepts, based on a worldview of ongoing, personal, and consensual relationships, did not give courts the conceptual tools to account for the costs of injuries.

The applicable legal framework available when railroads' practices began to be challenged accommodated neither the nature nor the volume of railroad accidents.[14]

> [T]he courts were confronted with recurrent injury situations having no close analogue in the earlier common law. Railroads and motor vehicles, for example, created a variety of risks to strangers that bore no obvious likeness to the harm caused by stampeding animals, stealthy poachers, or irresponsible innkeepers.[15]

Before the advent of the railroads, most accident victims simply endured the loss. At that time, "the general principle of our law was that loss from accident must lie where it falls."[16] People lived with calamity where there was often no one to blame—responsibility rested with the individual person.[17] Tort, the concept of imposing a duty of care to prevent unintended harm to third persons, was not a coherent concept prior to railroads and industrialization.[18] In the mid-1800s, in fact, there were few clear legal concepts that injured plaintiffs might advantageously use to recover damages. Lawsuits for damages tended to be resolved based on the relationship between the parties, often arising out of status, property, or contract considerations.[19] Before litigants could recover damages for an injury, they had to show that they were owed a duty which the alleged wrongdoer failed to meet. Unfortunately for an injured person, the law imposed very few duties that would permit damages.

Courts would "discover"[20] duties based on functional relationships, such as employer–employee, innkeeper–guest, or passenger carrier (also called a "common carrier"). Once a duty was owed, an injured party could recover damages in what amounted to the concept of strict liability. In strict liability, the defendant would be required to pay damages to the injured person regardless of fault, as long as there was some legally established relationship between the parties. A common carrier, for example, was held strictly liable for injuries to a passenger.[21]

Duties could also arise from the terms of a contract, although courts did not evaluate the intrinsic fairness of contracts. Parties to a contract were presumed to have equal bargaining power, and the contract was enforced strictly according to its terms.[22] For reasons that will become apparent when we talk about mass-produced goods, it was rare for an injured party to recover damages under a contract.

Finally, property considerations led courts to imply duties. Before the railroad existed, a property owner was generally required to use his or her property so as not to hurt neighbors. The owner's duty of due care to those entering the property depended on the classification of the person entering. Property owners owed a higher duty of care to those invited onto the property than to strangers (trespassers).

The railroad industry was thus born into a legal structure that was not particularly favorable to injured persons. In the mid-1800s, there was little liability for unintended injuries beyond the few categories of strict liability for common carriers. Concomitantly, the railroads' novelty confronted the courts with difficult legal choices: "[W]hether railroads would be held to a standard of negligence, strict liability, or something in between was in doubt."[23]

The judicial debate was over the legal standard that should apply to personal injuries resulting from the railroad's activities. Should the courts hold the railroads strictly liable for *any* injuries (without regard to fault) or should they be held responsible only for negligence (the failure to take expected precautions to avoid injury)? The courts chose the latter. By the second half of the nineteenth century, negligence was gaining a foothold as the proper legal standard under which to analyze the cases.[24] Tort principles (especially for negligence) developed as a coherent concept largely as a tool to enable courts to deal with the railroad issues.[25] Using the negligence standard made it more difficult for plaintiffs to recover damages than under strict liability, which would have been more favorable to the injured person. Under negligence, the burden was on the injured party to show that the defendant was at fault for the accident. With strict liability, fault was irrelevant. Stated another way, negligence is based on "the standard of the reasonable man," where perfection is not expected. Strict liability, if not requiring perfection, still allows little room for error.[26]

Clearly, the negligence standard was a victory for the railroad industry. Justifying the emerging negligence regime, Oliver Wendell Holmes noted that "the public generally profits by individual activity," and "[a]s action cannot be avoided, and tends to the public good, there is obviously no policy in throwing the hazard of what is at once desirable and inevitable upon the actor."[27] Holmes's words suggest a certain concern for the continuing health and vitality of the railroad industry. The perceptions of judges like Holmes were probably bolstered by the fact that "[t]he plain people loved the railroad passionately."[28] Even Walt Whitman celebrated it in poetry.[29] The railroad was generally regarded as a symbol of positive change.

To some degree, courts bowed to the favorable public attitude toward railroads by reducing the extent of the railroad industry's liability. In Georgia, for instance, the Supreme Court "was very concerned about 'excessive' liability, which was generally understood in economic terms: liability that would put railroads out of business."[30] Strict liability—a standard courts could have found applicable based on the maxim that one must use one's property so as not to injure another—was rejected because of the specter of draining the coffers of industrious enterprises.[31,32] Arguably, the rejection of strict liability alone may be seen as creating judicial rules more favorable to the railroads than to injured citizens. In Georgia, courts justified the rejection of strict liability expressly to protect railroads:

> Besides its oppressive injustice, [strict liability] would be grossly inexpedient, inasmuch as it would deny to the public the incalculable benefits of Railroads, for no company would long exercise franchises thus encumbered. . . . Railroads, by virtue of their charters, are exempted from the operation of the Common Law, as to liabilities for injuries done to property.[33]

The subsidiary rules developed to implement the emerging negligence standard offer another opportunity to analyze how the courts treated the industry (regardless of what legal historians think about the general liability standard that was developed). Several of the primary implementing rules—the fellow servant rule, contributory negligence, and assumption of the risk (explained below)—provided the railroads with what amounted to considerable immunity from injury litigation.

Because immunity is such an important aspect of the railroad, mass produced goods, and managed care stories, let us briefly discuss what it means. *Immunity* describes legal doctrine that tends to produce litigation outcomes more protective of the industry than what might otherwise be expected from either the logic of judicial precedent or statutory language. Courts may not intend to protect the industry from liability, but immunity may result from a court's reluctance to interfere with the market at an early stage of a new industry's development. *Immunity* may also be partial, with courts refusing to insulate the industry entirely from liability, while still offering extensive protection.

The first implementing rule the courts developed was known as the "fellow servant doctrine." Created at the birth of the railroad industry, this doctrine prevented a railroad employee from recovering personal injury damages due to the negligence of a co-worker.[34] Almost any negligent conduct resulting in a worker's injury was likely to occur because of a co-worker's activities (known in the law as a "fellow servant"). The fellow servant rule provided immunity because the rule relieved the railroad of bearing potentially heavy costs. What is most telling about its adoption is that the rule was contrary to the general "rule of agency," in which a principal (an employer) is liable for the acts of his agent (the employee). Courts that adopted the fellow servant rule effectively granted immunity at the time of the railroad's early development.[35]

Many judges also adopted other subsidiary rules favorable to the railroads, including "contributory negligence" and "assumption of the risk." Contributory negligence barred recovery for passenger and employee alike in the event that the injured person was at fault to any degree, hence insulating the railroad from liability in these situations. Even if the employee were only 1% at fault, he or she could not recover any damages. The nineteenth century saw the rise of the contributory negligence rule in most jurisdictions, which had the further effect of insulating railroads from liability.[36]

Nationwide, the doctrine of assumption of risk also immunized railroads from much liability. Courts determined that workers, by agreeing to employment in a dangerous industry, assumed the risk of their injuries and therefore could not recover from the railroad. This doctrine was applicable to those who willingly put themselves in a position of danger. Its use increased drastically in cases from the dawn of the railroad era, and some historians attribute the doctrine's growth to "spoon-feeding [the railroad] enterprise, the blind desire for economic growth."[37,38]

It is important to recognize that judges had a choice in developing the implementing rules because they were not bound or even guided by clear precedent. In common law, judges have enormous discretion in developing the rules of the game. That they consistently chose rules favorable to the industry may not be coincidental. "The thrust of the rules, taken as a whole, approached the position that corporate enterprise should be flatly immune from actions for personal injury."[39]

There was never complete immunity, however. In many instances, the courts depicted the railroads as being analogous to other common carriers. With regard to passengers, common carriers could be held to standards of strict accountability. The idea of liability for common carriers with respect to guests (passengers), one of the oldest ideas in the law, was easily transferred to the railroads. In Iowa, for instance, courts applied stricter legal accountability to railroads based on the analogy to common carrier liability.[40] Even so, railroads were able to take advantage of the more favorable subsidiary rules to prevent widespread legal liability, and could easily contract out of liability to passengers until the 1970s.[41]

In time, there was an inevitable public backlash against legal immunity. "Politically, the rage of the victims counted for very little in 1840, not much in 1860; by 1890, it was a roaring force."[42] In North Carolina, the general assembly changed the law regarding the burden of proof so that plaintiffs could win more personal injury cases.[43] Railroads started losing public favor, then public funding. Farmers organized in anti-railroad movements like the Grangers and the Populists.[44] Legislatures imposed more liability on railroads by statute, and some judges spoke about the "hardship and injustice" for which the fellow servant doctrine was responsible.[45]

While still fearing that too much liability might ruin commercial life, the courts adjusted the legal rules to favor railroads less and award damages for injuries caused by a railroad's activities.[46] In cases where the defendant's fault greatly outweighed that of the plaintiff, some courts modified the contributory negligence rule to allow a plaintiff's recovery of damages[47]—arguably the first step toward a more forgiving rule known as "comparative negligence"—allocating responsibility according to the percentage of the harm caused by any of the parties to the litigation. In some jurisdictions, comparative negligence replaced contributory negligence. Courts also created exceptions to mitigate the effect of the fellow servant rule and developed new counter-rules.[48] And the Supreme Court refused to allow railroads to contract out of common-carrier liability for negligence committed by their employees.[49]

A leading theory explaining the judicial response to the railroads, called the "Subsidy Thesis,"[50] maintains that nineteenth-century judges, for the first time, used the common law intentionally to achieve specific policy objectives; namely, to support and promote the existing economic and political powers. The railroads were the chief industrial beneficiaries. Judges provided the industry with a judicial "subsidy" by shifting some of the costs of operating the railroads to individuals, particularly poor and powerless individuals.[51] Courts altered the legal rules to make it difficult for workers or bystanders to recover damages resulting from railroad accidents.

The subsidy thesis has been widely criticized.[52] In examining cases from five states, one scholar found no evidence of a subsidy to industrial development in general or railroads in particular,[53] except perhaps in certain implementing (subsidiary) rules. Those opposing the subsidy thesis argue that the rules adopted to resolve railroad injury claims, far from being created by nineteenth-century jurists, had a long tradition in the law. Consequently, they argue, there was no shift in the liability standard. Instead, rules implementing the newly developing tort standard (liability in negligence) were "applied with impressive sternness to major industries and that tort law exhibited a keen

concern for victim welfare."[54] In turn, the revisionists' account has been criticized for the time periods employed, for generalizing from a limited sample
of states, and for the exclusive use of cases decided by courts of appeals (often
by a state's highest court).[55]

No definite consensus has emerged as to which, if either, of these accounts
is correct. For example, the historical evidence is mixed on whether the fault-
based negligence liability standard became newly widespread in the nineteenth century. In view of the mixed historical evidence offered by scholars
who have studied this area in depth, I cannot comment with any certainty
about whether, as a general matter, there was a shift in the liability standard
from strict liability to negligence, resulting in a subsidy to the railroad industry.[56] It seems advisable to focus instead on the subsidiary rules of that era,
which seem much more clearly to have benefited the railroad industry.
Whether the courts deliberately pursued legal doctrine favorable to the railroad industry is almost impossible to determine. Navigating a middle ground
therefore seems appropriate, without taking a strong position on how deliberate the changes in legal principles were. If anything, the legal doctrine protecting new industries developed either by happenstance, by confusion, or by
courts' being very cautious in the initial stages of litigation.

Regardless of how deliberate the initial legal rules were, as time went on
and courts became more familiar with the issues, a more nuanced set of rules
developed, allowing recovery for injuries. Certainty was out, accountability was
more or less in, and a body of doctrine had now formed imposing at least
some legal accountability through negligence on the newly matured industry.[57]

The Mass Production Story

Mass production is a name for

> ... the method of producing goods in large quantities at low cost per unit. ...
> The mass production process itself is characterized by mechanization to achieve
> high volume, elaborate organization of materials flow through various stages of
> manufacturing, careful supervision of quality standards, and minute division of
> labour.[58]

It is difficult for our purposes to pinpoint when mass manufacturing began.
Part of the problem is my own strategic decision not to focus on any particular
industry (e.g., automobiles) that used mass production techniques—a decision
forced by the paucity of legal scholarship on any one industry. Instead, what
follows is based on a combination of practices and product advancement dis-
tinctive enough to be labeled "mass production."

By the middle of the nineteenth century, some mass manufacturing had begun in isolated industries. These industries included sewing machines (1846), Yale locks (1855), and typewriters (1868).[59] None of these products appears to have presented any inherent dangers. Efforts to use scientific management to cut costs were still in a primitive stage prior to the turn of the twentieth century.[60] That changed in 1899 when Ransom E. Olds began mass production of cars in Detroit. Mass production came to its full fruition when Henry Ford's assembly line mass-produced the Model T in 1913. After Ford revolutionized the mass production process, it spread to other industries throughout the country. Product advertising shifted from a local to a national focus, and a range of national distribution systems was introduced to handle the newly available mass manufactured goods. As with the railroads, there is no dispute that mass production techniques radically transformed the manufacturing and distribution of goods.

The story of how the courts reacted to injuries resulting from these innovations begins with an explanation of the background legal context. When tort was coming together as a coherent subject in the years immediately preceding the mass production era, there was still no history of tort-like recoveries for injuries from defective products.[61] Where available, recoveries came in contract law.[62] A consumer had only one way to recover for a product-based injury.[63] An *express* warranty (i.e., an explicit, written guarantee of quality or performance) had to be part of the contract for the injured person to sue. If the contract included an express warranty of quality that was breached, the customer almost always recovered damages. This amounted to an early form of strict liability without regard to fault. Absent the express warranty, the consumer was stuck with the loss.

The operation of express warranties was further limited by an older legal concept: only those in privity with the producer or manufacturer could recover damages. "Privity" means two or more parties dealing directly with one another. Before goods were mass produced, most commercial transactions were based on privity—meaning that the consumer bought something from the person who made it. The concept of privity was premised on a world in which transactions involved personal, face-to-face encounters in the course of a continuing relationship. In mass production and distribution, a consumer no longer buys directly from the person who makes the goods, but from someone who sells them. Unfortunately, the lack of privity would prevent the customer from suing the manufacturer. The baseline rule where the contract was silent about warranties was *caveat emptor*—"let the buyer beware." Litigation for product injuries at the birth of the mass production industry began against a background of virtually no liability based on the prevailing concept of *caveat emptor*.

Before mass production techniques were available, both a privity limitation and a requirement of express warranties made sense in light of how goods were produced and sold. Most purchases were for items of necessity, and the consumer was reasonably able to judge acceptable quality.[64] Most commercial transactions occurred face-to-face where, by definition, privity was present, and did not function so often as a limitation on recovering damages for personal injuries. In the absence of bargaining power inequalities, requiring express warranties was not unfair given the nature of the direct relationships between buyer and seller. Without a doubt, there were disparities in bargaining power and other inequities in this pre–mass-production world. But those disparities paled in comparison with the vast wealth, power, and informational inequality existing between today's consumers and mass product manufacturing corporations.

An obvious mismatch between legal rules and the new mass production occurred because the world changed, but the legal rules did not. As injury claims from mass produced goods mounted, courts failed to adapt the old privity and contract disclaimer doctrines (where the contract specifically stated that there was no warranty) to the realities of the new industry. Judges were familiar with treating product defects as contract issues. They were reluctant to apply the tort theories developed to handle railroad injuries, apparently feeling that product injury cases arose under contract law to the exclusion of tort rules.[65] Yet the contract doctrines that had been developed in a bygone world of face-to-face encounters did not fit the conditions which existed in the early mass production era. By the time of the mass production era, the railroad industry had fully matured, facilitating distribution in a timely fashion over great distances. Mass production separated the producer from the consumer, weakening personal concerns of the seller that might have forced producers to consider more carefully the safety of their products.[66]

Once mass produced goods became available, the privity required for contract recoveries rarely existed because of the way the new system operated. As a consequence, the privity doctrine became a powerful source of immunity for the nascent industry, effectively limiting personal injury litigation against manufacturers.[67] As was the case with the railroad industry, the immunity was not total, but it was effective. Few cases were brought,[68] thereby achieving one of the acknowledged purposes of this immunity—to safeguard manufacturers against extensive liability to strangers, which was seen as too heavy a burden for industry to bear.[69]

Warranty disclaimers, standard in many contracts, provided another source of immunity. Courts at this time enforced disclaimers of warranty liability, which further prevented contract recoveries, even for those in privity.[70] Throughout the pre-industrial era and extending well into the advent of mass produced goods, contracts were strictly construed. Even if a defective product caused an injury, the absence of an express warranty meant no recovery for the plaintiff.[71] Prior to the 1960s, few recovered on a contract claim because manufacturers in the early decades of the mass marketing era generally included warranty disclaimers in their contracts. (As an aside: many contracts still contain warranty disclaimers, but legislation, including the Uniform Commercial Code, and judicial scrutiny of one-sided agreements may limit their effectiveness.)

Immediately before the mass production era, some tort-like liability for products that were imminently or inherently dangerous to human safety already existed. At the same time, the idea of tort law (in areas other than product liability) had begun to coalesce on account of the railroads, resulting in the eventual dominance of a negligence standard.[72] In 1916, these two trends came together in *MacPherson v. Buick Motor Co.*[73] In this case, the defendant manufactured a car that it sold to a retail dealer, who in turn resold it to Donald MacPherson. "While the plaintiff was in the car, it suddenly collapsed. He was thrown out and injured. One of the wheels (purchased by the defendant from another manufacturer) was made of defective wood and crumbled into fragments."[74] The court ruled that the defendant was liable for the injuries because it owed a duty to inspect the car before selling it. Judge Cardozo imported a general rule of negligence liability from railroad-driven tort law and applied it to product defects, despite the lack of privity. *MacPherson* is often cited as a watershed case, though its ruling was more cautiously limited to liability for products imminently or inherently dangerous to human safety, such as automobiles.[75]

At first glance, Cardozo's opinion appeared hostile to the nascent mass production industry. It was issued three years after Ford opened his assembly line and seemed to shift the liability standard from no liability to negligence. Although the opinion found general acceptance among other judges, its actual immediate effect was not that great. Recoveries for negligence on a tort theory were small: "[P]roduct defect claims, even after *MacPherson*, seem to have made modest demands on the legal system and to have gone unnoticed in the political forum."[76] *MacPherson* did not trigger a substantial increase in product liability litigation, since the negligence doctrine retained teeth that made recovery difficult.[77] Indeed, insurance premiums for product liability remained flat in the decades that followed *MacPherson*.[78] Also, mass producers could disclaim liability and courts would enforce the disclaimers. In an ironic way, then, this opinion actually contributed to mass producers' general immunity from tort damages.[79]

Eventually, as with the railroads, there was a reaction against the industries' immunity. This time, though, the backlash came from judges and legal academics, not from the public. It started in 1944 with a powerful concurring opinion in *Escola v. Coca-Cola Bottling Co.*,[80] which articulated the modern theory of strict product liability. In *Escola*, the plaintiff was severely injured when a soda bottle exploded as he was drinking from it. Arguing that an unsuspecting consumer was in no position to protect herself or himself against injuries from defective mass products, the opinion was based in large part on an innate sense of justice. The manufacturer was in the best position to take steps to avoid the defect and should therefore bear the legal responsibility for doing so. Legal scholars in the 1940s and 1950s also emphasized ideas of fairness. Their discussion of why contracts of adhesion should not be enforced—where the customer has no bargaining power to choose the contract terms—would strongly influence the subsequent cases that marked a significant change in legal rules.[81] After the *Escola* case, product injuries were regarded less as "accidents" to be borne by the consumer and more "as an inevitable consequence of routine activities" that the manufacturer should control.[82] The changing approach called for greater manufacturer accountability. Courts then moved away from all of the previous defenses and toward strict liability without regard to fault.

Changes in the rules to hold the industry accountable took place gradually, first in the subsidiary rules and then in the liability standard itself.[83] Beginning with recommendations by a distinguished panel of academic experts, attorneys, and jurists, judges more willingly applied negligence principles to product design defects, in addition to manufacturing defects.[84] (Defects that occur in every individual product manufactured, even though the product is made exactly as designed, are known as "design defects." Manufacturing defects arise when a product is not manufactured according to its design). An important adoption and extension of these recommendations occurred in 1944 when the Supreme Court of California permitted plaintiffs to invoke *res ipsa loquitur* for product defect cases. Using this doctrine effectively shifted the burden of proof to the manufacturer to show why the product was not defective.[85] From this case forward, the courts limited defendants' ability to contest defective product cases. Similar changes in the subsidiary rules created a system that was friendlier to plaintiffs' personal injury claims. The new rules resulted in full manufacturer accountability, even before the more abrupt changes in liability standards that occurred at the beginning of the 1960s.[86]

In the 1960s, the courts adopted revolutionary changes to product liability rules, effectively imposing pro-plaintiff tendencies. The changes arose most prominently in *Henningsen v. Bloomfield Motors, Inc.*,[87] where the New Jersey Supreme Court held both a manufacturer and a dealer strictly liable by finding an implied warranty between the manufacturer and the consumer, despite the lack of privity.[88] Equally, if not more importantly, the court also refused to enforce a disclaimer of liability. Following the lead of the California Supreme Court, the court based its decision on the changed conditions of production and distribution associated with the maturing mass production field, including the economic and informational power imbalances. Within three years after the *Henningsen* decision, the "implied warranty" approach essentially gave way to strict liability in tort.[89] Strict liability, of course, is accountability at its extreme because it severely limits the range of defenses a manufacturer can use to avoid legal responsibility.

From the mid-1960s through the mid-1970s, the doctrine of strict product liability spread rapidly and it has become a fixture of American law, much to the chagrin of product manufacturers.[90] In fact, "the general adoption of the doctrine [of strict liability] in this country from 1963 to the mid-1970s is one of the most rapid and dramatic doctrinal developments ever to occur in the law of torts."[91] It took a long time to traverse the distance, but the common law eventually moved from industry immunity for injuries to strict accountability for the consequences of product design or manufacturing defects.

In recent years, courts and legislatures, responding to the concerns of business, have retreated from the more aggressive interpretations of strict liability. Courts have not abandoned the tort standard, though they may be moving away from strict liability to negligence in product liability cases.[92] Courts have favored defendants by adding restrictions (through subsidiary rules) that fundamentally diminish the impact of strict liability.[93] For example, a number of courts now apply a so-called state-of-the-art defense that holds manufacturers liable only for product defects that they knew about or should have known about when their products were designed and manufactured. As we have seen, changes in subsidiary rules can greatly affect who wins and loses.

A Pattern?

The advantage of studying historical analogies is that they offer a different perspective on current areas of the law that are controversial and unsettled, such as with managed care. Doing so provides a context or framework to help clarify what might otherwise seem chaotic. Looking at the two historical examples suggests a general pattern of how courts develop legal doctrine with respect to nascent or dramatically transformed industries. Before discussing the pattern, a reader might legitimately wonder why these two examples were chosen and whether other examples would show different patterns.[94]

I chose railroads and mass production because the vast body of scholarly comment suggests something very different about their influence on the development of common law—more so than in any other industries. The development of negligence rules, which then expanded into strict liability, has dominated common law for the past century. The two areas represent the sweeping arc of how courts for over a century developed liability rules for private industry. If there are major departures from the pattern, they are hard to identify. I could not detect any instances where common law was actively hostile to new industries—confused, certainly (as with the Internet), but not antagonistic. No doubt, the law might not always follow this pattern and may well depart from it in the future. With some reservations, though, the pattern seems adequately to describe a general trend in how legal doctrine develops.[95] As we will see, this pattern seems broadly applicable to managed care.

To begin with, there is an underlying social or economic revolution and the birth of a nascent industry. When confronted with litigation challenging certain aspects of a new industry, the courts must rely on legal doctrine previously developed to resolve new and different types of problems. The courts' initial response has been essentially to immunize new industries from liability, permitting expansion and strong growth unimpeded by lawsuits. But then a backlash against the industry occurs, in part because of the immunity from liability. In response to the backlash, courts have changed legal doctrine and developed better mechanisms for holding industry accountable.

One hallmark of a nascent industry is its uneasy fit within established legal doctrine, because the existing rules are rarely applicable to the new types of issues presented. For that reason, the first reaction is generally for courts to attempt to apply the old legal rules, without changing them, to the new industry. Sometimes aspects of the old legal order provide an acceptable fit that remains good law for years with few adjustments.[96] More often, there is some tension—a mismatch between established doctrine and the new reality. One contemporary example of this mismatch is the difficult application of First Amendment protections to the Internet industry.

Courts are rarely blind to the mismatches. Faced with this dilemma, judges tend (implicitly or explicitly) to perceive public policy as favoring the nascent industry and then establish new legal doctrine or apply the old rules in ways that are favorable to the industry. Identifying or "finding" a "public policy" is a familiar way for a court to legitimize its position in a democratic society. Several sources may underlie this perception: the will of the legislature as expressed in statutory law and subsequent regulations; general policy considerations born out of the judge's (and as a somewhat homogenous group, the judges') understanding of the economic, political, and social context of the underlying industrial changes; and perhaps even the perceived tenor of popular opinion. Courts then foster a period of at least partial immunity from liability for the new industry. Immunized from liability, the new and favored industry is given a legally protected space in which to flourish. Contrary to other scholars,[97] my view is that the friendliness toward nascent industry may be animated as much by confusion as by design.

The next step in the pattern is the backlash against the industry in general and against the industry's legal immunity in particular. The sources of the backlash may be even more various than those from which the courts originally found a favorable policy. For example, the backlash may be expressed through public outcry, the media, scholars, or politicians. Even before the backlash triggers any change in doctrine, courts may participate in it by decrying the unfairness of the law in published opinions, while nevertheless applying the law strictly.

A new set of legal rules is then developed holding the industry more fully accountable for its operations. Legal accountability emerges at the point where the cost of adhering to the old rules, in the face of the backlash, becomes unbearable.[98] That cost may be reflected in judicial discomfort with the courts' inability to hold the industry accountable, or it may reflect a broader societal unease with that result. Within the greater accountability, there are also indications that courts may be advancing their own interests. When an industry is mature and the courts have a greater understanding of the types of legal issues presented, judges seem to reserve a fair amount of discretion for themselves by settling on flexible, rather than rigid, legal rules and principles. For instance, courts introduced vague concepts such as "proximate cause" and "due care" that, over time, were flexibly adapted in ways that did not necessarily favor industries.[99] Both vague doctrine and new trial practice rules suggest that courts reserve a certain amount of discretion that they did not have with the hard-and-fast rules available when they first confronted cases from new industries.

As the judicial reaction to strict liability shows, common law is never really fixed. Imposing patterns on a continually adapting and changing system runs the risk of seeming more deterministic than it really is. Nonetheless, describing patterns helps make some sense of the law's evolution and general direction.

It is time to turn to the present. How have the courts responded to managed care litigation? Does the general pattern outlined in this chapter apply to managed care? What role has Congress played in influencing case decisions? Why was the Andrews-Clarke case dismissed, while the Goodrich case resulted in a large damage award? Before answering these questions, let us consider some of the legal rules in greater detail, such as tort and contract, which form the basis of the managed care cases.

Notes

1. For an accessible overview of the historical development of the common law, see Cantor (1998).
2. Pacey (1990).

3. Lessig (1997).

4. From the start, a word of caution: The analysis of the railroad and mass manufacturing industries is drawn from studies by other scholars, most of whom have relied upon a review of appellate cases.

5. Croley and Hansen (1993), pp. 692–94.

6. See, e.g., *Chavez v. Southern Pacific Transportation Co.*, 413 F. Supp. 1203 (E.D. Cal. 1976); Rabin (1981). Strict product liability is a complicated and controversial area of the law. For our purposes, we need not delve into it extensively except to set the background for managed care litigation.

7. Prosser and Keeton (1984), pp. 257–262.

8. Friedman (1985), p. 471.

9. Klein (2001).

10. Friedman (1985), p. 478.

11. *Ibid.*, p. 479.

12. *Ibid.*, p. 468.

13. *State v. Tupper*, 23 S.C.L. (Dud.) 135, 141 (1838), quoted in Schwartz (1981), p. 652.

14. *Ibid.* "Existing tort law was simply not designed to deal with [railroad] accidents. . . ."

15. Rabin (1981), p. 947.

16. Holmes (1881), p. 94.

17. Friedman (1985), p. 470.

18. Friedman (1985), p. 299; Hackney (1995), p. 453; Hunt (1998), p. 397.

19. Hunt (1988), p. 424; Rabin (1981), pp. 933–45.

20. Rabin (1981). According to Rabin, the functional relationships tended to be based on contract or property.

21. Kaczorowski (1990), pp. 1129–30.

22. Rabin (1981), p. 946. "The mere existence of a claim based on a defective product, rather than any actual bargaining involving the injured plaintiff, led the common law judge to draw on a contract analogue." See also Horowitz (1977). Not until the 1960s would courts would void contracts through doctrines like unconscionability (i.e., a contract will not be enforced if it is so onerous that it shocks the court's conscience or violates public policy) and contracts of adhesion (i.e., where the customer has no bargaining power to choose the contract terms).

23. Hunt (1988), p. 426.

24. Prosser and Keeton (1984), p. 161. Rabin (1981) disputes the claim that negligence became the *de facto* liability standard this quickly, arguing that the no liability principle was dominant throughout much of this period.

25. Friedman (1985), p. 468. Friedman attributes the emergence of tort as a coherent concept to the rise of railroads. "Railroad law and tort law, then, grew up together." See also Winfield (1926), p. 195.

26. Friedman (1985), pp. 468–70.

27. Holmes (1881), p. 97.

28. Hawke (1988), p. 232.

29. Pacey (1990).

30. Hunt (1998), p. 427.

31. Rabin (1981).

32. *Ryan v. New York Central R.R. Co.*, 35 N.Y. 210, 216–17 (1866). The following evidence from several other states also seems to reflect courts' favorable treatment of

railroads when the existing doctrine met new factual scenarios created by the railroads. In Maryland, courts were resistant to choosing a liability standard that would impose the greatest duties and costs on railroads (Schwartz, 1981). Several times, the courts interpreted liability statutes considerably more leniently than the legislature intended, leading to immediate statutory amendments that expressly required the higher standard that the courts had rejected. In Georgia, courts resisted the higher liability standards that legislatures preferred, and endorsed a shift away from strict common carrier liability (Hunt, 1998). By enforcing the industry's contractual disclaimers of liability (which they had previously not enforced), the Georgia courts made it almost impossible for plaintiffs to prove that the railroad was negligent. In North Carolina, the doctrine also tended to produce verdicts for the railroad defendants, and the language and reasoning of the cases were clearly pro-railroad (Hunt, 1988).

33. *Macon & W.R.R. Co. v. Davis*, 13 Ga. 68, 85–87 (1853), *quoted in* Hunt (1998), p. 395. In the *Davis* case, the court was interpreting legislation that chartered railroads to determine the appropriate standard of liability.

34. Friedman (1985), pp. 301–302.

35. It is interesting to note that once the courts permitted more expansive personal injury damages, industries persuaded Congress to enact worker's compensation laws. These laws provide scheduled damages to workers injured on the job, but at much lower levels than juries might award.

36. Friedman (1985), p. 471; Hunt (1998), pp. 413–14. But see Honson (1996), pp. 819–20 (arguing that in Iowa the contributory negligence rule did not favor carriers over passengers).

37. Friedman (1985), pp. 472–73.

38. Additionally, the once legally moribund idea that a tort action was personal, and ended when the injured person died, was resurrected for the purpose of protecting railroads from wrongful death actions.

39. Friedman (1985), p. 475.

40. Honson (1996).

41. Horowitz (1977), p. 206.

42. *Ibid.*, p. 476.

43. Hunt (1988), p. 429.

44. DiBacco (1987), p. 142.

45. Friedman (1985), p. 481.

46. Hunt (1988), pp. 431–32. Friedman points out, however, that the courts did not go so far as they might, given that the famous case of *Rylands v. Fletcher*, L.R., 3 H.L. 330 (1868), if adopted in this country, might have called for a rule of absolute liability for industrial accidents. Fear of crippling the new industries helped prevent the adoption of such a rule. See Friedman (1985), pp. 485–86.

47. Prosser and Keeton (1984), pp. 469–70.

48. Friedman (1985), pp. 483–84.

49. See, e.g., *Railroad Co. v. Lockwood*, 84 U.S. (17 Wall.) 357, 384 (1873), examined in Kaczorowski (1990), p. 1155.

50. Horowitz (1977), p. 253.

51. *Ibid.*, pp. 99–100; see also Friedman (1985).

52. Kaczorowski (1990), p. 1199; Schwartz (1981), p. 1718; Schwartz (1989).

53. Schwartz (1989), pp. 664–65; Schwartz (1981), pp. 1773–75.

54. Schwartz (1981), p. 1720.

55. See, e.g., Hunt (1988), p. 423 n.28; Hunt (1998) p. 381. "[I]nsistence on broad

generalization, limited chronology, and a dichotomous winners and losers approach for the entire century may have distorted accounts of early negligence law."

56. See Rabin (1981) for a detailed argument that there was no shift because of limited historical support for this proposition. Rabin, a leading torts scholar, appears to lean toward confusion as the source of developing legal doctrine in this area. "But the consequent erosion of harsh industrial liability rules reflected more confusion than consistency . . ." Rabin (1981) p. 947.

57. As to railroad employees, at the beginning of the twentieth century, state and federal statutes such as FELA and worker's compensation began to replace the state tort rules. Friedman (1985) p. 484.

58. Kranzberg (1997).

59. Pacey (1990), p. 146.

60. DiBacco (1987), p. 142.

61. Rabin (1981), pp. 936–38; Prosser and Keeton (1984), p. 679.

62. Prosser and Keeton (1984), pp. 679–80.

63. Calamari and Perillo (1990), p. 588.

64. Kintner (1978), p. 9.

65. Rabin (1981), p. 937.

66. Hackney (1995), p. 465.

67. Rabin (1988), p. 7.

68. Schwartz (1983), p. 797.

69. Prosser and Keeton (1984), p. 682.

70. Prosser and Keeton (1984), p. 681; see also Wade (1989), pp. 8, 53.

71. Prosser and Keeton (1984), p. 682. Even before the mass production era, there were some exceptions to the no-recovery rule for items that were imminently or inherently dangerous to human safety.

72. Holmes (1881), pp. 76–77.

73. 111 N.E. 1050, 1052–1053 (N.Y. 1916).

74. *MacPherson v. Buick Motor Company*, 111 N.E. 1050, 1051 (N.Y. 1916).

75. Schwartz (1983), p. 798; Croley and Hansen (1993).

76. Rabin (1988), p. 8.

77. Epstein (1989), pp. 2199–2200.

78. *Ibid.*, p. 2199.

79. Cardozo's opinion actually cut off a line of authority developing toward strict liability under a contract theory and in itself represented a kind of immunity. Recovery on a contract theory would have been preferable to plaintiffs, because in theory breach of contract meant a standard of strict (i.e., no-fault) liability. The inability to recover on a contract theory remained a form of immunity for mass market manufacturers from 1916 to 1958. Wade (1989), p. 11 (noting an early products liability line of authority that tended toward strict liability but was cut off by development of negligence); see also Galligan (1995), p. 467. This kind of immunity was not a necessary outcome, occasioned by the immaturity of doctrine and/or social and legal thinking. Even before *MacPherson*, there were decisions imposing strict liability for one mass-produced product: food for human consumption. See, e.g., *State v. Kelly*, 43 N.E. 163 (Ohio 1896); Restatement (Second) of Torts §402A cmt. b (1965).

80. 150 P.2d 436, 440 (Cal. 1944).

81. Epstein (1989), pp. 2200–2201; see also Kessler, (1943), pp. 631–32. Contracts of adhesion are often used by commercial entities such as banks and stockbrokers that provide terms on a printed form on a non-negotiable basis.

82. Rabin (1988), pp. 8–9, 12.

83. Schwartz (1983), pp. 799–804. Schwartz argues that it was not strict liability itself, but the demise of the pro-defendant subsidiary rules (contributory negligence, assumption of risk) and the extension of the duty to warn of design defects that has resulted in the pro-plaintiff, full-accountability posture of post-1960s products liability law (pp. 802–803).

84. Restatement of Torts §398 (1934). Restatements of the law are developed by the American Law Institute, a non-partisan group of academics, attorneys, and judges who summarize the state of the law and make recommended changes. The changes are not binding on courts, but are often authoritative and gain wide acceptance. See also Schwartz (1983), pp. 799–800.

85. *Escola v. Coca-Cola Bottling Co.*, 150 P.2d 436, 438–439 (Cal. 1944).

86. Schwartz (1983), pp. 804–806.

87. 161 A.2d 69 (N.J. 1960).

88. Although the concept of implied warranty has its origins in warranty (contract) law, it is really quasi-contractual and somewhat tort-like, in the sense that the "implied warranty" is not found "in" the contract but rather in the law of contract. Prior to *Henningsen*, implied warranties could be negated by disclaimers (unlike tort rules in the usual case). See Prosser and Keeton (1984), pp. 690–691.

89. Prosser and Keeton (1984), pp. 692–693.

90. I am indebted to Robert S. Adler, J.D., for the observations in this paragraph.

91. Keeton, Owen, and Montgomery (1980), pp. 196–97.

92. In a few cases, the courts have explicitly rejected strict liability after initially embracing it. *Feldman v Lederle Laboratories*, 625 A.2d 1066 (N.J. 1993). Some courts have demonstrated reluctance to impose strict liability in design defect cases, reasoning that this would expose defendants to unfairly broad liability.

93. Henderson and Eisenberg (1990).

94. If so, this would suggest a selection bias that might compromise the pattern being described.

95. See Jacobson and Pomfret (1999). The analysis of these two industries relies on the work of other scholars and does not come from an analysis of the underlying cases themselves. My focus, therefore, is on whether the evidence could plausibly support the model, not on whether the model is a better description of the evidence than those presented by other scholars. Also, many have pointed out that an analysis of only appellate opinions, particularly with regard to the railroads and mass production, is flawed by the fact that the needs and history of each state were different. At a time when the railroads were in favor in the West, for instance, they were subject to backlash in the East. It is not clear that scholars have paid adequate attention to this issue, which may undermine any global conclusions.

96. Common-carrier liability rules for railroads were drawn from earlier English and American precedents applicable to stagecoaches and other forms of transportation. Kaczorowski (1990), p. 1150.

97. Horowitz (1977), pp. 99–101.

98. Lessig (1997), p. 1795.

99. Galligan, Jr. (1995), p. 468, stating that proximate cause has been used "not only to protect defendants from unlimited liability but also to shield defendants from full liability."

5

The Courts and
Managed Care—
Establishing the Rules

WHEN someone (the plaintiff) brings a lawsuit to recover damages from another party (the defendant), the plaintiff must allege both a set of facts showing wrongdoing and a legal theory (i.e., set of legal principles such as contract or property rights) that supports the case. To win, the plaintiff must prove the facts by a preponderance of the evidence (meaning that the scales of justice tip at least ever so slightly in his or her favor) and that the facts fit the elements of the legal theory. In contrast, the defendant will argue that the facts are wrong, the facts do not support the legal theory, or the plaintiff relied on the wrong legal doctrine.

In the Andrews-Clarke case, for example, Diane Andrews-Clarke brought claims against the MCO for breach of contract, medical malpractice (tort), wrongful death, loss of parental and spousal consortium, intentional and negligent infliction of emotional distress, and specific violations of the Massachusetts consumer protection laws. Teresa Goodrich filed similar claims. Listing numerous legal bases for the claim is typical of the trial process. After the complaint is filed, the case usually gets narrowed to a more manageable number of legal claims as the parties prepare for trial.

In many health-care cases, the claims really rest on breach of contract and medical malpractice (tort) allegations. Contracts, as we have seen, constitute voluntary agreements between parties for mutual benefit. A contract stipulates in advance what goods or services will be provided, how much they will cost, and what the consequences (i.e., damages) will be for breach of contract. Torts involve injuries from a failure to maintain the appropriate standard of care, such as liability for negligence, and are brought after the fact to recover suitable damages.

A key issue for the courts in managed care litigation is to choose the appropriate legal rules to guide the case. Most often, the choice will be between contract and tort law, although there are other rules courts can consider. In contract law, the will of the parties (as expressed in the health insurance agreement) controls the case. But under current law, courts often impose a tort standard of due care on the parties, regardless of what contractual arrangements they may make on their own.

The choice is not always one or the other. Depending on the type and organization of an industry, tort and contract will often operate together. As we will see, managed care presents some aspects especially amenable to contract and others to tort. Sorting out where one or the other should be applied is not necessarily an easy or straightforward task.

This chapter introduces the most important legal concepts and terms that ultimately help determine who wins and loses in managed care litigation. It also addresses various proposals for how the law should assign responsibility in the managed care system. After taking a closer look at the applicable legal principles, we will examine the debate over tort versus contract. The specific focus is on whether litigation against MCOs should be governed by tort doctrine, by contract law, by some combination of these two approaches, or by an alternative legal theory. The goal in this chapter is to illuminate the nature of the debate and explain why it matters.

To revisit the litigation context briefly, in the fee-for-service (FFS) system, the professional and legal responsibilities of physicians, as well as the role of payers and purchasers of health care services, reflected generous and largely uncritical payment systems.[1] Basically, the physician controlled most of the health care resources and the insurer paid for the recommended treatment. The law presumed that physicians were required to deliver a uniform standard of care to all patients, regardless of costs or patients' ability to pay.[2] In the fee-for-service era, insurance and health care delivery functions were distinctly separate. A patient purchased insurance from a commercial carrier and then chose his or her physician separately. Each function was largely covered by a different set of legal rules. Purchasing health insurance was a contractual arrangement governed by contract law, while any problems with the physician's clinical decisions were litigated under tort law. If an insurer in the fee-for-service system failed to pay for hospital or physician care already provided, the patient would sue the insurer in state court for breach of contract. If the health care resulted in an adverse outcome, the patient would sue the physician or hospital for negligence, also in state court.

In managed care, the insurance and health care delivery functions are combined into one entity, changing the litigation context.[3] An MCO's refusal to pay for recommended treatment is tantamount to denying health care altogether for those without independent means of paying. In their capacity as insurers, MCOs may deny health care recommended by the patient's physician or may agree to provide only limited funding for certain clinical interventions. If the patient suffers an adverse outcome as a result, which legal regime should resolve the dispute—tort or contract? Since health care is rapidly becoming just another market commodity, should the relationship be guided, as most market transactions are, by contractual arrangements and concepts? Or does this market reality require greater oversight through tort concepts? As an alternative, are there legal strategies for bridging the gap between tort and contract that would more effectively guide the judicial response to managed care?

At this point, a reader unfamiliar with the intricacies of legal maneuvering might be tempted to ask what difference it makes. Regardless of whether tort or contract "prevails," contracts are an integral part of health care delivery and always have been. If there is a legitimate claim, of course the injured person should recover. A reader may also dismiss this as an arcane topic designed to keep lots of young attorneys and scholars busy.

Not so fast. It makes a big difference whether a tort or a contract standard prevails. The debate between tort and contract has significant practical implications for patients, along with significant public policy considerations about whether and how government should intervene.

The choice of the controlling legal rules will influence who wins and loses. The patient has a much better chance of a successful outcome in court if permitted to sue under tort law than under contract law.[4] For patients, the different legal theories generate vastly divergent solutions if something goes wrong. Monetary damage awards under breach of contract tend to be more limited than under tort. It is rare, for instance, to recover for pain and suffering under breach of contract, but standard in a negligence action. Disparities in bargaining power between health plans and patients mean that patients' ability to challenge delayed or denied health care will be much more difficult under a contract regime. Depending on how the contract is written, individual challenges to the operation of cost-containment programs will be limited, if not eliminated altogether, under contract-dominated legal rules.[5]

Beyond these differences, contract and tort represent a fundamental philosophical and political divide regarding how to hold private sector firms and institutions accountable for their actions. What are the appropriate roles of the private sector and government intervention in addressing concerns about the health care delivery system? We might think about contract law as supporting a market-based approach, while tort implies government oversight or regulatory functions. Proponents of a market-based health care system argue that contractual arrangements should determine what level of care a patient should receive and how any subsequent dispute should be handled. They view tort as a form of governmental intervention in matters that should best be left to the marketplace. Proponents of tort (though few actually reveal themselves publicly, except for trial attorneys) contend that the market will not protect patients and that MCOs will take advantage of superior bargaining power to avoid responsibility for adverse medical outcomes. They view tort as a needed deterrent and potential corrective to the market's excesses.

To the extent that contracts dominate the legal rules, the balance of power between MCOs and physicians or patients will shift toward MCOs. Large institutions can use superior bargaining power to set the contractual terms. A system governed by tort law will provide some recourse for patients challenging cost-containment programs and also provide leverage against an MCO's decision to deny care.

Because the legal rules in health care were designed to respond to a system with separate financing and care-giving functions, a new approach is needed to govern the hybrid nature of managed care.

> Part of the challenge to the legal system is to ensure that liability rules are conducive to good overall performance by the industry, creating appropriate incentives to prevent patient injuries while not impeding efforts by employers, health plans, and physicians to define and implement efficient levels of spending.[6]

Whether contract or tort, or a combination of the two, can meet this challenge is an open question.

Overview of the Applicable Legal Principles

Torts are civil, non-contractual wrongs, such as negligence, where the injured person seeks monetary damages from the one who caused the injury.[7] Typically, tort suits are private civil actions brought to recover damages for the injury. Automobile accidents, slip and fall cases, and medical professional liability (medical malpractice) are typical examples of tort cases. In this book, we are concerned with unintentional torts (medical liability), but torts can also be intentional (such as defamation or battery). Tort liability is based on an after-the-fact (*ex post*) understanding of what went wrong. An *ex post* analysis allows a jury to consider what the defendant should have done under the circumstances to avoid the injury.

Tort litigation serves three basic purposes: compensation, deterrence, and accountability. Patients use private tort litigation to obtain damages, but may also desire to induce internal policy changes in how MCOs conduct business. The ability of private litigation to achieve broad policy changes may be limited,[8] though tort law mimics regulatory oversight in monitoring quality of care.

For an injured patient, the most obvious function of the tort system is to compensate for harm suffered as a result of the defendant's conduct. The injury could occur through failure to diagnose a problem, by not performing the intervention correctly, or by delaying or denying care. Compensation includes economic damages (actual medical expenses, for instance), but it can also include non-economic damages for pain and suffering. This may be thought of as the law's corrective function, and it is determined through liability standards, as discussed below.

The second function of the tort system is to deter future wrongdoing. In medical liability litigation, deterrence would include attempts to diminish the likelihood of future harm from medical intervention.[9] In theory, the physician or MCO being sued for medical liability would adopt corrective mechanisms or procedures to avoid subsequent errors. For example, a hospital found liable for failing to monitor drug–drug interactions would devise better systems to detect pharmaceutical errors before they occur.[10]

A closely related function is accountability, or holding persons and institutions responsible for the harms (and, in some cases, the unreasonable risk of harm) they inflict. By establishing rules to assess liability, the tort system provides a mechanism for society to hold wrongdoers accountable for their actions. The accountability function of tort law will be especially important as the courts begin to assess the consequences and available remedies for aggressive cost containment initiatives.

At its simplest, tort law establishes standards of reasonable behavior that individuals are expected to meet. It is basically the legal standard of care that the community establishes to set appropriate rules of conduct. When a person's or an institution's conduct falls below the minimum standard of care expected, the injured party (the plaintiff) may sue the alleged wrongdoer (the defendant) for appropriate damages. In general, tort law is based on showing that the defendant was at fault for the injuries.[11] To meet the burden of proof for a damage award, the plaintiff must prove the following four elements by a preponderance of the evidence: 1) a defendant's duty of due care; 2) breach of that duty; 3) the defendant's conduct caused the injuries; and 4) the injury produced actual damages.[12] Each state court system establishes its own body of negligence law, although all states use this basic framework. This means that legal doctrine will vary across states, so that what may be considered negligent in one state will not necessarily be considered negligent in another.

To begin, the plaintiff must show that the defendant owed a duty of care to protect others against the unreasonable risk of harm.[13] The basis of tort law is that people must conform to standards of reasonable conduct by taking steps to avoid foreseeable harm. Most often, the duty owed is uncontroversial. For example, a store owner has the duty to clean spills from the floor to protect customers from slipping, and a property owner owes a duty to invited guests to protect against known hazards. The more difficult issue is determining the second element, breach of duty.

A breach of duty occurs when the defendant's actions fall below the standard that a reasonable person would maintain. To determine whether a defendant has breached his or her duty of due care, courts often look to custom in the industry, and, in the absence of custom, to whether the defendant's conduct was reasonable. How would a reasonable person have acted under the circumstances?[14] The reasonable person standard allows the jury to make an informed decision about whether the defendant's activity met the community's standard of due care or created an unreasonable risk of harm. If the defendant knew or should have known that his or her conduct posed a risk of harm, then he or she has breached the standard of care. In some cases, the courts will overrule industry custom if the industry is slow to adopt technologies or systems that would avoid injury.[15]

The defendant's conduct must also *cause* the harm. Causation is one of the most controversial areas of the law. In general, courts have held that there are two types of causal relations—proximate (or legal) cause, and cause in fact. To determine whether the defendant's conduct caused the plaintiff's harm, courts use one of two tests. The first is known as the "but for" test: but for the defendant's conduct, no harm would have occurred. The other is the "substantial factor" test: was the defendant's conduct a substantial factor in causing the accident? As many have pointed out, everything is related to everything else, leading to an endless series of causal connections. That is why courts limit, on policy grounds, the extent to which causation will be applied. To recover damages, the harm must be foreseeable: would a reasonable person have foreseen or anticipated that the defendant's behavior would place others at risk of harm? If not, the defendant is not liable. For example, it is foreseeable to someone driving an automobile that a pedestrian may cross at a crosswalk. It may not be foreseeable that a bicycler will run a stoplight and ride into traffic. The driver may be liable for hitting the pedestrian, but may not be liable for hitting the bicycler.

Finally, negligence liability requires actual loss or damage—no harm, no foul! Most of the time, courts require some indications of actual loss, such as a physical injury, lost time from work, or treatment in a hospital emergency room. In extreme cases, emotional harm alone will suffice.

In the example about spills, the store owner has a duty to protect customers from potential slip-and-fall situations, and must act reasonably to remove the risk of harm. That does not mean cleaning the spill instantly, but it does mean that an unattended spill (say for more than an hour) might be considered unreasonable by a jury. It is foreseeable that uncleaned spills will result in other customers' slipping and injuring themselves, even if it is not foreseeable that a particular customer will spill a product. If the customer suffers damages, such as stitches to repair a wound, he or she can successfully bring a negligence case.

Establishing medical liability involves each of the four elements just described, with one important difference. Unlike the situation with general negligence, where the community sets the legal standard of care based on industry custom or what a reasonable person would expect, the medical profession itself sets the legal standard of care in medical liability cases. It is then up to the jury to determine whether the physician met the standard of care when applied to the facts of a particular case. The medical profession sets the standard of care based on what is customary and usual practice, as established through physician testimony and medical treatises. A typical statement of the law is that each physician must "exercise that degree of skill ordinarily employed, under similar circumstances, by the members of [the] profession."[16] In effect, this means that the same level of care must be provided to all patients, regardless of resource constraints.[17]

The primary reason why medical liability diverged from general negligence is that courts did not feel capable of second-guessing customary medical practice. Courts held that non-physicians do not have sufficient training to establish customary and reasonable medical practices.[18] Many physicians, nonetheless, deride the standard of care as being a legal construct rather than representing a medical standard. For the most part, they view care as being provided along a spectrum of options, not a fixed standard. Physicians reject the idea that there is one clear practice standard.

Each physician must exercise the degree of skill ordinarily practiced, under similar circumstances, by members of the profession. Physicians with special knowledge, such as cardiologists, will be held to customary practices among those of similar skill and training. If there is more than one recognized course of treatment, most courts allow some flexibility in what is regarded as customary treatment, known as the "respectable minority" rule. In relatively rare instances, courts will allow a plaintiff to challenge the adequacy of customary medical practice, resulting in a higher standard of care than determined by the profession.[19] Under the general rules of tort law, physicians are not guarantors of perfect health-care outcomes. The standard of care requires reasonable and ordinary skill—not the highest degree of proficiency in the profession. Physicians will not necessarily be held negligent for errors in judgment, and certainly not for every adverse clinical outcome, regardless of fault.[20]

When these rules were originally established, courts relied on customary practice within the physician's local area. Only physicians familiar with local practices could testify on behalf of an injured patient—but many physicians were unwilling to testify against local friends and colleagues. Most state courts have abandoned the locality rule to avoid the harshness of its results and because medical schools now use a uniform national curriculum. The customary-practice standard is now based on national practices. Physicians from anywhere can testify to what the national standard of care is. In most states, an expert witness must have sufficient expertise about the type of care provided to testify. For example, a radiologist would be expected to testify whether another radiologist properly read a CT scan. A general practitioner would not ordinarily have enough knowledge about radiology to testify.

Courts are reluctant to substitute their judgment for that of the medical profession, even when a new, safer technology is being considered.[21] Despite this deference to medical professionals, the tort system operates as a quality control mechanism over medical care in providing incentives for meeting the standard of care and sanctions against providing substandard care.

Health-care litigation, such as patients' suing physicians or hospitals to recover monetary damages for medical injuries, is usually resolved by state courts. Since the mid-1960s, state courts have held hospitals legally responsible for adverse medical outcomes, either directly for their own actions (such as negligent oversight of physicians) or indirectly (vicariously) for actions committed by physicians controlled by the facility. In the managed care environment, the issue is whether and how courts will apply established liability principles to the various managed care organizational forms and cost-containment innovations, both within the ERISA context and when the litigation is not preempted.[22]

Health-care institutions, including MCOs, may be held liable for their own negligence or for substandard care practiced by their employees, either under a theory of direct liability or under agency principles (vicarious liability). As a general rule, health-care institutions may be held directly liable for the failure to: 1) maintain safe and adequate facilities; 2) select and retain competent physicians; 3) oversee all patient care within the institution; and 4) ensure quality care.[23] MCOs can also be held indirectly liable under vicarious liability and agency principles for malpractice committed by physicians who are independent contractors. An independent contractor is a physician who has staff privileges to practice at a hospital but is not on the hospital's staff. In determining vicarious liability, the courts look to the MCO's control over the physician, how the plan markets its physicians, and how patients perceive the relationship between the physician and the MCO. The greater the indicia of control and the more the plan markets the quality of its physician panel, the greater the likelihood that the MCO will be held vicariously liable.

In the leading case of *Boyd v. Albert Einstein Medical Center,*[24] for example, the court held that an IPA could be found liable for an individual physician's medical malpractice because the patient reasonably believed that the IPA exercised some control over the physician's clinical decisions. Through the defendant's advertising campaign, the patient believed that the physician was part of the plan. The court rejected the plan's argument that it was not liable because the physician was an independent contractor, holding that the physician could still be the plan's agent with respect to the patient. A key element in such cases is whether the MCO has sufficient control, such as through utilization-review arrangements, to override a physician's clinical judgment.[25]

Contract law is primarily concerned with establishing and enforcing promises that are freely arranged by competent adults who understand the nature of the agreement. By designing rules that protect freedom of contract, courts enable individuals to bargain with others to purchase or sell goods and services under mutually agreed terms and circumstances. In the language of economists, contracts establish the expectations of the parties *ex ante* (from the beginning). When the contract is signed, people agree to be bound by its terms regarding benefits, rights, and responsibilities, even if their personal circumstances and desires change.

Freedom of contract is a fundamental concept in American political, economic, and legal traditions. Politically, freedom of contract is the foundation of a market economy and a stable democracy. In many ways, the use of contracts is what demarcates the boundary between the public and the private sectors. Most transactions that support our economy are based on contractual arrangements. In a democracy, the freedom to contract is the favored mechanism for citizens to express their preferences about social and economic arrangements. Courts and legislatures have been reluctant to interfere with the right to contract, unless the bargain is either so unfair that it was not freely entered into, or it violates public policy. An example would be contracts to pay for surrogate motherhood (beyond reasonable expenses), which courts have ruled are contrary to public policy.

Health care is no exception to the importance of contracts. Much of the structural change in health care delivery during the past decade, including the relationship between physicians and hospitals or health plans, results from the flexibility inherent in contractual arrangements. For instance, IPAs contract with MCOs to provide physician services to the MCOs' patient population. Joint ventures between hospitals and physicians are based on contractual definitions of how the venture will be organized and governed, how risk will be shared, and how the proceeds will be distributed. Hospital by-laws guide how the organization will be structured and governed, and define the terms for granting and retaining staff privileges. Hospitals may contract with certain specialty groups to provide all of the hospital's needs for that service (such as radiology or pathology). These are known as *selective contracting arrange-ments* because they exclude other physicians or groups from providing that service.

For our purposes, the most important contractual arrangement is between patients and health plans. The selection of a health insurer or a health plan is a contractual arrangement that sets the scope and limits of expected health-care coverage. In return for a set premium, the health care benefits defined by the contract will be provided. That contract forms the basic understanding of what benefits will be provided (the benefit package); how decisions regard-ing health care are made (medical necessity); what alternatives exist regarding out-of-network coverage; the gatekeeper role of the primary-care physician; how patients can challenge the denial of medical care (grievance procedures); and available remedies to resolve any disputes (arbitration). The available ben-efit packages for employees of most large firms (more than 100 employees) are relatively similar, with insurers and MCOs competing on price.[26] There is much greater variation in the benefit packages for employees of small firms (fewer than 50 employees) or those purchasing individual health insurance coverage from a commercial insurer.

In either case, patients usually sign a standard contract setting forth the terms and conditions on a take-it-or-leave-it basis. In theory, the employer negotiates the best available package of benefits and price, but the employer and employee have different interests and incentives, as we will see. A major problem for employees is that it is difficult to define important terms—in-cluding limits on benefits such as experimental therapy—with enough detail to avoid arguments over what is covered.

When interpreting contracts, courts first look to determine whether there was a meeting of the minds (that is, mutual assent to the terms and obligations in the contract) between the contracting parties. As long as the terms of the agreement are clearly stated and there was reasonably equal bargaining power, courts will not overturn the contract reached. To determine whether a "meet-ing of the minds" occurred, courts will look to the parties' intent, as indicated by the plain language of the agreement. As one court noted,

> . . . the objective in construing [a contract] is to ascertain and carry out the true intentions of the parties by giving the language its common and ordinary mean-ing as a reasonable person . . . would have understood the words to mean.[27]

How courts interpret contracts will play an important role in the managed care industry's ability to implement various cost-containment initiatives. More to the point, how courts balance between tort and contract will shape how aggressively MCOs can implement these programs. Historically, courts have tried to hold parties to the basis of their contractual bargain. Beginning in the late 1960s, however, some courts questioned how freely consumers entered into certain relationships; these courts were willing to void contracts based on the doctrine of unconscionability. Under this doctrine, if the contractual terms are so one-sided and the bargaining power between the two parties so unequal, courts would not enforce the contract, leading some experts to proclaim the "death of contract."[28]

More recently, courts have moved away from the doctrine of unconscionability and have generally upheld contractual arrangements even where there is no equality of bargaining power and the terms are one-sided in a standard-form agreement.[29] The one area where this trend is less clear is the doctrine of *contra proforentem,* which means that ambiguity must be interpreted against the drafter. This doctrine has been especially important in cases challenging the denial of experimental treatments. Since it is difficult to specify every conceivable health-care contingency up front, health insurance contracts exclude coverage for most experimental treatments, but cannot list or define all treatments likely to be excluded. Some courts have required coverage where the exclusion is not specific, leading some scholars to complain about "judge-made insurance coverage."[30] In these cases, ambiguity is interpreted against the drafter of the contract, usually the insurer.

The courts' consideration of equal bargaining power is somewhat problematic for an employee who is covered by employer-sponsored health insurance. For most employees, the employer negotiates the contract with the insurer or health plan. Courts then assume that there is equality of bargaining power, and hold patients to the terms of the agreement (such as submitting to arbitration to resolve disputes). In reality, employer and employee interests are not necessarily in agreement, and employees have little say over what is included in the health insurance contract. Undoubtedly, employers have an interest in a satisfied work force and employees can negotiate better terms in subsequent employment contracts. Nonetheless, it is perhaps a necessary fiction that individual patients and health insurers have a "meeting of the minds" when the contract is signed. Otherwise, it would be very difficult for employers to arrange health benefits for their employees because it would be hard to sign binding agreements.

When parties to a contract disagree about its terms or meaning, courts are asked to determine whether a promise contained within the contractual agreement has not been performed or whether the agreement has been breached. Here, courts must ask whether the injured party has been deprived of a benefit that he or she reasonably expected. In the health-care context, potential contractual breaches arise when patients allege that a health plan failed to provide benefits included in the patient's benefit package, or failed to provide medically necessary care as recommended by the treating physician. To determine whether the plan breached the contract, a court will examine the terms of the agreement and interpret them according to the parties' intent and the common meaning of the terms.

If a court finds a breach of contract, the next step is to assess how to compensate the injured party adequately. The basic remedy for breach of contract in the Anglo-American legal system involves awarding damages to compensate an injured party for the loss. In certain cases, courts could compel specific performance of the contract, meaning that a plan would be required to provide a benefit that was otherwise denied. Specific performance is an equitable remedy that is available when monetary damages would not be adequate. If, for example, a plan denies a bone marrow transplant and thereby breaches the health insurance contract, a court could order the plan to provide the transplant.

Another type of remedy is that of punitive or exemplary damages, which are designed to punish the offending party and to deter similar conduct in the future. Exemplary damages are reserved for cases where the defendant's conduct is tantamount to fraud, malice, or oppression. They are not available for breach of contract in most jurisdictions, but may be appropriate where a defendant acts in bad faith.

One area where tort and contract law overlap is with the concept of *bad faith breach of contract*. Suppose that a patient presents with anorexia nervosa, with insurance coverage for 70 days of inpatient psychological treatment.[31] If the plan has no comparable provision for an inpatient eating disorder program, the treating physician may recommend referral to an out-of-network program. The MCO may approve a total of six weeks of inpatient therapy, but then discontinue coverage over the treating physician's objections. In response, the patient may sue the plan for bad faith breach of contract.

The bad faith claim arises from an alleged breach of contract, but has a different legal basis. Unlike the traditional suit for breach of contract, bad faith is a tort claim separate from the breach of contract allegation:

> The rationale underlying a bad faith [claim] is to encourage fair treatment of the insured and penalize unfair and corrupt insurance practices. By ensuring that the policyholder achieves the benefits of his or her bargain, a bad faith [claim] helps to redress a bargaining power imbalance between parties to an insurance contract.[32]

To win, the plaintiff must show that the refusal to provide coverage was either malicious or recklessly disregarded the terms of the contract. If bad faith can be shown, the patient can recover both compensatory and punitive damages. The import of bringing a tort action for bad faith as opposed to a breach of contract case is in the damages allowed and in forcing the MCO to show a reasonable basis for its actions in order to avoid liability.

Contract vs. Tort

The distinction between tort and contract law in the context of the changing health-care environment has been the source of scholarly and judicial debate for many years, closely matching the shifts we examined with the railroads and mass production. What stands out in the literature is the striking dominance of proponents favoring contract over tort law for resolving health-care disputes.

In some situations, managed care's combined care-delivery and financing functions will make little difference as to which doctrine will be applied. Selecting a set of health care benefits only involves defining the terms of the health insurance contract; disputes can usually be resolved by contract principles. If a patient pays a lower premium for a plan with fewer benefits, the plan should be held only to the contracted benefits, not those the patient subsequently decides he or she should have purchased. Likewise, an MCO that employs a physician (usually a staff model HMO) cannot avoid liability for a physician's substandard care. Individual clinical decisions, which have traditionally been governed by tort concepts, will most often be matters of clinical judgment rather than contract interpretation. It is difficult to see how contract principles could easily resolve whether a particular 45-year-old should have been given a CT scan for a head injury unless a CT scan for that diagnosis is specifically excluded from coverage.[33]

Most of the contentious disputes will emerge from the mixed managed care functions, where the distinctions between financing and care delivery are blurred. As an example, let us look at the issue of financial incentives for physicians, a situation unlikely to arise under fee-for-service medicine. One of managed care's primary cost-containment measures is to provide physicians with financial incentives, perhaps an end-of-the-year bonus based on health care resources used, to limit health care services such as referrals to specialists.

Suppose, for example, someone presents with classic symptoms of coronary artery blockage, including chest pain radiating into his or her arms and shortness of breath, but is discharged after a thallium stress test proves negative.[34] Later, the pain recurs and another plan physician recommends an angiogram, which the treating physician rejects based on the thallium test. The patient then dies of a heart attack. Suppose the treating physician had an arrangement with the patient's plan that any money remaining in a fund designed to provide necessary tests and referrals to specialists would be distributed between the physician and the health plan on a 60–40 basis. If the patient suffers an adverse outcome from medical intervention, he or she is likely to sue the physician and the MCO for negligence, alleging that improper financial incentives interfered with the care. The MCO is likely to defend on the basis that the incentives played no role in the patient's health care. The patient has a much better chance of recovering damages if permitted to sue under tort law than if a court rules that the case is governed by contract law (though bad faith breach of contract remains a distinct possibility). Many of the disputes over how cost containment programs are implemented will fall into this category, so case outcomes will be very dependent on which legal rules, tort or contract, courts adopt.

As another example of where it is difficult to separate managed care's hybrid functions and where the choice of the controlling legal rules will influence case outcomes, take *utilization review* (UR). MCOs rely heavily on UR techniques, such as preauthorization for high-cost medical interventions, to reduce costs. These decisions involve a mix of benefit determinations (contract) and individual clinical decisions (tort). Legal challenges to UR decisions require courts to determine whether contract or tort is the proper rule.

Let us assume that an obstetrician recommends bed rest for the final months of a pregnancy and then requests pre-certification for conducting 24-hour inpatient monitoring near the delivery date.[35] Based on an independent medical review (either through an external grievance panel or through internal utilization review), suppose the plan determines that ten hours of in-home nursing care is sufficient and refuses to pre-certify the hospitalization request. If, during a period of time when no nurse is on duty, the fetus goes into distress and dies, what recourse would the parents have against the health plan? The defendant will no doubt claim that it was simply making a benefit determination and therefore should not be held responsible. In fact, as the court found, this type of choice involves both clinical judgment and benefit decisions. If the court sees the case as a contract dispute, the litigation is likely to be resolved in favor of the plan. Patients would then have little recourse when clinical decisions are influenced by cost considerations. If the court sees the case as a tort suit for negligence, the result may be more favorable to the parents. The litigation might then limit the ability of MCOs to maintain cost-containment programs. This situation is a variant of the issues at stake in both the Andrews-Clarke and Goodrich cases.[36]

Table 5–1 lists the primary health-care and financing functions in the fee-for-service and managed care systems. The table demonstrates two important relationships. In the fee-for-service era, most cases would arise under the tort system. With the exception of interpretations of covered benefits (financed by independent commercial insurers), the cases were resolved by tort rules. By contrast, most of the managed care functions are of a hybrid nature, where it is not clear whether tort or contract should govern. Financial incentives, utilization review, and drug formularies are central to managed care's attempts to control health-care costs, and did not exist in the fee-for-service system. The choice of legal rules will influence how effective these strategies will be.

The scholarly literature discussing the intersection between law and health care overwhelmingly supports a market-based (i.e., contract) approach. The

TABLE 5–1. Managed Care and Fee-For-Service

	MANAGED CARE		
	TORT	CONTRACT	HYBRID
Provider selection	X		
Financial incentives			X
Plan selection		X	
Utilization review			X
Drug formularies			
Benefits			X[a]
Clinical care			X[a]
Information			X

[a]Some scholars would still place benefits as a contractual claim and clinical care as a tort claim in the managed care context.

	FEE-FOR-SERVICE		
	TORT	CONTRACT	HYBRID
Provider selection	X		
Financial incentives			NA
Plan selection			NA
Utilization review	X		NA
Drug formularies			NA
Benefits		X	
Clinical care	X		
Information	X		
Information ads			NA
Informed consent	X		

basic argument for contract rules is that the market will provide the type and level of choices that consumers want:

> In the managed care marketplace, if plans compete on price, choice, and quality, they have incentives to cover services . . . that are worth their costs to consumers. Patients who want comprehensive coverage can choose high premium plans. . . . Consumers self-select to different types of health plans based on their preferences for cost, coverage, copayment, prompt access to new technologies, restrictions on choice, and so forth. Thus consumers' choices among health plans reflect their preferences and willingness-to-pay. . . . [37]

While there is no single contract viewpoint, proponents share a belief that some form of market-based health care grounded in contract law is both economically efficient and will produce higher quality health care than a system based on tort law. Contract proponents also share a belief that legal rules must encourage physicians to take into account the cost constraints imposed by

MCOs at the behest of employers and other purchasers of health-care services. In the most comprehensive form of this system, contracts would be used to set all aspects of the health-care relationship, including benefit determinations and liability standards.[38] In the dominant scholarly view, contracts would not establish all the terms of the relationship, but would become the primary mechanism for ordering the relations between health-care providers, insurers, and patients.

The rationale for the primacy of contract is that consumers can directly exercise power over cost, quality, and service. As an instrument of market arrangements, contract rules will force health-care providers to compete on both price and quality to retain customers. Purchasers have an incentive to choose an efficient plan, defined as "... one that provides all cost-justified care and no more."[39] Also, contracts allow individuals to decide how much they desire to spend on health care rather than other commodities. In turn, contract proponents argue, this would help bring spiraling health-care costs under control without sacrificing quality of care.

More extensive use of contracts would provide market alternatives to the current "Cadillac" (i.e., high-benefit, high-cost) plans now available. According to contract proponents, society allocates too many resources to health care, in part because courts are reluctant to uphold sometimes vague contracts that attempt to limit benefits. Unless the people who purchase health insurance can contract for a set of benefits and limitations that they are willing to pay for, the threat is that legislatures will set mandated benefit packages or that courts will impose benefit coverage regardless of cost.[40] As long as patients understand what benefits will or will not be provided when they get sick, they should be able to select plans providing fewer benefits at lower cost. In this way, the market will set the desired benefit–cost levels through a series of contractual choices that individual patients make.

A related argument is that a contract-based system returns responsibility for health-care decisions to the patient where it belongs. Patients have a duty to assume accountability for the consequences of their health care choices.[41,42] Patients who are more involved in health decisions would have an incentive to learn about their individual needs and which plan would be most appropriate. Over time, they would demand fewer unnecessary interventions because they would have a financial stake in the outcome. Patient satisfaction should be higher and the number of malpractice lawsuits should be reduced. Indeed, the premise behind medical savings accounts (MSAs), which are savings accounts patients would use solely for health care, is that patients, rather than physicians, insurers, or employers, should take control of the process.

In response to objections that patients lack adequate information to make efficient benefit decisions, contract proponents maintain that consumers purchase numerous goods whose workings they do not necessarily comprehend fully. Few people understand how an automobile functions, but that does not inhibit the use of contracts to set the terms of the exchange.[43] They still remain bound by the signed agreement.

Contract proponents also contend that the market, via the process of selecting health insurance plans, is the appropriate vehicle for making health-care rationing decisions.[44] Accordingly, the type of insurance plan purchased indicates a patient's desired level of insulation from the costs of treatment.[45] If an employee purchases a classic HMO model, he or she has signaled a desire for some form of bedside rationing, given the explicit exclusions in the insurance coverage. Market proponents postulate that such choices validate the use of financial incentives that encourage physicians to minimize unnecessary health care.

An important underlying factor in the case for contracts is a deep aversion to the tort system as a mechanism for imposing accountability.[46] For our purposes, we need not explore in depth the reasons why contract proponents oppose the tort system. In brief, these commentators believe that the tort system is inefficient and random in providing compensation, has high administrative costs, does not deter wrongdoing, sets standards of care too high, and provides benefits that consumers would generally not be willing to pay for in the market. Some severely injured patients receive too little compensation, while less-injured patients are awarded too much. And the evidence is thin that the tort system deters substandard care.[47] Opponents of the tort approach argue that it produces higher costs, which will undermine the very cost savings rationale that is the *raison d'être* of managed care.[48] Applying the tort system's use of the customary standard of care governing medical liability to MCOs is inefficient, they contend. Tort concepts require the unitary level of care developed under the fee-for-service system where there were no cost constraints, and encourage the provision of unnecessary care.[49]

To avoid the problems presented by the tort system, some contract proponents would permit patients and health plans to establish liability contractually, entirely bypassing the tort system. Contract reform would eliminate the high expenses of the traditional tort system, including the cost of medical malpractice insurance, by allowing parties to bargain for less liability protection in return for lower premiums. The parties could also negotiate for more efficient and less costly alternatives for resolving disputes, such as mediation or arbitration.[50,51,52] That is, the patient and health plan or physician could determine through the contract the applicable standard of care or how disputes over the care provided would be resolved. A reformed system would expand the number of patients compensated for substandard care, while limiting the size of recoveries and eliminating duplicate benefits from collateral sources.

On one level, the case for the dominance of contract is strong and coherent. Yet when its component assumptions are scrutinized more closely, there are several serious deficiencies that limit how well it would actually work.

At the heart of the pro-contract case is the assumption that customer choice will force greater emphasis on quality and efficiency of care. That assumption depends on the availability of adequate information, regardless of whether "the customer" is the employer or the individual seeking insurance. The most powerful argument against contracting in health care, in fact, is the absence of adequate patient information. In most consumer contracts, the customer can anticipate his or her needs and assess the costs and quality of the product being purchased. Not so in health care, where most patients are unable to anticipate their medical needs or assess the likely quality-of-care when the contract is signed. Perhaps more significant, most consumer contracts provide for the delivery of a specific good in return for a monetary payment. In health care, the arrangement assumes an ongoing set of needs that depend on the individual's health status and the advancement of medical technologies and interventions, neither of which patients can easily anticipate when buying health coverage.

Patients cannot obtain sufficient information about quality of care before knowledgeably signing a contract. It is neither practical nor efficient for patients to become highly educated about the kind of medical care they might need. Even if patients could judge certain aspects of quality care; namely, the amenities or the interpersonal aspects, ". . . they usually lack both the information and the knowledge necessary to judge whether the *technical* quality of the product is unacceptably low."[53] Medical information would need to be unduly simplified to be accessible to the average patient, potentially leading to misunderstanding or the misuse of accurate information. The result would be worse decisions than now observed.[54] The complexity of health-care delivery makes it difficult to reduce the clinical encounter to a simple contractual arrangement. The uncertainty and unpredictability inherent in medical care make it difficult to provide sufficient information and to anticipate ahead of time (*ex ante*) what the contract should include or exclude. Too many patients might try to save a few dollars in health insurance costs and purchase inadequate coverage when they need it most.

To be sure, patients should expect to be involved in decisions about their health care, especially where the physician must rely on the patient's preferences, such as whether to test for prostate-specific antigen (PSA) or how much end-of-life care to provide. Most of the time, it is difficult for patients to know what care is likely to be needed or what the best medical options are, in order to bargain over it in advance. An example is a woman who could not find out from five of the six HMOs she contacted whether they would continue her breast cancer treatments.[55]

The combination of lack of information, inability to evaluate medical risk, and unequal bargaining power between the patient and the medical system is a powerful rejoinder to the contract viewpoint. And there are additional problems with relying on contract rules to regulate MCOs. By governing all managed care decisions through contracts, MCOs would not be held accountable for their influence over quality of care unless the contract included a term specifically covering liability. Furthermore, reliance on contracts ignores the vulnerable psychological state patients are in when they are sick.[56] Patients are unlikely to appreciate information provided at the time of treatment. Full disclosure must occur prior to treatment. The proper time to inform managed care patients about what their contract contains is when they enroll in the MCO.[57] At that point, plan enrollees can at least try to weigh the contract terms against other health care options.

Accepting a contract based on full disclosure when enrolling in an MCO assumes that the information problems can be best corrected through contract rules. For health insurance coverage, the employer arranges a set of benefits at a certain price for all its employees. That arrangement allows individual employees to obtain health care at lower group rates than any individual can find on his or her own in the commercial insurance market. But employers have an incentive to reduce health-care benefit costs and may be no more adept at assessing or bargaining over quality of care than any individual employee.[58] In fact, the employer's incentives may not be in the individual employee's best interests.[59] This is known as an *imperfect agency problem*. In agency theory, an individual relies on another to act in his or her best interests. The reality of modern health-care purchasing is that employees have only a limited voice in the benefits available and employers might not purchase benefits individual employees would select on their own. Freedom of choice is not available for most employees. In any event, it is not clear how employers could effectively monitor each plan's medical decisions to make the market work.

Nor is a physician able to be the patient's perfect agent in the managed care era. The physician no longer has the luxury of providing Cadillac care to all patients and must balance the needs of the individual patient against those of the patient population. While the physician retains an obligation to be the patient's advocate, changes in the organizing and financing of health care have altered the traditional fiduciary relationship between patient and physician.[60] Thus, physician and patient interests are not entirely congruent in the managed care environment.

Bridging the Gap Between Tort and Contract

To this point, tort and contract have been presented as opposing and irreconcilable antagonists. Standing alone, neither tort nor contract rules seem adequate for resolving managed care disputes. Aside from other legitimate critiques of the tort system, tort is inadequate because it does a poor job on the cost-containment side.[61] Juries may not be sympathetic to health plan arguments regarding cost controls and cost-effectiveness.[62] On the other hand, contract is inadequate because its deficiencies are manifest in the situations that are of greatest concern to patients—namely, hybrid financing and health care decisions.

In truth, tort and contract are likely to operate in tandem to shape common law rules in managed care. Several scholars recognize the need to bridge the gap between tort and contract to create a more coherent and comprehensive legal framework. Even one of the leading contract proponents has decided that some form of tort liability is needed to impose accountability on the managed care industry.[63] At present, there is no agreement on how contract and tort would operate together, though several examples of what I term "bridging strategies" between tort and contract have been proposed. Let us start with an idea that has been on the policy agenda for the past decade.

The national debate over health reform in the early 1990s first focused public attention on the concept of enterprise medical liability (EML). Under EML, legal accountability for medical malpractice is directed away from the individual physician and toward the health-care organization administering both the financing and delivery of care.[64] The enterprise (that is, the MCO) would be responsible for any negligent acts, including its own or those of its affiliated physicians. Physicians and other health professionals practicing as employees of, or under contract to, health plans would be immune from suit. In return for increased liability exposure, MCOs would retain greater authority over physicians to reduce costs and improve quality of care.[65]

According to proponents, EML creates incentives for MCOs to ensure that care provided under their auspices meets appropriate standards of quality. Proponents of EML would encourage the use of arbitration, no-fault arrangements,[66] and other alternatives to litigation to allow health plans to compensate a greater percentage of injured patients quickly and more consistently.

Despite its advantages, there are several criticisms of EML. The most significant is that EML substantially limits physicians' autonomy and ability to advocate on behalf of the patients. That is why the American Medical Association opposes legislation to implement EML.[67] Also, EML might make it difficult to maintain a record of poorly performing physicians and share it with other institutions. Another objection is that certain tort claims fall outside the logical scope of enterprise liability. With the shift from inpatient care to in-office and outpatient settings, it is not clear how the MCO can be held responsible for actions it has no ability to control.[68]

A second bridging approach argues for retaining tort law for "deficiencies in medical expertise" (a term encompassing technical skill, effort, advocacy, knowledge, judgment, and conscientiousness) and using contract rules to set the level of benefits or resource use.[69] The legal standard of care would be bifurcated. Issues involving clinical expertise would be governed by tort law, while issues involving resource use would be governed by contract.[70] Contract law would define an MCO's benefit obligations and the level of service patients can expect; tort standards would address departures from expected clinical expertise and technical skill. Both health plans and physicians would owe patients the customary standard of medical expertise concerning professional knowledge and skill. But since both health plans and physicians operate under resource constraints, the terms of the contract would set the levels of expected resource use. In this way, tort and contract law principles would apply together.

For disputes regarding health plans' and physicians' knowledge, skill, and effort, little change to the traditional tort approach is needed. Unlike resource issues, technical skill and expertise are completely within the physician's control and fall within classic tort concepts. Tort law should also apply to health plans on matters of expertise, such as the procedures by which decisions are made and providing information to the right people at the right time. MCOs have a further responsibility to take due care in selecting physicians and authorizing care.

Legal standards for resource use raise more complex issues. A health plan's or physician's resource obligations are largely defined by a contract, which usually promises to cover defined benefits that are medically necessary or appropriate, and identifies various exclusions from coverage.[71] Lawsuits against health plans or physicians for denying benefits or for exercising cost containment strategies would be brought in contract, and the plan or physician would be able to use the resource constraints specified in the contract as a defense.

Under current rules, the legal treatment of cost-containment programs places an undue responsibility on physicians, even where resources are actually controlled by the health plans. Where a health plan may survive judicial scrutiny for a particular decision under contract law, a physician may be found liable in the same case under tort law. To prevent such inconsistent outcomes, suits alleging wrongful denials of resources should be litigated as contract disputes and not as malpractice torts.[72]

On many levels, this approach is very attractive, though implementing it to resolve managed care litigation will not be easy. As the cases litigated to date demonstrate, the distinction between technical skill and resource utilization is unlikely to be as clear as proponents maintain.[73] Issues such as utilization review vex current litigation and are likely to be problematic for this approach as well.

A third bridging strategy recognizes that the narrow legal doctrines of contract and tort are not equipped to account for managed care's hybrid roots.[74] This strategy begins by drawing a distinction between the protection of man-

aged care enrollees as patients, and their rights and responsibilities as consumers. Patients' rights focus on the relationships among patients, physicians,
and other providers, with tort law as the tool for protecting patient rights.
Medical care requires specialized knowledge that patients do not have. The
law protects patients against the misuse of this expertise by imposing a common law duty to provide an acceptable standard of care.[75] Consumer rights,
instead, are related to purchasing decisions prior to the formation of a physician–patient relationship.

In some respects, the patient versus consumer distinction is similar to the
resource versus expertise dichotomy just described and similar as well to contract proponents' focus on *ex ante* benefit selection. The proposed solution—
what one scholar terms "the doctrine of informed reasonableness"—is very
different. Under the informed reasonableness formulation, the plan's obligations ". . . would be those that reasonable managed care organizations, and
reasonable patients, with equal bargaining power and good information, would
expect as fair and reasonable for the stated price."[76] The tort element is to
permit negligence lawsuits against an MCO; the contractual element is in
allowing financial limitations to be specified in the contract. Contrary to what
contract proponents advocate, this approach would limit the extent of the
contractual restrictions while recognizing the need to operate within resource
constraints.

The strategy sounds suspiciously circular and difficult to apply. Health plans
could specify limits, but the limits would not be enforced unless "they were
expressly and knowingly agreed to by the individual."[77] No doubt this waiver
provision would be incorporated into all health plan contracts, and would
quickly overwhelm the reasonableness standard.

A fourth approach to the problem is similar to enterprise medical liability.
Courts would use a tort-based implied warranty of quality to hold MCOs liable
as sellers and arrangers of medical services.[78] A warranty is a guarantee by the
seller that the product or service being sold meets the promised quality standard. Unlike the express warranty concept described in the context of the
pre–mass production era, the courts would impose an implied warranty of
quality arising from the contract between the patient and the MCO. With the
warranty, MCOs would be liable for negligently provided health care services.[79] As with enterprise medical liability, the MCO takes full legal responsibility for adverse outcomes.

An implied warranty of quality is conceptually similar to strict liability in
the modern mass production industries. Just as manufacturers are in the best
position to evaluate safety and induce consumers to buy products based on
an assumption of safety, MCOs are in the best position to guarantee quality
and prevent medical injuries.[80] MCOs are also in a better position than individual physicians to bear the risk and cost of malpractice judgments.

The major drawback to this proposal is that it does nothing to avert the MCOs' argument that they are not providers of care, only insurers. Another potential problem is that because warranties are based conceptually on contract, nothing prevents judges from turning this into a contract standard, with the same problems we saw in the pre–mass production era.

The Reality of Managed Care—Individualized Clinical Decisions

The case for contract assumes an easy separation between benefit decisions, customarily a matter for contract interpretation, and medical treatment decisions, usually overseen by tort law's standard of care. In theory, it is possible to list managed care functions that would be entirely governed by contract law, particularly the benefit package, and those governed by tort law, especially quality of care. But the reality of managed care is that the two functions are inextricably intertwined, making distinctions between the two seem arbitrary. "It is becoming impossible to characterize components of managed care as wholly contractual or wholly tort, which makes it quite difficult to determine which body of law governs."[81] Those who favor using contract law alone ignore this hybrid nature. Most of the contentious, litigated disputes arise from the mixed managed care functions, where the distinctions between financing and care delivery are blurred. These disputes are likely to be about specific clinical determinations rather than whether a specific benefit was provided by the contract. Utilization review decisions (such as a premature discharge from inpatient care) often present difficulties in separating whether the decision to deny care is based on a determination of benefits or on individual clinical considerations.

Some situations, such as requests for experimental procedures, undoubtedly involve contractual interpretations and are less likely to be provided under a contract regime than in tort. Other circumstances, including interpretations of whether an available benefit should have been provided to an individual patient, are governed by tort concepts and are not directly influenced by the terms of the contract. Since these clinical decisions do not usually depend on interpretations of available benefits, contract law may have little to say about how they are resolved.

Even so, contract proponents have a strong argument that the purchase of health insurance is without doubt a contractual arrangement and that disputes about the terms of the agreement should be resolved by contract law, not through tort. If, for example, a patient purchases a benefit package that specifically limits, let us say, inpatient stays to 30 days per year, courts should be reluctant to overrule the arrangement through tort law. The problem is that most employee benefit packages are written in much broader language, usually guaranteeing medically necessary inpatient care. This makes it difficult to describe in advance what treatments will be covered for individual circumstances. The rapid pace of change in medical technology means that what is expected when the contract is signed might be obsolete when the intervention is needed.[82]

Contracts are extraordinarily flexible agreements, but can be used by parties with superior bargaining power to impose terms that the tort system would find objectionable. Contracts can include waivers of rights that would otherwise be available through the tort system. For example, managed care enrollees can be required to submit disputes to arbitration, where damage awards are usually far lower than obtainable in court. But relying on contracts does not necessarily insulate MCOs from liability and may not remove the courts from becoming involved. Quite the contrary. Any contract is susceptible to a range of interpretations that courts must resolve. In an oft-cited case, *Fox v. Healthnet, Inc.*, a jury reached a verdict for $89 million ($77 million in punitive damages) for bad-faith breach of contract, not negligence, suggesting that a predominantly contract regime will not be a panacea for health insurers or providers.

Both tort and contract law doctrines will most likely be used to address relationships within the modern health care industry. One does not necessarily eclipse the other, and many complaints against MCOs raise both contractual and tort claims. A significant example is that of delayed and denied care. An MCO's processes for responding to patients' needs for care is at first glance an issue falling within the administration of the plan, and therefore governed by the contract between the patient and the MCO. If that process results in delayed or denied care, it begins to look more and more like a medical treatment decision that should be examined through the lens of tort law doctrine.[83] This is similar to what happened in *Payton v. Aetna/US Healthcare*,[84] where a dispute over health care coverage under the contract led to both breach of contract and tort damages claims. Following a drug overdose, Robert Payton repeatedly asked Aetna/US Healthcare (USHC) for inpatient clinical dependency treatment. Although Payton was covered for this care, USHC initially denied it because he had not purchased a necessary rider to the insurance contract. Payton filed a grievance with USHC, but subsequently died from a second drug overdose. Eight days later, the USHC grievance committee determined that the inpatient care should have been approved. Payton's estate then sued USHC for breach of contract and tort damages. USHC argued that the tort claim should be dismissed because the dispute was really about a breach of contract and whether the grievance process operated properly, rather than a dispute over appropriate medical treatment. In refusing to dismiss the tort claim, the court held that USHC had a duty to act expeditiously in meeting its contractual obligations. But the court determined that USHC had not made medical decisions in this case.

It is certainly possible that greater reliance on contract rules would generate the variety of health plan options contemplated by proponents, especially a health care market competing on different premium amounts for differing benefit packages. Contracts could also specify in advance a process for how disputes over individual clinical decisions should be resolved. For instance, health plan enrollees could agree that the MCO is permitted to deny care that is not cost-effective, so long as there is a process in place to monitor how such decisions are made. So far, the anticipated competition over plan options has not developed. The real utility of contracts is to induce a change in health care purchasing patterns, perhaps leading to low-price, low-benefit options in the marketplace. Having those options would be a substantial achievement, but it would not eliminate the need for tort law remedies.

Contract is valuable as a reminder that parties agree to certain benefit levels when they enroll in an MCO. It remains inadequate because it departs too much from reality to be sustainable. Tort remains viable for accountability and retains a fundamental role in monitoring health care delivery in the managed care era. It remains suspect because of its potential to undermine legitimate cost-containment programs. On balance, a contract regime will favor institutions (in part because of superior bargaining power and information resources), while tort, for all of its shortcomings, helps level the playing field by holding institutions accountable for their decisions.[85] Neither contract nor tort, nor even a needed bridging strategy, adequately addresses the conflict between the needs of the individual patient and those of the patient population. In Part III we will consider whether a new alternative to the continuing battle between tort and contract, rooted in the concept of fiduciary duty, might be more appropriate.

For the foreseeable future, tort and contract rules are likely to operate somewhat uneasily together in managed care litigation. Inevitably, one approach will come to dominate the development of legal doctrine in managed care litigation. On average, an MCO will be in a better position to defend its cost-containment and care delivery choices in a regime dominated by contract than in a regime dominated by tort. In tort, each cost-containment initiative is subject to subsequent challenge.

Having now described the conceptual interaction between tort and contract, let us consider how the courts have used tort and contract law in responding to managed care litigation. That brings us straight to the mystery known as ERISA and its powerful influence over the health-care system.

Notes

1. Today's smaller commercial health insurance market works the same way, with the exception that commercial insurers now pay greater attention to cost controls.

Employees who lack employer-sponsored health plans and self-employed individuals purchase health insurance from a commercial plan and arrange for their own physicians.

2. Havighurst (1995); Morreim (1987), p. 1725.

3. An important aspect of managed care litigation is that MCOs can invoke protection from liability under the Employee Retirement Income Security Act of 1974 (ERISA). ERISA's preemption provision blocks state courts from considering the case. See Chapter 6.

4. In fact, a state court tort suit raising issues relating to covered benefits would be preempted if the patient is insured by an ERISA benefit plan.

5. Litigation against an MCO involving an interpretation of the benefit contract (i.e., whether the patient was entitled to a particular medical service) may be preempted by ERISA. If preempted, the patient could only recover the amount of the denied benefit.

6. Havighurst (1997), p. 594.

7. *Black's Law Dictionary* (1991) defines tort as "A legal wrong committed upon the person or property independent of contract."

8. Rosenberg (1991); Jacobson and Warner (1999).

9. Lucian Leape notes that in the risk-management context, injured patients often want an assurance that the same thing will not happen to others. Patients want to find some meaning (such as quality improvements) in an otherwise meaningless tragedy. Personal communication, 1 December 1999.

10. Leape (1994).

11. As we saw in Chapter 4, modern products liability law introduced the concept of no-fault liability, where the manufacturer of a mass-produced good can be held liable for injuries even if the manufacturer was not at fault.

12. The *preponderance of the evidence* standard means that it is more likely than not (even if 50.1% to 49.9%) that the facts favor the plaintiff.

13. As Gostin (2000) notes, the law does not impose liability for all possible harm, since all human activity involves some risk. Instead, only unreasonable risks are considered negligent behavior.

14. Negligence law is not concerned with the individual actor's intent or motives. The standard is based on the mythical "reasonable person" as determined by the jury.

15. See, e.g., *The T.J. Hooper*, 60 F.2d 737 (2d Cir. 1932), *cert. denied*, 287 U.S. 662 (1933).

16. *Lauro v. The Travelers Insurance Co.*, 261 So.2d 261 (La. 1972); Prosser (1978).

17. Morreim (2001, p. 31, argues that "traditional malpractice law expects physicians to commandeer other people's money and property."

18. Prosser (1978). The rare exception is that courts will allow jurors to make a determination when the dispute is about issues that are within a juror's everyday common knowledge.

19. *Helling v. Carey*, 519 P.2d 981 (Wash. 1974).

20. Southwick (1998); see also Morreim (2001).

21. Jacobson and Rosenquist (1988); Jacobson (1989). During the past 20 years, numerous states have enacted tort reforms, such as limitations in damage awards, to address what some scholars believe is an out-of-control tort system. Most of the legislative reforms have been pro-defendant, partly in response to a loosening of procedural rules that were perceived to be pro-plaintiff.

22. The ERISA preemption doctrine will be considered in detail in Chapter 6.

23. *McClellan v. HMO of Pennsylvania*, 604 A.2d 1053 (Pa. Super. 1992). Other

courts agree. See, e.g., *Petrovich v. Share Health Plan of Illinois, Inc.* 719 N.E.2d 756 (Ill. 1999); *Jones v. Chicago HMO Ltd.* of Illinois, 730 N.E. 2d 1119 (Ill. 2000).

24. 547 A.2d 1229 (Pa. Super. 1988); see also, *Shannon v. McNatty,* 718 A. 2d 828 (Pa. Super. 1998).

25. Furrow (1997). Although the independent contractor doctrine (insulating institutions from liability for the acts of independent contractors) appears to be eroding, it retains some vitality. See, e.g., *Baptist Memorial Hospital System v. Sampson,* 969 S.W.2d 945 (Tex. 1998); Liang (1998).

26. This is particularly true for firms participating in business health-purchasing coalitions (Jacobson et al., 1996).

27. *Healthcare America Plans, Inc., v. Bossemeyer,* 1998 U.S. App. LEXIS 31323 (10th Cir. 1998).

28. Gilmore (1974).

29. Mooney (1995); Mariner, (1998).

30. Morreim, (1997); Abraham (1981).

31. These facts are derived from *McEvoy v. Group Health Cooperative of Eau Claire,* 570 N.W.2d 397 (Wis. 1997).

32. *McEvoy v. Group Health Cooperative of Eau Claire,* 570 N.W.2d 397 (Wis. 1997).

33. Clark Havighurst and others maintain that one barrier to a contract regime is that the courts are unwilling to uphold contracts. Along with Mark Hall, Havighurst claims that courts routinely require plans to provide any beneficial care regardless of the contractual language. This is because many such contracts are ambiguous and courts interpret ambiguity against the drafter (i.e., the doctrine of *contra proferentem*). What Hall and Havighurst want is for plans to negotiate tighter contractual limitations with managed care enrollees and for courts to defer to the contractual agreement. As discussed in Chapter 8, courts are in fact deferring more to contractual agreements.

34. These facts are taken from *Neade v. Portes,* 739 N.E.2d 496 (Ill. 2000).

35. Taken from *Corcoran v. United HealthCare, Inc,* 965 F.2d 1321 (5th Cir. 1992), *cert. denied,* 506 U.S. 1033 (1992).

36. As we will see in Chapter 6, the court ruled that this was a benefit determination, which meant that the lawsuit was preempted by ERISA.

37. Danzon (1997).

38. Epstein (1997).

39. Rubin (1999).

40. Havighurst (1986a, 1995). The empirical evidence for this proposition is slim. In the early 1990s, the Robert Wood Johnson Foundation funded a demonstration project to test the hypothesis that employees would purchase low-cost, low-benefit plans if they were available in the marketplace. The results did not support the hypothesis, and the demonstration was abandoned (Helms, Gauthier, and Campion, 1992; McLaughlin and Zellers, 1992). A variant of this strategy, medical savings accounts (MSAs), has been somewhat more successful, but has not galvanized public attention as much as its backers anticipated.

41. Morreim (1994a). Morreim (1994b) also advocates greater patient responsibility in health care decisions based on her theory of "contributive justice," whereby health plan enrollees are granted entitlements based on their status as contributors to a common pool of resources. Morreim argues that contributive justice recognizes that needs of vulnerable individuals, including the underinsured, must be balanced with the need to protect the legitimate expectations of others whose contributions create the common resource pool.

42. Morreim (1994b, 1989, 1987). Morreim does not necessarily advocate that patients should pay out-of-pocket.

43. This may be true, but it ignores the importance of repeat business in understanding what a consumer needs to know about the product. With most medical interventions, there is little opportunity or need for repeat business.

44. Hall (1997b). Hall articulates an extensive ethical justification in favor of physician rationing at the bedside based on the patient's initial contractual benefit selection.

45. Hall (1997a) calls this the theory of economic informed consent, meaning that patients give prior assent to cost-control mechanisms (such as limitations on marginally beneficial care) at the time they purchase insurance coverage.

46. For a recent analysis questioning the appropriateness of tort accountability in managed care, see Hyman (1999a).

47. Jacobson (1989); Weiler, et al. (1993).

48. Rubin (1999); Epstein (1997); Danzon (1997).

49. Havighurst (1986b); Morreim (2001).

50. Havighurst (1995). Unlimited reliance on contracting authority would presumably include the right to change other legal provisions, such as contracting out of liability or fiduciary duty standards.

51. Rubin (1999).

52. Epstein (1997); Hall (1989); Morreim (1997, 2000); Havighurst (1986b). *Dukes v. U.S. Healthcare*, 57 F.3d 350 (3rd Cir. 1995) specifically notes this possibility.

53. McLaughlin and Ginsburg (1998), p 739.

54. *Ibid.*

55. Korobkin (1999).

56. Of course, many health plan enrollees are not sick when they choose a health insurance plan, and those with chronic illnesses have an incentive to learn as much as possible about coverage and benefit limitations. Indeed, Hall's economic consent argument suggests an ability to make such choices at the time when the plan is purchased to avoid problems of making decisions under the stress of illness. Nevertheless, the choice of an insurance plan remains an enormously complicated decision.

57. Hall (1993).

58. Jacobson et al. (1996); Meyer et al. (1996); McLaughlin, Zellers, and Frick (1994).

59. Empirical evidence on the employee–employer agency relationship is mixed. Peele et al. (2000) reported survey and focus group results showing that employers may act as good agents for employees, in particular that employees would not be better served by purchasing their health insurance directly. But Legnini et al. (2000) found that this might not hold true for small employers. Moreover, Chernew and Scanlon (1998) report limited employer involvement in helping employees interpret quality of care report cards. Until further evidence supports the Peele et al. results, I remain skeptical that employers are adequate agents for employee health choices.

60. Rodwin (1993); Sage (1999a); Jacobson and Cahill (2000).

61. A legitimate critique of this presentation is that it overemphasizes the deficiencies of contract without an equivalent emphasis on tort's shortcomings. The primary reason for the disparity is that the case against contract has not seriously been examined, while the opponents of torts dominate the scholarly literature. Also, public policy in recent years has been decidedly antithetical to tort recoveries. This is not to suggest that tort is superior to contract, only that the virtual exclusion of tort in managed care would limit whether and how MCOs could be held accountable.

62. For an extensive discussion of this concern, see Jacobson and Kanna (2001).

63. Havighurst (2000b).

64. Sage (1997b); Abraham and Weiler (1994a and b); Havighurst (1997).

65. Havighurst (1997).

66. In no-fault systems, an injured patient would be able to recover damages from adverse medical outcomes regardless of the physician's culpability in causing the injury.

67. Morreim (2000) argues that under EML physicians will perversely be rewarded for not challenging clinical practice guidelines or for not raising potential quality-of-care problems.

68. Abraham and Weiler (1994b).

69. Morreim (1989, 1997). For an excellent summary of these arguments and of the general development of tort and contract law in managed care, see Morreim (2001).

70. Morreim (1997).

71. *Ibid.*

72. Morreim (1994a).

73. As we will see, this strategy has some resemblance to the quantity/quality distinction under ERISA that has troubled judges and commentators alike (see Chapters 6–8). This is not to equate the expertise/resource distinction with the reviled quantity/quality distinction—the former is conceptually superior to the latter. It is simply to note that the expertise/resource distinction still needs to be implemented, which will not always be easy to do.

74. Mariner (1998).

75. *Ibid.*

76. *Ibid.*, p. 43.

77. *Ibid.*, p. 47.

78. Brewbaker (1997).

79. *Ibid.* Applying the implied warranty of quality to MCOs is simply to use "conventional principles of commercial seller accountability for personal injury."

80. *Ibid.*

81. Mariner (1998), p. 27.

82. Korobkin (1999).

83. See, e.g., *In re: U.S. Healthcare, Inc.*, 193 F.3d 151 (3rd Cir. 1999), where the court rejected an ERISA preemption argument to litigation challenging the plan's refusal to provide visiting nurse service for a recently discharged neonate.

84. 2000 N.Y. Misc. LEXIS 91 (N.Y.S.Ct. 2000).

85. For somewhat different viewpoints, see Krause (1999); Rubin (1999).

6

Immunity

FOR the past several years, Congress has been debating proposed patients' rights legislation that would give disgruntled managed care patients an opportunity to sue for delayed or denied care. Both Republicans and Democrats have supported some form of legislation, but the two parties disagree profoundly on critical details, especially a patient's right to sue an MCO for damages. A reader not versed in this debate may wonder why it is happening at all. From what has been discussed so far, it would seem fairly obvious that dissatisfied patients can sue MCOs, either for breach of contract or for negligence. Thanks to a complex federal law—the Employee Retirement Income Security Act of 1974 (ERISA)—that is not the case for some patients.

ERISA is an extremely complicated statute that patients and physicians would no doubt prefer to ignore. Yet it plays such a central role in insulating MCOs from liability litigation and state regulatory oversight that it is important to understand what ERISA is, how it operates, and how it influences clinical decision making in the managed care era. At a minimum, the context of the ongoing policy debate about patients' rights legislation and state oversight of managed care requires at least some understanding of ERISA. Beyond that, any proposed policy solutions to managed care's shortcomings must take ERISA into account or risk exacerbating rather than alleviating the problem.

ERISA has clearly been the most dominant factor in the existing healthcare environment. The statute not only shapes the public debate over managed care regulation, it has probably been the most important influence in shaping the courts' development of legal doctrine in managed care. In essence, ERISA has created a regulatory vacuum by preempting (that is, preventing) state regulation of MCOs. It only provides minimal federal regulation in place of state oversight, and drastically limits state medical liability lawsuits against MCOs.[1] The most important problem for patients is that ERISA (and how courts have interpreted its preemption provision) insulates MCOs from lia-bility for delayed or denied care. While not the only source of immunity, it is far and away the most significant, and accounts for the managed care indus-try's intense opposition to patients' rights legislation.

The theme in this chapter and the next is that managed care litigation follows the same general pattern of developing legal rules described earlier for railroads and mass-produced goods. One significant difference from the general pattern is that legislation plays a much more dominant role in man-aged care litigation than in the previous examples. In the railroad and mass-production cases, the courts provided immunity on their own, and could therefore change legal doctrine in response to concerns about the lack of accountability. In managed care litigation, the industry has also obtained sub-stantial immunity from tort litigation. In this instance, immunity is a combi-nation of legislation—namely, ERISA's preemption provision—and how the courts have interpreted it. Several years of inconclusive congressional debate have kept ERISA's preemption mechanism in place, leaving the courts with less flexibility to overturn immunity on their own initiative.

Another important difference from the historical pattern is that we are still reasonably early in the managed care litigation cycle. Many of the more com-plex resource-use conflicts have yet to be litigated, and courts have not settled on clear lines of accountability (i.e., tort vs. contract). With the advantage of hindsight, the direction and pattern of legal doctrine in the railroad and mass-production examples is relatively easy to see. In the midst of the managed care story, the twists and turns are more evident than the evolving patterns. Looking at managed care at this point allows us to see that legal rules do not develop in a straight line.

Let us start with revisiting the managed care story and then backtrack some-what to examine ERISA's intricacies. After establishing the ERISA framework, we will look at how the courts have interpreted ERISA to the managed care industry's advantage.

The Managed Care Story

Like the previous emergence of railroads and mass-produced goods, managed care burst on the scene in ways that radically departed from how medical care had traditionally been provided. Much of this story was told earlier (see Chap-ter 1) and will not be repeated here, except to place the shift to managed care within a legal context.

Managed care represents both conceptual and practical changes that influ-ence the legal context of managed care litigation. Conceptually, the entire structure of the managed care enterprise departs strikingly from the prior fee-for-service model that dominated health care from after World War II until the mid- to late 1980s. The overt emphasis on having someone other than the physician monitor how health care is delivered separates managed care from the past. Equally important, managed care alters the focus from providing (unlimited) care to an individual to concerns about the costs of health care for the MCO's entire patient population. Practically, the way health care is now delivered to patients is dominated by large institutions, not by physicians, and is governed primarily by market-based arrangements. The changing nature of managed care organizational structures differentiates it from the stable hospital-based care in the fee-for-service era. Even if one were to argue that the changes are not altogether radical, the sheer complexity of the current system and its varied organizational forms and stakeholders separates it from the health care system of the past.

In concept, managed care is a needed corrective to the unsustainable cost increases of fee-for-service medicine. Although critical commentary is mixed and public antipathy to it has grown, managed care offers quality medicine at a generally affordable price. Its focus on preventive care is as important as its emphasis on containing costs. Arguably, managed care's shortcomings are more in how it has been implemented than in its overall design. If not fairly administered, its cost-containment programs can potentially harm patients by placing limits on access to hospital and specialty care, limiting the availability of pharmaceutical choices, delaying diagnosis, and denying care.

Managed care is not a static concept. Media reports indicate a constant stream of innovations that may well presage further structural changes in health-care delivery, perhaps even the decline of the managed care model.[2] It is changing in response to employer and employee preferences, in reaction to legislative and political factors, and to the changing economics of health care. Under pressure from physicians and patients, for example, the early emphasis on preauthorization before care could be provided has been relaxed (if not abandoned altogether). Direct referrals to specialists are much more frequent than many MCOs had originally permitted. Organizationally, the managed care environment is also changing, with more point-of-service plans (allowing greater patient freedom to seek care outside the MCO's network) and fewer traditional staff model HMOs.

Regardless of how the managed care model evolves (or even if it is superseded by another approach), the fundamental legal issues presented are likely to remain salient, at least in the near term. The clash between cost containment and access to health care remains the defining theme in contemporary health policy, inevitably raising conflicts between individual patient needs and preserving assets for the patient population. Patient demand for unlimited care persists despite the cost control imperative. For the foreseeable future, the legal system will be responding to that tension—unless Congress enacts a universal health insurance program (a highly unlikely scenario).

At the dawn of the modern managed care industry, many doubted that the courts would support its cost-containment programs. After all, neither the courts nor the legislative branch had welcomed previous attempts to impose institutional controls over physicians. The legal system relied on the "corporate practice of medicine" doctrine to block institutional controls. One study of previous efforts in the fee-for-service system to limit costs and physician autonomy led to the ominous prediction that the cost-containment innovations in managed care would not survive judicial scrutiny.[3] To many observers, the courts were poised to disrupt the core premises of the new managed care industry's financial incentives.[4] Without doubt, these predictions were based on sound interpretation of judicial attitudes at that time. What the scholars were unable to account for were changes in judicial attitudes, fundamental ways that managed care cases would depart from fee-for-service litigation, and how ERISA would undercut all previous expectations.

By the time the managed care industry overcame its roots as a limited, prepaid health-care system, negligence principles were fully applicable to hospitals and physicians. Since the 1960s, hospitals have been held legally responsible for the negligence of their employees and often of their independent contractors. When the contemporary managed care system arrived, the legal question was whether negligence principles would be applicable to MCOs or whether new liability rules would be needed. From the outset, the managed care environment exposed a new set of issues to be litigated. Judges were confronted with conflicting policy objectives, particularly the tradeoff between access to health care and cost containment, that were not present when the current medical liability rules were developed. Consistent with the situation when both the railroad and mass-produced goods industries arose, the courts in managed care litigation initially faced a radically reformed health-care industry where the old legal rules did not clearly apply.

At first, courts seemed uncomfortable with determining how to define managed care and how to apply existing liability principles. Judges were somewhat confused by the idea that MCOs are often more than insurers of health care (that is, they perform dual functions as insurer and provider). Some decisions held that MCOs perform two distinct functions, while more sophisticated opinions recognized that the administrative (financial) and care delivery functions are intertwined.[5] The symptoms of judicial discomfort and lack of familiarity with managed care concepts showed early on: courts routinely referred to MCOs and prepaid health plans as "insurance," and seemed unsure how to characterize utilization review for liability purposes.[6] As recently as

1991, courts felt it necessary to define in their opinions what exactly this strange beast known as a "health maintenance organization" was.[7] Indeed, courts routinely referred to all managed care organizational types as Health Maintenance Organizations (HMOs), regardless of their actual form.

McClellan v. HMO of Pennsylvania is a good example of this problem.[8] The issue in this case was whether an independent practice association (IPA)[9] should be included within the statutory definition of "health care provider" for purposes of a motion to compel the disclosure of certain documents to ascertain liability. On a three-to-three tie vote, the court upheld the lower court's decision that an IPA did not meet the statutory definition. The judges voting to affirm the decision viewed the IPA strictly in relation to the older forms of health-care delivery, stating that "an IPA cannot be regarded as a health care provider because it cannot oversee patient care within its walls." In contrast, the three dissenting judges noted that this conclusion "ignores the reality of health care today." A corporation operating a health-care facility may not necessarily be in a place where it can oversee patient care "within its walls."

Discomfort and confusion were further manifest when courts decided challenges to utilization review (UR) practices. Recall that UR covers a wide range of techniques designed to reduce health care costs and inappropriate care. Legal challenges to utilization review decisions require courts to determine which entity is responsible for any adverse consequences from a UR decision to delay or deny treatment: the UR firm, the MCO, the treating physician, or a combination of these participants? In the early utilization review cases, courts seemed unable to come to grips with the reality that utilization review entails clinical decision-making. For this reason, they either denied that UR decisions are medical,[10] or they recognized the hybrid nature of UR but held that the administrative aspect trumped the medical aspect.[11] Both confusions initially benefited MCOs.

Problems in characterizing and defining the managed care enterprise also affected early attempts to apply liability principles developed for fee-for-service medicine to managed care. Courts struggled with how to apply legal rules designed for the fee-for-service system (where the individual patient's interests were preeminent) to a system where the individual's needs must be balanced with the allocation of plan resources to the patient population. Both concerns led courts to move slowly before holding MCOs vicariously or directly liable.[12] As courts began to confront the new types of litigation disputes, the judicial tools to resolve the disputes appeared to be inappropriate for the task. There was, in short, a mismatch between the established legal rules and the nascent managed care industry. That mismatch led to a period of judicial confusion over the applicable legal rules in managed care litigation, eventually resulting in considerable immunity for the managed care industry.

Two particular problems magnified the mismatch. The first was that the conceptual approaches judges generally use to make decisions are problematic for resolving health-care resource allocation disputes. In the traditional case, an individual litigant brings suit against an individual defendant to protect a right or entitlement, or to recover damages. The current medical liability rules were formulated in an era where one patient sued one physician, and later, a hospital. A more recent litigation framework has been developed for mass personal injury litigation, including the mass toxic tort cases, where multiple parties and conflicting interests are the norm. Mass tort cases are usually litigated as class actions, frequently involving thousands of injured workers, to resolve common issues of law and fact. An example of this type of case is the litigation against asbestos manufacturers for exposing workers to fibers that cause asbestosis and mesothelioma. Often, mass tort litigation is oriented toward reaching global settlements that serve the collective interests of all claimants, rather than the specific interests of individual claimants. For many reasons, this approach has only been partially successful in the mass tort context and has generated considerable dissatisfaction among defendants and claimants alike.

With no easily adaptable mechanisms available, courts have struggled to develop suitable alternatives for resolving the resource allocation disputes that increasingly dominate managed care litigation. One drawback with relying on the traditional litigation framework is that resource allocation disputes are conceptually different from previous cases, falling in-between the one plaintiff–one defendant and the mass tort judicial decision-making models. Unfortunately, neither legal approach seems intuitively satisfactory for addressing the issues. Judges need to consider whether either framework can be suitably applied to health-care cases, or whether alternative approaches might be more appropriate.

The second problem, most observers have argued, is that law and medicine operate on sets of underlying values that are not necessarily congruent or adequately recognized by the courts. Judges and attorneys view the disputes very differently than physicians and health care administrators. Certainly, the two professions share many important social and professional values, including dedication to the patient's or client's well-being, the importance of maintaining practice autonomy, and responsibility for meeting ethical obligations to society.[13] But there is an important difference in medicine's concern for preserving health and the law's concern for individual liberty. This difference can generate deep misunderstanding in the adversarial context of litigation, as we will see in Chapter 9.[14]

As the managed care revolution took hold, the challenge for courts and health policy makers became clear: to develop an analytical framework that takes both the legal and the medical perspectives into account in understanding how judicial and medical values interact to shape health-care policy. Otherwise, there would be a real possibility that litigation would lead to inconsistent legal doctrine and subsequent distortions in how resources were allocated. Thanks to ERISA, distortion is exactly what has occurred (though the consequences were quite unintended). Once again, the difficulty of using the existing legal framework to resolve disputes arising from a new industry was immediately apparent. That challenge was only exacerbated by ERISA.

ERISA Dominates and Complicates

To this point in the book, we have been more concerned with examining the regulatory and judicial aspects of the relationship between law and medicine than with the legislative involvement. To have a better understanding of how courts have ruled in managed care litigation, we need to examine in some detail the interaction between the courts and the legislative branch at both the state and federal levels.

Earlier, we looked at the growing federal presence in health care after 1965. As far as the development of managed care and judicial responses to it are concerned, ERISA is the most important of the federal health care statutes, looming like a colossus over the managed care environment. Originally enacted to control employer-sponsored pension plans, the statute also covers employer-sponsored health-care benefits. One reason ERISA is so important is that most people in the United States receive their health insurance coverage through an employer-sponsored health plan.

According to Department of Labor estimates, ERISA covers approximately 125 million Americans, most of whom are employed by large businesses. Large employers usually pay for and arrange employee health insurance benefits under an ERISA-covered plan.[15] Health insurance benefits are an integral part of labor negotiations over wages and benefits and a great concern to both labor and management. In the automobile industry, for example, health benefits in 1998 constituted nearly $950 per General Motors vehicle, and GM spent $3.9 billion on health care in calendar year 2000.[16]

By contrast, most small employers do not offer or arrange ERISA-covered employee health benefits. Unlike large employers, they usually only provide limited financial support, with the cost falling largely on the employee. People lacking employer-sponsored insurance either purchase more expensive commercial insurance, buy from a state-sponsored plan, or go without. Commercial and state-sponsored plans are not covered by ERISA and remain subject to state law. State and federal government employees are also not covered by ERISA. This creates an anomaly where individuals with health insurance not provided through an ERISA-covered plan retain the right to sue in state court, while employees covered under ERISA do not. In a conceivable, if unlikely scenario, two patients can suffer the same care denial by the same MCO. One patient could seek damages in court, but the other could not.

ERISA's Provisions Explained[17]

To oversimplify for the moment, ERISA has three major components of interest to us. First, ERISA prevents states from regulating MCOs and patients from suing them for delayed or denied care. This is the key concept to keep in mind in reading this section. Second, ERISA imposes a fiduciary duty on the ERISA plan administrator to make decisions on behalf of the beneficiaries (i.e., the employees). Third, ERISA limits the amount of money a patient can win if ERISA preemption is invoked. Taken together, these components insulate MCOs from liability exposure.

Part of the problem with explaining ERISA is that applying these basic elements to real disputes between a patient and an MCO is very confusing. One reason is that ERISA's terms are vague and not well-defined. Another part of the problem with ERISA is that its framework does not easily apply to health care. Congress enacted ERISA primarily to regulate pension plans. Reflecting a period of time in which thousands of workers, after a lifetime of work, lost vested benefits due to plan insolvency or mismanagement,[18] ERISA shifted regulatory responsibility from the states to the federal government. Its goals were to redress pension plan abuses by establishing uniform national standards, safeguarding employee benefits from loss or abuse, and encouraging employers to offer those benefits. To achieve these objectives, ERISA imposes strict requirements on pension plan administrators for reporting and disclosure,[19] participation and vesting,[20] funding,[21] and performance of fiduciary obligations.[22] ERISA does not mandate that employers provide benefit plans, but it provides a structure for national uniformity of administration once such plans are offered.

The statute also applies to employer-sponsored employee benefit plans (EBPs),[23] which include health care and other non-pension benefits (e.g., medical, surgical, hospital, accident, and disability coverage). Somewhat surprisingly, the inclusion of health benefits appears to have been an afterthought. Congress never really pursued the consequences of regulating both health and pension plans under one statute, and the specific pension plan requirements are not generally applicable to health care. Members of Congress who recited the problems that motivated the bill never identified health benefit problems. Nor could Congress have predicted in 1973 the eventual importance and dominance of the managed care model. Health care industry officials did not even recognize immediately that ERISA could be used in their favor to defeat a patient's lawsuit. Accordingly, ERISA provides no substantive regulation of employer-sponsored health plans comparable to that of pension plans.

The lack of an adequate framework to govern health benefits has not prevented ERISA from dominating the managed care environment. Quite the contrary. Three interrelated provisions that were originally designed for pension plan oversight, but that apply to health plans, help explain ERISA's complexity and its influence on health care. These provisions are the preemption clause, its limited remedies, and a fiduciary duty obligation.

To encourage employers to offer health benefits, ERISA provides for a uniform national administrative scheme as opposed to meeting 50 separate state requirements. For a large employer with employees in a number of states, national uniformity allows the company to offer similar benefits to all employees without worrying about state-to-state variation or regulatory interference. The explicit preemption of state law was among the methods chosen to encourage employers to offer employee benefit plans.[24] ERISA's express preemption clause provides that ERISA "shall supersede any and all State laws insofar as they may now or hereafter relate to any employee benefit plan."[25] In this context, "preemption" means that state laws purporting to regulate health plans may not be enforced in any court. The preemption provision is central to achieving ERISA's statutory purposes by prohibiting state regulation of employee benefit plans. Courts have consistently ruled that MCOs are included under this protection as a part of health insurance coverage.[26]

State laws include not only regulations, such as those mandating particular benefit coverage, but also most state tort liability actions targeting MCOs and other related organizations that administer health plans.[27] Courts have interpreted the preemption clause broadly to prevent enforcement of state laws ranging from medical malpractice litigation to laws governing an MCO's ability to limit the number of physicians in its network (selective contracting). The courts have held that Congress intended such broad preemption of state law to allow a multistate employer to offer a single, nationally consistent plan to all its workers without the cost and inconvenience of complying with contradictory state regulations, legislation, or litigation. Most courts have interpreted congressional intent as keeping the costs of administering a health benefit plan low so that employers will continue offering health insurance benefits.[28]

In assessing whether a particular state law is prohibited, courts look sequentially to each of the three parts of the preemption provision. First, courts decide whether the state law "relates to" an employee benefit plan. If it does, the law is preempted. The Supreme Court has held that any state statutory reference to ERISA or any state law requiring a court to interpret the terms of a health plan meets the "relates to" test.[29] Any attack on an "ERISA plan's administrative structure, system, operation, and management" triggers preemption.[30] A critical question courts consider in determining the "relates to" language is whether the challenged law burdens the administration of plan benefits or has only a remote impact on them. Laws that bind employers or health plan administrators to particular benefit choices or preclude the uniform national administration of a health plan will probably be treated as a burden on the plan administrator.[31] If a law has only a remote or incidental effect on plan administration, such as a surcharge on hospital services, it may not "relate to" the benefit plan.

An example of preemption in action is a state lawsuit that challenges a benefit determination, perhaps an MCO's denial of coverage for additional hospital inpatient days beyond the terms of the benefit plan. The litigation relates to a health plan because that challenge would require the court to interpret the plan's benefits. A decision to require the additional coverage would be a burden on the plan administrator because it might require a change in the benefit package for all members. Therefore, the litigation would be preempted, barring the patient's state court challenge.

The focus on plan administration explains why ERISA, a statute designed to govern employee health benefit plans, also encompasses MCOs. Courts have universally reasoned that the various functions MCOs perform—utilization review, claims processing, and medical necessity determinations—constitute the administration of plan benefits and are consequently covered by ERISA. Judges have also noted that MCOs hit with damage awards would pass the costs on to the employers with whom they contract. On the other hand, physicians are not considered to be administering plan benefits and hence are not covered by ERISA. Including MCOs but excluding physicians occurs because Congress failed to define two important terms in ERISA— *plan* and *benefit*—allowing courts to interpret whether MCOs and physicians administer plan benefits. It also leaves the physician fully exposed to liability, while insulating the MCO from being held responsible.

In most instances, whether a law is preempted will depend on how courts interpret the "relates to" phrase. The vast majority of judicial challenges to MCO cost-containment practices will be resolved based on how broadly courts interpret the "relates to" language. Determining whether state laws designed to regulate managed care will be preempted involves interpreting two adjoining provisions in ERISA, the "savings" clause and the "deemer" clause.

Even if a state statute relates to a health plan, it is not necessarily preempted. Insurance regulation has always been a state-based function, and the federal McCarran-Ferguson Act limits federal involvement in this area. The savings clause allows states to continue enforcing state laws governing the business of insurance. It "saves" state regulation of health insurance, including financial solvency requirements, from preemption. For example, if a state law mandates solvency requirements for all health insurers—including MCOs—it would be saved.

In turn, the savings clause is qualified by what is known as the deemer clause. The deemer clause prevents states from deeming or characterizing an ERISA-covered plan as "insurance." States may not "deem" an employer-sponsored plan to be an insurer in order to circumvent the preemption clause and regulate the plan under the savings clause. Effectively, the deemer clause limits the savings clause to commercially insured (non-MCO) benefit plans.[32] In a sense, Congress "giveth" through the savings clause, and then "taketh" away through the deemer provision.

As an example of how these terms interact, consider a state law mandating certain health insurance benefits: e.g., coverage of yearly mammograms for women over age 40. The law "relates to" an ERISA plan since it would involve the structure of plan benefits. The legislation would be "saved" from preemption insofar as it regulates a state's insurance policies. It would still be preempted if a state attempted to apply the statute to an employer-sponsored health-benefit plan that contracts with an MCO. In that instance, the "deemer" clause means that the health plan cannot be characterized as an insurer. The patient would then be forced to sue in federal court under ERISA's more limited civil enforcement scheme. (No one ever said ERISA is easy!)

A key part of comprehending the ERISA preemption process is to understand who actually determines whether preemption should be invoked. Health care claims are usually filed and litigated in state courts. After a state court lawsuit against an MCO is filed, the MCO will argue that the case should be removed (transferred) to federal court to determine whether ERISA preempts the state court from deciding the litigation. A federal trial court judge then makes the initial preemption decision. If the federal court decides that ERISA does not preempt the case, it will be returned to the state court for trial. If the federal court decides that preemption applies, the case remains in federal court.

By itself, removing state courts from considering liability litigation against MCOs and transferring the case to federal court would not mean very much if patients could still seek the same range of damages as available under state law. The problem is that ERISA greatly restricts the patient's available remedies in federal court. Even if victorious in the federal court case, an ERISA-covered patient can usually recover only the amount of the benefit that should have been provided, as well as certain incidentals, including attorneys' fees—a drastically more limited remedy than is usually available under state law. In state courts, the patient might be able to recover damages for any economic losses, non-economic damages for pain and suffering, and possibly punitive damages (especially in cases alleging bad faith insurance denial—though punitive damage awards in health care litigation are unusual).[33] In effect, the MCO is insulated from exposure to monetary damages, except what it would have paid (the amount of the denied benefit) in the first place. That is a crucial reason why employers and the managed care industry are so opposed to amending ERISA to allow employees to sue in state courts.

An additional practical effect of ERISA preemption is that liability may be borne entirely by physicians. MCOs often control resource allocation, while physicians (and patients) bear the costs when decisions to deny or delay care produce adverse outcomes. In cases preempted by ERISA, the patient's only realistic remedy is to sue the physician, regardless of how much control over the clinical decision the physician actually exercised. For patients, there are thus very real and practical consequences if an MCO can successfully invoke ERISA preemption in a lawsuit challenging a benefit denial.

Many state law actions are preempted, though ERISA does provide some remedies to health plan participants through its civil enforcement scheme. A health plan enrollee may seek to enjoin practices that violate ERISA or the terms of the plan. Most often, this is likely to arise when a patient challenges an MCO's decision to deny care based on a breach of ERISA's fiduciary duty provision (see below). For instance, a patient may request a court to issue an injunction barring the plan from denying a bone marrow transplant recommended by the treating physician.[34] If issued, the injunction would force the MCO to provide the treatment—if it is not already too late for the benefit to make a difference. To date, a few courts have issued injunctions in cases requesting autologous bone marrow transplants.[35]

Another essential part of ERISA is how the benefit plan will be administered and what criteria the administrator must follow when making benefit coverage decisions. Because of an MCO's power to deny or delay recommended treatment, those who make discretionary decisions on behalf of the benefit plan are subject to a fiduciary duty under ERISA. Discretionary decisions include whether to approve a physician's treatment recommendation. In general, a fiduciary is someone entrusted with a duty of loyalty to act on behalf of another. ERISA fiduciaries must perform their discretionary functions "solely in the interest of the participants and beneficiaries" of the plan (i.e., the employees).[36] Regrettably, this ambiguous phrase has not been clarified by the courts. On its face, the language would seem to imply a balancing between individual patient treatment needs and preserving assets that will be available for all the other patients in the health plan. The statute does not clarify how to balance those obligations, especially with regard to the role of non-medical factors (i.e., cost concerns) in the decision. The plan administrator must not allow non-medical factors to interfere with the obligation to act on behalf of the plan beneficiaries. (For clarification, the ERISA fiduciary duty bears no relation to a physician's common law fiduciary duty to his or her patient. The two fiduciary duties represent separate professional obligations. See Chapter 10.)

Increasingly, disappointed health plan members have sued for breach of fiduciary duty, often in the context of challenging the denial of physician-prescribed benefits. In many, but not all, cases,[37] courts have held that MCOs are subject to ERISA's fiduciary duty requirement when reviewing treatment recommended by health plan physicians.[38] To determine whether an MCO breaches its fiduciary duty when denying plan benefits (i.e., that the denial is not "solely in the interest of the participant"), courts employ different levels of scrutiny based on the level of discretion implicitly or explicitly granted to the MCO. Generally, courts are very deferential, upholding most MCO decisions as long as they are not "arbitrary and capricious" (even where, in the court's view, the MCO has interpreted the plan's terms incorrectly). If the employee benefit plan expressly names the MCO as the plan administrator, the courts defer to the MCO's discretionary power to make these decisions. Where an MCO bears (or shares) the financial risk of providing health care services, and potentially benefits financially from withholding care, courts employ a more rigorous—but still deferential—level of scrutiny.

So far, courts have rejected most fiduciary duty challenges. In most cases, courts simply ensure that the MCO followed the terms of the benefit plan.[39] While MCOs have won most of the fiduciary duty cases, this is not to say that courts never rule against MCOs. In situations where MCOs profit from denying care, plaintiffs may win. For example, in *McGraw v. Prudential Insurance Co.,*[40] the MCO's medical director refused to pay for recommended care without ever reviewing McGraw's medical records. Without too much difficulty, the court held that the decision was arbitrary and not in accordance with the terms of the plan.

The effect of this very limited definition of fiduciary duty and deference to the plan administrator is that MCOs retain power *vis-à-vis* physicians by controlling how the plan's terms are interpreted. When clinical decisions are reviewed to determine their medical necessity, the plan administrator's interpretation will usually prevail over the treating physician's recommendation. Just as important, MCOs and employers are generally not subject to the fiduciary standard when creating or amending the terms of the benefit plan, or in setting compensation and incentive structures between the MCO and physicians.[41] How the plan is established and structured is a business decision that does not give rise to any fiduciary duties.

For physicians and patients, ERISA preemption has indirectly caused courts to favor MCOs' cost containment initiatives over established notions of physician autonomy.[42] The treatment a physician recommends is vulnerable to a managed care utilization review process largely unimpeded by fear of state law liability or accountability. One upshot is reduced physician autonomy; another is a patient's inability to sue the MCO for delayed or denied care.

Nevertheless, ERISA has undoubtedly achieved many of its original goals and has had some positive influences. For one thing, it has attained Congress's goal of encouraging employers to offer employee benefit plans. ERISA has allowed large employers to offer standard health-care benefits to employees across the country without worrying about state-by-state health benefit mandates. For another, ERISA has contributed substantially (and may have been the primary stimulus) to the rise of managed care as an alternative to the increasingly costly fee-for-service system. Absent ERISA, it would have been much harder for managed care to obtain and sustain its current preeminence in the health-care marketplace.

ERISA's complexities are evident, as are the politics surrounding it. The policy issue is how to retain its beneficial attributes while restoring a patient's right to seek damages for improperly denied or delayed health care. How courts interpret ERISA's preemption provision is of paramount importance in this complicated situation.

Judicial Immunity

As previously described, the early managed care litigation showed considerable judicial confusion about how to define managed care. The initial cases also provided MCOs with extensive immunity from liability, just as we have seen with litigation involving railroads and mass-produced goods. Immunity resulted largely because of ERISA preemption. The combination of judicial confusion and ERISA preemption gave managed care considerable space to operate, with minimal intrusion from the legal system. To demonstrate this, we can explore three specific case types where courts protected the managed care industry's cost containment innovations: challenges to specific compensation arrangements (that is, financial incentives to reduce health care use), liability challenges against MCOs, and antitrust cases.

Immunity (or at least near immunity) from specific legal challenges to cost containment programs is indispensable if managed care is to succeed. Using ERISA preemption as the lodestar, judicial decisions have explicitly favored MCOs' cost-containment initiatives, assuming that the MCOs are legal, desirable, and favored by public policy. Courts have also preempted litigation alleging that the structure of a health plan was responsible for poor medical outcomes.

For example, courts have consistently rejected the claim that an MCO's financial incentive arrangements with its physicians violate ERISA. A good example is *Weiss v. Cigna Healthcare, Inc.*, where a physician brought a breach of fiduciary duty challenge against an MCO's financial incentives because they were designed to reduce patient care.[43] The court ruled that ERISA preempted the claim, determining that the case "is tantamount to a claim that risk-sharing arrangements in managed care are inherently illegal, a position that is refuted by federal and New York law."[44] Upholding these claims would render managed care illegal—a result courts find absurd, given federal and state laws encouraging managed care. In another case, the court used a similar (if somewhat tautological) argument to defeat a claim: every plan does it this way, every plan cannot be illegal, therefore this plan is not illegal.[45,46] As we will see in the next chapter, the Supreme Court has emphatically confirmed the judiciary's view that public policy clearly supports managed care and its attendant cost containment initiatives.

For MCOs, the innovation of utilization review (UR) has been a crucial component of their cost containment strategy. But it can be a controversial approach. To the extent that UR decisions are economic in nature, the needs of the individual patient could be subordinated to cost-containment objectives. The more courts uphold UR decisions, the less control the treating physician has over the patient's medical treatment.

Courts have generally not impeded the use of UR for containing costs, especially under ERISA. No court has ruled that UR programs violate public policy, and several cases have explicitly upheld preauthorization arrangements, retrospective review, and coverage determinations. ERISA preemption clearly shields MCOs from liability in state courts for UR decisions, even when these are arguably medical and not merely administrative in nature. Federal courts have uniformly held that UR decisions relate to benefit plans and are preempted, regardless of whether medical care recommended by the treating physician is denied. For instance, in *Dukes v. U.S. Healthcare, Inc.*,[47] a case otherwise favorable to the plaintiff, the court supported the prevailing view that a utilization review dispute was preempted by ERISA because it was a dispute over medical benefits, not medical care.[48] The stated reasoning was that ". . . only in a utilization review role is an entity in a position to deny benefits due under an ERISA . . . plan."[49]

A case that exemplifies the difficulty of interpreting ERISA in the UR context is *Corcoran v. United Health Care, Inc.*[50] In this case, the court concluded that a challenge to United's UR program, in which a fetus died after hospital care had been denied, was preempted as a benefit determination. What might have been an unfortunate outcome of a reasonable benefit determination was complicated by the fact that it was made in the context of a medical decision. The court agreed with Corcoran that United's UR program involved clinical decisions, while also agreeing with United that part of its actions constituted a benefits determination. Since there was no way to split the difference, the court chose to characterize the UR process as a benefit determination rather than a clinical decision. Hence, the court provided wide latitude for health care plans to control costs at the possible expense of both individual access to health care services and the treating physician's clinical autonomy. The problem is that the court never explained what benefit was actually at issue, why United's action constituted a benefit determination, or why the aspect of the UR plan incident to a benefit decision should predominate over the clinical aspects.[51] The ERISA cases supporting this analysis fail to analyze the legal and practical significance of the hybrid form of combined clinical and cost-containment decisions made through the UR process.[52]

State litigation against UR firms (not covered by ERISA) has fared only slightly better, still usually shielding them from liability. An early California case, for example, placed the ultimate responsibility of UR decisions on the treating physician.[53] In a subsequent case, however, the California Supreme Court ruled that the UR firm should not be exempt from the consequences of its decisions, and could be held liable if its decision was a substantial factor in causing a patient's injury.[54] Later cases ruled that a jury should determine whether the UR decision was a substantial factor in causing the adverse outcome.[55] The Wyoming Supreme Court extended this reasoning in permitting litigation against the UR firm to proceed, holding that the UR process involves medical decisions.[56] Nevertheless, liability for UR decisions has been rare.

What makes this line of analysis significant is that most of the contentious litigation in the future will involve mixed clinical and financial decisions. The cases where the separation is clear probably will not be litigated. The hard cases, like *Corcoran,* where the separation is difficult to see, will require greater nuance in judicial scrutiny than was evident in the early cases. In the same way that it is largely impossible to separate an MCO's financing functions from its health-care delivery functions, the dual functions served by UR cannot easily be reduced to discrete decision processes.

Another important cost-containment mechanism used by MCOs is to provide financial incentives to plan physicians to restrain costs. "Salary withholds" and bonuses are used as compensation incentives for limiting referrals to specialists and other high cost procedures. Not surprisingly, attacks on the operation of financial incentives have been an important part of managed care litigation almost from the beginning. To date, no court has ruled that these financial incentives violate public policy, although some non-ERISA cases have permitted challenges to be tried before a jury. In one instance, a court ruled that the plaintiff could sue a physician for negligence on the theory that financial considerations motivated the physician to deny referral to a specialist and to discharge the plaintiff prematurely from the hospital.[57]

For many reasons, a similar result will not occur in an ERISA case. ERISA does not regulate how MCOs create incentive structures to motivate contracting physicians to comply with cost-containment measures. MCOs are under no fiduciary duty of loyalty to employees regarding the business decision of how to set compensation arrangements. These are treated strictly as arrangements between the MCO and the employer (who pays a dominant share of the cost), to be regulated by market competition. As a contractual arrangement between the employer and the MCO, it is almost impossible for a patient to challenge how the plan is structured. In any event, the U.S. Supreme Court has convincingly shut the door on similar ERISA challenges. (See Chapter 7.)

ERISA preemption also prevents states from trying to regulate the compensation and incentive arrangements through tort law or legislation. A typical case is *Lancaster v. Kaiser Foundation Health Plan of Mid-Atlantic States, Inc.*[58] In *Lancaster*, the court held that ERISA preempted the plaintiff's state law claim alleging negligence for the establishment and operation of an incentive program that encouraged physicians not to prescribe certain expensive tests and not to refer to specialists. The plaintiff alleged that this program was a substantial factor in her physicians' failure to diagnose her brain tumor for five and a half years until it had invaded 40 percent of her brain. The court characterized the establishment and operation of this incentive scheme as an administrative decision affecting the provision of benefits, and therefore the claim was preempted.

Not all courts have agreed.[59] In *Pappas v. Asbel,* the Pennsylvania Supreme Court ruled that an HMO could be sued for negligence based on treatment delays allegedly caused by the HMO's cost-containment program. In this case, the HMO denied the physician's request for a referral to a non-network hospital. The physician determined that the plaintiff's neurological condition could best be treated at a university hospital that was not part of the HMO's network. The court held that ERISA preemption did not apply and allowed the state law challenge to proceed to trial. Following an appeal, the U.S. Supreme Court remanded the case to the Pennsylvania court for reconsideration in light of the Supreme Court's definitive rejection of challenges to financial incentives based on a breach of ERISA fiduciary duties.[60] After reconsideration, the Pennsylvania Supreme Court upheld its prior decision.

A closely related cost-containment issue that has received extensive public attention is whether MCOs and physicians must disclose their financial incentives to patients. MCOs have argued vigorously that these economic incentives do not interfere with the exercise of their physicians' clinical judgment and should not be disclosed to patients. Courts are currently split on this issue. In one case, a court allowed health plan members to sue for nondisclosure of economic incentives as a violation of ERISA's fiduciary duties.[61] The court held that the HMO's financial incentives, including incentives discouraging treatment referrals, constituted material facts that must be disclosed as part of ERISA's fiduciary duties. Other courts have rejected this reasoning. Without taking a position on the effect of compensation arrangements on treatment, one court ruled that no disclosure was required. The court found that ERISA does not require such disclosure and the court would not find an implied duty to disclose; rather, the court encouraged plaintiffs to address their arguments to Congress by seeking an amendment to ERISA.[62] And in *Weiss v. Cigna Health Care, Inc.,*[63] the court explicitly declined to require disclosure.

The Supreme Court has not yet resolved the split between the Circuit Courts of Appeals, but added an intriguing footnote to its opinion in *Pegram v. Herdrich,* saying that

> Although we are not presented with the issue here, it could be argued that . . . [an ERISA] . . . fiduciary is obligated to disclose characteristics of the plan and of those who provide services to the plan, if that information affects beneficiaries' material interests.[64]

Several class actions have been filed to require disclosure, with no definitive rulings so far.

Class actions contesting financial incentives and the failure to disclose them to patients are increasingly part of the judicial landscape. In an attempt to circumvent ERISA preemption, the class action lawsuits challenge managed care's financial incentives as fraudulent, as a violation of racketeering laws, or as implemented in ways designed to deny legitimate benefits. Physicians have also filed class actions alleging that MCOs continually deny medically needed care, arbitrarily reduce reimbursement claims, and interfere with physician autonomy. Courts have been conspicuously resistant to these cases, almost uniformly rejecting them, and providing an important source of immunity for MCOs.[65]

An analogous problem to financial incentives in managed care relates to potential conflicts of interest physicians face. The ethics of medical practice, which require a physician to act in the best interests of each individual patient, conflict with managed care's expectations that physicians have responsibilities to the broader patient population as well. Judges have not interpreted ERISA's ambiguous language to require some deference to this medical professional ideal (perhaps by limiting rewards for withholding care). Instead, courts have given plan administrators wide leeway to serve the interests of plan beneficiaries as a whole. What this means is that the conflict between the individual and the patient population shifts in favor of cost control, regardless of the plan's justification for denying care. More important, the failure to consider the physicians' ethical dilemma is another source of judicial immunity for MCOs.

In reviewing plan decisions to deny treatment under ERISA, courts have used flawed reasoning in their conflict-of-interest analyses.[66] Judges have failed to factor in the reality that health plans have financial interests and incentives of their own that might bias their decisions against the individual patient. The judicial rulings are also problematic because they fail to recognize that ERISA's fiduciary duty provisions do not readily accommodate the professional norm of loyalty to individual patients. Fiduciary duties are owed to employees as a group, requiring health plan managers somehow to mediate among beneficiaries' competing resource needs. Absent closer judicial oversight of an MCO's fiduciary duty decisions, the health plan has no incentive to develop criteria so that the individual patient is not disadvantaged during the process. (See Chapter 10.)

Liability challenges to managed care's involvement in clinical decisions is the second type of case where courts have provided MCOs with at least partial immunity. Just as the courts had to adapt medical liability principles to hospitals, the same process is now underway with regard to the organizational forms comprising managed care. Sorting out which party is legally responsible for delayed or denied care and the acceptable level of care resulting from cost containment strategies remains a work in progress. Resolving these issues is complicated by a multiplicity of actors in any given case, and by the evolving nature of managed care's organizational structures.

From a liability perspective, MCOs face the same risks as insurance companies, i.e., patients' litigation over what is covered or excluded. MCOs face additional potential liability for the conduct of their employees or affiliated physicians, as well as potential direct liability exposure for the operation of cost-containment programs and utilization review decisions.

Most of the initial liability claims against MCOs were either preempted or rejected. Led by early Supreme Court cases holding that ERISA intended broad preemption, lower federal courts interpreted the phrase "relates to" very broadly by preempting most state law tort suits challenging health plan innovations and medical decisions. Before 1996, courts repeatedly held that challenges to delayed or denied care were preempted as relating to an ERISA plan.[67] Since 1996, however, as we will see in Chapter 7, many courts have departed from a strict application of ERISA preemption to benefit denial challenges.

Tolton v. American Biodyne[68] is illustrative of the many pre-1996 cases preempting similar challenges. In this case, Tolton was a drug addict who requested inpatient psychiatric care. Tolton's plan rejected inpatient care, but offered outpatient treatment instead. After several failed outpatient episodes, Tolton committed suicide. His heirs sued the plan for damages. Without much ado, the court characterized the tort and breach of contract claims as clearly relating to the administration of the benefit plan. Relying on what was then the predominant legal analysis, the court did not consider the clinical consequences and ruled that ERISA preempted the lawsuit.

A different and more nuanced pattern emerges in cases where ERISA was not applicable. Initially, courts rejected liability lawsuits against MCOs, but that immunity is slowly eroding. MCOs were able to raise several defenses against liability. In many states, they could point to statutes prohibiting corporations from practicing medicine. In others, they could show that the physicians were independent contractors not under their control. Perhaps the strongest early barrier to MCO liability was that many courts refused to hold that MCOs influenced or made clinical decisions.[69]

The evolution of liability in Illinois and Pennsylvania provides a nice illustration. In the 1992 case of *Raglin v. HMO of Illinois, Inc.*,[70] an Illinois appellate court held that the HMO could not be held vicariously liable for its physician's negligence because the physician was an independent contractor. Then, in 1999, the Illinois Supreme Court ruled in *Petrovich v. Share Health Plan of Illinois, Inc.*,[71] that an HMO could indeed be sued for vicarious liability (if the plaintiff can demonstrate requisite control over the clinical decision) even where the physician was an independent contractor. The Illinois Supreme Court then expanded MCO liability in *Jones v. Chicago HMO*,[72] ruling that the MCO could be sued directly for its own negligence. In this case, the plaintiff was allowed to proceed to trial to prove her allegation that the HMO assigned too many patients to its physician. The physician was too busy to see the plaintiff's daughter, misdiagnosing over the phone what was actually bacterial meningitis that resulted in permanent disability.[73]

A similar evolution is apparent in Pennsylvania. The first case, decided in 1992—*McClellan v. HMO of Pennsylvania*[74] (discussed earlier in this Chapter)—ruled that an IPA did not meet the statutory definition of a health care provider because it did not oversee patient care within its walls. The plaintiff's liability claim was therefore dismissed. Six years later, the same court ruled in *Shannon v. McNulty* that "We see no reason why the duties applicable to hospitals should not be equally applied to an HMO when that HMO is performing the same or similar functions as a hospital."[75] In this case, the liability claim was allowed to proceed to trial.

Not all states have followed or will adopt a similar pattern. Prior to the mid-1990s, the picture was mixed, with some states imposing liability and others rejecting liability claims.[76] Even in Pennsylvania, a 1988 case allowed a liability claim against an IPA to proceed to trial.[77] But these illustrations indicate that where ERISA preemption is not available to a defendant, courts are willing to apply traditional liability doctrine to MCOs where they exert control over physicians' clinical decisions.[78] In contractual disputes outside of ERISA protection, courts have been more lenient in ordering treatment coverage for unproven therapies. Some juries have also awarded punitive damages for what might be considered routine decisions or ordinary mistakes (though punitive damage awards remain an exception in health-care cases). For example, in one non-ERISA case, a jury awarded damages to a physician who was fired in violation of a California statute for providing too many tests and spending too much time with patients.[79]

As with most areas of the law, there is considerable variation in the state liability cases. In part, this variation explains why one might argue that the courts were initially hostile to managed care and that applying liability principles to MCOs represents judicial hostility to managed care rather than immunity. Up to a point, that is an accurate assessment. In the 1970s and early 1980s, the law was at least partially unreceptive to managed care's forerunners (i.e., prepaid care in HMOs). After that time, antagonism quickly gave way to substantial immunity from liability. A separate analysis of non-ERISA cases in state courts shows that MCOs still win about as much as they lose, indicating that managed care enjoys at least partial immunity even without the benefit of ERISA preemption.[80]

The key to expanded liability will be the extent to which courts consider MCOs to be involved in making medical decisions and the ability of injured patients to prove that MCOs controlled or influenced clinical decisions. At this point, MCOs have not been held liable in many cases. What the courts in Pennsylvania and Illinois have done is merely to permit cases to be scheduled for trial. Where there is strong evidence of MCO control over the clinical decisions, MCOs may settle the case or juries may impose damages.

Managed care's early favorable judicial treatment was not limited to liability claims. It extended to antitrust decisions as well. Antitrust litigation in health care did not become a major force until the 1980s. Since then, courts have applied traditional antitrust principles to health care markets, helping stimulate the movement toward more efficient organizational forms.[81]

Physicians have attempted to use antitrust principles to block cost-containment initiatives. Physician groups have also filed antitrust challenges to force health plans to open their physician panels to competition. Neither effort has generated or found much support in the courts. Courts have dismissed antitrust actions attacking selective contracting (i.e., an exclusive arrangement with one group to provide specialty care), with explicit deference to the managed care form. In *Ambroze v. Aetna Health Plans of New York, Inc.*,[82] anesthesiologists brought a restraint of trade action under Section 1 of the Sherman Act challenging the defendant's exclusive contracting arrangement with another physicians' group. After determining that a valid antitrust violation had not been alleged, the court attacked the heart of the plaintiff's case:

> It is worth repeating the fact that the plaintiffs' principal target here is the very concept of managed care. The fact that HMOs have their critics does not obligate

the courts to create a novel application of the antitrust laws. Judicial restraint in this highly charged area of law and policy is the best recourse.

In addition, courts have given MCOs wide authority to control staff-privilege determinations, an area now dominated by contractual interpretations. MCOs have argued that an important aspect of controlling health-care costs is limiting the number of physicians who are eligible to participate in the plan and applying economic criteria to staff selection and retention decisions. For the most part, courts have upheld the use of economic credentialing and the use of selective contracting. In *Maltz v. Aetna Health Plans of New York*,[83] the court upheld the MCO's change in network physicians based solely on cost containment reasons, despite the disruption to long-term physician–patient relationships. In this instance, physician–patient autonomy yielded to cost containment dictates.

As we have seen with the railroad and mass-production industries and with liability trends, immunity is not absolute. An important issue in antitrust cases is how to characterize MCOs for purposes of determining whether planned mergers between hospitals should be permitted. Mergers that lack market power are usually upheld. In antitrust analysis, courts determine whether a firm can use market power to increase prices or otherwise stifle competition. To define "market power," courts look at the particular product or service involved (e.g., inpatient services) and the geographic area that would be affected. Judicial decisions regarding mergers have focused on systems integration and economic efficiencies to determine whether an activity violates the antitrust laws.[84] If consumers can find adequate substitutes within a reasonable geographic distance, there is usually no antitrust violation because the price increase will not prevent patients from seeking care elsewhere.

The antitrust question for managed care cases is how to define the relevant market; that is, how to characterize MCOs for purposes of analyzing competition. One of the issues for courts to decide is whether managed care constitutes a separate market for health services distinct from other providers. If so, this would insulate MCOs from competition. Two important cases have ruled that MCOs do not constitute a separate health care market for antitrust analysis, in part because physicians have other market alternatives for selling their services.[85] In the leading case of *Blue Cross & Blue Shield United of Wisconsin v. Marshfield Clinic*,[86] the court held that managed care is simply one form of organizing health care services that competes against all other organizational arrangements, and hence should be open to market-based competition.

In Chapter 8, we will explore the reasons for the slow development of managed care liability. For now, it is sufficient to note that the key consequence of ERISA preemption is that people with similar claims against an MCO may leave the courthouse with dramatically different results. To bring us back to where the book started, many patients have been caught in ERISA's complex web. One particular family covered by an ERISA health plan was the Andrews-Clarke family. As the reader may have surmised, ERISA provides the key to understanding why Andrews-Clarke lost and Goodrich won, and is the source of Judge Young's lament about whether anyone cares. The short answer to why Ms. Andrews-Clarke failed in her litigation while Ms. Goodrich succeeded is that Andrews-Clarke was covered by ERISA and Goodrich was not. Regardless of the merits of the two lawsuits, Andrews-Clarke never got the opportunity to present evidence because ERISA preempted her case, preventing the state court from even holding a trial. Since Goodrich was not covered by ERISA, her case could be tried in state court. Who knows whether Andrews-Clarke would have won had she been able to present her case to a jury? In some ways it does not matter. What matters is the palpable unfairness of treating similar claims very differently. The differential treatment raises fundamental questions about a patient's right to seek judicial redress to resolve disputes, the legal system's ability to monitor managed care, and a doctor's autonomy in treating patients.

Judges interpreting ERISA have felt obligated to provide almost absolute immunity, though many judges have publicly chafed under the perceived injustice of denying injured patients at least the opportunity to prove their claims. Many judges, including Judge Young in the Andrews-Clarke case, have expressed bitterness and frustration at these results, and literally have pleaded with Congress to amend ERISA. Believing themselves to be bound by the statute, however, judges usually preempt the litigation.

As with the railroad and mass-produced-goods litigation, courts have provided MCOs with substantial immunity from judicial challenges. In early cases involving managed care, courts were particularly reluctant to subject MCOs to liability for implementing cost-control innovations. Although courts have backed away from conferring almost absolute immunity, MCOs still retain considerable immunity from tort litigation. Courts have strongly protected managed care's financial incentives, suggesting that it is up to Congress to change the law.

Even though it is relatively early in the litigation cycle, MCOs have retained much of their initial advantage. But the inevitable backlash, fueled in part by judicial hostility to the harsh results of ERISA preemption, has begun.

Notes

1. Gostin (1993).
2. See, e.g., Robinson (2001).

3. Hall and Anderson (1992).

4. Hall and Anderson (1992); Hall (1988); Ferguson, Dubinsky, and Kirsch (1993).

5. Compare *Lancaster v. Kaiser Foundation Health Plan,* 958 F. Supp. 1137 (E.D.Va. 1997) (claiming that HMOs perform two "independent" functions) and *Corcoran v. United Healthcare, Inc.,* 965 F.2d (1321 5th Cir. 1992) (noting the functions are inextricably intertwined) with *Crocco v. Xerox Corp.,* 956 F. Supp. 129 (D.Conn. 1997), 137 F.3d 125 (2d Cir. 1998) and *Murphy v. Board of Medical Examiners of the State of Arizona,* 949 P.2d 530 (Ariz. App. 1997) (both holding that MCO decisions are medical, not financial).

6. See, e.g., *Wota v. Blue Cross and Blue Shield of Colorado,* 820 P.2d 1137 (Colo. App. 1991), where the court referred to a prepaid health plan as "insurance" throughout.

7. *Chase v. Independent Practice Association,* 583 N.E.2d 251, 252 n.3 (Mass. App. 1991).

8. 604 A.2d 1053 (Pa. 1992). Six years later, as discussed further on in this chapter, the court abandoned this reasoning in *Shannon v. McNulty,* 718 A.2d 828 (Pa. Super. 1998).

9. An IPA is a group of physicians (such as a multi-specialty group) that contracts with managed care firms and commercial insurers to provide medical services.

10. *Jass v. Prudential Healthcare Plan,* 88 F.3d 1482 (7th Cir. 1996).

11. *Corcoran v. United Healthcare, Inc.,* 965 F.2d 1321 (5th Cir. 1992).

12. *Raglin v. HMO Illinois, Inc.,* 595 N.E.2d 153 (Ill. App. 1992).

13. Hadorn (1992).

14. Annas (1989a). This issue will be discussed in greater detail in Chapter 9.

15. In limited circumstances, employers who purchase health care coverage from a third-party insurer may also be covered by ERISA.

16. Personal communication with Tom Weatherup, Director, General Motors Health Care Initiative, January 2002. See also Millenson (1997), pp. 168–170; Califano (1986).

17. Even implying that I can explain ERISA is nothing short of hubris. To the best of my knowledge, nobody really understands this beast!

18. Legislative history of the *Employee Retirement Income Security Act* of 1974, Vol. 2, p. 3456 (1976).

19. 29 U.S.C. Art. 1021–1031.

20. 29 U.S.C. Art. 1051–1061.

21. 29 U.S.C. Art. 1081–1086.

22. 29 U.S.C. Art. 1101–1114.

23. Langbein and Wolk (1995), pp. 418, 508.

24. *Aetna Life Insurance Co. v. Borges,* 869 F.2d 142, 144 (2d Cir. 1989).

25. 29 U.S.C. Art. 1144(a).

26. *Nealy v. U.S. Healthcare HMO,* 711 N.E.2d 621 (N.Y. 1999).

27. Large employers often contract with firms called third-party administrators (TPAs) to handle employees' health insurance benefit claims.

28. Jordan (1996).

29. Jacobson and Pomfret (1998).

30. *Carpenter v. Harris Community Health,* 154 F. Supp. 2d 928, 931 (N.D.Tex. 2001). See also *District of Columbia v. Greater Washington Board of Trade,* 506 U.S. 125, 129–130 (1992), holding that ERISA preempts state laws with any reference of connection to benefit plans.

31. *Moreno v. Health Partners Health Plan*, 4 F. Supp.2d 888 (D.Ariz. 1998).

32. Chirba-Martin and Brennan (1994).

33. *McEvoy v. Group Health Cooperative of Eau Claire*, 570 N.W.2d 397 (Wis. 1997).

34. 29 U.S.C. Art. 1132.

35. See, e.g., *Marro v. K-III Communications Corp.*, 943 F. Supp. 247; *Mattive v. Healthsource of Savannah, Inc.*, 893 F. Supp. 1559 (S.D.Ga. 1995); and *Dosza v. Crum & Forster Insurance Company*, 716 F. Supp. 131 (D.N.J. 1989). See also an interesting discussion in *Pryzbowski v. U.S. Healthcare, Inc*, 245 F.3d 266, 273–274 (3rd Cir. 2000), where the court strongly implied that the plaintiff should have sought an injunction to accelerate the defendant's approval of out-of-network surgery.

36. 29 U.S.C. §1104 (a)(1).

37. *Kyle Railways, Inc. v. Pacific Administration Services*, 990 F.2d 513 (9th Cir. 1993); *Klosterman v. Western Gen. Mgmt.*, 32 F.3d 1119 (7th Cir. 1994).

38. *Reilly v. Blue Cross and Blue Shield United of Wisconsin*, 846 F.2d 416 (7th Cir. 1988). A health plan participant (or beneficiary) may also bring a civil action against an administrator who fails to comply with a request for information about the plan, to recover benefits due, to enforce rights under the terms of the plan, or to clarify rights to future benefits. See also *Maltz v. Aetna Health Plans of New York*, 114 F.3d 9, 12 (2d Cir. 1997) and *Weiss v. Cigna Healthcare, Inc.*, 972 F. Supp. 748 (S.D.N.Y. 1997).

39. *England v. John Alden Life Ins. Co.*, 846 F.Supp. 798, 801 (W.D. Missouri 1994). In most cases, courts have equated compliance with the terms of the benefit plan as acting by definition "in the interests" of the plan.

40. 137 F.3d 1253 (10th Cir. 1998).

41. *Curtiss-Wright Corp. v. Schoonejongen*, 115 S.Ct. 1223, 1228 (1995); *Maltz v. Aetna Health Plans of New York*, 114 F.3d 9, 12 (2d Cir. 1997).

42. Jacobson (1999).

43. *Weiss v. Cigna Healthcare, Inc.*, 972 F. Supp. 748 (S.D.N.Y. 1997).

44. *Ibid.*, p. 753. The court noted that the compensation arrangements require physicians to balance their economic interests and ethical obligations to patients, presenting a danger of abuse. But the court added, (p. 752) that: "to the extent that a doctor takes advantage of financial incentives and withholds necessary care from his or her patients, that doctor's ethical breach is not attributable to CIGNA. The profit motive created by the HMO does not make such violations 'inevitable.' " See also Morreim (2001). Perhaps, though, this underestimates the influence of these financial incentives on physicians' clinical decisions.

45. *Hartman v. Northers Services, Inc.*, No. C1-96-135, 1996 WL 438810 (Minn. Ct. App. Aug. 6, 1996).

46. In concept, this is similar to Bovbjerg's argument that the standard of care for an MCO should be the care provided by a similar MCO (Bovbjerg, 1975).

47. 57 F.3d 350 (3rd. Cir. 1995).

48. *Tolton v. American Biodyne, Inc.*, 48 F.3d 937 (6th. Cir. 1995).

49. *Dukes v. U.S. Healthcare, Inc.*, 57 F.3d 350, 360–361 (3rd. Cir. 1995).

50. 965 F.2d 1321 (5th. Cir. 1992).

51. For a similar analysis, see Rosenblatt, Law, and Rosenbaum (1997).

52. *Ibid*.

53. *Wickline v. State of California*, 192 Cal.App.3d 1630 (Cal.Ct.App. 1986).

54. *Wilson v. State of California*, 271 Cal.Rptr. 876 (Cal. 1990).

55. *Berel v. HCA Health Services of Texas, Inc.*, 881 S.W.2d 21 (Tex.App. 1994).

56. *Long v. Great West Life & Annuity Insurance Co.*, 1998 Wyo.LEXIS 62 (Wyo. 1998).

57. *Paul v. Humana Medical Plan*, 695 So. 2d 700 (Fla. 1997).

58. 958 F. Supp. 1137 (E.D.Va. 1997).

59. *Oulette v. The Christ Hospital*, 942 F.Supp. 1160 (S.D. Ohio 1996).

60. *Pegram v. Herdrich*, 530 U.S. 211 (2000).

61. *Shea v. Esensten*, 107 F.3d 625 (8th Cir. 1997).

62. *Ehlmann v. Kaiser Foundation Health Plan*, 198 F.3d 552 (5th Cir. 2000), *cert. denied*, 530 U.S. 1291 (2000).

63. No. 96 Civ. 1107 (SHS), (S.D.N.Y. 1997).

64. 530 U.S. 211 (2000).

65. Several class actions have been brought against MCOs under the Racketeer Influence and Corrupt Organizations Act (RICO) alleging that MCOs fraudulently induce employees to subscribe when the MCO has no intention of providing the promised benefits. So far, these claims have been rejected. See, e.g., *Maio v. Aetna, Inc.*, 221 F.3d 472 (3rd Cir. 2000). Many commentators oppose the concept of class action litigation in health care, in part because the statutory basis for many of these cases, RICO, does not apply to managed care practices. See Havighurst (2001). As we will see in Chapter 11, I agree with the criticism about using RICO but disagree that class actions are an inappropriate response to a range of managed care practices.

66. Morreim (1998a).

67. See, e.g., *Pilot Life v. Dedeaux*, 481 U.S. 41 (1987); *Metropolitan Life Insurance Company v. Massachusetts*, 471 U.S. 724 (1985); *Kuhl v. Lincoln Health Plan*, 999 F.2d 298 (8th Cir. 1993), *cert. denied*, 510 U.S. 1045 (1994); Jacobson and Pomfret 1998); Jordan (1996). To be sure, some cases, including *Pacificare of Oklahoma v. Burrage*, 59 F.3d 151 (10th Cir. 1995), rejected ERISA preemption. But the vast majority of pre-1996 challenges to delayed or denied care were preempted. As one commentator noted, "Early cases focused on a literal interpretation of the 'relates to' language . . . and suggests a broad and almost limitless preemptive reach." Hammer (2001), p. 779.

68. 48 F.3d 97 (6th Cir. 1995). Technically, the case arose under the plan's utilization review process. But the court specifically stated that it was analyzing the issues as a benefit denial case.

69. Noble and Brennan (2001).

70. 595 N.E.2d 153 (Ill. App. 1992).

71. 719 N.E.2d 756 (Ill. 1999).

72. 730 N.E.2d 1119 (Ill. 2000).

73. For an interesting examination of the Illinois cases and their implications, see Noble and Brennan (2001), p. 300.

74. 604 A.2d 1053 (Pa. 1992). See also *Chase v. Independent Practice Association*, 583 N.E.2d 251 (Mass. App. Ct. 1991), and *Harrell v. Total Health Care*, 781 S.W.2d 58 (Mo. 1989).

75. 718 A.2d 828 (Pa. Super. 1998).

76. See the cases noted in Noble and Brennan (2001), endnotes 75, 89, 106.

77. *Boyd v. Albert Einstein Medical Center*, 547 A.2d 1229 (Pa. Super. 1988).

78. Furrow (1997); Noble and Brennan (2001); *Boyd v. Albert Einstein Medical Center*, 547 A.2d 1229 (Pa. Super. 1988); *Petrovich v. Share Health Plan of Illinois, Inc.*, 719 N.E.2d 756 (Ill. 1999).

79. *Self v. Children's Associated Medical Group*, Cal.Super.Ct., No. 695870 (1998).

80. Jacobson, Selvin, and Pomfret (2001).

81. Greaney (1997).

82. 1996 WL 282069 (S.D.N.Y.), rev'd on other grounds, 107 F.3d 2 (2d Cir. 1997).

83. 114 F.3d 9 (2nd Cir. 1997).

84. Greaney (1997).

85. *Blue Cross & Blue Shield of Wisconsin v. Marshfield*, 65 F.3d 1406 (7th Cir. 1994); *U.S. Healthcare, Inc. v. Healthsource, Inc.*, 986 F.2d 589 (1st Cir. 1993).

86. 65 F.3d 1406 (7th Cir. 1994).

7

The Backlash

THE perceived injustices of ERISA preemption have prompted numerous judges to complain bitterly and to look for ways to correct or overcome ERISA's constraints. It is not just the case outcomes that are troublesome. Legal opinions interpreting ERISA are bewildering in their complexity, often the product of tortured reasoning, and impenetrable even to many who study the area closely. It is all but impossible for the average citizen to comprehend individual case opinions, let alone the convoluted legal doctrine that has emerged.

Not only are patients covered by ERISA treated differently from non-ERISA patients, there are now two categories of ERISA patients. Some patients who raise allegations about quality of care may be able to proceed to trial in state courts. But those who challenge benefit determinations (*quantity* of care) still find their claims preempted. The result is a set of absurd distinctions and case outcomes that are not sustainable or explainable to anyone but a few experts. (Frankly, even the experts cannot adequately explain these decisions and what they mean!) Along with visible public antipathy toward managed care and the predictable political response, these judicial opinions have helped initiate the same type of public backlash seen earlier with railroads and mass-produced products.

Public Misgivings

At the beginning of the twenty-first century, managed care has become the dominant approach to providing health care.[1] Yet the concept of managed care is constantly changing as a result of market forces and regulatory demands, and hardly resembles the early models of prepaid health care. Many of the

152

evident changes in managed care result from a natural evolution of the concept. What was fashionable five years ago now no longer exists or is deemphasized (such as extensive pre-certification review requiring the MCO to certify a medical treatment before it can be provided). New approaches and organizational arrangements have replaced the original prepaid concept, making the system even more confusing to patients.

Other changes were essentially imposed on the industry, at least partially resulting from the inevitable negative reaction to managed care's domination and to its operations. Under steady physician and public attack, MCOs have been forced to adapt. Physicians, who have long chafed under managed care's treatment controls and bureaucratic delay, are now rejecting capitation payment arrangements (a fixed sum of money per member/per month for medical care) and have gained some bargaining power back from MCOs. In response to patients' demands for a greater choice of providers, more MCOs are using point-of-service plans that allow patients to see out-of-network physicians. However, point-of-service plans are not as effective in reducing the use of health care resources as more stringent cost-control techniques. Many plans have also relaxed their previous opposition to direct patient access to specialty care.

One scholar has already announced the death of managed care.[2] Perhaps this will happen. At a minimum, there is a serious debate going on about the future of managed care and what might replace it. Many observers have expressed increasing concern that managed care is not working as its proponents expected. During the economic boom of the mid- to late-1990s, employers were reluctant to force employees to accept higher costs or lower benefits. Instead, employers used generous health-benefit packages, with fewer restrictions, as a recruiting tool. Now that cost savings from managed care's innovations have all but eroded, with cost increases back to double-digit margins, employers are again looking to curb health-care spending.

To reduce their costs, employers are seeking alternatives to the current system of providing health insurance benefits. Some employers are considering providing a fixed amount of money for health benefits (called *defined contribution programs*) and allowing employees to shop for their own health-care coverage.[3] Defined contribution programs shift more of the health-care cost to employees than under the current defined benefits system, where most of the cost is absorbed by employers. If successful, this would certainly influence the structure and operation of MCOs.

But even if the concept of managed care as envisioned by its proponents is in decline, consolidation among existing MCOs has created tremendous economic power.[4] In certain geographical areas, MCOs "have aggregated to the point that some are moving toward monopoly."[5] In any event, there does not appear to be a feasible alternative model for controlling costs. Whatever substitute might emerge will still be burdened with the need to control costs, so the dynamic discussed in this book will not change much, no matter what type of new health care system arises.

Several factors have contributed to and fueled the backlash against MCOs. Patients have reported increasing dissatisfaction with them, in part because of bureaucratic delays and uncertainty about whether care would be provided, and in part because the industry has done little to explain its decision-making processes to patients.[6] The press has joined the bandwagon by reporting on the most egregious managed care shortcomings.[7] Numerous horror stories about needless bureaucratic delays in paying for recommended treatment have generated considerable public antipathy and concern. Ironically, these anecdotal horror stories contradict a more important story. Most research has concluded that managed care's quality is roughly equivalent (i.e., there are no significant differences in most areas) to quality of care in the fee-for-service system.[8] The horror stories also contradict surveys demonstrating that patients generally like their own MCO even while distrusting the concept of managed care.[9]

Physicians are a major source of the backlash. Since the early 1990s, physicians have complained about MCOs' antagonism toward their clinical choices and constantly being second-guessed by non-physician managed care administrators. Most of all, physicians complain about their loss of autonomy and managed care's interference with patient care. The vast amount of paperwork and bureaucratic delay associated with managed care is an added irritant. Both physicians and nurses have complained that proper medical care has taken a back seat to corporate profits.[10] Physicians treating managed care patients feel pressured to reduce the average time per patient visit to achieve greater economic efficiency as opposed to focusing on quality of care. (To be fair, the loss of physician income under managed care no doubt plays a role in their dissatisfaction.)

Finally, legal scholars and judges have criticized the MCOs' favored position in legal challenges to the operation of cost-containment programs.[11] Like the backlash against railroad immunity, judges have been prominent in voicing their misgivings. Several judges have been particularly vociferous in complaining about harsh results and the lack of flexibility when interpreting ERISA. Judicial opinions—"in light of modern health care"[12]—have condemned laws that insulate MCOs from liability, especially for improper utilization review or other practices that delay or deny medically necessary care. Skeptics on the bench have been vocal in their denunciations:

> This [result], of course, is ridiculous. The tragic events set forth in [plaintiff's] complaint cry out for relief. Under traditional notions of justice, the harms alleged—if true—should entitle [plaintiff] to some legal remedy. Nevertheless,

this Court has no choice but to pluck [plaintiff's] case out of the state court in which she sought redress, and then, at the behest of [defendant MCO], to slam the courthouse doors in her face and leave her without a remedy.[13]

Some courts have seemed to criticize the "management" aspect of medical care in general.[14] "The 'market forces' the dissent refers to hardly seem to have produced a positive result in this case—Herdrich suffered a life-threatening illness (peritonitis), which necessitated a longer hospital stay and more serious surgery at a greater cost to her and the Plan. [W]e are far from alone in our belief that market forces are insufficient to cure the deleterious affects of managed care on the health care industry."[15] As will become apparent later, judges have complained loudly but have not necessarily acted on their distress to rule against MCO immunity.

Unlike the reaction against mass production, where academics led the assault, scholars are divided on managed care's immunity status. In fairness, many scholars and judges actively support the managed care concept and believe that its cost-containment strategies are entirely appropriate. Some go farther and argue that managed care has not been stringent enough in reducing costs.[16]

The managed care industry has compounded its adverse publicity by opposing reasonable regulations and by failing to include the public (and managed care enrollees) in the process of cost containment. MCOs have done very little to bring in the public, either to explain why cost containment is essential or to solicit the public's views on how to fairly implement cost-containment programs. When the industry has taken action, such as voluntarily developing grievance procedures, it has done so only after intense political or anticipated legal complications.[17] Without a doubt, managed care's image has been battered in the courts and in public opinion. Not surprisingly, politicians have been paying attention.

Congress has not yet enacted legislation that would remove MCOs' ERISA protection, but certain actions to address public concerns have been taken without congressional approval. The Clinton administration issued an executive order to implement a patients' bill of rights shortly before leaving office. Because only Congress can amend ERISA, the executive order stopped short of allowing patients to sue, and was limited to participants in Medicare, Medicaid, and various other federal health insurance programs.[18] Even so, the Bush administration promptly rescinded the order as applied to Medicaid. Also, the Department of Labor issued regulations requiring MCOs to make coverage decisions quickly and provide meaningful information about patients' rights and benefits.[19] Perhaps most important, the rules require MCOs to consult with an independent health-care professional, who has appropriate training and expertise, when responding to a denial of requested care. But the rules do not require external grievance panels to resolve disputes, nor do they permit the right to sue for delayed or denied care. The right to sue an MCO for delayed or denied care can be achieved only through congressional action or by judicial reconsideration of ERISA preemption.

As part of the backlash against managed care, many state legislatures have tried to safeguard the attributes of physician autonomy by enacting laws that restrict an MCO's review of a clinical recommendation. State legislation has ranged from prohibiting gag clauses (provisions that prevent physicians from explaining plan options to the patient) to comprehensive reforms designed to limit the primacy of cost-containment strategies. In many instances, courts have ruled that these state laws are preempted by ERISA (although the decisions are by no means consistent or uniform). ERISA preemption has therefore negated many state legislative attempts to restore physician autonomy and has reinforced health-plan control over clinical decisions.

Take, for example, Any Willing Provider (AWP) laws as a proxy for a range of state legislative attempts to regulate MCOs. AWP laws would require MCOs to contract with any physician willing to meet the MCO's established criteria and are intended to preserve the patient's choice of physician. MCOs oppose these laws because they eliminate at least one cost-reduction mechanism—a plan's ability to choose physicians who will be willing to offer lower prices in return for guaranteed patient volume. AWP laws affect another cost reduction mechanism, the power to control quality of care by restricting membership in the plan's network to physicians meeting rigorous quality standards. Without the ability to select participating physicians based on cost and quality standards, MCOs argue that they cannot as easily monitor the quality of care.

In ERISA preemption cases, AWP laws have had a mixed reception. All courts hold that AWP laws relate to employee benefit plans (and are therefore potentially preempted).[20] Courts have split on whether AWP laws should be saved from preemption as regulating the business of insurance. Some courts have held that such laws are not preempted by ERISA because they apply to all health insurers, not just MCOs.[21] As a result, they fall under the state's traditional regulation of insurance. Other courts have concluded that the AWP laws apply specifically to ERISA-covered plans and are preempted. In the language of ERISA, the laws are "not saved" and therefore cannot be applied to any ERISA-covered health plan.[22]

The most extensive attempt to regulate MCOs is a Texas statute requiring an external appeals process for health care denials and allowing patients to sue the MCO for poor-quality health care (mainly raising vicarious liability claims for actions by affiliated physicians). The law does not grant the right to sue for delayed or denied care, but if upheld against an ERISA challenge, the law would probably become a model for other state legislatures. A federal Circuit Court of Appeals upheld the limited right to sue, for reasons discussed in the next section, but overturned the external grievance process as preempted by ERISA.[23] The fact that the court viewed the external review process as a law relating to a health plan is an indication of the ERISA-created hurdles facing state laws that try to bolster clinical autonomy.

Just as troublesome, the uncertainty in ERISA litigation makes it difficult, if not impossible, to predict which state laws will be preempted. For instance, some recent decisions have reduced the scope of preemption, not only of state tort actions but also of other state legislative initiatives. In one case, a federal Circuit Court of Appeals rejected an ERISA preemption challenge to a Washington State law mandating that certain benefits must be provided. The court reasoned that because the legislation only covers a product an ERISA plan may buy, it did not "relate to" a benefit plan.[24] And another Circuit Court of Appeals upheld an Illinois state legislative mandate for an external grievance procedure against a similar ERISA challenge (in contrast to the ruling in the Texas case).[25] The court ruled that since the external grievance process requirement pertained to insurance regulation, it was a matter for state insurance law, not ERISA. The Supreme Court has agreed to review the Illinois decision.[26]

One strategy designed in part to circumvent ERISA preemption has emerged. The state board of medical examiners can use its licensing authority to investigate complaints that MCO medical directors interfere with treatment recommendations during the utilization review process. If successful, this strategy would hinder the plan medical director's ability to reject treatment recommendations without inviting challenges to the medical director's license to practice medicine. Some courts have upheld this approach,[27] but others have rejected it.[28] Potentially, licensing board oversight provides a powerful tool for states to monitor the utilization review process and intervene when the process unfairly disadvantages individual patients.

Overall, the uncertainty about how courts will rule on which state laws and regulations ERISA preempts makes it difficult for patients, as well as health care administrators, to anticipate what will survive. It also makes it difficult to develop a coherent state-level regulatory approach to managed care. To respond to public concerns, legislators may be under pressure to pass more laws than necessary, hoping that a few will survive ERISA preemption challenges. (Or, more cynically, some legislators might vote for laws they otherwise oppose anticipating that they will not survive an ERISA challenge.)

New Rules?

Legal rules are not static, and there are some indications that courts are now moving away from substantial immunity to partial immunity. Consistent with the backlash—and the pattern described in Chapter 4—there have been hints that courts are changing legal doctrine in ways that may result in greater accountability for managed care organizations. The major judicial break-through occurred in 1996 with the Supreme Court's decision in *New York State Conference of Blue Cross & Blue Shield Plans v. Travelers Insurance Company.*[29] The Court permitted New York State to impose a tax on all in-surers except Blue Cross and Blue Shield, reasoning that a uniform tax only tangentially related to ERISA plan administration. This signaled a willingness to scale back the breadth of preemption, particularly in determining whether the challenged law or practice actually burdens the administration of plan benefits or has only a remote impact on them. After *Travelers*, courts have been less vigorous in finding ERISA preemption.

The most important trend following (and largely inspired by) *Travelers* is that courts have erected a critical distinction between state law tort challenges to the technical quality of care (i.e., liability claims for substandard clinical care) and state law challenges to the quantity of care (involving improper plan benefit decisions). Most claims alleging delayed or denied care will still be preempted and must be brought in federal court, subject to ERISA's limited remedies. Yet the quantity–quality distinction has allowed patients to sue MCOs in state courts for their physicians' substandard care, and may result in significant verdicts against managed care.

In essence, the quality–quantity distinction—a distinction only tenuously based on the reality of managed care decision-making—reduces the industry's ability to use preemption to block judicial scrutiny of care provided by plan physicians. By narrowing the types of cases that are preempted, MCOs are more likely than before *Travelers* to find cases returned to state courts. State courts, which historically have been more patient-friendly than federal courts, will decide whether patients can recover damages. Through the quality–quan-tity distinction, lower courts have increased the likelihood of full MCO ac-countability to injured patients. The more courts define as quality challenges what previously would have been considered preempted benefit determination challenges, the more the industry's immunity is reduced.

A notable example of how legal doctrine has changed in ways reducing MCO immunity since the *Travelers* case is *Bauman v. U.S. Healthcare, Inc.*[30] In this case, Michelle Bauman gave birth to a baby girl. Two days later, the parents noticed that the baby was ill and requested an in-home visit by a pediatric nurse. The request was denied. Later that day, the baby contracted an undiagnosed strep infection that developed into meningitis. She died that day. The parents sued the MCO under various legal theories (similar to those used by Andrews-Clarke and Goodrich). U.S. Healthcare defended by denying culpability and by arguing that ERISA preempted the lawsuit. The court ruled that the parents' challenge asserted substandard quality of care rather than a denial of benefits. "In performing these activities, the HMO is not acting in its capacity as a plan administrator but as a provider of health care, subject to the prevailing standard of care."[31] In rejecting the MCO's characterization of the case as a "quintessential" challenge to a benefit denial, the court clearly signaled a new willingness to weigh mixed questions of plan administration and health-care delivery in favor of the patient.

In practice, the quantity–quality distinction is difficult to maintain, as many clinical decisions involve both aspects. Take the simple example of discharging a patient two days early. The discharge may represent a clinical decision, or it may be a based on a benefit determination. It is a quality issue because the patient will argue that the discharge was medically inappropriate. At the same time, the plan will define it as a benefit determination because the discharge constituted an interpretation of plan benefits. Before *Travelers*, courts almost uniformly preempted these types of cases because even a mixed quality–quantity determination involved an interpretation of plan benefits.[32] After *Travelers*, courts have shown greater willingness to characterize the claim as a traditional medical liability action (i.e., a quality-of-care complaint) that does not implicate a benefit determination, and therefore should not be preempted.[33] The Pennsylvania Supreme Court has already concluded that negligence claims against an MCO (an HMO in this case) do not "relate to" an ERISA plan and are not preempted.[34]

But as quickly as the courts created an opening, subsequent decisions have suggested the limits. To demonstrate how confusing ERISA's distinctions have become (not to mention how unsustainable they really are), consider the case of *Pryzbowski v. U.S. Healthcare, Inc.*,[35] decided in 2000 by the same court that ruled in the *Bauman* case just a year earlier. Linda Pryzbowski sought treatment for severe back pain, following several previous back surgeries. A CT scan revealed disc degeneration and herniation. After a lengthy series of delays regarding referral to an out-of-network surgeon, U.S. Healthcare agreed to the referral. Unfortunately, the delay exacerbated the disc degeneration and the surgery left the plaintiff in constant pain. Pryzbowski sued the defendant for negligence in delaying approval for the surgery.

The facts of this case sound suspiciously like those in *Bauman*. But the court disagreed and ruled against Pryzbowski. To the court, the claim fell between a clear quality-of-care case (for delayed surgery) and a benefit determination (eligibility for out-of-network placement). Taking a step back from the *Bauman* case, the court held that Pryzbowski's claims regarding the delay in approving benefits fell within the plan's administrative functions and were preempted by ERISA. But what was delayed was a decision "about how to provide care that is covered as a benefit," not just about eligibility for a particular benefit.[36] In this case, the medical condition was covered; the treatment was delayed, not the benefit coverage. The court's emphasis on form over function is disturbingly reminiscent of early ERISA preemption cases.

Whatever actual difficulty courts might have in implementing the quality–quantity distinction, the mere fact that the distinction exists signals a nascent trend toward holding MCOs accountable, at least in some circumstances. As their liability expands, MCOs may begin to reconsider the ways in which clinical decisions are reviewed. It is one thing to deny treatment when potential liability rests with the treating physician; it is another to deny the claim when the organization itself might also be held responsible. More potential MCO liability may mean more deference to physician autonomy.

Consider, for example, state litigation seeking to hold an MCO indirectly liable for the malpractice of a physician affiliated with (but not employed by) it. Because a claim alleging substandard care is litigation about the quality of care, not the quantity of benefits, the case may survive ERISA preemption and be heard in state court. Because state courts require MCOs to have a certain amount of control to hold them indirectly liable, MCOs may seek to avoid liability by loosening their control below the threshold required by state law. The possible result: increased physician autonomy and greater access to services for individual patients.

One consequence of the changing judicial landscape is to embolden lawyers to bring new challenges to managed care's cost-containment programs. Several class actions have been filed under the Racketeer Influenced and Corrupt Organizations Act (RICO),[37] charging that MCOs fraudulently mislead subscribers into believing that they will be provided high quality care when the financial incentives dictate undertreatment. So far, these class actions have not been successful. As we will see below, the Supreme Court has opened the way for a less sweeping class action against an MCO's failure to disclose its incentives.

Even the question of remedies has revealed hints of judicial reluctance to stick to ERISA's strict terms. In *Varity Corp. v. Howe*,[38] the Supreme Court suggested that certain common law remedies might be available for a breach of fiduciary duty. Common law remedies would often far exceed ERISA's more limited approach. Despite this, several federal Circuit Courts of Appeals have rigorously enforced the limited ERISA recoveries.[39] In some instances, courts have even refused to force entities who make bad faith denials of coverage to disgorge what they should have paid for denied care.[40,41]

Aside from ERISA, another area curtailing MCO immunity that is gaining some judicial adherents, though not widely adopted to date, is a due process standard. In this approach, the private sector retains decision-making authority subject to basic due process requirements. Some courts, particularly in California, New Hampshire, and Pennsylvania, have imposed fair process require-

ments, including a fair hearing, as a condition of severing a physician's contractual relationship with a facility or terminating staff privileges. Even if the
physicians signed a contract waiving the right to notice prior to termination,
some courts have nevertheless required hospitals to hold a fair hearing before
taking action. In *Potvin v. Metropolitan Life Insurance Company,*[42] a physician
challenged his termination from a provider network without due process. The
court cited previous California cases to hold that private organizations must
provide due process when they control important economic interests.

Without specifically defining what would constitute important economic interests, the court noted several factors in this case that should be considered:
the importance of the product (i.e., health care) to the public; legislative recognition of its public nature; the industry's representations to the public about
the product; and managed care's economic power over patients and physicians.
The court added that the public has a substantial interest in the "unique
relationship among an insurance company, its insureds, and the physicians who
participate in the network.[43] Usually due process only applies where the government, or an entity acting on the government's behalf, acts in ways that
violate due process. In this case, the private organizations were treated as
having "quasi-public significance," which opened them to fair procedure requirements. Stating that the health plans in this case were "tinged with public
stature or purpose," the court held that a fair hearing must be provided prior
to termination.

But another court rejected a due process challenge to the hospital's termination of the physician's contract. The contract permitted unilateral termination of the agreement by either party. Relying on this provision, the court
ruled that the hospital did not violate the physician's liberty interest and was
not required to provide due process prior to termination.[44]

To date, the cases imposing fair process have not gone beyond procedural
requirements, suggesting that terminating a physician's staff privileges (known
as "deselection") may proceed in these states once the procedural requirements have been satisfied. Similar procedural requirements in peer review
determinations have not impeded hospitals from terminating staff privileges.[45]
Indeed, courts have not yet held that clauses permitting termination without
cause violate public policy. One court has remanded a case for trial on whether
such clauses violate public policy,[46] another court overturned an arbitration
panel's decision because the panel was not fair and impartial,[47] and at least
one state, New York, has done so legislatively.

For physicians and patients, the due process standard is attractive because
it provides some leverage against arbitrary actions and facilitates continuity of
care. A due process approach does not prevent MCOs from taking action
against a plan physician or against a physician's recommendation. Before it
does so, the MCO must provide adequate due process protections that allow

the affected physician or patient an opportunity to present his or her case. Undoubtedly, this is a limited approach that will help individuals but will not address the systemic market deficiencies that still exist. Without additional judicial support, it is premature to call the due process approach a new rule. It is, nonetheless, a promising development that protects the continuity of the physician–patient relationship without unduly limiting MCO decision-making. It might also be extended to require fair process before health care is denied.

Although the judicial and political backlash has resulted in some tentative movement toward reducing managed care's immunity from liability and in developing new lines of accountability, we are still largely in a period of immunity with regard to cost-containment policies. Despite a lessening of complete immunity and a trend toward partial immunity, the burden is with the ERISA-covered patient to demonstrate that the case is a quality-of-care challenge. If not, the case will most likely be preempted. There is no major change in legal doctrine so far. The most recent Supreme Court opinion to deal with compensation arrangements and disclosure of incentives, two issues critical to managed care's success, makes the limitations of the judicial backlash to ERISA preemption very clear.

ERISA Revisited

In view of the post-*Travelers* narrowing of preemption and the attendant increase in litigation, it was inevitable that the Supreme Court would need to resolve whether ERISA preempts challenges to managed care's financial incentives. During the period of MCO immunity from litigation, attorneys tried alternative strategies to attack adverse outcomes from delayed or denied care. Aside from direct assaults on managed care's financial incentives, which accelerated after *Travelers*, many lawsuits charging MCO misconduct have been cast as breaches of fiduciary duty under ERISA rather than as (potentially preempted) state law liability lawsuits.[48] As Part III of this book will explore, the fiduciary duty obligation provides a unique way of reconciling various tensions within the managed care context. Oddly enough, ERISA provides at least a partial framework for how alternative legal doctrine might be developed. If properly interpreted and implemented, ERISA's fiduciary duty provision can be a mechanism for resolving the tensions between the needs of the individual patient and those of the MCO's patient population.

For now, most courts have explicitly refused to be the agents of a major overhaul of ERISA, preferring to leave that role to the legislative arena. For example, courts continue to preempt direct challenges to MCO-physician compensation arrangements. With direct attacks on financial incentives seemingly blocked, breach of fiduciary challenges offered an alternative that might allow courts to enjoin the denial of care (essentially forcing them to provide it), even if it might not result in damages. That alternative has been seriously undermined by the Supreme Court.

In *Herdrich v. Pegram*,[49] a Federal Circuit Court of Appeals held that a patient could sue for breach of ERISA's fiduciary duty based on an allegation that the nature of the financial compensation arrangements between the MCO and the physicians caused her to be deprived of proper medical care. Herdrich's claim asserted that the plan's financial incentives for physicians led her doctor to delay an abdominal ultrasound. During the delay, her appendix ruptured, resulting in peritonitis. The patient also alleged that the MCO and the physicians reaped economic benefits from the denial of care, and therefore had a palpable conflict of interest. According to Herdrich's complaint, the physician group acted as the health plan's fiduciary and breached its fiduciary duty because of the conflict of interest.

The trial court rejected Herdrich's ERISA claim, but the appellate court reinstated it, warning in sweeping language that rewards to physicians for withholding care endangered the quality of American medicine.[50] In an opinion that directly and somewhat intemperately attacked managed care, the appellate court ruled that the operation of the economic incentives in this case amounted to a breach of fiduciary duty. Even though the court specifically noted that the mere existence of economic incentives would not automatically be tantamount to a breach of fiduciary duty, the ruling nevertheless had the potential to erode the core of managed care's financial incentives.

Swayed by two stinging appellate court dissents[51,52] and the managed care industry's warning that subjecting physicians' financial incentives to liability would mean the end of managed health plans,[53] the Supreme Court agreed to review the decision. That set off a variety of responses among the most directly affected groups and organizations. Ms. Herdrich and many scholars urged the Supreme Court to interpret ERISA as setting boundaries on physicians' financial incentives to limit treatment. In turn, the managed care industry had competing objectives. It first wanted to prevent plaintiffs' lawyers from using ERISA to attack the delegation of cost control to treating physicians. The industry also hoped to preserve ERISA as a shelter against liability for plan administrators' utilization review decisions. Likewise, the medical profession was deeply divided between two contending positions. One group viewed financial incentives to withhold care as ethically troublesome and thus an appropriate target for federal regulation. Another group, including the AMA's leadership, feared federal liability for physicians (and physician-owned health plans) and thus sided with the managed care industry.

In June 2000, the Supreme Court issued a ruling in the now-titled case of *Pegram v. Herdrich*[54] that has significant policy consequences for congressional reconsideration of patients' rights legislation and for a patient's ability to challenge managed care's financial incentives. With stunning candor, the Court proclaimed that health care rationing is not only routine in America but a matter of national policy. Writing for a unanimous Court, Justice David Souter said "inducement to ration care goes to the very point of any HMO scheme" and that Congress has for 27 years promoted the formation of HMOs and thereby endorsed "the profit incentive to ration care."

For several reasons, this opinion merits in-depth consideration. It forecloses judicial attacks on the foundations of managed care, essentially confirms at least partial judicial immunity, and explicitly shifts responsibility to Congress for alleviating public anger toward MCOs.

The decision has three parts that can be stated rather succinctly. First, the Court ruled that ERISA preempts challenges to the way physicians are paid (i.e., managed care's financial incentives). Even the egregious operation of financial incentives to deprive a patient of care cannot be challenged under ERISA. Congress, not the courts, should resolve any dissatisfaction with managed care's financial and organizational structure. Second, the Court explicitly confirmed that rationing health care is accepted national policy. Again, challenges that basically attack what public policy permits do not belong in the courts. Third, the Court severely limited challenges based on ERISA's fiduciary duty provisions. In a portion of the opinion that is very difficult to interpret, the Court held that mixed treatment and benefit eligibility determinations are not fiduciary duty decisions under ERISA. This means that since most of the contested ERISA claims will fall under mixed treatment-benefit decisions, the Court's opinion may remove breach of fiduciary duty as a viable ERISA litigation strategy. As we will see in a moment, there is considerable dispute over what this part of the opinion means.

At least for now, the Court seems to consider the quality–quantity distinction as an acceptable development, although that distinction was not directly raised in this case. (Instead of these terms, the Court used "eligibility" for a benefit determination, and "treatment" for quality-of-care. The new terms are functionally equivalent to the old ones but may be somewhat easier to apply.)[55] Equally important, the opinion does not foreclose similar challenges at the state level for non-ERISA patients. Most likely, state courts will seriously consider the Supreme Court's reasoning before venturing in a different direction, particularly on challenges to compensation arrangements. For fiduciary challenges under a state's common law, however, this opinion may not be as persuasive.

On its face, the Supreme Court's decision in the case was a big win for managed care and a return to immunity from litigation. At a minimum, the Court has removed ERISA-based challenges to managed care's financial incentives. Whether such challenges might be mounted under state law remains in doubt.

The Court rejected the use of ERISA as a mechanism to attack MCOs, holding that the statute's fiduciary-duty provisions do not apply to financial arrangements between plans and physicians that reward the latter for withholding treatment. Justice Souter's opinion accepted the industry's claims that federal suits against managed care for offering financial incentives would "precipitate" a health care "upheaval." Congressional promotion of HMOs since 1973[56] constitutes endorsement of these incentives, the Court held, and exposing physicians to the costs of their clinical decisions is integral to the managed care model. More bluntly than the industry's leaders might have preferred, Justice Souter said that MCOs must balance medical risks against costs, and that Congress is better suited than the courts to make "social value" judgments about the balances health plans should strike.[57]

In ruling that public policy has encouraged the use of financial incentives to reduce health-care costs, the opinion removes any doubt about the judicial acceptance of managed care's cost-containment programs. The Court's approach also suggests that managed care's hybrid financial and benefit decision making is not susceptible to a fiduciary duty challenge. Consequently, the *Pegram* case does little to restore physician autonomy with respect to managed care organizations. The Court is clearly deferring to Congress and to the market to set the terms of health-care delivery.

In many ways, the Court went too far in treating the conflict of interest presented by financial incentives as being beyond judicial scrutiny and in removing challenges to ERISA's fiduciary-duty provision. As we will see, the Court emphasized its own institutional concerns over those of patients and physicians. Thus, the decision was a rebuff to those who looked to ERISA's fiduciary duty provisions to limit pressure on physicians to depart from the ethical ideal of undivided loyalty to patients.[58] Magnifying the import of this defeat is the continuing congressional failure to amend ERISA by enacting patients' rights legislation. As of this writing, no federal regulation of physician incentives in employer-sponsored health plans has been enacted.

Ironically, the industry's victory could prove bittersweet. Ambiguous language in the opinion regarding mixed clinical and financial decisions may invite litigants to argue that state law can impose constraints on cost-control programs. Some scholars have interpreted the opinion as permitting challenges to mixed financial (benefit) and clinical treatment decisions to proceed in state courts. If hybrid financial-clinical decisions are no longer subject to ERISA preemption, more cases will go to trial in state courts, especially utilization review determinations that previously were immune from liability lawsuits. Perhaps unintentionally, the *Pegram* decision may have opened the way for patients to sue their health plans for denying coverage.

The ambiguity in the Court's language reflects a central tension in the Court's treatment of health care—between the justices' generally favorable stance toward market-driven change and their support for shifting regulatory authority over the health sphere from federal to state government. Whether (and to what degree) *Pegram* will become the basis for expanded state legal authority over medical cost control will largely depend on how lower courts interpret the Court's ambiguity concerning the question of state versus federal power. Where a state has explicitly enacted a statute allowing patients to sue an MCO for the improper operation of financial incentives, e.g., Texas,[59] patients' lawyers may have a clear shot at the industry. It may be much more difficult to win such a case in a state without a law specifically permitting the litigation.

One state court opinion lends credence to the view that *Pegram* will result in greater MCO vulnerability to state court liability lawsuits. In *Pappas v. Asbel,* a case involving a refusal to permit a referral to a non-network hospital, the Pennsylvania Supreme Court initially ruled that ERISA did not preempt the litigation. The court determined that the referral question was a mixed eligibility and treatment decision that should properly be decided under state law. After deciding the *Pegram* case, the U.S. Supreme Court remanded the *Pappas* case back to the Pennsylvania Supreme Court for reconsideration in light of *Pegram*. Once again, the Pennsylvania Supreme Court confirmed its previous ruling and allowed the case to proceed to trial in the Pennsylvania trial court.[60]

On the other hand, *Pegram's* ambiguity about the kinds of hybrid clinical and benefit coverage decisions that should be subject to state law permits health plans to argue that the Court intended no such thing. As a result, current law preempting health plans from state suits for negligent determination of benefits should stand undisturbed. The overall tone of the Court's opinion—highly favorable toward managed care and not at all solicitous of further litigation—supports this contrary interpretation. The industry can also argue that if the Court had intended a change as dramatic as curtailing health plans' immunity from suit, the justices would not have suggested it so circumspectly. Already, one lower court has basically accepted this argument by stating that "we do not read *Pegram* to entail that every conceivable state law claim survives preemption so long as it is based on a mixed question" of coverage and treatment.[61] Perhaps an even more telling signal is the progression from *Bauman v. U.S. Healthcare, Inc.,* to *Pryzbowski v. U.S. Healthcare, Inc.*, decided in successive years by the Third Circuit Court of Appeals. Before *Pegram*, the Bauman case expansively interpreted the quality–quantity distinction against preemption. Citing *Pegram*, the same court, in the *Pryzbowski* case, retreated from its expansive interpretation to decide that a similar challenge was preempted. In support, one commentator has even suggested that courts could interpret *Pegram* to expand ERISA preemption of hybrid claims, which would invalidate the quality–quantity distinction.[62]

This odd result is entirely consistent with the history of ERISA litigation and in keeping with the judicial pattern we have been considering. Even after the Supreme Court's attempt to clarify, what will follow in the lower courts (or in Congress) is not at all predictable. Suffice it to say at this stage of the managed care litigation cycle that the movement to new legal rules has not occurred. If anything, *Pegram* represents a step away from the judicial backlash and back toward the immunity phase. But the opinion's ambiguity regarding a patient's ability to challenge a mixed determination of treatment and benefit administration might indicate the beginning of a slow shift toward developing new doctrine. Should they choose to pursue it, the opinion provides lower court judges with a rationale for expanding the trend away from immunity. Since many judges are already disaffected with ERISA preemption, they may use the ambiguous language to permit lawsuits in state courts. That will not be clear until we see additional lower federal and state court opinions. So far, lower court cases interpreting *Pegram* have, as usual, conflicted with one another.[63]

Further legal troubles for managed health plans may lie ahead as a result of a footnote in *Pegram* suggesting that they can be held liable under ERISA for failure to tell subscribers about physicians' financial incentives. "It could be argued," the Court said, that a plan "is obligated to disclose characteristics of the plan and of those who provide services to the plan, if that information affects beneficiaries' material interests."[64] Disclosure of financial incentives to withhold care has been required by at least one lower court based on this theory,[65] which is also the basis for some of the federal class action suits now pending against HMOs. *Pegram* thus breathed life into cases challenging the failure to disclose financial incentives.

Andrews-Clarke and Goodrich Revisited

At this point, it seems appropriate to take a closer look at the Andrews-Clarke and Goodrich cases in light of the quality–quantity distinction and the subsequent rulings on utilization review and financial incentives. The Andrews-Clarke and Goodrich cases are good examples of how federal legislation can shape litigation outcomes. Both cases arose because of the changes in health care delivery and organization. Neither patient received the health care he expected because of the intense pressure the MCOs exerted to lower health care spending. In the fee-for-service era, the requested treatment most likely would have been provided. If the insurer had then failed to pay, the resulting litigation would have been about reimbursement, not about the failure to provide needed health care.

The two cases were litigated at a time when tort law was already firmly established as a legal theory applicable to health care disputes. At first glance, this looks like a simple extension of the pattern seen earlier with railroads and mass produced goods where courts would need to choose between tort and contract as the guiding standard in developing legal doctrine. But as we have also seen, this might not necessarily be an easy or straightforward task. The multiplicity of actors and organizational forms in managed care virtually assures a difficult application of the tort and contract concepts to managed care cases.

Recall that Mr. Clarke requested additional inpatient care for chronic alcoholism, which was denied by the utilization review firm. The MCO upheld the denial, refusing to provide additional inpatient care. To Ms. Andrews-Clarke, this was strictly a matter of substandard quality of care, for which the MCO should be held responsible. In short, this should have been a routine medical malpractice case where the issue would have been whether the MCO met the proper standard of care in denying additional inpatient care. Nothing in ERISA, however, is routine.

Despite considerable agonizing, the judge decided with very little analysis or extensive discussion that the challenge was to a benefit denial. Under ERISA, any state court challenge to a benefit denial is preempted. In reaching this conclusion, the court said that Andrews-Clarke's complaint arose from allegedly improper benefit claims processing, not from a treatment decision. Under this somewhat tautological reasoning (it is a benefit because it is a benefit), ERISA preemption was the only option.

Yet there is nothing inevitable about the court's decision. At a minimum, the case involves both a claim for substandard treatment (a quality-of-care claim for medical malpractice) and a claim regarding denial of benefits (a quantity issue). When both are intertwined, why should the quantity claim trump the quality claim? Nothing in the court's opinion suggests an adequate answer. In fact, there was no disagreement that Mr. Clarke was entitled to inpatient benefits. No one suggested that he should be provided with more inpatient days than covered in the health plan benefit package. Instead, the disagreement was about the medical need for inpatient care to control his chronic alcoholism, which appears to be a claim about quality of care.

Judge Young was right to be distressed by feeling compelled to dismiss the Andrews-Clarke case. Did he reach the correct result? As the case law developed in the period following his ruling against Ms. Andrews-Clarke suggests, there is reason to question Judge Young's decision. It certainly seems unduly harsh to dismiss the claim, and arguably an incorrect legal decision as well. Since the case was decided after the *Travelers* decision, Judge Young had wider latitude to reject immunity. Had the court defined Ms. Andrews-Clarke's case as a challenge to the quality of care, it could have remanded the case to state court for trial. The defendant might then have appealed, forcing a more definitive ruling by a higher court.

Compare the tragic result in the Andrews-Clarke case with the different results in the Bauman and Goodrich cases. Under reasonably similar facts, Andrews-Clarke's challenge was preempted while the Goodrich and Bauman cases proceeded to trial. What changed? For Goodrich, the case was not covered by ERISA, so there was no impediment blocking a state court trial. For Bauman, the short answer is that the *Travelers* case provided enough room for lower courts to weigh the quantity–quality distinction in favor of patients. Had the Andrews-Clarke situation arisen later in the litigation cycle, it is entirely possible that Judge Young would have ruled in favor of proceeding to trial, based on the reasoning in the Bauman case.

By the time the Andrews-Clarke case arose, the judiciary, as expressed by Judge Young's strong condemnation of ERISA preemption, was ready to address managed care's judicial immunity. Unfortunately for Ms. Andrews-Clarke, the judicial backlash against immunity was just beginning.

It is exactly cases like *Herdrich* and *Bauman* that delineate the contours of the law, change the prevailing legal doctrine, and force the appellate courts to come to terms with both the harsh results engendered by ERISA and the inherent contradictions of the quantity–quality distinction. If law is to serve its function of changing in response to social conditions, it seems appropriate for judges to err on the side of protecting the right to proceed to trial. At trial, it is entirely appropriate for MCOs to use cost-containment as a defense. What seems illegitimate is to deny the opportunity to seek compensation for medical injury arguably caused by those very cost-containment programs.

Then again, it is cases like *Pryzbowski* that confuse the situation and demonstrate how unsatisfactory the ERISA preemption doctrine has become. The courts have a long way to go before eliminating managed care's immunity and before ERISA rulings are at all predictable.

Observations on the Development of Legal Rules

We have now reviewed the development of legal doctrine during three points of significant industrial change. Several observations are especially applicable to managed care. First, courts adjust legal doctrine to meet changing social and organizational arrangements. The common law is a supple instrument that allows judges significant flexibility to adapt legal rules to changing circumstances.

One point to keep in mind is that the common law is always evolving. To speak of a general pattern is somewhat misleading. As our examples imply, there is a constant ebb and flow to the development of legal doctrine—periods of stability followed by periods of upheaval and change. We can still discern general directions and patterns, but there are few absolutes, which may be unsettling to those who expect the law to be stable and predictable. Like the economic and social conditions that form the context in which the common law develops, change and ambiguity are more often the reality than stability and predictability.

Second, the pattern described can be used to predict the various stages courts will go through before arriving at a reasonably stable set of rules. While the pattern does not predict the outcome of the process, it will help place the development of legal rules in a broader context that could assist judges in achieving stable and predictable rules. The pattern predicts that eventually courts will select a set of principles and rules to impose more legal account- ability on the mature industry than on the industry in its nascent phase.

Third, the examples indicate that because courts are reluctant to interfere with emerging market arrangements, they end up protecting new industries. The common law is generally reflective of a pattern of favoring markets and thereby facilitating innovation. To suggest that courts tend to favor industrial innovation is not to imply a Marxist analysis where courts simply favor the ruling class. At least to some extent, courts may be taking a wait-and-see approach to assess the implications of the market transformation. It takes judges time to understand the policy and market implications of a new in- dustry. As we have seen in each of the examples, courts have trouble initially in understanding the innovations. Further complicating the judicial response is that judges must react to the early cases by using legal doctrine developed for a previous set of circumstances

Fourth, the question remains as to which legal regime, liability standard, and subsidiary rules are most appropriate for holding the industry account able—tort or contract, or a mix of both. The historical examples imply that it is not an either/or question. For the most part, tort and contract operate in tandem, allowing courts to choose from a variety of legal options depending on the goals to be achieved. But since one approach is likely to be used to establish baseline principles for judicial thinking, it is important to understand how and why tort or contract rules become the operative legal rule. Even within tort or contract, choices need to be made both as to the liability stan- dard and its subsidiary rules. For example, courts could have imposed strict liability in the railroad example and negligence for mass-produced products, resulting in very different accountability mechanisms.

In both of the selected historical examples, tort law emerged as the domi- nant—but by no means exclusive—method for achieving accountability. For railroads, the courts adopted a negligence liability standard; for mass produc- tion, the courts chose strict liability. If the historical examples are broadly representative of how courts operate, judges will eventually select some form of tort liability to hold MCOs accountable. So far, that has not happened. Courts have applied hospital liability principles to MCOs, but they have not yet adopted tort doctrine in considering challenges to cost-containment initiatives. Cracks in ERISA preemption may presage a potential shift to tort.

Remember, the changes in legal rules in the railroads and mass production were achieved over a long period of time. Viewed after the fact, the pattern and direction are reasonably clear. We are still relatively early in the litigation cycle for managed care, so it should not be surprising that there is little stability, predictability, or accountability in the rules. Viewing the ongoing development of rules, as we now try to assess managed care litigation, presents a much murkier and more ambiguous picture. The shift from immunity to tort liability for the railroads took several decades. The change from contract to strict liability for mass-produced goods took about 50 years. In the historical examples, shifting to tort liability addressed the needs of the courts by providing a structure that was "more adaptable" than contract. Much as occurred in railroads, with the use of subsidiary rules that provided judges with greater flexibility in resolving personal injury claims, moving away from contract rules in mass production provided greater judicial flexibility.

How and why one rule emerges instead of another remains an important and inconclusive area of legal scholarship. It is also important for stakeholders. In managed care, for instance, the assignment of liability rules will affect the power balance between physicians and MCOs, as well as the ability of plan subscribers to challenge cost-containment initiatives. A contract-based legal regime will most likely restrict a patient's ability to challenge cost-containment initiatives, while a tort-based regime will most likely be more patient-friendly.

Even if the historical precursors are generally applicable, there are two possible ways the judicial response to the managed care industry may diverge from the patterns seen in the earlier examples. We live now in the "Age of Statutes,"[66] with legislation playing a greater role in setting legal standards and in constraining courts from developing incremental common-law doctrine. Though statutes influenced the direction of doctrine in the other two industries, particularly with regard to the railroads, legislative and regulatory intervention was not as pervasive. More than ever before, the development of common-law rules takes place through a dialogue between the courts, stakeholders, and legislators. Legislators in particular play an important role in shaping the direction and outcome of the courts' deliberations in managed care litigation. Changes in legal doctrine—at least to the extent that it is the product of judicial initiative—may be altered by legislative intervention, perhaps leading to a different path altogether.

Another difference is that the theory and style of judging has probably changed from the heyday of railroads and mass production. Considerable evidence suggests that judges now perceive their role to be far more restrained in judicial creativity and activism. There seems little doubt that the judiciary as a whole is now more deferential to the legislative branch. Throughout the ERISA cases, in which MCOs achieve immunity from liability despite evidence of their wrongful conduct, the constant theme is that the injustice must be curbed by Congress, not the courts.[67] The legitimacy of a judge's "imposition" of his or her own "policy" choices is under sustained attack.[68] The contemporary perception of the judicial role may result in a preference for more rigid rather than more flexible doctrine in which discretion is allocated to the elected legislature rather than the judiciary.

It seems fair to conclude that the courts have generally supported managed care's immunity from liability. As with the railroad and mass production industries, immunity is hardly complete, and there are signs of increasing judicial willingness to challenge the managed care industry's immunity. Overall, though, there is little indication that courts have yet developed an alternative approach that would impose greater accountability. The ambiguity and inconsistency in legal rules make it difficult for patients, policy makers, physicians, and health-care administrators to predict what the courts will preempt and what they will permit. Even so, there has been enough litigation to examine trends and their policy implications, which will be the subject of the next chapter.

Notes

1. Gabel (1997).

2. Robinson (2001).

3. For a discussion of the defined contribution strategy, see Blakely (2001) and Jacobi and Huberfeld (2001).

4. Gabel (1997) p. 138

5. Robinson (1999); Landa (2001).

6. Gabel (1997), p. 144; Millenson (1997); Anders (1996).

7. Church (1997).

8. Miller and Luft (1994; 1997).

9. For a review of public attitudes over a 50 year period, see Blendon and Benson (2001). They find that public attitudes are contradictory. On the one hand, people express dissatisfaction with managed care and a mixed public–private system. But on the other hand, surveys show that the public is satisfied with their own medical arrangements. See also, Ginsburg and Lesser (1999).

10. Ad Hoc Committee to Defend Health Care (1997); see also, Luft (1999).

11. Dorros and Stone (1995); Cunningham (1996); Pittman (1994); O'Neil (1994); Conison (1994); Fisk (1996); Jordan (1996).

12. *Pomeroy v. Johns Hopkins Medical Services*, 868 F.Supp. 110, 116–17 (D.Md. 1994).

13. *Andrews-Clarke v. Travelers Ins. Co.*, 984 F. Supp. 49 (D.Mass. 1997).

14. *Herdrich v. Pegram*, 154 F.3d 362 (7th Cir. 1998) pp. 375–78.

15. *Herdrich v. Pegram*, 154 F.3d 362, 374–375.

16. *See, e.g.*, Robinson (2001); Havighurst (2001); dissenting opinion in *Herdrich v. Pegram;* 170 F.3d 683 (7th Cir. 1999) (Easterbrook dissenting).

17. Bloche (2001).

18. Pear (1998), p. A7.

19. 29 CFR Part 2560, *Federal Register*, Vol. 65, No. 225, Tuesday, 21 November 2000, pp. 70246–70271.

20. *Stuart Circle Hosp. Corp. v. Aetna Health Management*, 995 F.2d 500, 502 (4th Cir. 1993), *cert. denied*, 114 S.Ct. 579 (1993).

21. *Blue Cross and Blue Shield v. St. Mary's Hospital*, 426 S.E.2d 117 (1993).

22. *CIGNA Healthplan of Louisiana, Inc. v. Louisiana*, 82 F.3d 642 (5th Cir. 1996); *Texas Pharmacy Ass'n v. Prudential Ins. Co. of America*, 105 F.3d 1035, 1039 (5th Cir. 1997).

23. *Corporate Health Insurance, Inc. v. Texas Department of Insurance*, 215 F.3d 526 (5th Cir. 2000).

24. *Washington Physicians Service Ass'n v. Gregoire*, 147 F.3d 1039 (9th Cir. 1998).

25. *Moran v. Rush Prudential HMO*, Inc, No. 99–9574 (7th Cir. 2000).

26. *Rush Prudential HMO v. Moran*, 230 F.3d 959 (7th Cir. 2000), No. 00–1021, *cert. granted* (U.S. June 29, 2001),

27. *Murphy v. Board of Medical Examiners of the State of Arizona*, 949 P.2d 530 (Ariz. Ct. App. 1997); *Long v. Great West Life & Annuity Insurance Co.*, 1998 Wyo. LEXIS 62 (Wyo. 1998).

28. See, e.g., *Crocco v. Xerox Corp.*, 956 F. Supp. 129 (D.Conn. 1997), 137 F.3d 125 (2d Cir. 1998).

29. 514 U.S. 645 (1995).

30. 193 F.3d 151 (3d Cir. 1999), *cert. denied*, 2000 U.S. LEXIS 4177 (2000).

31. 193 F.3d at p. 162.

32. *Corcoran v. United Healthcare, Inc.*, 965 F.2d 1321 (5th Cir. 1992).

33. See, e.g., *In re: U.S. Healthcare, Inc.*, 193 F.3d 151 (3d Cir. 1999), *cert. denied*, 2000 U.S. LEXIS 4177 (2000). *Dukes v. U.S. Healthcare, Inc.*, 57 F.3d 350 (3rd Cir. 1995) actually started the trend, but it accelerated after the *Travelers* case.

34. *Pappas v. Asbel*, 724 A.2d 889 (Pa. 1998). As noted below, the case was reviewed by the United States Supreme Court and remanded for reconsideration based on the U.S. Supreme Court's opinion in *Pegram v. Herdrich*, 530 U.S. 211 (2000). On remand, the Pennsylvania court essentially upheld its previous ruling [*Pappas v. Asbel*, 768 A.2d 1089 (Pa. 2001)].

35. 245 F.3d 266 (3rd Cir. 2000).

36. Mariner (2001), p. 261.

37. 18 U.S.C. §1961 et seq.

38. 516 U.S. 489, 515 (1996).

39. Some lower courts appear to be stretching the limits imposed by the Supreme Court (Stoecker, 1997). See *Fotta v. Trustees of United Mine Workers of Am. Health Retirement Fund* of 1974, 67 U.S.L.W. 1392 (3d Cir. December 18, 1998) (permitting recovery of interest for period of which benefit was improperly denied, even though not specifically authorized in ERISA); *Pickering v. USX Corp.*, Civ. Nos. 87-C-8387, 88-C-763J, and 91-C-636J, 1995 WL 584372, at °34 (D. Utah May 8, 1995) (stating

that relief lies in restitution and thus is equitable in nature where it "restore[s] the status quo and return(s) the amount rightfully belonging to another"); *Reid v. Gruntal & Co.*, 763 F. Supp. 672 (D. Me. 1991) (permitting recovery of consequential damages under ERISA §502(a)(3)); *Weems v. Jefferson-Pilot Life Ins. Co.*, 663 So. 2d 905, (Ala. 1995) (permitting extracontractual and punitive damages under ERISA), *cert. denied*, 516 U.S. 971 (1995). See also, *Russell v. Northrop Grumman Co.*, 921 F. Supp. 143, 152 (E.D.N.Y. 1996), noting that while restitution is generally awarded to prevent unjust enrichment to the defendant, this is not required in every case. Additionally, it is not necessary that restitution be made in kind, "for a court may restore the plaintiff to the position he formerly occupied 'either by the return of something which he formerly had or by the receipt of its equivalent in money.' "

40. See, e.g., *Bast v. Prudential Ins. Co. of Am.*, 150 F.3d 1003, 1011 (9th Cir. 1998) (refusing to impose a constructive trust to hold ill-gotten gains from a breach of fiduciary duty).

41. A good example of the backlash in how the technical legal rules are developed can be found in decisions arguing that the term "health plan" does not equate with an "ERISA plan." Instead, the ERISA plan is simply the promise to purchase insurance rather than everything that is contained in the insurance contract and provided by the health plan. This means that the ERISA plan is merely the contract and the MCO is not itself part of the plan. If this view were to take hold, preemption would be narrowed considerably. The Pegram case hints at this distinction, as does an opinion by the high court in New York State (*Nealy v. U.S. Healthcare HMO*, 99 N.Y. Int. 0035 (N.Y. 1999)). Such a reinterpretation would be the equivalent of changes in the subsidiary rules seen in the railroad and mass produced products examples. But courts could adopt this position and still hold that the MCO would "relate to" an ERISA plan. See also McClean and Richards (2001).

42. *Potvin v. Metropolitan Life Insurance Co.*, 997 P.2d 1153 (Cal. 2000).

43. *Potvin v. Metropolitan Life Insurance Company*, 997 P.2d 1153, 1160 (Cal. 2000). In contrast, the court in *Austin v. American Association of Neurological Surgeons,* 252 F.3d 967 (7th Cir. 2001) held that a neurosurgeon's suspension from the defendant professional association for irresponsible expert testimony did not constitute a sufficiently important economic interest.

44. *Clark v. West Shore Hospital*, 2001 U.S. App. LEXIS 17231 (6th Cir. 2001).

45. Blum (1996); See also, *Scheiner v. New York City Health and Hospitals Corporation,* 1999 U.S. Dist. LEXIS 15028 (S.D.N.Y. 1999).

46. *Harper v. Healthsource, Inc.*, 674 A.2d 962 (N.H. 1996).

47. *Rudolph v. Pennsylvania Blue Shield*, 717 A.2d 508 (Pa. 1998).

48. *Ince v. Healthsource Arkansas, Inc.*, 1997 WL 591117 (E.D.Ark.).

49. 154 F.3d 362 (7th Cir. 1998). See also 170 F.3d 683 (7th Cir. 1999) (Easterbrook dissenting).

50. *Pegram v. Herdrich*, 154 F.3d 362, 375–78 (7th Cir. 1998), rev'd 120 S.Ct. 2143 (2000).

51. 154 F.3d 362, 380–84 (7th Cir. 1998) (Flaum, dissenting).

52. 170 F.3d 683, 683–87 (7th Cir. 1999) (Easterbrook, dissenting from denial of rehearing *en banc*).

53. American Association of Health Plans, The Health Insurance Association of America, The Association of Private Pension and Welfare Plans, and the Chamber of Commerce of the United States, Brief of Amici Curiae in Support of Petitioners, 1999 WL 1054919, °4–8 (U.S. Amicus Brief, 1999).

54. 530 U.S. 211 (2000). In the Supreme Court, the name of the challenging party (i.e., the loser in the lower court) goes first.

55. Hammer (2001).

56. Health Maintenance Organization Act of 1973, 42 U.S. C. §300e et seq.

57. Ms. Herdrich's HMO tried to characterize the treating physician's cost management decisions as purely clinical judgments, distinct from the administration of plan benefits. The strategy was to preserve ERISA's shield against state tort liability for coverage denials while still evading ERISA as a means of attack. If it worked, the strategy would have put the decisions beyond the reach of ERISA lawsuits, leaving them susceptible (like all treatment decisions) only to state malpractice suits. At the same time, the strategy would have left untouched the lower courts' reigning view that lawsuits challenging hybrid clinical and coverage decisions by health plan officials remote from the bedside are preempted by ERISA because these decisions involve plan administration. What ensued was a double win for the industry.

58. Bloche (1999).

59. Tex. Ins. Code Ann. §20A.14(k) (West 2000); Tex. Ins. Code Ann. Art. 3-70-3c, sec. 7(d) (West 2000).

60. *Pappas v. Asbel*, 768 A.2d 1089 (Pa. 2001). The case, now known as *United States Systems of Pennsylvania Inc. v. Pennsylvania Hospital Insurance Co.*, has been appealed to the U.S. Supreme Court (U.S. No. 01–200, *petition for certiorari filed*, 1 August 2001).

61. *Corporate Health Insurance, Inc. v. Texas Dept. of Insurance*, 215 F.3d 526 (5th Cir. 2000).

62. Mariner (2000).

63. Contrast *Pappas v. Asbel*, 768 A.2d 1089 (Pa. 2001) with *Corporate Health Insurance. Inc. v. Texas Department of Insurance*, 215 F.3d 526 (5th Cir. 2000).

64. *Pegram v. Herdrich*, 530 U.S. 211, 227 n.8 (2000).

65. *Shea v. Esensten*, 107 F.3d 625, 628–29 (8th Cir.), *cert. denied*, 522 U.S. 914.

66. Calabresi (1985).

67. *Turner v. Fallon Community Health Plan, Inc.*, 127 F.3d 196, 200 (1st Cir. 1997); *Kuhl v. Lincoln Nat'l Health Plan, Inc.*, 999 F.2d 298, 304 (8th Cir. 1993); *Corcoran v. United HealthCare, Inc.*, 965 F.2d 1321, 1338–39 (5th Cir. 1992).

68. It is unlikely that the Earl Warren-led Supreme Court of the 1960s would have reacted the same way. For an elaboration of this point, see Jacobson and Selvin (2002).

8

Managed Care Litigation— Shaping Policy and Health-Care Delivery

WE have now explored the various judicial and legislative attempts to monitor managed care. At this point, we need to address what all of this activity means for physicians, patients, and policy makers. The purpose of this chapter is to try to make sense of the legal system's involvement in managed care and to place it within a broader policy context. Then we can examine a possible strategy to answer the question of where we should go from here. Before addressing that question, though, let us consider the significance of the trends to date.

When the contemporary managed care era began in the mid-1980s, the conventional wisdom was that the courts would undermine cost-containment initiatives. That has not happened. Whatever problems the managed care industry faces, the industry's fears about judicial intervention have largely been unfounded. Legal challenges to the managed care industry have proven more difficult to win than expected.

It is understandable that physicians and patients initially expected the courts to protect the physician–patient relationship from interference by managed care plans. After all, the essence of the health-care system lies with physicians' autonomy in medical decision-making, and courts had protected physician dominance (and hence the sanctity of the physician–patient relationship) in the past. But courts have not done so in the managed care era. To the extent that physicians have been able to secure some gains through the courts, it has largely been through fair process protections and retaining the often-maligned legal standard of care.

While the ultimate contours of the judicial and legislative responses to managed care have yet to be established, several themes with important public policy and health-care-delivery implications are already evident. By not interfering with managed care's financial incentives, the courts and Congress have allowed the dictates of the marketplace to define who controls the health care enterprise. The marketplace will also determine the scope of physician autonomy and whether the physician–patient relationship will remain central to health-care delivery. Another theme is that MCO liability has developed slowly. Most patient or physician challenges to MCO practices have failed. A third theme is the possible development of fair process standards that might be useful to patients and physicians in future litigation against MCOs.

Judicial reluctance to support challenges to managed care's programs has been essential to the successful implementation of cost-containment innovations. For those who support managed care's cost-containment objectives or believe that the courts should play only a limited role in forming social policy, the news from the courts is quite favorable. For those who advocate greater MCO accountability and yearn for the era when the judiciary was more engaged in forming social policy, the news is less welcome and not particularly reassuring.

Overall Litigation Trends

Even though judges have struggled with some aspects of managed care, the judicial decisions present a clear, overriding theme: courts are facilitating the market-based arrangements that drive managed care. In most aspects of health-care litigation, courts treat the health-care field as they would any other industry. What this amounts to is deference to prevailing market principles in health-care delivery, as courts have shown no inclination to reflexively overturn market decisions. The clearest evidence is in courts' increasing acceptance of contractual arrangements, in physicians' litigation against MCOs, and in antitrust cases where courts are not protecting MCOs from competitive forces in the health care market.

Within the history of the law–medicine relationship, the fact that the courts are supporting managed care as the market winner is ironic. For years, observers complained that the law actually supported physicians' dominance over the health-care delivery system by deferring to doctors in developing standards of care for medical malpractice cases.[1] Now the courts are supporting the managed care industry's dominance over physicians. To the extent that the common law protects market arrangements, the results are entirely consistent. When physicians were dominant, they were supported by the legal system. As control shifted to managed care, so did the courts—in a variety of areas.

The first and most important way the courts have facilitated the scope of market principles in health care is by relying on contractual arrangements to determine the extent of the parties' obligations and responsibilities. Judges have shown considerably more deference to contracts in recent years than previously.[2] During the 1960s and 1970s, courts often decided not to enforce a contract if it resulted from unequal bargaining power or if its terms were too one-sided (unconscionable) or ambiguous. That happens much less frequently now. In a range of health-care cases, including most decisions regarding physicians' staff privileges and many patients' contractual challenges to benefit denials, contract language is being more strictly interpreted. At one time, courts found ambiguity in the contract to justify requiring a health plan to provide treatment. More and more, judges are rejecting claims of ambiguity in favor of upholding the terms of the agreement.

For example, judges are increasingly supporting contractual limits on benefits instead of compelling treatment, which is a very favorable development for MCOs. MCO cost-containment programs could be vulnerable when patients sue to compel contractual coverage of certain high cost or experimental treatments. A typical case might involve denial of high dose chemotherapy with autologous bone marrow transplant as an experimental medical intervention. Although one study found that courts ordered treatment in 57 percent of the coverage cases reviewed,[3] the sample included few managed care cases. Consistent with what we have seen, the authors also found that courts compelled treatment at a significantly lower rate in cases brought under ERISA. Nothing in more recent ERISA cases suggests that MCOs will be compelled to provide similar benefits; ERISA preemption will block most challenges to MCOs' coverage decisions. More to the point, courts in subsequent non-ERISA cases have been less likely to rule in favor of patients, deferring instead to contractual arrangements limiting coverage.[4]

A good example of the deference to contract, admittedly somewhat tangential to managed care litigation, is *Baptist Memorial Hospital System v. Sampson.*[5] In this case, the Texas Supreme Court confronted the issue of a hospital's liability for the negligence of an emergency department (ED) physician. Rhea Sampson was bitten by a spider and sought treatment at the defendant's emergency department. After twice having the problem diagnosed and treated as an allergic reaction, her condition deteriorated and she was properly diagnosed and treated at another hospital. Sampson continued to suffer from recurrent pain, and sued Baptist Memorial for negligence. Before being treated, Sampson signed a consent form acknowledging that each physician in the emergency department was an independent contractor. Also, signs were posted indicating that the ED physicians were independent contractors. Based on the signs and the consent form, the court rejected Sampson's claim that the hospital should be liable for the treating physician's negligence. Here, contract trumped the tort claim.

The trend toward contract rules is neither unlimited nor uniform, but it represents a potentially significant departure from the cases in the fee-for-service era where courts showed greater willingness to scrutinize and overturn contracts based on contractual ambiguity. This does not necessarily indicate a trend to supplant tort law with contract law in managed care liability litigation. It simply means that MCOs will be able to use the contract as a defense to physician or patient challenges to certain activities, especially denying health care benefits based on contractual limitations. At this point, though, it is too early to detect which way courts will go. Despite the urgings of scholars who want the courts to use contract law to determine all aspects of health care, only one case has even alluded to the possibility of using contract law to determine liability.[6]

In another area dominated by contractual interpretations—staff privileges determinations—courts have given MCOs wide authority to operate. MCOs have argued that an important aspect of controlling health care costs is limiting the number of physicians who are eligible to participate in the plan and in applying economic criteria to staff selection and retention decisions. For the most part, courts have upheld the use of economic credentialing and the use of selective contracting (where an MCO contracts with one medical group to provide all of its specialty care, such as cardiology).[7] An MCO's decision to contract with one group and not another, based solely on economic factors, has not been successfully challenged. Generally, courts do not factor into their decisions the potential disruption to long-term physician–patient relationships, meaning that both physician and patient autonomy yield to cost-containment goals.

A fairly typical case is *Bartley v. Eastern Maine Medical Center*,[8] where the court ruled that doctors could not successfully challenge an exclusive contract to provide emergency department services even though the physicians had been providing the services for the previous ten years. A less typical but potentially more significant case is *Maltz v. Aetna Health Plans of New York*.[9] The court upheld an MCO's change in network physicians based solely on a cost-containment rationale. In this instance, the court explicitly favored cost-containment considerations over the continuity of the physician–patient relationship.

An area that will help define how far courts will go in deferring to contract rules is the interpretation of arbitration clauses in managed care contracts. These clauses require that grievances against the plan be handled through arbitration rather than through litigation, and could be applied to prospective and retrospective denials, medical liability claims, and coverage disputes. Arbitration clauses are potentially significant limitations to litigation challenging benefit denials. Two California cases interpreting Kaiser-Permanente's arbitration provisions demonstrate both the willingness of courts to uphold contractual arrangements and some of the limits courts might set when they interpret contracts.

In *Toledo v. Kaiser Permanente Medical Group*,[10] the court upheld Kaiser's arbitration provision against a challenge claiming that Kaiser did not adequately inform the plaintiff of the provision. Relying on the plaintiff's signature just below what the court termed a "clear and conspicuous" arbitration clause, the court rejected the challenge. In *Engalla v. The Permanente Medical Group, Inc.*,[11] the California Supreme Court refused to rule that the arbitration clause violated public policy (as inherently one-sided, or as an unconscionable agreement). But the court allowed the plaintiff to avoid arbitration in this case because Kaiser's manipulation of the process prevented the arbitration from taking place in a timely manner. *Engalla* is an important case that will probably be followed by other state courts. If so, it indicates that state courts will be reluctant to overturn contractual provisions while closely scrutinizing how arbitration clauses are implemented to avoid unfairness or overreaching by MCOs. The arbitration clause must be unmistakable and clear in describing what other rights might be waived.[12]

Antitrust law (restraint of trade) is the third area where courts have facilitated market arrangements in health care. Starting with *Arizona v. Maricopa County Medical Society*,[13] the courts opened the way to the new organizational arrangements and to a more competitive marketplace by ruling that health care is not immune to antitrust considerations. The established antitrust doctrine, supported by specific federal antitrust guidelines, has worked well when applied to health care,[14] and has been an important contributor to the expansion of managed care. In general, courts have applied traditional antitrust principles to health care markets, helping stimulate the movement toward more efficient organizational forms.

Physicians have tried unsuccessfully to use antitrust law to challenge staff privilege denials or exclusive contracts. Neither claim has garnered much support from judges. The antitrust claim is that an exclusive contract amounts to a group boycott between the hospital and the selected group against physicians who are not part of the group. (A group boycott is an agreement between two or more parties to refuse to deal with a competing firm). Courts have been no more receptive to this argument than to using antitrust to overturn staff privileges decisions.

Interestingly, most courts have also rejected MCOs' claims for protection under the antitrust laws. A dramatic increase in the number of hospital mergers has been one of the characteristics of the new health care order. As hospital bed occupancy has declined and as pressure from MCOs to reduce costs has intensified, hospitals have entertained merger opportunities for leverage in negotiating contracts with MCOs. The antitrust issue to be decided is whether the merged facility would accrue too much market power so that it could raise prices. If patients then have no health care alternative (substitute) within a reasonable geographic area, competition would be reduced and patients would be compelled to pay higher prices.

For the most part, the courts have been reluctant to interfere with the merger process and other market-based changes, viewing them as pro-competitive. Merger decisions have focused on systems integration and economic efficiencies to determine whether an activity violates the antitrust laws. In several high-profile antitrust cases where the Department of Justice and the Federal Trade Commission have opposed mergers, courts have permitted them to proceed.[15] While some of the specifics have been controversial, such as permitting a 73-mile primary care geographic area in one case,[16] courts have generally demonstrated that they understand the underlying market changes and have adapted traditional antitrust doctrine to those changes.

In two important cases[17], the courts have ruled that MCOs do not constitute a separate health care market for antitrust analysis. For all practical purposes, these cases have ended the debate over MCOs competing in a managed care market. Because doctors have other market alternatives for selling their services to insurers and MCOs, managed care is treated as another market competitor under the antitrust laws. If the courts had ruled that managed care constitutes a separate market, the judges would have provided broad immunity from competition with non-MCO health-care entities. By ruling that all providers compete in the marketplace for patients, the courts are not protecting any particular type of health care organizational form against competitive pressures in the health-care market. In this area, at least, MCOs have not benefited from judicial immunity. At the same time, the cases are entirely consistent with the general trend of deferring to the marketplace. Antitrust enforcement has contributed to the erosion of physician dominance, even if it has not resulted in the competitive health care system proponents had hoped to see.[18]

A second theme evident from the litigation is the slow development of MCO liability. Neither physicians nor patients have been successful in directly contesting managed care practices. Patients and physicians have brought a wide range of challenges to managed care's cost-containment programs, most of which have been unsuccessful. As we have seen, patients have sued MCOs, alleging negligence for injuries resulting from delayed or denied care or from the improper operation of financial incentives to limit care. Primarily because of ERISA, these challenges have usually been futile. Even outside of ERISA, plaintiffs have not won a majority of cases.

Several federal courts have specifically deflected to Congress allegations that managed care incentives violate public policy, and the Supreme Court made it very clear in the *Pegram* decision that similar challenges under ERISA will be rejected. If given the opportunity, state courts may be more willing than federal courts to hold MCOs accountable for their improperly implemented cost-control decisions, especially when the incentives for undertreating patients are excessive. Having the opportunity depends largely on the erosion of ERISA preemption. Still, it seems equally unlikely for state courts to rule that financial incentives to control costs are automatically illegal or inherently unethical.

Physicians have not fared much better in challenging MCO practices. Except for some inroads on fair procedures, courts have been unsympathetic to physicians' arguments. Where physicians have been primarily put at a disadvantage is in liability challenges to MCO practices. Largely because of ERISA, patient challenges in state courts to delayed or denied care have often been preempted, leaving the treating physician exposed to liability without being able to "share" responsibility with the MCO. Also, courts have upheld the use of utilization review for controlling costs, especially under ERISA, regardless of the treating physician's recommendation. In limited circumstances, physicians have incidentally benefited from patients' lawsuits. In non-ERISA disputes over benefit coverage denials, courts have occasionally deferred to the treating physician in ruling for patients, though patients still lose many of these challenges.

In cases not controlled by ERISA, courts are slowly applying traditional medical liability concepts to the new organizational forms, including HMOs, IPAs, and PPOs, despite variation in the state cases decided to date. Depending on the actual amount of control MCOs have over the practice of medicine, courts are willing to impose liability for inappropriate clinical decisions. After an initial period of focusing on the MCO's insurance role, courts increasingly view MCO actions as involving the practice of medicine.

Victories over MCOs outside of ERISA are hardly guaranteed, however. This is why the erosion of ERISA preemption is so important. If MCOs must face potential liability litigation in state courts, both physicians and patients will be able to exercise greater power over how cost containment is implemented. As their liability expands, MCOs may begin to reconsider the ways that clinical decisions are reviewed. For example, some observers argue that the threat of liability may induce changes in MCO behavior, including taking more safety precautions to enhance quality of care and changing physician incentives.[19] Or, when confronted with liability, MCOs could back away from influencing medical decisions altogether, at the risk of increasing their costs.

Physicians have made some inroads against MCO practices in a narrow but potentially significant area—due process. One of the mechanisms judges use to monitor economic and social arrangements is ensuring that procedures are fair and fairly administered. In a long line of public benefit cases, the Supreme Court has determined that benefits, once granted, cannot be removed unless the government sets forth and follows procedures that provide the beneficiary with a fair hearing to contest a benefit denial. In theory, due process is a constitutional requirement that will not be imposed absent some sort of governmental involvement. An inchoate theme in health care litigation and regulation is to mandate fair procedures before certain actions are taken regardless of governmental involvement. Fair procedures include, at a minimum, the right to be notified before an adverse action is taken, the right to a hearing to determine whether the action is proper, and the right to present and examine any witnesses called.

What is not clear at this point is whether and how these requirements will protect physicians from the loss of network participation or staff privileges. Nor is it clear whether other state courts will follow the lead of the few state courts mandating due process protections. In fact, the trend appears to have stalled for the time being. At best, these cases should be viewed as an exception to the trend toward strict contract interpretation.

Taken on their own terms, this line of cases stands for the proposition that procedural protections are required when private organizations control important economic interests. Several courts, most persuasively in the *Potvin v. Metropolitan Life Insurance Company* case, have held that managed care constitutes precisely such an important economic interest. In this area, at least, courts have allowed physicians to challenge certain aspects of managed care practices. While not framed in the context of the physician–patient relationship, assuring that physicians do not arbitrarily lose valuable hospital staff privileges certainly facilitates the continuity of the physician–patient relationship.

Where fair-procedure protections are required, physicians will have added leverage to challenge arbitrary terminations. Courts imposing fair process requirements have done so based on an explicit public policy rationale, and they are likely to insist on proper procedural mechanisms to protect individual patients.[20] The unresolved issue is whether courts will eventually defer to procedures established by MCOs,[21] or whether judges will essentially impose stringent procedural requirements that limit how cost-containment programs will be operated.[22] Courts may well seek a middle ground, though such a compromise position has yet to be articulated.

Another area involving fair procedures of great interest to physicians and patients is the ability to challenge an MCO's treatment decision by appealing via an external grievance process. States have been aggressive in mandating grievance processes permitting a patient to challenge a denial of care. Most require the MCO to obtain expert opinions from physicians (usually three) who are not part of the plan. In some instances, plans have provided the care even if only one of the three external reviewers determined that the treatment should be provided. Judicial opinions in ERISA challenges to state-mandated external grievance processes are split. One Circuit Court of Appeals ruled that they are preempted by ERISA, while another upheld them.[23] The Supreme Court has agreed to resolve the split.

Congress has not mandated an external grievance process, but many states have done so. Also, the Department of Labor (DOL) has issued regulations under ERISA that begin to address the absence of fair procedures in managed care decision-making. By requiring an independent evaluation, these states and DOL indicate the need for patient protection through fair process requirements when health care is denied.

Future expansions of fair process rules could focus on continuity of care and could well be expanded to protect patients from arbitrary health care denials. The managed care industry has generally opposed external grievance procedures, though an increasing number of plans have voluntarily implemented them. It is too soon to determine how these voluntary arrangements will operate.

Explanations

With these trends in mind, it is useful to explore the factors that might account for them. What explains the trends, especially those that were unanticipated? Obviously, ERISA preemption tops the list, with the judicial shift to stricter contractual interpretations a close second. But there are additional (and less obvious) explanations that play a role.

One explanation for the slow development of MCO liability is that courts struggled at first to understand the changes in health care delivery. As with all new areas that courts must confront, there is an inevitable learning curve at work. At first, judges are unfamiliar with the terms and concepts of the new area. Combined with the need to apply legal doctrine developed for different types of social and economic arrangements, the unfamiliarity leads to early decisions that seem unsophisticated. When courts become more conversant with the new terminology and concepts, subsequent decisions are more refined and reflective.

The evolution of judicial thinking in both Pennsylvania and Illinois (described in Chapter 6) provides a nice illustration. In both states, early decisions largely discounted an MCO's role in the clinical decision and refused to permit liability lawsuits to go forward. At that point, the judges were not comfortable with the language and arrangements of the new industry. As their exposure to the managed-care environment grew, these courts became knowledgeable about how managed care operates and much more sophisticated in their rulings. To their credit, these state courts were willing to reconsider their initial rulings in subsequent cases, allowing liability challenges to proceed. What changed in the interim few years seems clear: judges determined that when MCOs perform similar functions as hospitals, they should be held similarly accountable. As the court noted in *Jones v. Chicago HMO Ltd. Of Illinois,* "because HMOs undertake an expansive role in arranging for and providing health care services to their members, they have corresponding corporate responsibilities as well."[24]

Judicial understanding, as demonstrated through written opinions, depends on whether the type of case is an extension of the world that already exists or presents a new experience altogether. Where the changing health care environment still fits within an established framework of legal rules, the courts have adapted fairly easily. Antitrust law is a good example. Managed care presents few new antitrust challenges that cannot be decided by applying established law. Determining how managed care operates within a competitive environment involves the application of customary legal principles rather than the need for new rules.

In contrast, where courts are confronted with an entirely new set of issues and circumstances, judges have not adapted as smoothly. When courts struggle to understand the new dynamic, they experience difficulty either in using existing legal rules or in establishing new ones. At the outset, not surprisingly, courts varied widely in how well they comprehended the shift to managed care. The initial cases ignored the complex reality of how managed care operates in favor of the industry's attempts to characterize managed care organizations as merely health insurers. Utilization review (UR) cases represent a clear example. Once again, the problem has been how to characterize UR's combined functions—as a benefit determination and as a review of medical treatment recommendations.

Early on, judges often viewed MCOs as mere financers of health care rather than understanding the MCOs' mixed health care delivery and insurance functions. The resulting confusion allowed MCOs to distance themselves somewhat from the full consequences of their actions as providers.

That has changed. For example, subsequent UR and other cases have either questioned or rejected the MCOs' arguments for strictly separating clinical and financial functions, ruling instead that MCOs in fact make medical decisions. The shifting understanding of how MCOs function may lead to closer judicial scrutiny of the MCOs' role in clinical decision-making, and hence greater difficulty in avoiding liability. None of this necessarily means that MCOs will automatically lose as judges become more knowledgeable. It merely implies that the industry's operations will be more closely scrutinized over time.

The early struggle to understand the new organizational entities resulted in decisions exalting the *form* of the transaction instead of viewing *functional* or *operational* relationships. Focusing on the form of the transaction (initially, how the activity was characterized by the MCO) is easier than trying to understand its operational nuances. If the court looks to form, MCOs will almost always win because form ignores the combined insurance and health care delivery functions, and the MCO controls how the form is defined. Failing to consider the hybrid functional relationships, where MCOs are more vulnerable, has been tantamount to immunity from liability. In the ERISA context, for instance, courts have generally looked to the form of the transaction to define UR narrowly as a benefit determination, even where the administrative decision is incidental to reviewing a physician's clinical recommendation.

The judiciary's initial focus on form over function allowed a deft managed care industry to have it both ways—insurers only in one type of case, but insurers and health care providers in another. For purposes of defending liability litigation, MCOs argue that they are insurers only and have nothing to do with clinical intervention. For purposes of ERISA preemption, especially regarding UR functions, MCOs argue that their actions involve the review of clinical recommendations as benefit determinations, which means that they are not strictly insurers. The reason is that if they act as insurers they are covered by ERISA's savings clause, making MCOs subject to state insurance regulation. This is a neat (though cynical) balancing act that MCOs have pulled off brilliantly.

Another explanatory factor that is often overlooked in commenting about the courts is the reality of the judiciary's own institutional interests. While courts are neutral arbiters of the litigation, judges are also aware that the judiciary as an institution of government has certain interests that must be taken into account, including caseload management, political considerations, and theories of judges' responsibilities. Any effort to use or rely on the courts to challenge managed care's shortcomings must confront and overcome the stark reality that the courts' own institutional considerations impose substantial impediments.[25]

For our purposes, the *Pegram* opinion accurately illustrates the difficulty of using the courts to redress the perceived unfairness of managed care's operations. As a philosophical matter, the Court based its unanimous opinion on the doctrine of the separation of powers. On a more practical level, the Court cited institutional considerations beyond separation of powers for rejecting Herdrich's challenge. The opinion does not fully detail the Court's institutional concerns, but the language used indicates the Court's underlying concern for avoiding policy debates.

The federal courts are like any other agency petitioning Congress for funds,[26] but judicial resources do not necessarily grow in tandem with increasing caseloads. Judges have repeatedly expressed concerns about court congestion resulting from increased litigation and the costs to the judicial system.[27] To avoid these problems, judges approve plea bargains in criminal cases and sealed settlements in civil litigation, even when the public is not informed of serious public safety hazards.[28] As a result, Supreme Court justices must take into account the volume of litigation likely to surge if the Court were to retain an institutional oversight role in the operation of managed care's financial incentives. For example, the Court noted that if it were to permit Herdrich to challenge how the financial incentives operate, it would open the courts to endless litigation in trying to fine-tune market mechanisms.

To the Court's credit, it was quite explicit in the *Pegram* decision about some of these practical concerns, especially the potential explosion of litigation. What is troublesome about the opinion for those concerned with how managed care operates is that the Court went further than necessary to resolve the *Pegram* case. The Court easily could (and should) have retained an institutional oversight role to ensure that financial incentives operate fairly. But it will be difficult, if not insurmountable, to convince the judiciary that its overreliance on institutional reasons to justify abjuring an oversight role leaves patients vulnerable and inequities festering.

A closely related concern is that judges are very protective of the courts' institutional legitimacy. Far more than the other branches of government, the judiciary relies on its legitimacy to secure public compliance with judicial decisions. Aside from its political and social legitimacy, the courts have very little ability to enforce their decisions. As Andrew Jackson said after a Supreme Court decision that he did not like, "John Marshall has made his opinion, now let him enforce it."[29] When Chief Justice Earl Warren was assembling his unanimous opinion in *Brown v. Board of Education*, he had to confront two aspects of the legitimacy issue.[30] On one hand, he had to deal with recalcitrant colleagues who felt that the decision to integrate the schools should be made by Congress and that the Court's constitutional mandate would be publicly viewed as illegitimate (at least in the South). On the other hand, to gain legitimacy, Warren needed unanimity. In the end, he got both—a unanimous decision that sparked repeated calls to "impeach Earl Warren."

Under Chief Justice William Rehnquist's leadership, the current Supreme Court has articulated strong views about the separation of powers that run directly counter to Warren-era tendencies. The separation of powers doctrine constitutes a powerful restraint on the Court's willingness to use its powers to "legislate" from the bench. The guiding philosophy now is in part a response to "the institutional stresses brought on by the [Warren] era's most expansive ... decisions."[31] An instructive quote from the *Pegram* opinion demonstrates the separation of powers concerns that now motivate judicial thinking:

> ... any legal principle purporting to draw a line between good and bad HMOs would embody, in effect, a judgment about socially acceptable medical risk. A valid conclusion of this sort would, however, necessarily turn on facts to which courts would probably not have ready access. . . . But such complicated fact finding and such a debatable social judgment are not wisely required of courts unless for some reason resort cannot be had to the legislative process, with its preferable forum for comprehensive investigations and judgments of social value, such as optimum treatment levels and health care expenditure. . . . The very difficulty of these policy considerations, and Congress' superior institutional competence to pursue this debate, suggest that legislative not judicial solutions are preferable.

The Supreme Court has not always refrained from being involved in social policy. For a relatively brief period in the 1960s, it seemed as though litigation was the answer to society's most pressing and intractable social policy dilemmas. All it took to remedy racial discrimination was to issue a Supreme Court opinion declaring an odious practice—such as the refusal to serve blacks in a restaurant—unconstitutional, and justice would prevail. The judiciary eagerly accepted the challenges of economic and social unfairness. Invited by a welcoming Supreme Court under Chief Justice Earl Warren, liberals used litigation to achieve social goals when a more conservative establishment blocked other policy solutions, particularly legislative.

Whatever one may think of the Warren Court's constitutional doctrines, we now inhabit a fundamentally different legal universe than the one Warren and his supporters created. Social policy questions that the Warren Court aggressively attacked are now equally aggressively avoided. Quite the opposite approach is now the norm, as a much more conservative judicial philosophy has taken hold. One of the principal interpretive tenets or norms repeatedly stated by the current Supreme Court is that social policy should be made by the elected representatives, not by the courts. The separation-of-powers doctrine was much less important to the Warren Court, which was willing to push the bounds of legislative interpretation.[32]

Courts, it seems fair to say, take into account their own interests when making decisions. Judges function as an integral part of the American political system and are hardly immune from political and social influences and trends. In may ways, therefore, it is understandable why courts might not want to be at the forefront of instituting changes in how managed care operates.

Implications for Physicians and Patients

As a general rule, the courts have not treated health-care cases differently than they would in deciding any other legal challenge to a product or service. Regardless of expectations that courts might take into account the mortality and morbidity implications at the heart of health-care litigation, courts have refrained from developing legal doctrine that views health care as "exceptional." To be sure, courts do not uniformly view health care as just like any other commercial transaction. In bioethics disputes, especially those involving end-of-life care, there is a good deal of health care "exceptionalism." And in cases contesting benefit denials where the situation is life-threatening, courts may abandon strict contractual terms in favor of saving the patient's life. Even so, the evidence is striking that the vast majority of cases make no significant distinctions between health care and other industries.

In view of this general tendency, it is not surprising that one of the most important implications of the trends in managed care litigation is that the courts no longer treat the physician–patient relationship as sacrosanct. The courts' unwillingness to reject utilization review on public policy grounds accepts limitations on physician autonomy. Judicial interpretations ERISA also tend to diminish physician autonomy and favor managed care's cost-containment goals over the individual patient's needs. Perceiving themselves bound by ERISA, courts do not champion either physician autonomy or the patient–physician relationship. State legislatures have responded by enacting laws protecting physician autonomy, but these initiatives are often barred by ERISA preemption. Thus, Congress appears to be physicians' and patients' best hope for change or relief.

Even if courts defer to physicians on malpractice standards, the fact that judges have upheld economic credentialing, staff selection and retention restrictions, and utilization review decisions suggests that physicians will not retain their prior dominance over the allocation of health-care resources. The implication of the litigated cases is that the courts' traditional deference to the treating physician is not likely to be sustained.[33] Implicitly, the litigation trends reinforce the status quo of the health-care delivery market, and hence managed care's current market domination, including its ability to limit physician autonomy.

Physicians, who have long resented medical liability doctrine, may now attempt to hold onto it as the best mechanism for bolstering their autonomy in health-care delivery. Ironically, perhaps the strongest protection against loss of physician autonomy (at least where state courts have established MCO liability) may be the very same legal standard of care that has been so troublesome for physicians in the past. Physicians can argue that meeting the legal standard of care requires certain treatment recommendations that MCOs would otherwise prefer to deny.

What has changed over the past decade or so to cause the courts' shift from protecting physicians dominance to reinforcing managed care's dominance? At this point, the answer is somewhat speculative because of the limited number of cases. One possible explanation is that courts are simply responding to the expansion of managed care. As the nature of health care has changed, especially the prominence of cost-containment goals, it is perhaps not surprising that courts have begun to incorporate those goals in resolving managed care litigation.[34] The integration of cost containment as a factor in judicial decisions is an extension of how the common law adapts to changing social and economic arrangements.

At the heart of the cost-containment issue for courts is how to balance the needs of individual patients with legitimate concerns about how to contain costs. Both law and ethics are moving from individual physician–patient issues to issues of how to allocate medical resources for existing and potential patients. In 1987, one observer wrote that:

> [t]he obligation to put the patient's interest first, even above the physician's, is at the center of the physician–patient relationship. It is the ethical principle that separates the professions from the trade and commercial relationships. This principle applies to more than just avoidance of financial self-interest.[35]

Just ten years later, another commentator argued strongly that changes in health-care delivery and health law have altered these ethical precepts.[36] In defining the terms of this change, judges, legislators, managed care administrators, and ethicists are largely setting the ground rules, not physicians.

Reflecting both the ethical shift and the rationale for managed care, a striking fact about managed care litigation trends is that the patient seems to be the forgotten soldier. In case after case, the unspoken and ignored party is the patient. Even in due process cases, the courts talk about physicians and plan administrators or hospitals, but rarely about the physician–patient relationship. Some of that, no doubt, reflects the nature of the legal argument attorneys may be compelled to make under current law. More likely, much of it reflects the peripheral position patients occupy in managed care. The result is that the tension between managed care decisions favoring patient populations at the expense of individual access to services is being implicitly resolved in favor of patient populations. The trend seems to be against individual patients.

A good example is *Pegram v. Herdrich*, where the Supreme Court discussed at length the potential for financial incentives to interfere with a physician's clinical judgment and the proper role of the courts as distinct from the legislative branch in setting health policy. The Court explicitly accepted the need for rationing in health care, where the needs of the individual patient are secondary to the resources available for the broader patient population. Yet the Court never mentioned any concern for the physician–patient relationship. By ignoring an important aspect of the litigation, the courts are by default pushing the physician–patient relationship to the periphery, just as managed care organizations have done.

Consider, also, the case of *Doe v. SEPTA*.[37] During a routine check of pharmaceutical expenditures, the defendant's utilization review firm discovered that the plaintiff was HIV positive and disclosed this fact to the employer. Claiming an invasion of privacy, Doe then sued for damages. In defense, SEPTA maintained that the disclosure was unfortunate, but incidental to legitimate cost-containment activity. The court ruled in defendant's favor on two grounds. After setting forth several criteria for balancing between the individual's privacy rights and public policy favoring cost-containment, the court determined that the need for cost controls justified and outweighed the invasion of privacy. For support, the court noted that the invasion of privacy was minimal, and the plaintiff suffered no harm and was promoted after the incident. Aside from the questionable finding that the plaintiff suffered no harm, what is instructive is that the court was willing to insulate cost-containment even against a strong invasion of privacy claim.

As reflected in their opinions, judges are now well acquainted with the tradeoffs between access to health care and cost containment and seem quite willing to rely on policy considerations in reaching their decisions. MCOs win most benefit denial cases (the percentage is higher under ERISA) and when cost containment is given great weight in the judicial decision.[38] Conversely, plaintiffs are more successful when courts rely on claims of fairness (i.e., access), especially outside of ERISA.

One of the subtexts to managed care litigation is who can best frame the cost versus access tradeoff. Unfortunately, the factors that contribute to successful framing of the issues are not clear. What motivates a particular judge to give great weight to economic efficiency as opposed to fairness considerations? We do not know, for instance, whether attorneys presented the policy conflicts clearly in their arguments, or whether judges on their own decided to consider the policy choices in reaching a decision. That said, it is quite possible that judges are simply using policy considerations to justify results reached on other grounds.

Regardless of why the litigation trends have occurred, the import is that MCOs are largely insulated from liability for delayed or denied care. The obvious question, then, is what to do about the absence of MCO accountability. Deep philosophical differences between congressional Democrats and Republicans

render a legislative solution elusive. If one agrees that protecting the physician–patient relationship is a desirable social policy goal, it will be incumbent
on the courts to develop liability standards that impose accountability for managed care's involvement in clinical decisions.

There is no reason why MCOs should be legally absolved from the adverse
consequences of their economic decisions. If MCOs should be liable for cost-
containment programs, it follows that they should be permitted to argue that
the proper negligence standard should incorporate cost-based decisions.[39] In
essence, juries should be able to decide whether the MCO has appropriately
balanced the benefits of preserving assets for the patient population against
the harm incurred by the individual patient, as in any other industry. The
question is what standard should MCOs be held to in implementing cost-
containment programs. In considering the standard of care for MCOs, courts
could adopt one of several possibilities.[40]

First, the liability standard for MCOs could be based on customary practices
in similar organizations.[41] An argument favoring this standard is that it would
not be desirable to hold MCOs to customary standards of the fee-for-service
system when MCOs were organized on a different model. Doing so could
undermine their cost-control strategies. When the concept of the customary
MCO standard was introduced, it really applied only to HMOs. With the
expansion of the myriad organizational forms constituting the current managed
care environment, it might be a more difficult concept to apply. Still, the core
idea that the standard of care for MCOs would adjust for cost-containment
strategies remains attractive and is consistent with arguments encouraging the
industry to incorporate cost constraints into clinical decisions.

Second, the standard could be based on whether the plan made a reasonable attempt at applying cost-effectiveness analysis (CEA) in determining
which services to provide. In CEA, if the cost of health services exceeds the
net benefits, based on reasonable data and analyses, the care would not be
provided. Judicial review would be similar to the standard seen in government
regulation cases where courts defer to the regulatory agency when the agency
presents adequate documentation and justification in the record. By analogy,
courts would accept that MCOs make cost–quality–access tradeoffs and would
intervene only if the CEA were conducted in an arbitrary and capricious manner. In this sense, the courts' primary role would be to ensure that fair processes were followed. As we will see in Chapter 10, the use of CEA could
play an important role in implementing the fiduciary-duty framework. To date,
however, MCOs have not used an explicit cost-effectiveness rationale in making benefit-coverage decisions.

Third, courts could reverse their deference to professional custom and resolve liability questions under traditional negligence standards, which would
place cost–benefit tradeoffs at the core of the judicial inquiry. An advantage

is that MCOs could explicitly invoke cost-effectiveness and other cost-containment efforts as a defense. A disadvantage is that the court may second-guess the appropriateness of the methods and impose a higher standard of care.[42] Unquestionably, the potential for liability limits the extent of cost containment. By imposing general negligence standards, the courts would not be impeding cost-containment initiatives, but would be requiring plans to weigh the costs and benefits of implementing cost controls, given potential adverse medical outcomes. The courts would simply be playing their traditional role in setting limits and in monitoring private economic relations.

Fourth, courts might revert to the physician-dominated standard of care seen under fee-for-service litigation. Under fee-for-service, the physician's duties are to treat the individual patient and to increase the probability of a good outcome without worrying about resource constraints. In this approach, many cost-containment initiatives would constitute below-standard care unless they became part of customary medical practice.

A fifth possibility is that courts could abandon tort altogether in favor of contract, which is the preferred solution for many legal scholars and economists. To be viable, the contract would need to clearly specify procedures for using cost-effectiveness analysis and other cost-containment mechanisms, how they will be implemented, and how patients will be informed about their use. Absent more explicit contractual arrangements between plans and employers, courts are unlikely to shift to contract on their own. If, over time, plans and subscribers bargained for lower-cost plans with lower benefit levels based on explicit cost-effectiveness criteria or other cost-containment strategies, a contractual approach could be more feasible. Courts would then be compelled to address the use of cost-effectiveness from a contractual, as opposed to a tort, perspective.

Sixth, courts could develop a standard based on fiduciary duties. As will be developed in Part III, this standard would force the courts to develop criteria for balancing between individual patient needs and preserving resources for the patient population. Although the Supreme Court has for now foreclosed fiduciary challenges under ERISA in *Pegram v. Herdrich*, nothing prevents state courts from developing a common law of fiduciary duty in managed care litigation that survives an ERISA preemption challenge. Also, lower federal courts may well try to narrow the Supreme Court's interpretation even in cases raised under ERISA.

For the time being, ERISA preemption may limit state court experimentation with different standards of care. To the extent that state courts hear more managed care cases, it seems likely that variation across states among the above options will emerge. Judges will look to legal scholars and health policy analysts and researchers for guidance on the health-care policy and delivery implications of each standard.

Public Policy Considerations

Managed care litigation trends have important ramifications for a number of health policy and health-care delivery considerations. In view of the courts' explicit deference to the legislative branch of government to determine how policy in managed care should be set, the cases have implications for legislators and regulators. Public dissatisfaction will need to be remedied by the legislatures; the courts do not seem inclined to interfere with the marketplace. Physicians, too, will need legislative support to preserve their autonomy.

The unexpected consequences of ERISA preemption have generated a broad policy debate about how to regulate managed care. Though sometimes unstated, the crux of the debate is whether to rely on governmental regulation or depend on a market-based self-regulatory approach. Should state regulation be the model for managed care or should regulation be entrusted to the private sector, with entities like the National Commission on Quality Assurance (NCQA) and the Joint Commission on Accreditation of Healthcare Organizations (JCAHO) playing a dominant role? Either way, the central health policy concern remains how to limit the high cost of health care without unduly restricting individuals' access to needed services.

The most pressing and controversial congressional legislative debate has thus been over whether to amend ERISA to permit patients to sue MCOs for delayed or denied care, and to allow greater state regulation over MCOs. If enacted, the legislation would help restore the primacy of the physician-patient relationship. Several issues are in dispute: control over physicians' clinical decisions; a patient's ability to challenge improperly operated cost-containment programs; and generally how managed care should be regulated (if at all). As we have seen, physicians are caught between patient demands for more care and health plan demands to contain health-care spending. For now, ERISA tilts this precarious balancing act heavily toward containing costs for a health plan's patient population at the expense of health-care services for an individual patient. Reforming ERISA would alter that balance and at least give the individual patient an opportunity to prove his or her case.

At several points during the past three years, Congress seemed close to enacting a compromise, only to see it collapse every time. The reason why amending ERISA has proved elusive is that powerful interests oppose any changes. Both the managed care industry and large employers, two politically powerful and savvy interest groups, have adamantly opposed patients' rights legislation, preferring a market-based approach. They argue that amending ERISA would undermine a large employer's ability to offer one standard national plan for all employees and force small businesses to avoid offering health insurance to employees. Both large and small employer groups argue that amending ERISA would raise the cost of providing health insurance benefits, and would result in increased numbers of people without any health insurance coverage. Supporters of the legislation argue that it is basically unfair to allow those who are not in ERISA-covered insurance plans to sue for damages, when others with similar claims who are covered by ERISA are prevented from doing so. Physician organizations also support reform so that their clinical autonomy will not be compromised by cost-containment imperatives. But the combined political strength of the employee and industry groups has foreclosed congressional action, despite considerable popular support for holding MCOs accountable. Managed care's cost-containment initiatives reflect current congressional policy, so there is little chance of major ERISA revisions either to include additional federal remedies or to limit (or eliminate altogether) the reach of ERISA's preemption provision.

If ERISA demonstrates anything, it is the resilience of the law of unintended consequences. When ERISA was enacted, managed care was limited to a few traditional HMOs and was an improbable candidate to dominate health care. What began as a statute to reform pension practices and policies has, as a result of what amounts to an afterthought, arguably stimulated a market revolution in health-care delivery. Through liberal interpretations of ERISA preemption, courts have served as a catalyst of the revolution, even as individual judges have complained bitterly about unjust results. The managed care revolution might have occurred anyway, but there seems little doubt that Congress and the courts have played an important facilitating role. By not acting to amend ERISA in the face of critical commentary from scholars, patient advocates, and judges, Congress has clearly signaled its satisfaction with the ensuing health care environment.

MCOs should nevertheless be held accountable both for financial decisions that affect clinical treatment and for their role in making medical decisions. It is also important that doctors not be left in an untenable position where they are responsible for cost-containment provisions over which they have almost no control. Exposing MCOs to similar liability considerations means that MCOs will not be able to influence medical decisions with impunity, which should enhance physician autonomy. Congress should therefore overturn ERISA preemption, in part because ERISA's goals have been achieved, and in part because of preemption's fundamental unfairness.

Short of revoking ERISA preemption, Congress could take several actions in favor of the patients' right to sue. For instance, Congress could expand on the available remedies under ERISA, while still blocking state court litigation. Consistent with the goal of maintaining national uniformity, Congress could retain preemption but allow individuals to sue for monetary damages in federal court for an ERISA violation. Congress could also direct the Department of Labor (as the appropriate regulatory agency) to develop regulations that would more effectively protect the physician–patient relationship. Regulations could define some of ERISA's more ambiguous terms, including fiduciary duty and what constitutes a health plan. Other regulations might address a patient's right to notice of a denial of care and to an external grievance panel.

The current uncertainty in how courts will interpret ERISA preemption is an advantage to the managed care industry in retaining its control over health-care delivery for two reasons: Efforts to enact state legislation may be undermined by ERISA preemption. And, as long as ERISA protects cost-containment innovations, there is no incentive for MCOs to defer to the treating physician over clinical decisions.

For physicians, it seems clear that medical practice autonomy would be better served by supporting changes to the current ERISA law. A downside is that supporting changes to ERISA would enhance state regulatory mechanisms that could also impede physician autonomy. The question is whether physicians believe that they have more to gain by eliminating ERISA preemption than they have to lose by being subject to state legislative oversight. Most state laws have favored greater physician autonomy at the expense of MCO control over clinical decisions, so such laws should only present a minimal threat to doctors.

This review of managed care litigation raises the question of whether there is a better way to proceed at this point. Since neither tort nor contract laws is likely to provide a satisfactory approach to the conflicts presented by managed care, it seems reasonable to offer an alternative strategy. To counter the trends explained in Part II, the proposed fiduciary-duty approach is designed to restore the physician–patient relationship to its rightful place at the center of the health-care encounter. Part III explains why a fiduciary-duty approach is superior, both for resolving managed care litigation and for reconciling the tension between law and medicine.

Notes

1. Kapp (1985); Havighurst (1995).

2. Mooney (1995).

3. Hall et al. (1996). The Hall et al. regression analysis attributes this result to being in federal court rather than to ERISA. For a critique of these results, see Sage (1998).

4. Morreim (1997), p. 46, footnote 148.

5. 969 S.W.2d 945 (Tex. 1998).

6. *Dukes v. U.S. Healthcare, Inc.*, 57 F.3d 350 (3rd Cir. 1995)

7. *Mateo-Woodburn v. Fresno Community Hospital*, 221 Cal. App. 3d 1169, 270 Cal. Rptr. 894 (Cal. App. 5th Dist. 1990).

8. 617 A.2d 1020 (Maine 1992)

9. 114 F.3d 9 (2d Cir. 1997).

10. 987 F. Supp. 1174 (N.D.Cal., 1997).

11. 938 P.2d 903 (Cal. 1997).

12. *Garfinkel v. Morristown Obstetrics & Gynecology Associates*, 773A.2d 665 (N.J. 2001).

13. 457 U.S. 332 (1982).

14. Greaney (1997).

15. *Federal Trade Commission v. Butterworth*, 946 F. Supp. 1285 (W.D.Mich. 1996); *United States v. Mercy Health Services*, 902 F. Supp. 968 (N.D.Iowa 1995).

16. *Federal Trade Commission v. Butterworth*, 946 F. Supp. 1285 (W.D.Mich. 1996).

17. *Blue Cross & Blue Shield of Wisconsin v. Marshfield*, 65 F.3d 1406 (7th Cir. 1994); *U.S. Healthcare, Inc. v Healthsource, Inc.*, 986 F.2d 589 (1st Cir. 1993). See also, Sage (1997a).

18. Hairghurst (2001b), p. 953.

19. Noble and Brennan (2001), p. 300.

20. Hadorn (1992); and Hall and Anderson (1992).

21. Hall and Anderson (1992) have proposed this approach.

22. See, e.g., *Potvin v.Metropolitan Life Insurance Company*, 997 P.2d 1153 (Cal. 2000). *Shalala v. Grijalva*, 526 U.S. 1096 (1999).

23. *Moran v. Rush Prudential HMO Inc.*, 230 F.3d 959 (7th Cir. 2000); *Corporate Health Insurance, Inc. v. Texas Department of Insurance*, 215 F.3d 526 (5th Cir. 2000).

24. 730 N.E.2d 1119, 1128 (Ill. 2000). For similar observations, see Mariner (2001) and Noble and Brennan (2001).

25. Jacobson and Selvin (2002).

26. Resnik (2000).

27. See, e.g., Peterson and Selvin (1991). RAND's Institute for Civil Justice has studied this issue extensively. See, e.g., Kakalik et al. (1996); Hensler (1999); see also Resnik, (2000).

28. See, e.g., France (2000), p. 42.

29. Sellers (1991), p. 311.

30. Kluger (1976).

31. Judge Wilkinson's concurring opinion in *Brzonkala v.Virginia Polytechnic Institute and State University*, 132 F.3d 949 (4th Cir. 1997). "Finally, our role in this modern era is not as substantive adjudicators, but as structural referees. The due process decisions of the *Lochner* and Warren eras, as well as the individual rights rulings of the latter, attempted to remove the subject matter of those cases from the political debate altogether."

32. See Tushnet (2000); Powe (2000).

33. An exception to this is *Muse v. Charter Hospital of Winston-Salem, Inc.*, 452 S.E. 2d 589 (Ct.App.N.C. 1995), a case that did not involve an independent utilization management firm. The court deferred to physician autonomy where the plaintiff was discharged when his insurance coverage expired. The court held that the treating physician's recommendation of continued hospital stay should have been honored, leaving open the question of who pays for the continued hospitalization given current economic incentives. Arguably, this result is more consistent with cases decided before the expansion of managed care. See, e.g., *Van Vactor v. Blue Cross Association*, 365 N.E.2d 638 (Ill.App. 1977).

34. In *Doe v. SEPTA*, 72 F.3d 1133 (3rd Cir 1995) and *Creason v. State Department of Health Services*, 957 P.2d 1323 (Cal. 1998), the courts made this tradeoff explicitly. See also Morreim (1995).

35. Capron (1987), at p. 19.

36. Hall (1997b).

37. 72 F.3d 1133 (3rd Cir. 1995).

38. Jacobson, Selvin, and Pomfret (2001).

39. "There is no theoretical impediment to configuring a medical malpractice standard that is ... sensitive to available patient resources" (Henderson and Sciciliano, 1994).

40. I am indebted to Arnold Rosoff for suggesting this line of analysis.

41. Bovbjerg (1975).

42. *Helling v. Carey,* 519 P.2d 981 (Wash. 1974); Schwartz and Komesar (1978).

PART III

Restoring the Primacy of the Physician-Patient Relationship

9

Mutual Distrust Between Attorneys and Physicians

THE relationship between law and medicine is complex, uneasy, and unsettled. Mutual recriminations over medical malpractice have stifled productive lines of communication and cooperation, often to patients' detriment. Quite simply, the conventional wisdom is that the two lack a common vocabulary, a common policy agenda, and a framework for cooperation. As usual, the conventional wisdom reflects only one part of the story, and the most negative one at that.

Policy makers need not choose between polarized options of unfettered physician autonomy (which resulted in excessive health care costs in the fee-for-service era) versus strict cost containment (which restricts access to health care services under managed care). Instead, there is an alternative approach that maintains managed care's ability to control costs, but in a way that is far more deferential to physician autonomy and restores the primacy of the physician–patient relationship.

As alluded to throughout the book, the alternative approach is the concept of *fiduciary duty*. This approach is designed to encourage the development of judicial doctrine that is informed by health policy concerns, and the formulation of health policy that is cognizant of likely judicial responses. For this approach to take hold, it must appeal to physicians, health-care administrators, and the judiciary. It is, of course, an ambitious agenda to suggest that these stakeholders might agree on the fiduciary duty approach. Yet the rapidly changing health-care delivery system and the judicial response to the managed care system provide a perfect opportunity for a broad discussion about law and medicine. The fiduciary-duty concept offers an opportunity to move beyond the current terms of the debate to provide courts and health policy makers with a useful framework for thinking about the relationship between law, health-care delivery, and health policy.

Previous scholars have argued that the problems between law and medicine can be resolved by fairly simple and direct mechanisms. One group would rely on contract law to reform the health care system by allowing market mechanisms to reduce costs. Another group would impose enterprise liability and place full legal responsibility for health care with MCOs.[1] As we have seen, these strategies have a superficial attractiveness. They also have serious limitations, not the least of which is the assumption that the health care system is susceptible to simple and direct solutions.

In contrast, my approach assumes that problems facing the health care system are complex. In truth, there is no obvious or simple solution. One scholar captures this reality in observing the moral quandary physicians face in an era of changing medical ethics:

> The need for myriad contextual moral judgments precludes resolution by a simple elegant algorithm. We would make more progress . . . by . . . constructing an ethics of role conflict in more modest terms as an ongoing effort to mediate, case by case, between clinical fidelity and medicine's social purposes. We could thereby come to appreciate conflict between medicine's caring and social purposes as in need of ongoing management, rather than as a problem to be solved once and for all.[2]

The fiduciary-duty model is just such an approach, depending, as we will see, on case-by-case determinations.

To develop an approach that avoids the polarity between unfettered physician autonomy and rigid cost controls, three things need to occur. First, there needs to be some reconciliation (or at least accommodation) between attorneys and physicians so that a common approach can be considered in a cooperative atmosphere. Reducing the level of antagonism between the two professions is a precondition to a productive dialogue. Second, the fiduciary-duty approach needs to be viewed as something worth contemplating from both a conceptual and a practical standpoint. Third, the public needs to accept that cost containment, while important, is not the only value to be pursued in health care.

The purpose of Part III is to address these issues directly. It will offer a foundation for the legal and medical professions to engage in a productive dialogue over how to resolve the difficult philosophical issues presented in the current health-care environment. This chapter will describe ways of improving communication and cooperation between attorneys and physicians. Chapter 10 will outline the fiduciary-duty approach. And Chapter 11 will discuss the policy implications and advantages of this strategy, even if the nature of the health care enterprise changes over the next few years.

Restoring the physician–patient relationship to the center of the medical enterprise will not be easy under the best of circumstances. The obvious question is how to accomplish this goal. As long as cost containment remains the dominant health-care policy concern, physicians will be under pressure to limit patients' access to health care services. Neither the courts nor Congress seem anxious to restore physician autonomy to its previous levels. All of this makes it even more imperative for physicians and attorneys to reach some sort of accommodation.

The Juxtaposition of the Professions

Ars longa, vita brevis—"Art is long, life is brief"—is how Hippocrates, the founder of medical ethics, described the practice of medicine. This maxim could apply to any profession, but it seems to have special resonance for the legal and medical professions. Their trades take a long time to learn well, and are defined by the ongoing development of expertise and skill.

Most commentary focuses on what divides the two professions. The limited commentary on their commonalities says little about shared values and practices.[3] One observer remarked on a series of California Supreme Court decisions on medical and hospital practice by noting that

> . . . when values of a legal or judicial nature clash with ethical or practice values in medicine, this court seems to impose the legalistic value without adequate regard for the effect on medical practice and values.[4]

Others add that the two professions have different world-views,[5] and that the difference between medicine's concern for preserving health and the law's concern for individual liberty can generate deep misunderstandings in the adversarial context of litigation.[6]

These assessments are incomplete. They overlook a shared set of core social and ethical values that help define physicians and attorneys as professionals. The two professions share respect for the individual, the need to make case-by-case decisions under uncertainty, and a commitment to reason, professional judgment, and experience as the basis for decision-making.[7] The tension between law and medicine is not over differences in core values but over different approaches for resolving the inevitable conflicts that arise. Nevertheless, the fact remains that physicians and lawyers tend to focus on their differences to impugn the other profession during disputes (i.e., the battle over medical error and defensive medicine). Shared values and experiences that might improve health-care delivery and policy are ignored.

This chapter examines what those shared values and experiences are and how they might serve to revive communication and cooperation between attorneys and physicians. The goal is to understand better why the antagonism between doctors and lawyers persists and what steps can be taken to accommodate their mutual values and experiences. To bridge the gap between the two professions, the focus must be on areas where cooperation and accommodation could improve health-care policy and patient care. Recent changes in health care delivery invite new ways of facilitating cooperation.

At the outset, it is important to summarize briefly why encouraging more cooperation is important. Clinical decisions made out of fear of attorneys or the legal system may sometimes reduce neglectful behavior, but often can put patients at risk. Better public policy decisions will be made if attorneys and physicians, two groups with major influence over health policy, can engage in meaningful dialogue rather than useless finger-pointing.

Along the way, the interests of patients have gotten lost in the struggle between attorneys and physicians for supremacy over the medical enterprise. As we saw with the litigation trends, where the patients' interests seemed, at best, to be a judicial afterthought, the patient is too often vulnerable to disputes between attorneys and physicians that are only tangentially related to patient care.

The tension between law and medicine does not occur in a vacuum. It is, first, the product of the historical relationship between attorneys and physicians, along with physicians' general dissatisfaction with a seemingly unfriendly legal system. Just as important, the tension exists in the broader context of how individual physicians and attorneys view and abide by their professional responsibilities. Another factor is changing perceptions about what constitutes a profession and the professional relationship to the patient or client.

The relationship between law and medicine has not always been this contentious, as we have seen.[8] Despite the failure to develop a specialty in legal medicine, the two professions have been interdependent on many aspects of medical practice and health policy. Both professions' claims to new and ever-expanding areas of practice, and their constant professional contact, may be the root of their propensity to battle over health-care delivery.

At times, especially during the past 30 years, that interdependence has led to considerable conflict between physicians and attorneys over the perceived intrusiveness of the legal system—including judicial decisions, legislation, and regulation—into the clinical domain. The conflict has been exacerbated in recent years with the decline of physician dominance and authority over health-care delivery and the rise of managed care.[9]

The struggle between lawyers and doctors is not just about setting medical practice standards or health policy. At the core of their adversarial relationship is the battle for professional and social supremacy between two fiercely independent professions. During the nineteenth century, legal practice was held in great esteem, while medicine was viewed by many with considerable skepticism. By the mid–twentieth century, medicine had undergone a social transformation that placed its practitioners at the pinnacle of American society.[10] For much of the second half of the twentieth century, attorneys and physicians have vied for preeminence in social and economic status. Physicians actually supplanted attorneys in social and economic stature after World War II, dominating health-care delivery and health-care policy.[11]

Since the emergence of medicine as a high-profile profession, physicians and attorneys have contested for dominance in defining the role of law in medicine and medicine in law. Physicians need to understand the nature of the legal process and why courts rule as they do, while judges and attorneys need to understand the nature of clinical decision-making and the values that motivate and underlie medical and health-care policies and practices.

During the past decade, both professions have suffered attacks on their preeminence and professional autonomy. For physicians, managed care has surmounted their dominance over medical care, non-physician practitioners have demanded more authority in clinical practice, and the public perceives them as receiving excessive compensation for their work. For attorneys, public cynicism about their avarice and gamesmanship reached a pinnacle during the O.J. Simpson trial and the squabbling over enormous fees from litigation against the tobacco companies. Today, paralegals are demanding a greater scope in providing basic legal services.

Recall that the legal system played an important role in securing physicians' social prominence and control over health-care delivery. Regardless of their discordant dialogue, the legal system facilitated the establishment of modern medicine.[12] Throughout the post–World War II period, the courts actually supported physician dominance over health-care delivery[13] and acted as a conduit for the expansion of the medical industry.[14] One scholar suggests that

> [b]ecause the law absorbs and reflects the values and relationships of traditional medicine, it has codified the ethic of professional dominance, effectively shielding physicians from the institutional influence contemplated by revolutionary changes in health care policy.[15]

This statement, clearly accurate when it was written in 1988, is no longer viable, though it is fully applicable to the law's treatment of the now-dominant managed care approach.

The status of any given profession is a privilege, not a right, granted by the state: "At the heart of every profession is a legally sanctioned control over a specialized body of knowledge, and a commitment to service."[16] By definition, this technical, specialized body of knowledge lies beyond the average citizen's ability to comprehend fully. Without going into the theoretical disputes over what constitutes a *profession,*[17] it is generally agreed that certain functions define a profession:[18]

- Possession of a discrete body of knowledge and skills as controlled by members of the profession
- Development of ethical guidelines for the professional's practice
- Responsibility for determining education, training, and requirements for admission into the profession
- Workplace autonomy
- Social responsibility
- Responsibility for professional discipline

A fundamental aspect of professional status is autonomy and the right to self-regulation. Autonomy means that professionals practice independently, but are subject to a code of ethics that enshrines the patient's or client's and society's welfare above the professional's economic interests.[19] Professional status is also subject to state licensing laws and, for physicians, rules of government regulatory agencies and the various accreditation bodies.[20] The keys to what constitutes a profession apply equally to law and medicine.

The state's involvement in licensing physicians and attorneys, and hence conferring legitimacy, is a double-edged sword. Licensing gives physicians and attorneys unique authority to practice, but permits legal oversight of their practices and fitness to practice. Even though the medical and legal professionals choose their peers by setting the admissions qualifications, first to medical or law school and then to medical specialty boards and the bar, government grants the basic permission to practice and imposes sanctions on the failure to meet licensing standards.

Professions are not static endeavors. They are subject to external economic and social pressures and internal dynamics that continually redefine how their professional responsibilities and functions are met. In fact, scholarly commentary has not always been kind or adulatory toward the professions. Some scholars contend that professions are mere trade monopolies and self-interested groups no longer serving the public interest.[21] A result of this has been what some call a loss of legitimacy in the professions.[22]

During the past three decades, external economic forces have transformed the working environments of both law and medicine.[23] Increasingly, these professionals practice within large institutions. Well into the twentieth century, solo practitioners or small group practices dominated both professions. Now, both are characterized by institutional arrangements—large law firms for attorneys and managed care organizations (MCOs) or large multi-specialty groups for physicians. Solo practitioners have virtually vanished from both professions, with at least some sacrifice of professional autonomy in exchange for the economic benefits of large-scale organizations.

More intense economic competition and personal anxiety among professionals have created a charged but troubled workplace in many instances.[24] For most of the twentieth century, senior partners at the end of their law firm careers did not need to produce new business but could rely on newer associates to sustain the partners' income. All partners are currently expected to generate income or retire gracefully. A similar reality dominates the medical profession. Under managed care, physicians' clinical decisions are subject to reversal by executives who may decide not to pay for further medical intervention. The era of hospitals as the doctor's workshop is over. At present, physicians share control of health-care institutions with (often) non-physician administrators.

The modern legal and medical professions are also characterized by endemic sub-specialization and by periodic cleavage between practitioners and researchers. The increasing sub-specialization means that members of a profession have different interests, economically and politically, than did the more homogeneous legal and medical professions of the 1950s and 1960s. In health policy debates over reimbursement or manpower development, for instance, surgeons and primary care physicians may have dramatically different interests, making it difficult for the medical profession to speak with a unified voice. Money available for one activity comes at the expense of someone else's program. The same is true for health policy. If state money is made available for expanding Medicaid eligibility, it may come at the expense of maintaining trauma clinics.

The ongoing changes within each profession seem largely parallel, further undermining the possibilities of cross-professional cooperation. But nothing inherently prevents the two professions from working together and learning from each other in hopes of improving health-care policy and delivery. Right now, the prospects for such alliance seem sadly dim, though increasing codependence and interaction offer opportunities for improved communication, cooperation, and mutual respect.

Professional Differences and Similarities

To set the stage for considering ways of cooperating, we should explore briefly the main attributes that are similar and different between physicians and attorneys. Let us look first at the differences and then explore the shared values and experiences.

Certain aspects of each profession engender conflict between physicians and attorneys. One commentator identifies the sources of mutual hostility as follows:

> The antagonism many physicians feel toward lawyers is the result of fundamental disagreement about five issues: the nature of authority; how conflict should be resolved; the relative importance of procedure and substance; the nature and significance of risk; and the legitimacy of politics as a method of solving problems.[25]

This astutely identifies the sources of the antagonism between physicians and attorneys—with one exception. Even if the two professions place different emphases on the role of politics in professional activity, the increasingly heavy involvement by medical organizations in state and federal politics suggests that this aspect is no longer a fundamental distinction.[26]

Reflecting on these points, one might easily contend that the thought processes of the professions are inherently at odds. The lawyer is skilled as an adversary by virtue of the Socratic method. In contrast, the physician, educated in science and trained through an apprenticeship with more-senior practitioners, acts professionally as an evaluator of objective truth. Physicians rely on laws set by nature; lawyers derive arguments from laws made by man. Medicine is, at least in part, an experimental science devolved from the natural sciences, while law originates mainly from the humanities through inductive reasoning. Though both professions suffer from not always having complete information before making a decision, the legal rules of evidence block certain information from being admitted into trial, whereas the physician can seek out all available data. And as others have observed, ". . . the physician as scientist is trained in the techniques of what may be termed objective inquiry in distinction to contentious disputation. The adversary method, the meat of the lawyer, may be the poison of the doctor."[27] In short, physicians are concerned with scientific proof (determined through observation and verification), whereas lawyers focus on relative truth as determined through the adversary process (i.e., who makes the most persuasive argument). When this dynamic tension arises "[t]he lawyer often does not seem to the doctor to be seeking the truth, but only to place blame."[28]

Equally important, physicians are generally unwilling to relinquish clinical authority and judgment to non-medical third parties, even as lawyers routinely expect third parties (judges and juries) to make reasoned decisions.[29] As such, physicians resent that the legal system (either at trial or in settling a claim) inherently emphasizes process over clinical outcomes. In either case, personnel not trained in medicine, often with vastly different risk perceptions, scrutinize a physician's clinical judgment. In fact, three of the five differences identified above (conflict resolution, the balance between procedure and substance, and politics) can be collapsed into one category—how to balance the legal system's concern for process with the medical profession's concern for appropriate clinical outcomes.[30]

The divergence in disciplinary standards explains some of the underlying tension between law and medicine and why doctors and lawyers have such a difficult time communicating. As any academic knows, disciplinary differences can be difficult to bridge. A common vocabulary is often lacking, as are shared approaches to knowledge and problem resolution. Terms and concepts whose meaning is seemingly obvious to one discipline can convey different meanings to another, further aggravating the antagonism. The problem is magnified because increasing subspecialization makes it more difficult to communicate even within the professions themselves, let alone across the law–medicine divide.

To take one example, the concept of causation has very different (and perhaps irreconcilable) meanings in law and medicine, with differing perceptions of acceptable risk. Many clinical outcomes, such as the birth of a neurologically impaired baby, that physicians would categorize as within reasonable risk of medical intervention or as lacking a clear causal correction, would be attacked as being preventable medical error by attorneys representing a client.[31] The result might be a contentious medical liability trial for something perhaps beyond the control of medical science. A cooperative approach to compensate the family would be a far better solution.

In this sense, a further distinction between law and medicine is important to consider. Preserving a client's individual choice (i.e., promoting self-determination) is the highest legal value for lawyers in serving their clients.[32] For physicians, by contrast, the essential goal is to preserve their patient's health. In many situations, especially in ethics disputes, these two objectives are incompatible. "Health care professionals devalue freedoms that compromise health, and lawyers oppose the rendering of health care that negates or jeopardizes individual choice."[33] Take, for example, the issue of a homeless mentally ill person who does not want to be institutionalized. A physician might argue that it is in the patient's best medical interests to be treated in an institution, while the lawyer tends to see the primary obligation as advocating for the patient's liberty. A pessimistic conclusion is that this disconnection undermines agreement on common goals.[34]

These types of disputes were more common in the 1970s and 1980s during the early battles and formative period of bioethics. Law and medicine disagreed, for instance, about when it was appropriate to remove life supports, how to define death, and who could speak on behalf of the patient. Since then, many of the contentious bioethical issues separating law and medicine have been resolved, or at least there is general agreement on the essential bioethical principles and how they should be applied. The AMA has adopted ethical guidance specifically sanctioning the patient's right to refuse treatment,[35] and the types of ethical disputes now being litigated do not necessarily pit attorneys against physicians.

To be sure, the doctor and the lawyer are entrusted with protecting different spheres of a person's being—the former with bodily integrity and the latter with rights under law—and these parallel obligations can result in conflict. The attorney's duty to represent his client creates the very adversarial tension that animates medical liability litigation and sometimes makes it seem as though attorneys are not interested in the search for scientific truth. Medical liability litigation may well remain the single greatest threat to rapport between the medical and legal professions because of the searing animosity generated by the adversarial nature of the legal system. This has consistently been the situation since the 1840s, and continues to be today, even considering the expanding interaction between law and medicine.

Viewing physicians and attorneys solely as adversaries risks overlooking their commonalities, shared values, and shared experiences as professionals, especially in times of conflict. For reasons that will become apparent, the core shared values and experiences are more fundamental and important than the attributes that differ. The similarities revolve around how attorneys and physicians function as professionals, their experiences, and ways of thinking that animate the actual practice of law and medicine. Attorneys and physicians may not necessarily share public policy views or agree on how an individual client or patient should be treated. Nor, however, do they operate on different sets of underlying values. Refocusing the dialogue on shared values and experiences and the professions' interdependence will help reduce the animosity now dividing them.

First, professional autonomy is highly valued in both fields. Without practice autonomy, much of what defines a profession becomes unsettled. Without much doubt, a considerable amount of the physicians' antipathy toward managed care is driven by its attempts to restrict physician autonomy. Attorneys face analogous challenges to their professional independence from the increasing concentration of legal work in large, bureaucratic law firms or other institutional settings.[36] In these settings, attorneys may not have the choice about whether and how a client will be represented. Both face encroachments into areas they previously dominated, mainly by paraprofessionals (such as nurse practitioners for medicine and paralegals for law). Though attorneys do not currently face similar constraints on their professional autonomy, an attack on one profession's autonomy may lead to similar attacks on the other's. Thus, health policy determinations that undermine physician autonomy may one day be used to justify public policies that undermine attorney autonomy.

Second, they both owe primary duties to the individual client or patient, respectively, as part of their canons of ethics. Taking responsibility for the quality of advice to, and care or representation of, the patient or client is common to how physicians and attorneys function. Central to their shared professional role is the concept of fiduciary duty; that is, they stand in relationships of trust to their patients or clients. The concept of fiduciary duty is particularly important in understanding the professions' shared values. Perhaps the ethic most common to physicians and lawyers is dedication to the individuals who seek their services. The perceived integrity of law and medicine as professions rests on the public's confidence that practitioners place the patient's or client's interest above other considerations, including financial remuneration. These duties are elemental to the professions and are assumed with the taking of oaths upon graduation from medical school or induction to the bar.

The key to taking responsibility lies in establishing relationships of trust where the client's or patient's interest comes first. In turn, a critical element of trust lies in the professional's responsibility to preserve the confidentiality of that relationship, which has developed beyond being legally enforceable to being etched into societal, as well as professional, expectations. Proper diagnosis or representation entails access to sensitive personal information that must be protected from being seen or used by anyone not privileged to review the file.

Third, both professions are devoted simultaneously to the betterment of society, as well as to the benefit of the client or patient. The lawyer has a duty to uphold the law, a core value that at times conflicts with a client's interests. For instance, a lawyer must withdraw from a case if he or she is aware that the client is not telling the truth under oath. Physicians have corresponding commitments to social purposes, including public health and non–health related social goals (e.g., military readiness or criminal justice).[37] These duties can also result in actions that the individual physician may oppose, such as refusing to provide certain services to patients (e.g., euthanasia, abortion, or futile care), or the requirement to report substance abuse. Both professions have ethical aspirations and legal obligations to provide services to the community and to individuals who cannot afford to pay them.

Public acceptance of professional autonomy and self-regulation depends on assurances that professionals are committed to balancing their loyalty to clients and patients with their obligations to public service and accountability to the public.[38] Lay acceptance of professional autonomy and self-regulation also rests on professional acceptance of public accountability.[39] Neither profession operates in a vacuum apart from social values and goals. Physicians operate within a changing health care system and lawyers operate under constant scrutiny from legislators, litigants, and judges. Preserving public trust is essential if both professions are to thrive and maintain their autonomy. Public trust is endangered when professionals appear to advance their own economic interests at the expense of societal or patient and client obligations. Continued bickering in public does little to inspire the community's trust in either profession.

Fourth, strong self-promulgated ethical codes and norms similarly guide the two professions. These codes enshrine the concepts of fiduciary duty and professional responsibility to the patient or client as the practitioner's highest ethical duty. While the codes themselves do not exactly have the same force (for example, the American Bar Association codes are intended to be adopted formally by state disciplinary boards, whereas the American Medical Association codes are intended to provide guidance to disciplinary authorities), they are nonetheless similar in their importance to practitioners and to the community. The codes uphold the professions' similar moral aspirations and explain to the public what constitutes ethical medical or legal professional behavior. Each code binds the practitioner with a set of ethical strictures.

Being a professional encompasses aspirations and ideals that transcend financial rewards and social status. A sense of purpose is an intangible attribute that the two professions share; it unites them philosophically. Their codes of ethics encourage that sense of purpose. The existence of comparable codes *per se* cannot resolve conflicts between the two professions, but it can serve as a platform for identifying and clarifying differences.

Fifth, physicians and lawyers find themselves increasingly subservient to their respective institutional environments. Institutional constraints are a shared experience in shaping the options and perspectives of medical and legal practitioners. For both, institutional norms and pressures increasingly conflict with traditional professional obligations and norms. An individual practitioner's ability to determine the type of patient or client he accepts (and what to charge) is restricted by organizational policies and concerns. In the fee-for-service system, by contrast, physicians were solely responsible for clinical decisions and quality of care. One of the problems patients face in the managed care era is that physicians may no longer have sole clinical authority, but must respond to managed care's cost-containment programs, especially utilization review.

Sixth, physicians and lawyers find themselves in similar predicaments in our increasingly consumer- and service-oriented post-industrial world. Professional sovereignty is being eroded by government regulations (in some cases, deregulation) and by consumers with access to information previously available only to professionals. Both professions are struggling to preserve their domains, as well as lay belief in their unique expertise, judgment, and skill. In the medical arena, physician assistants, nurse practitioners, pharmacists, and others are impinging on the primary care physician's role.[40] On matters involving the law, people may alternatively seek the counsel of consultants, accountants, or paralegals. The phenomenon of other occupations' encroaching on professional territory is a shared threat and, perhaps, a rallying cry. Attorneys and physicians must vigorously protect their domains, areas of unique expertise, and skill to practice.

One aspect of the current environment, conflicting loyalties facing the medical profession, is appreciably more severe than attorneys face. The current emphasis on reducing the cost of health-care delivery and the resulting conflicts between loyalty to the individual patient and concern for the patient population animate medical practice in the managed care era.[41] Attorneys do not currently face such a difficult ethical and professional quandary. Physicians may be tempted or forced away from serving the best interests of patients unless clear markers are established to thwart cost-containment pressures from interfering with medical services.[42]

Seventh, the very nature of conducting business is similar in both professions. Both rely on reputation and word of mouth to attract patients or clients. Within the ethical guidelines developed by each profession, both act with considerable autonomy in deciding whether and how to treat a patient or to represent a client. Both rely on coherent systems of decision-making to advance the patient's or client's interests, and both are solely responsible for the quality of services provided.

Finally, in important senses, both remain entrepreneurs who are marketing professional services and skills to people who select or entities who pay for their services.[43] Professional reputation is critical to the success of a physician or attorney, even within the institutional context in which they now mainly practice. Along with the ultimate legal and ethical responsibility for the patient's or client's well-being, professional responsibility separates attorneys and physicians from the practitioners without legal or medical degrees who would like to expand their legal or medical responsibilities. As the court in *Mandeville v. Harman*[44] noted, "Professional skill, experience, and reputation are things which cannot be bought or sold. They constitute part of the individuality of the particular person . . ." Attorneys and physicians receive social and economic rewards and recognition for their skills.

Developing More Productive Encounters

The extensive consideration of differences and shared values raises two questions: Should anyone care whether attorneys and physicians can develop a more productive dialogue over health-care delivery and health policy? And are these shared values and experiences useful in helping accommodate and reconcile the two professions?

Does it matter, one might legitimately ask, if the differences between the two professions have been overstated and the similarities understated? Even if one agrees that important shared values, experiences, and interests have been overlooked, the shared values are arguably more abstract than of practical significance. Cynically, one might view the shared experiences as reinforcing a sense of professionalism as a trade monopoly, with no inherently redeeming social or personal value. Certainly, money lurks as a factor in both legal and medical services, so the desire to stave off competing economic interests is mutual. Conversely, the differences present real impediments to cooperation. Just because the two share strong ethical codes and a concern for the individual they represent does not necessarily enable them to unite on contentious questions of public policy or clinical treatment. Nor do the shared values and experiences mitigate different perspectives on questions of medical liability. Even in a best-case scenario, there is unlikely to be congruence between the two professions about either patient care or health policy. Differences along the dimensions described are likely to remain. The question is whether these abstractions are useful in helping to forge a more productive dialogue over health-care delivery and health policy. The answer should be yes, because both patients and policy makers have a shared interest in improved professional cooperation.

From the patient's perspective, the antagonism between law and medicine subordinates appropriate medical care to other interests. If physicians are overly concerned about liability, they may take actions that jeopardize patient welfare, including excessive testing or unnecessary treatment. Likewise, public policy may suffer if the professions are unable to forge common policy goals, such as developing a better system to detect lapses in quality of care. It is difficult to determine the best way to reduce medical error or resolve controversial issues regarding data privacy if physicians and attorneys are blaming each other for causing the problem.

At the same time, there are considerable benefits to increased cooperation. The AIDS epidemic, for instance, has raised joint health policy and medical questions that require (and have received) cooperation between law and medicine.[45] Understanding the biological, psychological, and clinical mechanisms of HIV leads to more appropriate regulation and reduces individuals' risk of social stigma and employment discrimination. Cooperation on medical liability issues is more likely to yield reasoned public policy, as occurred in California when physicians and attorneys set aside their differences and agreed on legislative reforms to set a cap on medical liability damage awards.[46] And developing a cooperative strategy to return the physician–patient relationship to the center of the health care enterprise would help patients and provide a common goal for health policy.

For several reasons, the shared values and experiences can lead to cooperation between law and medicine. The shared concept of fiduciary duty is particularly amenable to facilitating a more productive dialogue. But there are several additional reasons for optimism.

The initial point to consider is that the differences were more important in the fee-for-service era, and the shared values and experiences are likely to be more germane in the managed care environment. To begin with, the relationship between the physician and the patient, and hence the roles of attorneys, have changed. When health care operated under the fee-for-service system, physicians' contact with attorneys was mostly confrontational over medical malpractice allegations and trials. In this context, the differences were magnified, triggering mutual antipathy. With the emergence of health care as a business and a regulated industry, physicians are increasingly reliant on attorneys to secure business advantages for themselves. As a byproduct of this changing circumstance, their shared values and experiences are likely to be magnified. The attorneys whom physicians encounter are often counsel to health plans or represent physician groups on regulatory matters and general business dealings. In many of these situations, attorneys are allied with, rather than antagonists toward, physicians. The imperative of working closely together to achieve business objectives tends to submerge differences and to underscore the shared professional values.

The managed care environment thus creates new alignments and opportunities for cooperation. At this point, the new alignments are tentative. One possibility is that the new divide will be institutional rather than professional. Future tensions might be between MCO physician-administrators and their attorneys on one hand, and those who treat and represent individual patients on the other. Physicians and attorneys within each of these groupings are likely to have shared positions on MCO accountability. Plaintiffs' medical malpractice attorneys may seek alliances with treating physicians against physician-administrators and MCO attorneys. Plaintiffs' attorneys and treating physicians are likely to be more supportive of physician autonomy (and patients' right to sue MCOs) than will physician administrators and plan attorneys, who are likely to be more concerned with preserving managed care cost-containment programs.

At one time, malpractice litigation was viewed as the primary threat to physician autonomy. That is what made the law's focus on self-determination (i.e., through informed-consent rules) so threatening to physicians. Now physicians are under increased scrutiny from several directions. MCOs use economic credentialing (i.e., weighing an individual physician's use of medical resources) in deciding whether to include the doctor as a member of the plan. The government and employers, whose financial contribution subsidizes medical care, want to make sure that their money is well spent, and closely monitor physician services. Economic considerations are already central to clinical decisions. The law's focus on patient self-determination is no longer a fundamental assault on physician autonomy and second-guessing of clinical judgments.

An interesting upshot of the managed care environment is that individual physicians sometimes need to hire attorneys to protect their interests against MCOs. Even state medical associations have come to recognize that physicians may now have some convergence with attorneys on some issues. Take, for example, what one physician said about a state medical association's litigation against an MCO regarding responsibility for medical treatment:

> I would never have dreamed that I would have turned to plaintiff's (*sic*) lawyers to help me regain control of my practice. . . . We doctors suddenly found ourselves in trouble, and the only place we could turn was to the trial lawyers for help. . . . We had to bury a lot of long-held hard feelings to do this. . . . [47]

Anecdotal? Certainly—and maybe not at all representative of physicians' attitudes. Still, this type of contact is bound to change attitudes and create potential new alignments, which can lead to a cooperative dialogue.

A second reason why shared interests are more salient now is that medicine is increasingly importing concepts from law in adapting to cost constraints, especially the use of "processes" (such as structured dispute resolution) and clinical outcome measures.[48] Examples include the use of clinical practice guidelines as "evidence" of best practices, and the establishment of external grievance processes to resolve differences among patients, physicians, and MCOs over clinical decision-making.[49] The growing physician demand for independent external review of insurance benefit coverage denials, which is equivalent to a legal due process model, is likely to erode the medical profession's resistance to legal process, thinking, and values.

Physicians may come to welcome the law's due process approach as protection against managed care's direct challenge to physicians' medical autonomy or other arbitrary actions against physicians. In some instances, as we have seen, courts have ruled that physicians are entitled to fair procedures, including a hearing, even if they have signed contracts waiving the right to notice before staff privileges can be terminated. It seems likely that physicians will increasingly rely on due process concepts to protect their interests against managed care's involvement in clinical decision-making.

Another commonality between law and medicine is the need to make decisions in the face of uncertainty and large gaps in available data. Physicians may decry the legal system's need to resolve disputes without clearly decisive evidence, but physicians must also make clinical decisions without complete scientific evidence. Most medical decisions do not rest securely on scientific data, and even a greatly expanded agenda of clinical outcomes research will not change this in the near future.[50] High-profile disputes over the efficacy of mammograms for women under 50 or PSA tests for men underscore the incompleteness of medicine's scientific basis.[51] Many legal scholars and judges share physicians' general distaste for the adversarial system as a means of resolving medical disputes and share physicians' preference for peer review solutions. Hence the enactment of tort reforms in many states—often over the objections of trial attorneys.

Physicians trained as healers are not entirely comfortable with having patients reject their medical advice or having attorneys challenge it in court.[52] Yet this does not demonstrate that different underlying values animate how the two professions function. It only shows the difficulty in bridging the conceptual gaps to reconcile shared professional values. Certainly, the disagreements over patient care will remain; medical liability litigation against physicians is hardly extinct. Nonetheless, some broad areas of agreement have emerged regarding what is needed to alter managed care's current lack of accountability. Both the American Medical Association and the trial attorneys are lobbying Congress for increased patient protections against MCOs. In the past, such a common policy agenda has been rare-to-unimaginable. Limited policy agreement decidedly does not mean a reversion to the era when the law supported physician dominance over health-care delivery. Instead, it suggests the application of some countervailing power to the managed care industry's current dominance over health-care delivery and policy.

An alternative consideration is that each profession's self-interest supplies a more powerful motivation for cooperation than shared ethical values. If so, such self-interest can yield socially beneficial cooperation. To help restore public trust, both professions have an interest in being seen as committed to improving health-care quality. Working together to improve quality and reduce medical error is in both professions' self-interest and promotes the public's welfare.

An additional factor in the professions' mutual distrust is that physicians may project on attorneys their disappointment with the judicial and regulatory systems and their intrusion into medical practice. Attorneys, in turn, resent physicians' resistance to the legal system's mandates. For doctors, it can be easier to blame legal disappointments on the system's agents and messengers—the lawyers—than to criticize abstract legal rules and procedures. These psychological factors may limit the possibility for accommodation and cooperation. A focus on shared values and interests could lead to a more rational, less hostile dialogue between the professions, even where the roles played and interests affected by individual physicians and attorneys will inevitably conflict, especially over liability allegations.

One might argue that this analysis is hopelessly naïve and relies on shared professional values of interest to academics, not practitioners. In the real world, the antagonisms will continue as long as medical malpractice litigation remains an omnipresent threat for physicians. But if the analysis is too optimistic, the pessimists are too despairing of the conditions that might stimulate a more productive dialogue.

The question is how the professions might best pursue accommodation. There is a pressing need for stakeholders—including professional and trade associations representing physicians, attorneys, hospitals, health plans, and insurers—to convene an ongoing forum for addressing the central problems facing law and medicine. A crucial issue confronting the American health system is how to set limits on resource use in a manner that accommodates respect for individual patient and physician autonomy and society-wide conceptions of fairness. A collaborative effort to identify the underlying health policy questions, pursue agreement on basic principles, and bridge disciplinary and professional differences would be a valuable start. The Institute of Medicine is a potential forum for this because it has the independence and stature needed to encourage stakeholder participation.[53]

Through this forum, stakeholders might explore mechanisms such as the role of fiduciary duty as an instrument for striking a balance between an individual patient's use of health services and the MCO's need to preserve assets for the entire patient population (i.e., the resource limit issue). Within the managed care model, there must be a compromise between clinical treatment decisions and cost containment. MCOs, physicians, health plan subscribers, and the courts face the challenge of developing acceptable approaches to such balancing. Physicians and attorneys have fiduciary duties to act in the best interests of their patients or clients. Health plans have a fiduciary duty under federal law to make resource allocation decisions in the interests of plan beneficiaries as a whole. Each group is trained to understand and apply the fiduciary duty concept in their everyday work.

Neither Congress nor the courts have provided clear guidance for mediating between these conflicting conceptions of fiduciary duty. Right now, the law is uncertain about how to balance the medical needs of individual beneficiaries with the finances of the plan as a whole. What the proposed collaborative effort could do is engage stakeholders with sharply differing perspectives and interests to come together, in an environment less polarizing than the legislative and judicial processes, to consider how to address this dilemma. As a common denominator, fiduciary duty can be the basis for fruitful discussion of how to manage conflicting interests between physicians and MCOs. In this way, cooperation between stakeholders has the potential to achieve desirable public policy objectives.

An indication of the potential for a collaborative approach is physicians' and attorneys' recent cooperation in attempting to enact patients' rights legislation. Other groups need to be included, but this collaboration represents the possibility of reaching common ground on a broader range of issues. It suggests that the challenge of addressing medical error can be included in an interdisciplinary, collaborative effort.

In the new medical marketplace, old antagonisms are likely to erode and new ones will emerge. Battles between attorneys and physicians over the responsibility of individual clinicians for bad outcomes are likely to be less salient, and alliances between physicians and their patients' lawyers are likely to form. Initial agreement between the medical and legal professional associations regarding patients' rights at least points to the possibility of common ground between the two professions in policy debates.

If attorneys and physicians begin to focus on their shared values and interests and identify ways to build on what they have in common, they can contribute to rational resolution of myriad contentious policy concerns. If instead, the two professions continue to fight old battles by accentuating their differences, they are unlikely to resolve pressing health policy concerns.

Unrelenting antagonism between law and medicine is harmful to patients and undermines the formulation of effective health policy. The shared value of fiduciary duty offers an opportunity to open a mutual dialogue between law and medicine. There may be better alternatives for cooperative dialogue than the fiduciary model, but there is no acceptable alternative to collaboration. Through the fiduciary duty concept, the law will be able to take into account core medical values without distorting them through the lens of the legal prism.

Notes

1. The Clinton Administration made enterprise liability an important part of its proposed Health Care Security Act in 1994, but this provision was adamantly opposed by the American Medical Association and subsequently deleted from consideration.
2. Bloche (1999), p. 272.
3. Blackmun (1987/1988).
4. Curran (1981).
5. Sage (1999a).
6. Annas (1989a).
7. Hadorn (1992).
8. Mohr (1993).
9. Fox (1987).
10. Starr (1982).
11. For an excellent and comprehensive history of this transformation, see Starr (1982). See also Krause (1996).

12. Hall (1988), p. 536.

13. *Ibid.*

14. Kapp (1985).

15. Hall (1988), pp. 447–48.

16. Cruess and Cruess (1997), p. 1675.

17. Freidson (1986).

18. The following is adapted from Cruess, Cruess, and Johnston (1999).

19. Starr (1982), p. 15. Starr notes that the attributes ascribed to professions are cognitive, collegial, and moral.

20. Cruess, Cruess, and Johnston (1999).

21. Stevens (2001); Larson (1977).

22. Krause (1996); Starr (1982).

23. Hazard (1997).

24. *Ibid.*

25. Fox (1987), p. 369.

26. Dreyfuss (1998).

27. Louisell and Williams (1960) p. 398. See also Gibson and Schwartz (1980).

28. Curran et al. (1998), p. 44. Sage (2001), p. 1188, adds that "Lawyerly process is a justice construct; the physician-patient relationship is based on care."

29. Gold (1981); Gibson and Schwartz (1980); Sage (1999a).

30. In a different but related context, William Sage characterizes these differences by noting that attorneys are rule-based; physicians are role-based (Sage, 1999a). According to Sage, this means that physicians are trained to operate by consensus and peer consultation, especially given the dramatic changes in medical technology, as opposed to attorneys' reliance on rules to govern behavior. In essence, the physician obtains whatever information is needed to help the patient, while the attorney's role is limited by the rules of legal process. But the reality of managed care's control over physician behavior minimizes the import of this distinction. Dan Lang criticizes this distinction as being a social judgment rather than being visible to physicians. To carry out medical care, certain relationships are still essential. (Personal communication, 27 August 2000).

31. Jacobson (1989).

32. Dickens (1987); Annas (1989a).

33. Dickens (1987), p. 112.

34. Annas (1989a).

35. American Medical Association Code of Medical Ethics, Council on Ethical and Judicial Affairs, Current Opinions with Annotations, 8.08 (1998). See also Oberman (2000).

36. Kronman (1993).

37. Rodwin (1993); Bloche (1999).

38. Cruess, Cruess, and Johnston (1999); Wynia, et al. (1999). David Blumenthal (1994) observes that "professionalism is an antidote to the inevitability of market failure in medicine, and it is an antidote that the public would dearly like to preserve. In this public desire lies the moral and ultimately political power of organized medicine." The same might also be said about the organized legal community.

39. Wynia, et al. (1999); Blumenthal (1994).

40. Jacobson, Parker, and Coulter (1998).

41. Hall (1997b); Bloche (1999).

42. Council on Ethical and Judicial Affairs, American Medical Association (1995).

43. Levy (1997).

44. 7 A. 37, 40–41 (N.J. Ch. 1886), cited in Levy (1997).

45. Fox (1987).

46. Jacobson (1991).

47. Curriden (2001).

48. Hadorn (1992). Sage (1999a) argues that this borrowing is not necessarily a good idea if one result is to make physicians into patient advocates.

49. Hadorn (1992). Sage (2001) p. 1185 notes that "bioethics pushed medicine towards a lawyer-like approach to fact-finding through formal deliberative bodies and frank judicial oversight."

50. Bloche (2001).

51. Sox (1999). Another example is the management of a critically ill patient with multisystem failure. As Dan Lang notes, "Technology notwithstanding, this situation is beyond the state of human knowledge" (Personal communication, 27 August 2000).

52. Bill Sage notes that "physicians sometimes ignore patients' preferences because they [physicians] consider themselves guardians of clinical resources. This position is in direct conflict with the role of the legal advocate." Sage (1999a) p. 1583.

53. Havighurst (2000a).

10

Fiduciary Duty

<hr>

THE cost-containment innovations offered by managed care have been
appropriate corrections to the excesses of the fee-for-service health-care
system. Still, implementing these innovations raises inevitable questions about
conflicts of interest regarding the allocation of resources under managed care.
Simply put, how can MCOs simultaneously conserve money and provide
needed health-care services? Will managed care's financial incentives and
profit motive interfere with physicians' treatment recommendations? Managed
care is particularly vulnerable to conflicts between costs and services because
of its combined financial and health care functions.

Concerns about the high cost of health care may well influence treatment
decisions. The sources of the conflict are the economic incentives that underlie
the managed care revolution, such as capitated funding arrangements, limitations on referrals to specialists, bonuses and withholds. In making individual
clinical decisions, physicians and health plan administrators could potentially
take into account their own economic interests at the risk of interfering with
clinical care.

Some practicing physicians and commentators reject the ethical legitimacy
of these economic incentives.[1] But the vast majority appears to accept their
validity, especially in attacking the excessive cost increases under fee-for-
service medicine. Even though the economic incentives are not inherently evil
or ethically dubious, there are serious questions about how they can be implemented without compromising clinical decisions.

Two basic factors underlie why some conflicts are unavoidable under managed care. One aspect is the reality of scarce resources, which necessitated
the development of the modern managed care system in the first place. It
simply is not possible to provide health care on demand without regard to
cost. Cost containment is an inevitable feature of health-care delivery for the

foreseeable future; the question is not whether there will be cost containment, but how to structure and oversee the process of cost containment. Neither the courts—to whom patients frequently turn when the general need for cost containment turns into the specific denial of treatment—nor anyone else can successfully resolve managed care disputes by ignoring or wishing away the fundamental fact of scarcity. The mission facing whoever arbitrates managed care disputes is to ensure fair, accurate, and efficient administration while also preventing a bias toward limiting available health care in the name of short-sighted financial considerations.

The other factor is how to form a binding agreement (contract) for health-care benefits that will be provided in the future for as-yet-unknown medical conditions. When medical needs arise, any contractual ambiguities or tensions lurking beneath the parties' various understandings of the health care benefit package come to the surface. At best, it is difficult to anticipate the future contingencies of medical care when a patient enrolls in a health plan.

If some conflicts are an inherent feature of managed care, we need to find effective ways to resolve them quickly and limit how they might arise in the future. Here is where the concept of fiduciary duty comes in. It is designed to balance the individual patient's needs with the concomitant goal of preserving sufficient financial resources for the health plan's patient population.[2] Conceptually, fiduciary duty is easy to define; implementing the concept, however, is more challenging.

A fiduciary—literally, one who is entrusted with the power to act for the benefit of another—owes a duty of loyalty and a duty to exercise care in making decisions.[3] For example, when someone writes a will and appoints a trustee of the estate, the trustee is expected to act solely on behalf of the estate. The trustee's own values or economic interests should not enter into investment or other estate-related decisions. If the trustee fails to meet that responsibility, he or she is vulnerable to a lawsuit for breach of fiduciary duty. Fiduciary relationships are particularly important in medical care where "the parties are unable to foresee the conditions under which one act produces better results than another,"[4] and where the parties lack adequate information to assess the quality of health care.

The task of using the fiduciary-duty framework to resolve health-care conflicts is complicated by the reality that there are different understandings of the concept. Before the managed care era, fiduciary duty in health care meant the duty of loyalty from a physician to a patient or from a hospital administrator (or trustee) to the institution. Both the physician and the administrator owed exclusive loyalties to the patient or the institution, respectively. When a breach of fiduciary duty occurred, it was usually because an administrator used the position to obtain personal financial benefits at the expense of the institution, or a physician charged insurers for unnecessary tests. There was no competing on conflicting interests that might have explained or mitigated the breach of fiduciary duty.

Managed care changes the context by adding a new layer of fiduciary responsibilities that might interfere with patient care. The new layer is the health plan's accountability to maintain an economically viable organization to provide care for the entire patient population. A health plan administrator must balance between loyalty to the plan as a thriving business enterprise and loyalty to the individual patient who is entitled to receive the health care benefits that he or she purchased. Physicians are subject to a range of processes limiting their ability to provide care. Neither of these constraints existed in fee-for-service medicine.

Thus, one meaning of fiduciary duty is the loyalty a professional (physician or attorney) owes to the patient or client. Another meaning is the use of fiduciary duty to balance conflicting responsibilities. These meanings are not mutually exclusive. To the contrary, developing a common understanding of fiduciary duty will provide policy makers and the courts with a mechanism for balancing the resource allocation tradeoffs. A fiduciary-duty framework preserves patient trust while recognizing that changes in the marketplace, including economic incentives to limit the use of health-care resources, are unavoidable, at least in the short term.

The fiduciary duty approach delegates decision-making power to an impartial authority, called the fiduciary, to resolve conflicts over resource allocation decisions. The plan fiduciary, who can be either a physician or a health plan administrator, will bear responsibility for balancing the needs and interests of the patients who receive care, the insurers who pay for care, and the physicians who provide care. In the managed care context, an impartial plan fiduciary is perfectly poised to make whatever trade-offs are necessary between clinical treatment and the cost of care. Other existing legal mechanisms (namely, tort and contract) are inadequate for making these trade-offs up-front. Patients lack the knowledge and information to assess their clinical treatment, and individual physicians are unable to assess the impact of specific care decisions on the overall costs to the health plan. By contrast, the United States Supreme Court has noted that the central purpose of fiduciary law is to govern the exercise of discretion in making decisions that are not, and cannot be, controlled in advance by legal means.[5]

The underlying justification for using the fiduciary-duty framework is that a patient's trust in his or her physician is the foundation of a morally acceptable health-care system. Patients expect and trust that physicians have control over the resources needed for their care.[6] Many aspects of this relationship of trust—including methods of balancing social and economic concerns and the aspects of a physician's relationship to the managed care plan that must be disclosed to patients—are subjects of intense dispute.[7] The basic need for trust, though, is incontrovertible. Absent trust, managed care cannot survive.

The Fiduciary-Duty Concept

As a point of departure, neither tort nor contract law is adequate for balancing resource allocation trade-offs. Both the tort and contract approaches as we have seen, have considerable shortcomings in terms of their conceptual or practical ability to handle the conflicts posed by managed care. Even the strategies bridging tort and contract, which recognize the need for both concepts to operate simultaneously, are troublesome.

Particular aspects of managed care closely resemble contract-governed or tort-governed activities, though it is not easy to separate the functions in practice and characterize a certain function as either tort-like or contract.[8] Also, the terms *tort* and *contract* reduce very complex decisions to one-dimensional ideological polarities. As a consequence, the tort–contract debate is a dead end in addressing managed care's potential conflicts. That is why we need to consider new alternatives such as the fiduciary-duty approach.

One way to give a broad sense of what a fiduciary-duty framework would entail is to sketch how it would differ from the traditional contract and tort views. Unlike the contract perspective (agreeing to a specific set of health plan benefits up front), the fiduciary model acknowledges the specific clinical choices involved in benefit decisions. Instead of asking the courts to apply ambiguous contract terms to a complex clinical determination, the fiduciary-duty approach would examine what factors the plan fiduciary considered in the decision. In contrast to the tort model's focus on the standard of care in an individual case to determine damages, the fiduciary-duty framework would evaluate the integrity of the process governing how decisions are made and whether the challenged decision complied with that process. At the same time, it is more efficient and less costly than tort-based rules because health care administrators, rather than the courts, would be making decisions in the first instance.

It is also useful to compare the fiduciary-duty framework to other competing possibilities for a system of decision-making and review, such as arbitration and mediation. Similar to arbitration, there would be a decision-maker who hears the evidence presented by both sides. The framework shares some of arbitration's goals, including lower litigation costs and encouraging a less adversarial process. But unlike the standard arbitration approach, the fiduciary framework is designed to accrue a set of decisions as precedent for subsequent treatment recommendation reviews. Equally important, the framework presumes a more active judicial monitoring role than arbitration, which often precludes judicial review.

Similar to mediation, a goal of the fiduciary framework is to offer an opportunity for the parties to resolve the dispute among themselves. If both parties act in good faith, they may be able to come to agreement short of litigation. In contrast to mediation, where the mediator only has authority to make suggestions, the fiduciary is charged with making a decision if the parties cannot agree.

A fiduciary relationship imposes two fundamental duties on the fiduciary: the duty of loyalty and the duty to exercise prudence.[9] Courts can resolve conflicts regarding managed care decisions by focusing on whether the plan fiduciary has performed these two duties. A court will not substitute its judgment for the fiduciary's unless a plaintiff can show a failure to exercise good judgment or that the decision conceals an improper motivation.[10]

The duty of prudence, often ignored in health care cases discussing fiduciary duty, requires that the fiduciary must exercise reasonable care and skill in making decisions affecting beneficiaries. In exercising the duty of prudence, the fiduciary is required to obtain all available information that would help inform the decision. Any challenge to the plan fiduciary's decision to deny care would need to assert a breach of this duty.

The duty of loyalty demands that the fiduciary not have any conflicting allegiances that might influence his or her ability to make decisions in the patients' best interests. In the fee-for-service system, the duty of loyalty to one's patient was clear and conflicts of loyalty were avoidable. In the managed care context, some might assume that the prohibition on conflicts would foreclose the creation of incentives to curtail costs, as these might be thought to encourage disloyalty to specific patients. But public policy recognizes that the clarity of the old system has eroded and that conflicts of interest in managed care are unavoidable.[11]

Accordingly, there is a need for a feasible set of standards for physicians and managed care organizations that explicitly recognizes the tensions involved in simultaneously serving the patient and the entire patient population. The fiduciary framework offers a means of resolving these difficult conflicts without undermining the legitimate policy objectives of controlling health-care costs or the physician's fiduciary duty to his or her patients. Fiduciary law contemplates that fiduciaries may need to balance competing interests, such as corporate officers serving multiple constituencies. "[T]he fact that physicians have obligations to third parties does not mean that they cannot be fiduciaries for patients. Obligations to third parties may merely limit the scope of fiduciary obligation. . . ."[12]

In most cases involving an MCO's denial of health care, the correct analysis of the duty of loyalty is not to ask whether the plan fiduciary has any conflicts or broad incentives to minimize costs generally. The issue is whether a decision in any specific case denying health-care services was in fact motivated by an improper conflict of interest that interfered with sound clinical judgment. To address the issue, we must ask what kinds of conflicting loyalties or responsibilities are acceptable, what kinds are not, and how they will be resolved.

Not every external influence on a clinical decision creates a conflict of interest. Scholars distinguish between a conflict of interest and a conflict of obligation. By definition, conflicting obligations are inevitable under managed care because resources spent for one patient are not available for another. These are not necessarily the types of conflicts that would violate the fiduciary duty.[13]

A useful definition is that a *conflict of interest* occurs when an individual's professional judgment is unduly influenced by personal financial gain.[14,15] The fiduciary's financial interests should be irrelevant to the merits of a clinical decision. Rules to minimize conflicts of interest are designed to prevent the financial factors (even where legitimate) from controlling or influencing professional judgment. In a conflict of interest, the fiduciary may have incentives to act in his or her own interests rather than those of the patient. For example, physicians with economic incentives to reduce health-care costs might not refer a patient to a specialist when the referral would reduce the physician's income.

In contrast, a *conflict of obligation* occurs when a physician must simultaneously consider obligations that might inconvenience a patient temporarily, without any consequences for the patient's immediate care. A physician might have a roomful of non-emergency patients, but shorten some individual patient visits to attend a child's ball game. No patient's care is likely to be harmed in this situation.

A patient may not immediately see the distinction, but it is an important one. Conflicts of obligation generally do not interfere with patient care. They may inconvenience a patient by putting a physician behind schedule, yet the care the patient receives is not affected. With a conflict of interest, the possibility exists that patient care will be compromised.

An important consideration is whether the operation of managed care's financial incentives creates conflicts of interest or obligation. The potential conflict is that physicians' and plan administrators' economic interests will interfere with sound clinical decisions. Even if the incentives themselves result in conflicts of interest, the courts have been clear that patients cannot challenge the incentives directly. Still, this leaves open how to resolve conflicts of interest so that the physician's or health plan's economic interests do not compromise patient care.

Identifying truly relevant conflicts is more difficult than it may first appear.

It is challenging to distinguish decisions motivated by conflicting loyalties from good-faith efforts to control costs in accordance with managed care's objectives. Acts undertaken to benefit the plan as a whole (i.e., to reduce costs and, therefore, the premium owed by each plan participant) often look the same as acts undertaken to benefit the managed care corporate entity (i.e., to increase profits and make shareholders wealthier).[16] In either case, the people choosing the plan also have a decided interest in holding down costs to ensure the plan's economic viability and efficient operation. In a competitive marketplace, lower costs will result in reduced premiums or expanded benefits— both of which are attractive to employers and employees. Of course, if employees are willing to pay more in return for receiving more benefits, the MCO will have no incentive to deny care arbitrarily.

Numerous disputes regarding whether and how the plan fiduciary meets his or her fiduciary duty arise in managed care. One frequent source of litigation is the common provision that a plan will cover care deemed medically necessary.[17] This provision is devoid of meaning until it is applied to the medical needs of a specific patient with a specific condition.[18] Determining whether the treating physician's clinical recommendation is in fact medically necessary often requires difficult medical choices and benefit coverage decisions. For instance, is a positioning device for a multiply handicapped child medically necessary if it provides only comfort and no therapeutic or restorative care?[19] Referrals to specialty care present similar concerns.

Another common dispute is that many plans include policies restricting the use of procedures that, although they may provide substantial benefits for certain patients, have considerable costs that would exceed their benefits if made available to all patients. One such procedure is the injection of more costly contrast agents for radiological procedures that provide significant benefits to high-risk groups but whose benefits do not justify the cost of using them in every case.[20] Likewise, some plans refuse to provide yearly mammograms for women under 40 because of low cost-effectiveness in that age group. The plan fiduciary would be responsible for determining whether a particular patient was sufficiently high-risk to justify the more expensive procedure despite the general plan policy restricting its use. Or, suppose that a physician wants to order a particular drug treatment that is not listed on the approved pharmaceutical formulary (the drugs the MCO will reimburse)? In each of these examples, the fiduciary must make a decision in situations where the health plan's financial interests may conflict with an individual patient's medical treatment.

The concept of using the fiduciary-duty framework to make trade-offs between individual beneficiaries and plan populations is hardly novel. Already, ERISA explicitly contemplates the need to balance competing interests.[21] The act recognizes that individual clinical decisions may sometimes be made in the context of a potential conflict with the goal of preserving resources for the managed care patient population. As we have seen, ERISA imposes a fiduciary duty requiring those who make discretionary decisions on behalf of an employee benefit plan (health insurance coverage) to act "solely in the interest of the participants and beneficiaries" of the plan.[22] Unfortunately, these terms are not defined either by ERISA or by the courts.[23] No one really knows what the "solely in the interest of . . ." language means when a fiduciary makes certain decisions, such as reviewing the appropriateness of a physician's treatment recommendation.[24] In exercising the fiduciary duty, one obvious problem the administrator faces is that the plan's participants may not share a single interest. Some patients will want to keep costs low to reduce insurance premiums, while others will want to have unlimited care when they need it.[25]

Courts, as we saw earlier, have only developed an outline of how to interpret ERISA's fiduciary duty language. To determine whether an MCO breached its fiduciary duty when denying plan benefits, courts have employed different levels of scrutiny based on the degree of discretion granted to the MCO under the employee health plan. Generally, courts are deferential, upholding the plan administrator's decision as long as it was not arbitrary and capricious.[26] Deference is granted in recognition that the plan administrator also owes a fiduciary duty to preserve plan resources for other employees (plan participants). Courts limit their review to ensuring that the MCO reasonably complied with the terms of the health benefit. In the example raised earlier about the medical need for a positioning device for a multiply handicapped child, the court would ask first whether the fiduciary reasonably interpreted the plan benefit language in denying the benefit. If so, the court would defer to the fiduciary unless the interpretation was arbitrary and capricious, a very difficult standard to overcome. As a result, MCOs retain power *vis-à-vis* physicians by controlling the interpretation of the health plan contract terms.[27] Where the plan profits directly from the denial, however, the potential conflict of interest must be considered as a factor in deciding whether there was an abuse of the fiduciary's discretion.[28] Unless the patient can show that the financial motive drove the decision to deny, it will be difficult under ERISA to show that the decision was arbitrary and capricious.

For the most part, courts have understood ERISA's fiduciary duty only as a mandate that plan administrators avoid improper financial incentives. The precise rules governing which institutional financial incentives are acceptable and which are not remain undefined, as do the standards for making trade-offs between patients and the plan in individual cases. Beyond holding that patients cannot directly challenge managed care's financial incentives as a breach of fiduciary duty, the courts have also made it clear that employees cannot use ERISA to challenge the terms of the health benefit plan. Every way a patient turns, the courts have limited the reach and usefulness of ERISA's fiduciary-duty structure.

By itself, the ERISA fiduciary-duty framework is insufficient to resolve the resource allocation trade-offs at the heart of managed care, though it provides an important foundation for a broader consideration of the concept. As a useful point of reference, ERISA recognizes and explicitly accepts the reality that managed care fiduciaries must balance a variety of potentially conflicting interests. One problem is that the Supreme Court unnecessarily emasculated ERISA's fiduciary duty provision in *Pegram v. Herdrich* by ruling that Congress did not intend to treat MCOs as fiduciaries when making mixed benefit eligibility and coverage decisions. The Court went on to note that allowing patients to challenge fiduciary duties under ERISA would be tantamount to attacking managed care's financial incentives and would be nothing more than another type of medical malpractice claim.

For several reasons, the fiduciary duty concept remains a viable alternative despite the Supreme Court's rebuff. Nothing prevents state courts from developing a common law of fiduciary duty in cases that are not preempted by ERISA. To the extent that lower federal courts erode ERISA preemption, state courts will have the opportunity to go in a different direction. Other approaches are plausible. Health plans and physicians could easily implement a fiduciary duty arrangement on their own—if both sides can be convinced that it is in everyone's interest to do so. *Pegram* may eliminate a judicial method to force its use, but *Pegram* certainly does not prevent its voluntary adoption.

An example of the possibilities, though not taken in this case, is *Neade v. Portes*.[29] The primary care physician, Dr. Portes, relied on the results of a thallium stress test and an EKG to determine that the plaintiff's husband, Anthony Neade, was not suffering from coronary artery disease. About a month later, Mr. Neade returned to the doctor complaining of stabbing chest pains. Although Dr. Portes's associate and another physician recommended a more specific test, Dr. Portes refused to authorize an angiogram. Mr. Neade died a few days later. The plaintiff alleged that Dr. Portes's failure to authorize the angiogram was because his group had a Medical Incentive Plan with an HMO to divide money that was not used for referrals or outside tests (on a 60–40 basis). That incentive plan was not disclosed to the plaintiff, who brought a lawsuit for breach of fiduciary duty. The lower court upheld the breach of fiduciary duty claim. But the Illinois Supreme Court reversed the decision by accepting the reasoning in *Pegram* that breach of fiduciary duty and malpractice claims overlap.

This conclusion ignores the different conceptual bases of the two claims and the different goals to be achieved by each. As a strongly argued dissenting opinion recognized, a jury could rule in favor of disclosure regardless of whether the physician was right to rely on the stress test. Other states could easily follow the dissenting opinion in subsequent cases.

At some point, ERISA preemption will end. Either the courts will erode it to the point where it has little vitality, or Congress will be compelled to allow patients to sue MCOs in state court. When that happens, the fiduciary-duty concept will be even more useful as a means of resolving disputes before patients are forced to sue. The patient's leverage of being able to sue in state courts will provide an incentive for MCOs to adopt voluntarily a mechanism where the patient, physician, and plan administrator can jointly decide what is best in a non-adversarial context.

Implementing the Fiduciary Framework

It is one thing to suggest why the fiduciary duty might work in theory; it is quite another to show how it can be implemented. Moving beyond the narrow confines of the ERISA fiduciary-duty framework offers both opportunity and challenge. The opportunity is to outline how a more expansive fiduciary-duty arrangement might work. The bottom line is recommending a system that places a more stringent burden on the fiduciary to justify a benefit denial than the courts have imposed so far. Before denying recommended clinical treatment, the fiduciary must meet certain requirements. The challenge is to make these requirements both workable and acceptable to patients, physicians, and health plan administrators. Of necessity, doing so presents a complex and legally technical situation that will take time and a willingness to make adjustments to implement. The reality, though, is that there is no simple solution to the resource allocation dilemma that provides adequate protection against arbitrary denials of health care while simultaneously encouraging cost containment. The health-care delivery system is complex. Attempts to impose obvious or easy solutions are likely to create a false sense of security that will only postpone the need to adopt more complex policy responses.[30] What follows is an overview of how the concept might work in practice.[31]

The fiduciary-duty approach arises from the possibilities and limitations available to the parties as they contract to form a plan. While the parties cannot determine cost-allocation issues in advance, they can specify who the appropriate person will be to make the decision. In other words, they can vest someone (the plan fiduciary) with decision-making authority and with concomitant responsibilities, including the duties to be prudent and loyal to the participants' interests. Most plans already name an administrator whose function is to make determinations regarding matters at the intersection of two vital components of managed care: financial management and health-care delivery.

The proper objective of the loyalty rule is to eliminate systematic bias in favor of the MCO rather than to aid particular patients after the fact.[32] The way MCOs currently review treatment recommendations raises serious concerns about how to separate the fiduciary's power to make decisions affecting medical care from his or her direct stake in the MCO's financial performance. At least to patients going through the process, the impression is that MCOs have a financial incentive to deny care. The failure to establish a clear structure for fiduciary decisions and informing patients about how decisions are made contributes to this impression.

The fiduciary framework attempts to define who should decide what is medically necessary, how the fiduciary should make that decision, and what role the court system would play in reviewing it. Implementing the framework, therefore, involves three sets of issues: the proper structure for selection and oversight of the fiduciary; the actual decision rules that will govern the fiduciary's exercise of authority; and the role of the courts in reviewing challenges to the fiduciary's decisions.

How can the fiduciary-duty concept be structured within a health plan to ensure proper decisions? The common-law duty of loyalty demands the selection of a plan fiduciary with no conflicting interests that would prevent him or her from making unbiased decisions in the beneficiaries' best interests.[33] Institutional safeguards are needed to assure that the fiduciary will be trustworthy. These safeguards include determining who may serve as a fiduciary and disclosing to the health plan sponsors (i.e., employees and employers) how the process will work. Ultimately, accountability rests with the plan sponsors, so they must participate in designing the organizational structure that establishes and monitors the fiduciary. Nothing prevents employers and health plans from agreeing up front on a set of policies and procedures that would guide the fiduciary duty process.

One fundamental question that this framework must answer, and that courts have struggled to answer, is who constitutes a fiduciary in managed care. Broadly defined, whoever exercises discretion in determining when and whether to approve medical treatment is acting in a fiduciary capacity.[34] Either a physician or a plan administrator can act as a fiduciary if the plan delegates discretionary decision-making authority to him or her.

A controversial issue is what information health plan participants should be given regarding the operation of financial incentives, along with the mechanics of providing the information. At a minimum, health plan participants should be informed of the financial incentives and other relevant characteristics of the health plan's fiduciary process before signing up for the plan.[35] The fiduciary duty approach presupposes that all parties to the managed care plan have voluntarily ceded decision-making authority to the fiduciary. As is generally the case in the law governing fiduciary relationships, even where there is only an appearance or likelihood of conflict, it is critical that potential conflicts be disclosed.

The courts have given this issue increasing attention, but are split on whether to require disclosure. An Illinois court ruled that an individual doctor did not breach his fiduciary duty by failing to disclose to patients the nature of his financial relationship to the MCO and the incentives that relationship created.[36] The court held that the claimed breach of fiduciary duty actually duplicated a medical malpractice claim. The court was also pragmatically concerned that physicians have too many managed care contracts to keep track of the payment incentives and rules for each contract. Neither reason is compelling. As the dissenting opinion points out, "If there is any possibility that the course of treatment recommended by the care provider may be affected by the remuneration he stands to receive . . . , the patient has the right to know about it and the care provider has the obligation to make the disclosure."[37]

Under ERISA, the situation is equally unsettled. One case arguing in favor of disclosure[38] noted that "[t]he duty to disclose material information is the core of a fiduciary's responsibility. . . ." Although other courts have disagreed, the Supreme Court may have signaled its position by noting instances where the ERISA fiduciary is obligated to disclose information.[39]

Disclosure is not without its problems, both as to what must be disclosed and when it should be disclosed. Few people receiving the information will know how to interpret it, and they may have few alternatives in any case.[40] Too much information may be as difficult to interpret as too little, yet the arguments against disclosure are not especially compelling. For those arguing in favor of a market-based health care system, information disclosure must be a central component. Certainly, those opposed to a market-driven system recognize the value and importance of making available to plan enrollees information about the plan's practices and incentives. Without full disclosure, the fiduciary duty concept is a non-starter. It is premised on full agreement between the parties about the process and the way conflicts of interest will be resolved.

Once the structure is put in place, the next job is to determine what rules will guide the process. The key to the fiduciary duty approach is to devise a set of substantive decision rules the fiduciary will use to resolve disputes. Among the questions to be addressed are how a conflict of interest will be determined and under what circumstances a fiduciary breaches the duty of loyalty. These rules will govern the plan fiduciary's decisions regarding clinical choices about the level of care to be provided under specific circumstances. The willingness and ability to devise flexible but predictable rules is the crux of how well a fiduciary approach would operate. The question to address is how the fiduciary exercises the broad scope of his or her authority to review clinical decisions. What must a fiduciary do, or prove, to make the decisions authoritative?

For the decisions to have weight and survive both judicial and plan sponsor scrutiny, the fiduciary must meet a minimum threshold. Before coming to a decision, the fiduciary must gather and analyze sufficient information to make a reasoned judgment. After the decision, the fiduciary must be able to objectively articulate the bases for that decision. Most important, these decisions must be publicly accessible and transparent. In this context, transparency means that the decision-making process and reasoning must be available on request. It is critical that the fiduciary provide fair process before denying a benefit. Borrowing from the standard in *Potvin v. Metropolitan Life Ins. Co.*,[41] these private organizational decisions have such important public consequences that fair process should be expected. Fair procedures must protect individuals from arbitrary decisions.[42] Arguably, this standard would apply directly to managed care. The private administrator would make an initial decision that would be subject to judicial review and reversal if it were "arbitrary and capricious" or an "abuse of discretion."[43]

To meet this standard, a two-part test can be used to evaluate a fiduciary's decision to deny care. The first part of the test is that the fiduciary must have a sound medical reason for denying the requested clinical treatment. A strong medical reason is crucial for proving that the fiduciary has satisfied the duty to exercise prudence in making decisions affecting the patient. The medical reason must be based on the best available medical evidence. It must be supported by clinical practice guidelines, the current standard of care, well-defined benefit exclusions, the medical literature, or some other clinical practice justification. Some plans now routinely convene external review panels consisting of independent physicians to advise the plan administrator on how to respond to specific denials of care.[44]

Furthermore, the clinical justification must be reasonable given the facts of the case at hand. Because the duty of prudence embraces an "element of initiative or effort,"[45] it must be clear that the fiduciary was familiar with all facts necessary to arrive at a proper medical decision. In *McGraw v. Prudential Insurance Company*, the medical director charged with reviewing the decision to deny coverage did not even undertake to review the patient's medical records.[46] Relying in part on this "egregious" failure, the court found the ultimate decision to deny coverage to be arbitrary and capricious. Under the fiduciary duty concept being developed in this book, the failure to review medical records would automatically foreclose any ability to show a medical justification for the decision when it was made and would therefore amount to a breach of fiduciary duty.

For the second part of the test, the fiduciary must have an administrative reason for the decision to deny care that will be a defense against a claim that the decision breached the duty of loyalty. The fiduciary can satisfy the administrative requirement by indicating a concomitant benefit to the patient population that justifies the denial of the individual patient's care. To borrow from ERISA's language, the plan fiduciary's responsibility in each instance is to make decisions "solely in the interest of the participants and beneficiaries" of the plan.[47] The fiduciary must not be serving only personal or corporate ends. There are many tools the fiduciary might use, including clinical practice guidelines and cost–benefit or cost-effective analyses, to demonstrate an appropriate administrative reason.

The fiduciary's task will be to develop guidelines or principles that will both assist in making decisions and provide a transparent process. Some of these principles can be stated up front to show how a decision will be made. For example, rules can be established to show when health care will be denied because its costs outweigh the expected benefits. (To date, health plans have used cost–benefit or cost-effective analyses very sparingly.)[48]

The key question is how much of a showing is necessary to demonstrate the fiduciary's decision-making rationale? The fiduciary must demonstrate an objective, plausible medical reason and offer some showing that this justification actually motivated the decision.[49] Merely stating that the care should be denied or that providing care would adversely affect the patient population would not fulfill the fiduciary's obligations. As with judicial review of administrative agency determinations, the fiduciary should not be allowed to merely provide the courts with a rationalization created after litigation has commenced. The fiduciary is responsible for maintaining a contemporaneous record providing the basis for denial that existed at the time of rejection, which could provide a set of precedents to guide future cases and ensure consistency.[50] It would also make plan decisions explicit so they could be subsequently reconsidered during contract renewal discussions between plans and employers.

Many cases that would otherwise have led to litigation will be resolved once the fiduciary duty mechanism is implemented. Even under the most optimistic circumstances, however, judicial review and oversight will be needed to make sure that the process works as planned. For the cases still under dispute, what will be the role of the courts in overseeing the fiduciary duty mechanism?

Judicial review will be based on applying the medical and administrative reasons for the denial of care. Courts will assess the sufficiency of the fiduciary's justifications. What counts as a sufficient basis for the fiduciary's decision will be defined in terms of evidentiary requirements and the level of scrutiny the courts will apply to the fiduciary's decision. The task is not to decide what might make a fiduciary's decision right or wrong in the abstract, but to determine what will make a fiduciary's decision survive judicial review.

It is clear that some deference is due to the fiduciary's decision under the common-law model of fiduciary duty.[51] To ensure fairness, courts must also retain sufficient oversight to assure that any particular decision does not violate the duties of prudence or loyalty, or is not compromised by conflicting financial interests. With respect to both elements of the fiduciary standard, namely, the medical basis and benefit to the patient population, the burden should be on the fiduciary to justify the denial. But how is the fiduciary to meet that burden? One argument asserts that to surmount a claim based on medical necessity the health plan should be required to present clear and convincing evidence (using clinical practice guidelines, perhaps) that the patient's desired treatment is not appropriate.[52] This burden seems too stringent, although other suggestions seem too deferential to the managed care decision maker. For instance, one analysis suggests that the insurer should design a process for reviewing clinical decisions that would be overruled only if a court determined that the insurer's decision was arbitrary and capricious.[53] Another approach would ask whether the fiduciary's decision was "reasonably justifiable under the terms of the health plan," essentially a good-faith approach that defers to the plan fiduciary.[54]

Some courts have recognized that efforts to lower costs can be interpreted either as useful attempts to benefit participants or as nefarious schemes to increase corporate profits. The judicial standard of review should depend on the extent to which a clear, ulterior, profit-making motive is present. One court noted, for instance, that "the degree of deference to accord [a fiduciary's] decision will be decreased on a sliding scale in proportion to the extent of conflict present." This court recognized the need for flexibility, given that "every exercise of discretion impacts [the MCO] financially. . . ."[55] Meeting this standard requires an inquiry directly devoted to examining the justifications behind specific administrative decisions.

The basic factor determining the level of scrutiny a court should apply to the fiduciary's decision is whether the medical and administrative aspects of the decision are "inextricably intertwined."[56] A threshold issue courts will confront before applying the two-part fiduciary-duty standard is the extent to which the decision necessitates a trade-off between the competing claims and needs of the patient and the health plan. The more a given decision involves both the administration of the plan and the practice of medicine, the more evidence the fiduciary must show to demonstrate that these goals have been legitimately balanced, i.e., to show that the decision was motivated by good faith.[57,58]

An added benefit of the fiduciary-duty framework is the flexibility it gives judges in providing remedies for a breach of such duties. At common law, a suit against a fiduciary would *lie in equity*, meaning that a court could command the fiduciary to undertake action or undo past action.[59] The courts could also award monetary damages for any unwarranted gain to the fiduciary.[60] In many cases, the proper remedy would be an injunction to force the plan to provide and pay for the benefit. Not only do the expanded common law remedies grant the court greater discretion, they also encourage private settlements and creative solutions between beneficiaries and plan fiduciaries.

To be sure, this process will not be a panacea and will not solve problems immediately. Over time, standards and decision rules will emerge to provide predictability and fairness of process that will minimize the conflicts. The fiduciary duty approach recognizes that clinical loyalties may conflict with medicine's broader social purposes (including issues of cost containment).[61] In this sense, the fiduciary-duty framework represents an opportunity to find the right balance between conflicting health-policy objectives. It encourages an ongoing deliberative process that is adaptable to changing circumstances. But it will not be a *once and for all* solution.[62]

It might be useful to demonstrate how this approach would be applied to actual disputes. For illustrative purposes, let us look at three cases: one case where the fiduciary-duty approach would reach a different result, one where the result would be similar, and one that raised the fiduciary-duty issue directly but rejected it over a strong dissent.

For the first case, suppose a patient sought and received medical care for chest pain.[63] The patient then filed a claim for reimbursement with her employee benefit plan, but the plan administrator (the plan's fiduciary) denied the claim based on a pre-existing condition. (Most insurance contracts deny reimbursement within a certain period, say the first six months after enrollment, for conditions that pre-existed the date of enrollment in the plan.) To recover the money, the patient filed an ERISA claim that the plan fiduciary abused his discretion in denying reimbursement. The lower court agreed, but the appellate court ruled in the plan's favor.

Without going into the medical details of the case, the issue was whether the patient's prior treatment for high blood pressure and a high cholesterol level was tantamount to a pre-existing heart condition. The treating physician stated that there was no evidence of pre-existing coronary artery disease. After several levels of review, including recommendations from outside physicians, the plan administrative committee denied the patient's request for reimbursement. The plan considered prior treatment for hypertension as being related to heart disease, and the patient took medication that is often prescribed for heart patients (though it also has other uses). The plan also considered some ambiguous notes written by the treating physician to indicate the presence of a pre-existing heart condition.

Despite the conflicting medical opinion, the court ruled that the plan fiduciary did not abuse his discretion in denying reimbursement. This seems to be a defensible, but curious, result given the treating physician's direct statements that heart disease had not been diagnosed or treated. Under the fiduciary-duty framework, the plan fiduciary would not have met his burden of providing a compelling medical rationale to overcome the conflict of interest presented. The case outcome would therefore have been different. Absent a more persuasive clinical rationale for denying care, the fiduciary should have deferred to the treating physician.[64]

In another case, the result would have been the same. After a child was born with severe cerebral palsy and spastic quadriplegia, the treating physician requested ongoing physical therapy to prevent muscle deterioration. Based solely on one published article, the plan fiduciary concluded that intensive physical therapy was not medically necessary and denied further coverage. Consistent with the fiduciary duty framework, the court found that the fiduciary's medical rationale was deficient. It was clear that the reviewing physician had little experience with the physical therapy needs of multiply handicapped children and hence could not determine the medical necessity of the claims.[65] In finding a breach of fiduciary duty, the court said, "To put it most charitably, we think it abundantly clear that [the fiduciary] at least 'unconsciously' put the [health plan's] financial interest above her fiduciary duty. . . ."[66] Explicitly, the court recognized the need to provide an independent medical rationale to show that the inherent financial conflict does not taint the decision-making process.

> Even the most careful and sensitive fiduciary in those circumstances may unconsciously favor its profit interest over the interests of the plan [beneficiaries], leaving beneficiaries less protected than when the trustee acts without self-interest. . . . [67]

In the third example, two plaintiffs sought their insurer's approval for extended hospitalization beyond the automatic coverage period under their respective plans. One of the patients (Musette Batas) needed additional care so that the severe intestinal swelling caused by her chronic condition could be monitored. The other patient (Nancy Vogel) needed to be observed following a difficult abdominal hysterectomy to remove two large tumors.[68] Both were denied coverage on the assertion that further hospitalization was not medically necessary. Later, Batas was rushed back to the emergency room, at which time her doctor requested pre-authorization for exploratory surgery. The insurer pre-authorized the surgery five days later—two days after Batas' intestine had burst, necessitating surgery to remove part of her colon. Following the surgery, Batas was again discharged, over her physician's protests, on the basis that further hospitalization was not medically necessary.

Batas and Vogel belonged to the same health plan, and brought a lawsuit claiming that the MCO's failure to disclose the standards by which they made medical necessity decisions was a breach of fiduciary duty. The trial court's dismissal of the fiduciary-duty claim was upheld on appeal. In contrast, the dissenting opinion identified the inadequacy of existing state law tort remedies and argued in favor of recognizing a state law action for breach of fiduciary duty.

As the dissent clearly appreciated, a fiduciary-duty framework is a better way of deciding these conflicts between financial and clinical areas than either tort or contract. The dissent concluded that "[w]hen we consider the nature of the health insurance industry, it becomes apparent that medical insurers, even more than most, should be held to a special standard of conduct toward their policyholders, beyond that required of parties to an ordinary, commercial contract."[69] A "standard of conduct"—whether formally styled as a "duty of good faith and fair dealing" or a fiduciary duty—should exist, and its contours should be defined by reference to the nature of fiduciary decisions required in managed care.

The Supreme Court, in the *Pegram* case, missed an opportunity to impose such a model using ERISA's statutory scheme and its fiduciary duties. State courts still have the opportunity to use the fiduciary framework, as these types of cases are not likely to go away. Judges should closely scrutinize a health plan's stated rationale before deferring to the plan administrator. Interestingly, one court extended the fiduciary-duty approach by stating that "A fiduciary with a conflict of interest must act as if he is 'free' of such a conflict. 'Free' is an absolute. There is no balancing of interests. . . ."[70] This absolutist language seems unrealistic in a world where public policy explicitly expects plans to make trade-offs between access and costs.

At this point, the reader might well ask what the practical changes would be if the fiduciary framework were adopted? The primary change is that institutions would have less control over health-care decisions, and doctors would retain greater clinical autonomy and authority. Implementing the fiduciary duty concept will not automatically restore physician autonomy, nor will it automatically result in decisions favorable to individual patients. The fiduciary duty approach would govern benefit denial challenges, such as utilization review decisions and failure to refer to a specialist, but it would not play a role in traditional medical malpractice cases. What it would do is force both sides, the physician and the MCO, to acknowledge that competing interests need to be heard and considered.

Physicians need to realize that their ability to recommend treatment will be limited by factors other than what is in the patient's best interests. Costs neither can, nor should, be eliminated as a concern in treatment recommendations. For their part, MCOs need to recognize that they can no longer arbitrarily deny care without providing compelling reasons for their actions. Just as physician autonomy will be limited, institutional authority to deny care without constraint will be limited. Under the fiduciary-duty approach, both sides will be forced to start with the individual patient, and then bring other considerations into the decision as appropriate.

Both the *Andrews-Clarke* and *Goodrich* cases would have benefited from the fiduciary duty approach. In *Andrews-Clarke*, the MCO would have been required to justify its refusal of inpatient psychiatric treatment for Mr. Clarke. Instead of the tragic situation where her claim was preempted by ERISA, the fiduciary-duty approach would probably have resulted in a compromise course of treatment that might have prevented Mr. Clarke's suicide. With *Goodrich*, the fiduciary-duty approach would have solved the problem that prevented additional cancer treatment. Eventually, the plan said it would pay for Mr. Goodrich's care. By then it was too late. Had the fiduciary-duty framework been available, the miscommunications that occurred might have been avoided.

A legitimate concern is that the fiduciary-duty framework is merely a fig-leaf for a return to the excesses of the fee-for-service system. Consider, however, that the result reached in the *Pegram v. Herdrich* case would be the same under the fiduciary-duty concept. In that case, Herdrich alleged that her physician breached the fiduciary duty when Dr. Pegram determined that Herdrich would need to wait eight days for an ultrasound at a plan facility more than 50 miles away instead of at a local facility that was not part of the plan. Herdrich blamed financial incentives for the delay. Had the case not been caught in ERISA's complex web, it probably would have been litigated in state court as a standard medical malpractice action.

We can still analyze the *Pegram* situation under the fiduciary-duty approach. The existence of financial incentives would not by themselves preclude a decision favoring the plan fiduciary. Dr. Pegram could have argued that there were sound medical reasons for the delay and that the benefit package clearly supported a within-network referral. The plan could have successfully argued that too many out-of-network referrals would drastically reduce the availability of plan assets for other patients. Absent a pressing medical need for an immediate referral, the plan's judgment to delay the care could have been defended to defeat a breach of fiduciary-duty challenge.

The fiduciary-duty framework imposes a form of communication and justification that can avoid the harsh results from ERISA preemption and the unconstrained cost increases of the fee-for-service system. It will not solve all cases, nor result in an acceptable compromise every time. But it will no doubt change the physician–patient–plan dynamic in ways that will benefit individual patients and release some of the political pressure on the managed care industry.

Those who advocate strong institutional control over medical decisions will view this as regressing to the unconstrained costs of the fee-for-service era.

That is not accurate—I am not advocating for a return to fee-for-service medicine, and there is no assurance that physicians and patients will be consistent
winners. In any event, the framework retains an important role for MCOs in
reviewing clinical treatment recommendations, and an institutional oversight
role for the courts. Managed care introduced a set of needed restraints on
physicians, but the system has veered too far in favor of institutional control.
The fiduciary-duty model forces the needed return to the centrality of the
physician–patient encounter.

Justifications for the Fiduciary-Duty Framework

There are several justifications for the fiduciary-duty framework. Using this
approach has practical benefits for patients and MCOs alike. Aside from being
less confrontational, it is a medically sound and procedurally fair way to resolve
disputes between MCOs and patients. The fiduciary-duty framework contains
no particular bias for or against the provision of care in specific cases.

> [A] fiduciary obligation . . . does not necessarily favor payment over nonpayment.
> The common law of trusts recognizes the need to preserve assets to satisfy future,
> as well as present, claims and requires a trustee to take impartial account of the
> interests of all beneficiaries.[71]

Neither side has a built-in advantage, and it forces both sides to focus on the
medical evidence. Implementing the fiduciary framework may also alleviate
political pressure to "do something" about managed care.

Neither contract nor tort law seems to offer an adequate set of principles
for resolving conflicts between individuals and populations. Their inadequacy
demonstrates the desirability of finding an alternative method. The concept
of fiduciary duty is based on a set of legal principles that seem particularly
applicable to the conflicts presented in managed care. Though the concept
itself is not new, broad application to managed care litigation would be a
departure from current judicial thinking. To date, the common-law principles
applicable to the fiduciary relationship have not received much attention from
courts or commentators as a possible analytical framework for managed care
law.[72]

Since attorneys, physicians, and health-care administrators are trained to
understand the concept of fiduciary duty, they are more likely to be comfortable with a framework that places fiduciary duties at the core of decision-
making. Also, a new alternative that is still rooted in traditional common law
concepts and doctrines may be easier to implement than a truly radical or
revolutionary approach. Another advantage is that the fiduciary-duty concept

is indifferent to how health care is organized. Much of the current debate centers on how managed care has changed the nature of the law–medicine relationship. The centrality of fiduciary duties can remain stable even if the environment changes. However managed care evolves or whatever system replaces it, we will still struggle with the conflicts of interest spawned by cost pressures. A flexibly designed fiduciary-duty approach is easily adaptable to new health care delivery systems.

A framework that focuses on fiduciary duty is practical because it harmonizes well with the existing statutory regime governing managed care entities. ERISA already imposes a fiduciary duty on plan administrators toward plan beneficiaries. Moreover, the Supreme Court has stated its belief that the common law of trusts should inform courts' interpretation of the duty imposed by ERISA on plan administrators.[73] Certainly, a fiduciary model cannot be justified merely by relying on the fact that ERISA imposes a fiduciary duty. But state courts can develop their own fiduciary law principles without the constraints of a federal statute. As a starting point, judges may want to look at ERISA. Nothing in ERISA prevents state courts from going much farther or in a different direction in developing fiduciary-duty principles.

A method of analysis rooted in an existing legal framework assures that the courts can fulfill their traditional institutional role of monitoring and facilitating social and economic arrangements. Courts have long been in the business of reconciling or balancing conflicting policy objectives, particularly in situations like managed care, where an external check on free-market financial incentives is needed. The courts must mediate relationships like those presented in the managed care situation, where the triad of provider, consumer, and payer interests sometimes overlap and sometimes conflict. Judicial review of a health plan fiduciary's decisions allows the courts to consider medical and health policy values without sacrificing the value of each individual case and litigant that the law prizes. As an institution, the judiciary is also capable of establishing stable rules over time.

Equally important, a fiduciary-duty approach would enable the courts to render better decisions or at least provide better justifications for the decisions they now struggle to reach. A fiduciary-duty perspective allows courts to support the viability of managed care as a method of cost containment. It also avoids the blunt instrument of contractual interpretation, which frequently produces the harsh outcome of denying care without any legal recourse, or tort, which has the potential to undermine managed care's cost-containment innovations. In the realm of administrative law, a similar strategy of deference exists for judicial review of regulatory agencies. When the agency can provide an adequate justification for its actions, the agency will usually be upheld.[74] Likewise, the fiduciary model vests initial decision-making authority, and the power to create and evaluate a factual record, in a party with expertise in the area. To avoid a situation where the MCO controls how the process will be implemented, the courts must retain a crucial oversight role.

A successful fiduciary model will reduce litigation. While the tort and contract rules rely on the courts to resolve conflicts, the fiduciary model creates a structure to resolve these conflicts within the managed care system. It offers the opportunity to reestablish relationships of trust between all the parties and to focus on the ethical foundations of physicians' and institutions' fiduciary duties to individual patients.[75] A fiduciary-duty framework places the physician–patient relationship at the center of the clinical encounter, not at the periphery. The fiduciary concept motivates all parties to talk about the same issue and to think about creative solutions rather than to scream past one another. In this sense, it operates as a form of safety net for patients because it assures that the plan fiduciary must consider each individual situation in decision-making.

The fiduciary duty strategy may also reduce MCO regulation. Implementing the fiduciary duty approach requires that plans, doctors, and patients communicate with one another throughout the process. If implemented properly, the fiduciary duty mechanism could well result in greater patient trust of the managed care concept. Administrators would be forced to justify their decisions in terms that patients can understand. From this conversation, patients may recognize that MCO administrators are not evil and may be struggling to achieve the right balance between costs and access. That conversation alone might ease the current atmosphere of recrimination.

Aside from the framework's complexity, an objection to it is that "The traditional concept of a fiduciary duty is one whose entire loyalty is to his beneficiary."[76] Quite clearly, managed care presents a different set of loyalties than seen in traditional fiduciary relationships. Nonetheless, even under traditional fiduciary relationships, the law contemplates that there may be multiple beneficiaries and conflicting interests. The role of the law covering fiduciaries is to assure that such conflicts are managed within acceptable bounds. In particular, ERISA, as a matter of public policy, contemplates that MCOs will have divided fiduciary loyalties that must be balanced. The key is to design a system that maintains transparency and neutrality in decision-making.

A second objection is that the framework does little to address the systemic deficiencies facing the health-care delivery system. By focusing on

> . . . diversions like 'Patients' Bills of Rights' or consumer protections . . . we run the very real risk of creating new bureaucratic structures that will provide consumers with only limited real protection, but which will effectively vitiate any benefits good managed care might have produced in the first place.[77]

Several observers accurately note that patients' rights laws and approaches that focus on individual patients are a distraction from the serious health-system reforms needed. Among other concerns, critics correctly note that patients' rights laws or the fiduciary-duty framework will do nothing to address fundamental deficiencies such as rising rates of the uninsured, and concerns about quality of care. Still, patients' rights laws or the fiduciary-duty framework would provide important protections during a period when political stalemate blocks systemic reforms. As a matter of fundamental fairness to patients who must deal with delayed or denied care, their concerns should not be ignored during protracted political gridlock. Regardless of what reforms may or may not be enacted, fairness demands assurances that patients will have an opportunity to challenge delayed or denied health care.

One potential drawback to this framework is that requiring a detailed record of the decision-making process will make that process itself more expensive, increasing the overall cost of the plan. If so, the fiduciary-duty framework would work only if there were a concomitant decrease in the costs of litigation of disputed claims. This is a testable empirical issue. It is worth noting that even if requiring a fiduciary process increases administrative costs, it offers considerable public relations benefits and may reduce litigation. While there may be some start-up costs, over time the costs should diminish as the plan fiduciary builds a portfolio of decisions that can guide subsequent considerations. The plan fiduciary will be able to rely on (or update) previous decisions, so the time invested to decide cases should decrease over time.

Another potential drawback is that the fiduciary-duty framework might be seen as promising to be the answer to all of our health-care problems. It is not. Nor is it such a flexible concept that it will always favor patients. The fiduciary duty framework relies on a set of principles that can help determine how conflicts of interest can be resolved. It is not an empty vessel into which courts can simply substitute their own health-policy preferences for those of the fiduciary.[78]

The concept of fiduciary duty offers attributes that can address some of the central concerns patients have about resolving the critical problems facing managed care. Admittedly, it is a complex solution and lacks the elegance of more easily applied approaches. What the concept lacks in elegance, it more than compensates for through its coherence and its ability to mediate the inherent conflicts posed by managed care. In that sense, it is a very pragmatic approach to what has been an intractable social problem.

It also provides a mechanism for resolving the resource allocation dilemmas that define managed care. Inevitably, the courts play a central role in deciding such policy questions. Without a framework that provides judges with a means of balancing the conflicting interests, courts will tend to move toward polarized solutions—either defendants will win most of the cases or plaintiffs will. The strength of the fiduciary-duty framework, though it admittedly suffers from its case-by-case development, is both consistent with the way legal doctrine normally evolves and provides a set of organizing principles that judges can use.

This framework may also offer a way to organize a new dialogue between law and medicine. Perhaps the most common ethic shared by doctors and lawyers is dedication to the individuals who seek their services. The very integrity of the professions of law and medicine requires that every practitioner be able to maintain client or patient trust and confidentiality, which is exactly what the fiduciary duty requires.

Using shared values of fiduciary duty offers an opportunity for a productive dialogue between the two groups. A stable health-policy environment depends on an effective collaboration between law and medicine. Whether fiduciary duties will achieve the desired reconciliation remains to be seen. At a minimum, it is a more promising approach than continued reliance on tort or contract law to mediate the conflicts between physicians and attorneys.

Of equal significance, the framework restores the physician–patient relationship to the center of health-care delivery. Without some mechanism for obtaining leverage against an MCO's coverage decision, patients have little recourse when care is denied, and MCOs have little incentive to focus on individual treatment needs. The fiduciary-duty framework will not automatically restore physician autonomy and the importance of the physician–patient relationship. But implementing the framework will make it difficult for MCOs to ignore an individual patient's concerns.

Notes

1. Woolhandler and Himmelstein (1995); Relman (1985).

2. Norman Daniels and James Sabin have been developing a similar approach, albeit in a different context. See Daniels and Sabin (1998a), p. 50 (discussing a movement in managed care reform to increase accountability to consumers); Daniels and Sabin (1998b), p. 27 (discussing how greater fairness in the decision-making process is needed when health plans are expanding experimental and last chance procedures); Daniels and Sabin (1997) (discussing the shift of authority over medical care from the patients to private organizations).

3. Cooter and Freedman (1991); Mehlman (1990) (discussing the rules of fiduciary contracting); Rodwin (1995) (examining the "metaphor of physicians as fiduciaries"); Morreim (1998a). For an excellent and accessible overview, see Schwartz and Horn (1999), Chapter 1 and Appendix B.

4. Cooter and Freedman (1991), p. 1048.

5. *Varity Corp. v. Howe*, 516 U.S. 489, 504 (1996): "Indeed, the primary function of the fiduciary duty is to constrain the exercise of discretionary powers which are controlled by no other specific duty imposed by the trust instrument or the legal regime." Recall the discussion in Chapter 5 regarding a managed care subscriber's lack of information to assess one's future health care needs.

6. Mechanic (1998).

7. See, generally, Havighurst (1995) (arguing that private contracts can be used to specify patients' legal rights in relation to health care providers); Rodwin (1993) (examining the relationship between professional ethics and economic interests in determining medical behavior); Bloche (1999) (reviewing the conflicts between the ethic of "loyalty to patients and pressure to use clinical methods and judgment for social purposes and on behalf of third parties"); Hall and Berenson (1998) (examining the ethics of medical practice under managed care).

8. Mariner (1998), p. 27.

9. Bogert (1987).

10. *Ibid.*, pp. 334–36 (stating that the lack of good judgment or improper motivation triggers a breach of fiduciary duty).

11. *Cf.* Sage, 1999a (presenting a case against doctors' providing lawyer-like advocacy).

12. Rodwin (1995), p. 256.

13. Morreim (1998a), pp. 524–28.

14. Thompson (1993). See also Kassirer (2001); Rodwin (1989).

15. This summary is adapted from Morreim (1998a) and Goold (2000), Chapter 8, pp. 93–102.

16. *Cf.* Hall and Anderson (1992), p. 1669: "[T]he only conflict the [self-insuring] employer faces is that between a single claimant and a pool of beneficiaries, the very conflict that should be foremost in the insurer's mind when assessing medical appropriateness."

17. See, e.g., *McGraw v. Prudential Ins. Co. of America*, 137 F.3d 1253, 1259 (10th Cir. 1998), holding that a decision to deny benefits is arbitrary and capricious if it is not a reasonable interpretation of the plan's terms.

18. See, e.g., Jacobson, Asch, Glassman et al. (1997).

19. See, e.g., *Bedrick v. Travelers Insurance Co.*, 93 F.3d 149 (4th Cir. 1996).

20. Jacobson and Rosenquist (1988).

21. 29 U.S.C. §§1001–1461 (1999).

22. *Ibid.* §1104(a)(1).

23. Jacobson and Pomfret (1998); Morreim (1998a).

24. Compare *Reilly v. Blue Cross & Blue Shield*, 846 F.2d 416, 423 (7th Cir. 1988), and *Kyle Railways, Inc. v. Pacific Administration Servs.*, 990 F.2d 513, 516–17 (9th Cir. 1993). It is agreed that MCOs and employers are not considered "fiduciaries" with regard to establishing or changing the terms of the plan.

25. *Firestone Tire & Rubber Co. v. Bruch*, 489 U.S. 101, 107–08 (1989).

26. *McGraw v. Prudential Ins. Co.*, 137 F.3d 1253, 1259 (10th Cir. 1998); Morreim (1998a) at p. 520.

27. *See, e.g.,* Hall and Anderson (1992), p. 1670.

28. *Killian v. Healthsource Provident Administrators, Inc.*, 152 F.3d 514, 521 (6th Cir. 1998).

29. *Neade v. Portes,* 739 N.E.2d 496 (Ill. 2000).

30. Bloche (1999).

31. For a more detailed analysis, see Jacobson and Cahill (2000).

32. Bogert (1987), p. 343 n.11.

33. *Varity Corp. v. Howe*, 516 U.S. 489, 506 (1996).

34. Cantor (1997).

35. A full discussion of disclosure is beyond the scope of this section. For such a discussion, see, generally, Sage (1999b); Hall (1997a).

36. *Neade v. Portes*, 739 N.E.2d 496 (Ill. 2000).

37. *Neade v. Portes*, 739 N.E.2d 496, 507 (Ill. 2000).

38. *Shea v. Esensten*, 107 F.3d 625, 628 (8th Cir. 1997); *Shea v. Esensten*, 208 F.3d 712 (8th Cir. 2000).

39. *Pegram v. Herdrich*, 530 U.S. 211, 227 (2000), footnote 8.

40. Sage (1999b).

41. 63 Cal. Rptr. 2d 202, 207 (1997) (quoting *Delta Dental Plan v. Banasky*, 27 Cal. App. 4th 1598, 1607 (1994)), *aff'd*, 2000 LEXIS 3717 (Cal. Sup. Ct. 2000).

42. *Ibid.* pp. 208–09.

43. Hall and Anderson (1992); Jacobson and Cahill (2000).

44. As noted in Chapter 6, some states have also mandated the availability of external review panels. These state mandates may not survive an ERISA preemption challenge.

45. Bogert (1987), p. 335. See also Bloche (2000).

46. 137 F.3d 1253, 1262–1263 (10th Cir. 1998).

47. 29 U.S.C §1104 (1994).

48. For more details, see Jacobson and Kanna (2001).

49. Thus, if the decision meets the first element of the test to such an extent that it satisfied not only the fiduciary duty of prudence but the stricter tort standard of care (i.e., that the decision was consistent with standard medical practice), the decision is clearly sound.

50. At least one federal court of appeals has read the Supreme Court's decision in *Firestone Tire & Rubber Co. v. Bruch*, 489 U.S. 101 (1989), to impose such a requirement on ERISA trustees. See *Cox v. Mid-America Dairymen, Inc.*, 965 F.2d 569, 574 (8th Cir. 1992).

51. See *Firestone Tire & Rubber Co. v. Bruch*, 489 U.S. 101, 111 (1989); *Varity Corp. v. Howe*, 516 U.S. 489, 514–15 (1996).

> [C]haracterizing a denial of benefits as a breach of fiduciary duty does not necessarily change the standard a court would apply when reviewing the administrator's decision to deny benefits. After all, *Firestone*, which authorized deferential court review when the plan itself gives the administrator discretionary authority, based its decision upon the same common-law trust doctrines that govern standards of fiduciary conduct.

52. Rosenbaum et al. (1999).

53. Hall and Anderson (1992), pp. 1698–1705.

54. Morreim (1998a), pp. 551–52.

55. *McGraw v. Prudential Insurance Co.*, 137 F.3d 1253, 1258–1259.

56. This phrase has been used in a variety of situations. See, e.g., *Swint v. Chambers County Comm'n*, 514 U.S. 35, 51 (1995); *Atlantic Richfield Co. v. USA Petroleum Co.*, 495 U.S. 328, 345 (1990). In the context of ERISA preemption of state law claims, courts have held that the "essential inquiry" is whether allegedly negligent medical advice or care was inextricably intertwined with administration of plan benefits. See, e.g., *Schmid v. Kaiser Foundation Health Plan*, 963 F. Supp. 942, 944–45 (D. Or. 1997). Here as elsewhere, there is a rough correlation (though by no means congruence) between the fiduciary-duty framework and the ERISA regime.

57. *See United States v. Nova Scotia Food Products Corp.*, 568 F.2d 240, 252–53 (2d Cir. 1977), deciding that where the FDA did not cite reasons for its regulation, the regulation was arbitrary and invalid.

58. When medicine and administration are not intertwined, there would not be a proper claim for breach of fiduciary duty. For instance, the claim could be exclusively about the quality of clinical care, or the refusal to precertify certain treatment because the benefit is specifically excluded. In those instances, the appropriate remedies would be either a standard tort claim (if the decision was medical in nature) or breach of contract claim (if the decision was administrative in nature).

59. Bogert (1987), pp. 549–50.

60. *Ibid.*, p. 289.

61. Bloche (1999), p. 268.

62. *Ibid.*, p. 272.

63. *Booth v. Wal-Mart Stores, Inc.*, 201 F.3d 335 (4th Cir. 2000).

64. For our purposes, there are two important aspects of the decision. First, the court adopted a standard of review that is less deferential to plan administrators. Instead of requiring the patient to show that the plan administrator's decision was arbitrary and capricious, an almost impossible standard to meet, the court said that "abuse of discretion" is the proper standard. This standard is consistent with the approach described here. Second, the court set forth criteria for determining whether the administrator abused his or her discretion. Of the eight criteria, four seem congruent with my approach: the adequacy of the materials considered and how far the materials support the decision; consistency with previous interpretations of plan benefits; whether the process was reasoned and principled; and any conflicts of interest the fiduciary may have. The other four criteria were: the language of the plan, the purposes and goals of the plan, whether the decision was consistent with ERISA's requirements, and an external standard relevant to the exercise of discretion.

65. *Bedrick v. Travelers Insurance Co.*, 93 F.3d 149, 153 (4th Cir. 1996). The court noted that "It is as important not to get worse as to get better."

66. *Bedrick v. Travelers Insurance Co.*, 93 F.3d 149, 154 (4th Cir. 1996).

67. *Doe v. Group Hospital & Medical Services*, 3 F.3d 80, 86–87 (4th Cir. 1993).

68. *Batas v. Prudential Insurance Co.*, 724. N.Y.S. 2d 3 (N.Y. App. DW. 2001).

69. *Ibid.* at p. 15 (Saxe, J., dissenting in part).

70. *Bedrick v. Travelers Insurance Co.*, 93 F.3d 149, 154 (4th Cir. 1996).

71. *Varity Corp. v. Howe*, 516 U.S. 489, 514 (1996).

72. Two commentators who have considered this approach are E. Haavi Morreim (1998a) and Maxwell Mehlman (1990). Mehlman discusses imposing the obligations of a fiduciary upon health care organizations for the purposes of patient-related decision-making and judicial review. *Cf.* Hall and Anderson (1992), pp. 1697–98, discussing, but quickly dismissing, the possibility of a "trust law model" for the judicial review of decisions.

73. *Varity Corp. v. Howe*, 516 U.S. 489, 497 (1996).

74. Models of judicial review based on fiduciary duties share similarities with models of review under administrative law, constitutional law, and the law of arbitration. A useful, though certainly inexact, analogy is to look at the active rational basis test employed in constitutional law to understand how judicial review would operate in the fiduciary duty framework. The rational basis test is used to determine the constitutionality of legislation. Under the rational basis test, courts will uphold a state's economic and social legislation as long as it serves any reasonable state interest. But in an active rational basis analysis, courts require states to provide additional justification for the legislation. See Jacobson, 1996; Hall and Anderson (1992) at p. 1696 (noting that fiduciary, administrative, and arbitration models of judicial review are "somewhat com-

peting and somewhat overlapping"); *Milner v. Apfel*, 148 F.3d 812, 816 (7th Cir. 1998) (explaining that in some instances a more searching "active" standard of review is used).

75. Bloche (1999); Mechanic (1998), p. 661.

76. Mariner (2001), p. 263.

77. Vladeck (1999), p. 1211. Many others have raised similar objections. See, e.g., Hyman (2000) and Angell (2001). Deborah Stone (1999), p. 1214 offers a more biting critique that Patients' Bills of Rights "tap into a grand democratic metaphor that has little relevance in health care. An individual, even one armed with procedural rights, hardly stands a chance against a corporation. . . . Patients need rights to the positive provision of care . . ."

78. An anonymous reviewer of this book raised the concern that ". . . fiduciary law magically unfolds as containing the good things the author favors and avoiding the bad things he disfavors." The reviewer is correct to suggest that the fiduciary duty framework would have some of these characteristics, but is incorrect to suggest such a deterministic outcome.

11

Strangers in the Night, or Conciliation and Cooperation?

L IKE strangers in the night, physicians and attorneys perceive the world differently. Sometimes they simply pass one another without mutual recognition; more often, they collide in mutual distrust. Actions physicians may perceive as barriers to needed treatment may be seen by attorneys as processes designed to protect patient autonomy. No doubt, the metaphor of strangers in the night only reflects a partial reality—indeed, it is more symbolic than real. Yet that partial reality has powerful implications for patient care and health policy. The metaphor evokes the reciprocal suspicion that has too often characterized how law and medicine interact, and reflects the underlying tension between physicians and attorneys. In reality, the two inhabit intertwined systems whose interaction is so comprehensive that it seems hard to imagine how they could ever be extricated from each other.

The imprint of the legal system's role in health care is unmistakable and pervasive. From the involvement of attorneys in complex business arrangements to resolving patients' challenges to benefit denials, the legal system plays a dynamic role in the organization, financing, and delivery of health care. Far from being an idle observer, it seems clear that the legal system is involved in all aspects of the modern health care enterprise.

The story being told in this book—about the relationship between law and medicine and why it matters—is still unfolding. The story has focused on the evolution of the relationship between law and medicine, how the seemingly intractable problems of the health care system surfaced, how the legal system adapted to the changing environment, and a possible strategy to deal with these problems.

Three related themes emerge from the basic story that offer suggestions for future dealings between law and medicine. The first theme is that attorneys and physicians share a number of values, experiences, and interests that can be the basis for conciliation and cooperation. The second theme describes how the concept of fiduciary duty can be the mechanism for restoring the physician–patient relationship to the center of health-care delivery. Fiduciary duty also offers the potential for reconciling the contentious relationship between attorneys and physicians that currently interferes with patient care. The third theme is fairness—in dealings between MCOs and patients, between managed care and physicians, in how courts treat the physician–patient relationship, and how attorneys and physicians interact. At the heart of the fiduciary approach is the need to treat physicians and patients fairly while operating a health care system at a reasonable cost.

Under the best of circumstances, the relationship between law and medicine is complex, and has been since the early days of the professional interaction between physicians and attorneys. The complexity arises from many sources, including the uncertain role the legal system should play in monitoring the health care system and the difficult policy challenges posed by the managed care environment. The professional conflict between them, which is neither inexorable nor desirable, has undermined a relationship that has more in common than either profession has been willing to admit. A significant factor is the mutual mistrust between physicians and attorneys. No matter how much physicians and health-care administrators need to rely on attorneys to conduct business arrangements, the confrontations of medical malpractice litigation lurk in the background. And looming astride the vexed relationship between attorneys and physicians is the managed care industry, which has transformed both that relationship and health care delivery. More than anything, ironically, the development of the managed care system has accentuated their interdependence.

The struggle between physicians and attorneys has unfolded against a background of public attitudes toward both law and medicine that seem strangely contradictory. We simultaneously exalt the concept of the rule of law and bemoan the law's intrusion into our daily activities. In the same way, we condemn attorneys for dreaming up the latest class action litigation, while dialing 1/800/CallSlim to hire a lawyer as soon as we suffer an injury. Public attitudes toward medicine and health care are equally incongruous. The public complains about the cost of health care, but each individual wants full access to the latest technology regardless of its cost. According to general public surveys, managed care is wildly unpopular, yet individual members of MCOs respond favorably to patient satisfaction surveys.

This cognitive dissonance is nothing new. After all, polls show wide public disregard for Congress coupled with continued support for "my representative," which results in high incumbent reelection rates. Add to this the public's conflicting attitudes toward government regulation, and it is no wonder that current health-care policy can best be characterized as gridlocked.

Not surprisingly, then, there are no easy solutions to the challenges raised by the intersection of law and medicine. Managed care is not a fixed system. Its contours adjust to both marketplace considerations and the legal system's response to managed care's policies and operations. Despite considerable public discontent with the managed care industry, there is no obvious replacement, and the industry can claim to have achieved at least some of its cost-containment objectives. As the managed care system adapts and evolves, new challenges will appear that will require flexible and consistent political and legal responses. Unfortunately, past responses have not always been consistent. At times, the political and legal systems have adopted different, or even conflicting, strategies. In the 1970s, the courts pushed access to health care while the political system pursued cost controls. Regulators now are concerned that policies to encourage cost savings (by providing financial incentives) may promote undertreatment (providing too few services).

To a degree not expected by most observers, the legal system has been generally reluctant to interfere with managed care's cost-containment programs. Courts have facilitated the transformation to managed care and its dominance in the health care marketplace. As a matter of public policy, Congress has consistently endorsed managed care's goals and methods. Viewed historically, the legal system's support for managed care should not be surprising. In other periods of radical social and economic transformations, as we have seen with railroads and mass-produced goods, the legal system supported the new industry and allowed the market to develop. Even within health care, the legal system sustained physicians' earlier market dominance. When physicians then lost power to managed care, the legal system deferred to the emerging market arrangements and generally offered little support for continued physician control.

For the past two decades, the dynamic between the judicial and legislative branches over health care has been particularly circular. Congress first preempted (perhaps unwittingly) lawsuits against MCOs under ERISA and has resisted public pressure to amend the law. Meanwhile, courts initially supported the new managed care industry with generous preemption interpretations. After some reconsideration, many courts have tried to find ways around ERISA preemption and have somewhat eroded its harshness. But the circularity was completed when the Supreme Court ruled that an overhaul of ERISA should originate from Congress, not the courts.

One result of this circularity is that many patients find it difficult, if not impossible, to hold MCOs legally accountable for their role in influencing clinical decisions. Physicians have fared no better in their attempts to challenge managed care's cost containment policies that they believe compromise patients' well-being. Courts have not been particularly friendly to these challenges, in part because judges fail to appreciate the complexities of modern health care delivery. Nor has the political system found a way to enact laws that protect patients without undermining managed care's financial incentives.

So far, at least at the federal level, the managed care industry has won every important political and judicial battle since the early 1990s. Right now, the managed care industry occupies an enviable policy position. Congress has not enacted a patient's right to sue law, ERISA blocks most state attempts to regulate managed care, there is no substantive federal regulatory presence, and *Pegram v. Herdrich* limits judicial oversight. All of this leaves the managed care industry in a strong legal and political position.

At the very height of its legal and political triumphs, however, the concept of managed care seems surprisingly fragile and vulnerable. It remains a vilified industry with few friends and defenders. One reason may be the relentless pursuit of cost reduction at the expense of other values people care about, mainly a caring system that puts patient health and well-being above economic considerations. In concept, managed care offers a good product and a reasonable corrective to the unsustainable cost increases of the discredited fee-for-service system. But two failures have exposed serious deficiencies in the industry's strategy. One is the failure to involve the public in how the concept operates in practice. The other lies in allowing the perception of caring only about reducing costs to fester in the public's consciousness.

What has been seriously eroded in the transition to managed care is the essential element of trust—patients' trust that the managed care system recognizes a responsibility to individual patients, and perhaps trust between physician and patient as well. Managed care is unlikely to survive in its present form without public trust. At a minimum, the failure to maintain trust certainly invites a heavy regulatory presence in "micromanaging medical decisions."[1]

> Increased distrust of the structures and orientations of health care also encourages public and private alternatives to trust. Identifying the proper balance between trust and regulation is a challenging task of public policy. Good regulatory policy makes trust more possible by deterring or controlling its most risky aspects and by reassuring patients that they can also trust safely. Measures to bolster trust between patient and clinician, whether originating from initiatives developed by clinicians and medical settings or from regulatory agencies, are stabilizing influences in the context of rapid change and uncertainty in health care.[2]

The legal system can impose accountability (through appropriate sanctions) for the adverse consequences of failing to maintain trust, but cannot produce trust on its own. The essence of trust must emanate from the health-care system itself. Financial incentives to limit costs are now a necessary part of the health care landscape, but they are not mutually exclusive with establishing trust. By themselves, these incentives do not necessarily impede trust, as long as they are implemented in a way that treats the physician–patient relationship as the core of the health-care system. The problem is that physicians and the public remain skeptical that the difficult cost–quality–access trade-offs are being made fairly.

What remains is to discuss several questions that follow from the relationship between law and medicine: Why should we care? Can legal principles be effective in producing a sustainable consensus on health care policy concerning resource allocation disputes? Can the law be an effective instrument for returning the physician–patient relationship to the center of the health-care enterprise? How do judicial decisions fit within the broader health-policy environment? Is there too much law in health care? The remainder of this chapter will address each question in turn, followed by some concluding thoughts.

Why Should We Care?

One judge's lament about the state of law and medicine led him to ask provocatively, "Does anyone care? Do you?" The most important reason why we should care is that the issues being raised involve life and death and reflect our basic values as a society. Good health makes it possible to achieve personal goals.[3] If treatment is denied or delayed, a patient may not recover as quickly or may die sooner. In health care, the way cases are decided may mean the difference between life and death or the alleviation of pain and suffering. In many other areas of the law, the fight is over monetary damages or property rights. People can survive such disputes even if they lose. This does not mean that the courts should necessarily treat health care any differently than they would other types of cases. Nor does it mean that patients should automatically win each challenge. It means instead that the development of legal doctrine in health care directly affects our physical and emotional well-being and our ability to obtain the health care we need. Above all, it means that the legal system should be very careful not to thwart legitimate access to the judicial process, with its bedrock emphasis on fairness.

We should care because the inevitable involvement of courts and legislatures directly affects how health care is delivered. Take, for instance, the legislative reaction to so-called drive-through deliveries (where maternity patients are discharged within 24 hours of giving birth). In response to numerous complaints, Congress enacted a law mandating that maternity stays must last at least 48 hours. Critics have derided congressional action as improperly interfering with the market and with physicians' control over clinical decisions.[4] The criticism of legislating by body-part may be correct, but Congress felt serious political pressure to take some action. Another example is how to deal with medical error. Though courts already maintain oversight of medical error through medical liability determinations, the political branches of government feel compelled by their constituents to play a significant role in designing policies to reduce the incidence of medical errors.

The law affects every feature of the health care enterprise, from how patients are treated to how health care is organized. In the past two decades, attorneys have moved from interacting with physicians mostly over liability allegations to involvement in all aspects of health care as a business. At one time, medicine was concerned only with how the legal system punished deviations from the standard of care. Attorneys and the law are now integral to health care as a business—either through interpreting regulations and accreditation standards, or advising physicians and administrators on business strategies.

Patients also have a stake in how the courts resolve challenges to cost-containment programs, as these decisions shape the extent to which cost containment becomes a permanent part of the health care delivery environment. The courts have the opportunity to determine whether the operation of cost controls goes too far. If the courts, as they have done, simply defer to the legislative branch, at least the responsibility for change is clearly defined.

Patients need to be concerned about how the legal system's response to managed care shapes relations among attorneys, physicians, and the managed care industry. Regardless of its problems, the managed care industry remains the dominant force in health care, allowing the industry to control the type and amount of care patients receive. That dominance is not likely to last forever. In the meantime, an important first step toward reducing the industry's power and leverage over health-care delivery would be to reduce the antagonism between doctors and lawyers. Cooperation between attorneys and physicians is important, but by itself will not suffice to alter deficiencies in the managed care approach. Nevertheless, the health policy implications of the failure of law and medicine to cooperate are significant. From disagreements over medical error and privacy rights to the proper scope of regulatory oversight, their inability to cooperate leaves patients vulnerable to arbitrary denials of care and the managed care industry vulnerable to a virulent public backlash.

A final reason to care is that the health-care system is not in good shape. Costs are rising steeply once again, and the number of uninsured Americans creeps steadily higher. Physicians remain dissatisfied with managed care, and patients are bewildered at the system's complexity and their difficulty in maneuvering through it. Even if managed care is merely the messenger bearing the news of the old fee-for-service order's demise, it seems increasingly likely that managed care will ultimately be viewed as a transition between the fee-for-service system and whatever comes next.

At the present time, there is no obvious successor waiting to take its place.

Shifting to a fully private system is as unlikely as replacing managed care with universal health coverage. For the time-being, we will muddle through. Whatever shape the new system takes, the lessons of how the law responded to managed care will be important to understand and assess. The difficult choices to be made under a new system will resemble those that led to the managed care litigation trends at the heart of this book.

The Legal System and Resource Allocation

Courts play a fundamental role as venues for balancing conflicting social policy goals and values. As an institution, the judiciary retains considerable public authority and legitimacy. One of the judiciary's strengths is the requirement that judges explain their reasoning and articulate the legal principles in a written opinion that can be reviewed by appellate courts and critiqued by legislators, legal scholars, and stakeholders. Judicial opinions are also available to the public. The ensuing dialogue between these groups results in a constant process of reassessing judicial doctrine in controversial areas of social and economic policy. Courts, therefore, offer an appropriate forum for addressing the difficult resource allocation issues raised by managed care.

The resource allocation question is how to meet the individual patient's needs without squandering resources for the entire patient population. On some level, patients care about having enough health resources to go around so that resources are available for all patients when needed. On a more fundamental level, though, an individual patient is probably not worried about resource allocation decisions when his or her request for treatment is denied to preserve resources for the patient population in general. In a market-based health-care system, the reality is that cost controls operate by limiting services to individuals.

While the judiciary's role in resource allocation decisions remains controversial, judicial decisions will certainly be a factor in how the trade-offs are resolved. Historically, the courts are the one institution where the individual's case has remained the primary concern. Unlike the political process, which is designed to consider a variety of options based (in theory, anyway) on what is best for the public, the courts retain their focus on the individual case being presented. Consequently, the judiciary is often the institution that will develop mechanisms for balancing conflicting policy objectives and setting limits on how the market will operate.

It would be foolish to suggest that this book will resolve the inordinately difficult challenges facing policy makers in solving resource allocation problems. These problems range from the failure to provide health insurance to some 44 million Americans to trade-offs between individual patients' access to care and reducing costs. Numerous commentators have wrestled with the difficult ethical and conceptual problems surrounding the resource allocation dilemma, with little agreement on how to proceed.[5]

Until there is greater agreement on the ethics of rationing medical care, the pragmatic measures recommended here may be effective interim solutions. Through the concept of fiduciary duty, the legal system offers the potential to advance public policy and facilitate the necessary process of balancing between individual patient needs and preserving assets for the patient population. The fiduciary-duty concept is not a simple fix—there is no magic in it. Without a radical overhaul of the entire health-care delivery system, perhaps through national health insurance (an unlikely event any time soon), there is no obvious solution. Short-term fixes are not the solution, and may well make matters worse.

The courts can go farther to provide a context in which the major stakeholders can work out their resource allocation differences in an orderly fashion without undermining public policy favoring managed care. Judges can accomplish this goal through the use of two legal principles to shift decision-making power to the stakeholders where it belongs, without usurping the proper legislative role in setting health policy. The first legal principle would be to expand due process requirements to protect physicians and patients from arbitrary actions by MCOs. In the short term, mandating due process will no doubt result in some increased costs for MCOs. In the longer term, improvements in plan–physician and patient–physician relationships will more than offset the initial costs.

The second legal principle is the concept of fiduciary duty. The fiduciary-duty concept forces attorneys and physicians to work together to develop adequate rules and procedures and does not rely on the political process to make the difficult choices. Another reason why the fiduciary-duty approach can be effective is that it includes the managed care industry. No serious change in health-care delivery can be accomplished without agreement from the managed care industry. The industry is too large, powerful, and important to have a solution imposed without its participation. Doctors and lawyers alone cannot resolve resource allocation issues. Together, the major stakeholders can control how the issue is resolved, with the courts retaining an institutional oversight role. A primary virtue of the fiduciary-duty concept is that it forces the major stakeholders to decide on how to allocate scarce health-care resources rather than relying on the courts or the political process to impose the answer. A forum where these major stakeholders can discuss and resolve their differences is essential.

In the end, the legal system will probably not provide the final answers to resource allocation dilemmas. What the legal system *will* offer is a set of processes that will allow stakeholders to design systems that recognize the need to balance competing policy objectives in ways that do not sacrifice costs to access or vice versa. If the judicial model seen in the railroad and mass production examples is followed in managed care, the legal system will eventually set limits on how the health care market operates.

The Legal System and the Physician–Patient Relationship

With apologies to Gilbert and Sullivan, a physician's lot is not an easy or happy one in the managed care era. True, doctors as a group are still doing quite well financially compared to median family income levels; but their financial success obscures the pressures and challenges they face in the new healthcare environment. Aspects of the physician–patient relationship that were once taken for granted may no longer exist. For patients, the lack of direct access to specialty care, inadequate patient protections, and seemingly arbitrary limitations on health care further reduce the importance of the physician–patient relationship in favor of reducing health-care costs. For physicians, the lack of clinical autonomy is their paramount complaint against managed care.

If the dispute affected only physicians and MCOs, one might be tempted to let them fight it out—and may the best side win. But the constraints on physician autonomy have a direct and considerable impact on patient care. A central premise of this book is that the physician–patient relationship should be the core of the health-care enterprise. For reasons having mainly to do with the cost excesses of the fee-for-service system, the physician–patient relationship has been pushed to the periphery. In a legitimate desire to lower health care costs, some sacrifice of unbridled physician autonomy was needed. Hence the advent of managed care and public policies designed to protect cost-containment objectives. The question is whether the system has gone too far toward cost controls at the expense of patient needs, and whether the gains from reducing physicians' autonomy outweigh the cost of pushing aside the physician–patient relationship.

Though not its primary cause, the legal system has facilitated the movement away from the dominance of the physician–patient relationship in two ways. First, courts have not discussed or relied on protecting the physician–patient relationship in their decisions, even where the decision has as much to do with continuity of care as it does with controlling costs. Second, the broad immunity provided to MCOs has eliminated most challenges to the improper operation of cost-containment programs. A consequence is that MCOs have fewer incentives to pay close attention to any individual patient's complaints.

Both of these are eminently correctable. The legal system can play a critical role in restoring a proper balance. For one thing, the judiciary can do a better job of factoring the patient's concerns for continuity of care into its decisions.

For another, Congress can amend ERISA to permit patients to sue an MCO for delayed or denied care. These changes would force the managed care industry to balance legitimate cost-containment objectives with the individual patient's legitimate treatment needs.

Arguably, it could be worthwhile to sacrifice the centrality of the physician–patient relationship for tangible benefits, such as universal health insurance or a compelling demonstration that patients have generally benefited from managed care. The former certainly has not occurred, and the latter remains a debatable proposition. As it stands, the managed care industry is the primary beneficiary of reducing physician autonomy. What we have seen over the past 20 to 30 years is a shift in power and control over resources away from physicians and toward corporate health-care entities, with no commensurate gains in access to health care or substantial improvements in quality of care. Even the effectiveness of managed care's early cost-containment efforts is now being eroded.

In short, the overall social gains from ceding control over health-care decisions to managed care executives have not been sufficiently compelling to justify continued subordination of the physician–patient relationship. To suggest that the physician–patient nexus be returned to the center of health-care delivery is neither to argue for a return to fee-for-service medicine nor for rejecting managed care's financial incentives to constrain health-care cost increases. The argument is designed to achieve a better balance between physician autonomy and cost controls.

The reality is that clinical care starts and ends with physicians, rather than with institutions. Significantly, there are indications that at least some physicians are reclaiming a measure of the autonomy and control over health-care delivery lost to managed care.[6] Some may regard this as an unfortunate development; yet there really is no alternative to reliance on doctors for clinical decisions. MCOs should retain a role in determining the appropriateness of treatment recommendations, but should be held to a reasonably high standard before denying recommended care, as suggested by the fiduciary-duty framework.

The Judiciary and the Health Policy Environment

Like it or not, the judiciary plays an important role in social policy. At a minimum, the Supreme Court's role in interpreting the Constitution assures it a central place in deciding some of the most contentious social policy issues. Unlike Constitutional decisions, where courts, particularly the Supreme Court, have wide discretion to engage in policy debates, civil cases are not easily amenable to judicial policy-making.

Without a doubt, the appropriateness and capacity of the judiciary to resolve social problems is controversial. One view is that the courts are effective in generating social change—what is called the *dynamic view*.[7,8] Proponents of the dynamic view argue that as independent institutions, courts can issue rulings (especially constitutional interpretations) that directly induce policy change when other institutions are politically stymied. The dynamic view postulates that courts can also induce policy change indirectly by educating the public, stimulating public debate, and serving as a catalyst for change.[9] In this way, the courts can influence the nature of the policy agenda, if not directly its outcome.

In contrast, opponents of an active judicial policy-making role—called the *constrained view*—maintain that inherent impediments inhibit courts from leading social change. In the constrained view, courts face three structural limitations: 1) constitutional limits on creating rights; 2) the lack of independence from other branches of government; and 3) the inability to establish, implement, and enforce policies. This view is quite skeptical about courts as policy-makers, arguing that judicial policy-making is undesirable, primarily because ". . . the judicial process is a poor format for the weighing of alternatives and the calculation of costs."[10]

Many commentators argue that the complex (and value-laden) policy judgments and trade-offs required in making health care policy should reside exclusively with the legislative branch. According to this view, courts lack the ability to define policy objectives, to interpret empirical data, and to select the "right" parties to the litigation or the "right" cases for policy judgments. Nor will courts understand the policy implications of their decisions, assess the economic impact of various policy choices, or obtain the proper information needed to resolve conflicting policy choices.[11] As unelected officials, courts threaten their legitimacy as impartial arbiters when attempting to go beyond their dispute resolution functions to impose public policy changes.

All of this is certainly problematic for judicial policy-making, but it is not the only view. In deciding cases, judges often have little choice other than to balance conflicting social policy objectives. Not all cases can easily be resolved on the facts alone, without having to confront the underlying policy conflicts. For any given case, a court will not have access to the range of policy options that a legislature would have. Over a wider range of disputes, however, courts receive feedback about their decisions and have the opportunity to adjust the legal rules.

There are three ways courts could shape health-care policy. Under the Constitution, the U.S. Supreme Court could rule that there is a constitutional right to health care. Not even the aggressive Warren Court of the 1960s went this far, let alone the more conservative Rehnquist Court. A more conceivable approach would be for courts to use common law to impose limitations on the market that would be tantamount to policy determinations. As we have seen, the incremental accretion of common law allows policy makers to debate the emerging standard, adjust to new rules, or seek legislation to overturn such decisions.[12] The third way for courts to shape health policy is through the traditional means of statutory interpretation.

In responding to the enormous amount of health care legislation over the past 20 years, the judiciary has had a clear opportunity to use its interpretive responsibility to help shape health policy. When congressional intent is not clear, courts can interpret legislation expansively and invite further litigation. Likewise, by narrowly interpreting legislation, courts signal that further litigation is unlikely to achieve the desired objectives. The clearest example of this in health care is how the courts have interpreted ERISA to provide MCOs with a great deal of immunity from liability. Through questionable interpretations of congressional intent regarding ERISA preemption, the Supreme Court essentially provided immunity to managed care organizations.

A recurrent problem with judicial intervention to shape health policy is that courts are in a weak strategic position to order social policy changes, especially when compelling a state legislature to spend money or raise taxes. Judicial reluctance is not simply based on political ideology, but reflects legitimate concerns about judicial capacity to order social change. Shaping health policy would require exactly the kinds of affirmative steps that the courts are least willing to provide. The instances in which the judiciary can unilaterally determine policy are likely to be very limited.[13]

For these (and other) reasons, the courts have been reluctant health policy makers at best. Instead of seizing the opportunity to shape social policy in the early stages of managed care, the courts avoided sweeping policy rulings in favor of setting rules that are more deferential to the political process. This may reflect uncertainty about the desirability of imposing liability at the expense of cost containment, deference to the underlying policy judgments made by the market and by the legislatures, or a willingness to put the needs of the patient population above those of the individual patient. From a policy perspective, the result is functionally equivalent: at the present time, accountability resides with the legislatures, not the courts.

One of this book's central conclusions is that the courts have generally played a less-direct role in health policy than many anticipated. By deferring most of the challenges to managed care's policy choices to Congress or the marketplace, the courts have displayed a reluctance to engage in the policy process. The courts have supported the market winner—managed care—and have reaffirmed the status quo by not impeding managed care's cost-containment initiatives. Regardless of numerous opportunities and entreaties to intervene, Congress has also chosen to let the marketplace work. More than that, the judiciary has largely refused to treat health care as a special case, despite the argument often heard that health care is different. Opponents of legal intervention in the market should be heartened that the courts have not made an exception of the health-care industry.

By contrast, courts have been willing to make decisions in bioethics cases that many argued were best left to the legislature, even when legislators were unable or unwilling to do so. In the types of cases discussed throughout this book, courts are sending the message that restrictions on managed care innovations should be made by the legislatures, not by the courts. Why the difference?

The primary reason is changes in judicial attitude. Courts were more willing during the 1960s and 1970s to participate actively in the policy process than they are now. Another difference is changes in the political climate. Judges are very sensitive to political charges that they are overstepping their authority and intruding in areas best left to elected officials. Avoiding attacks on judicial legitimacy may be one factor driving the deference to elected officials. Finally, policy-makers persistently refused to deal with the bioethics issues, leaving the courts with no alternative. With managed care, Congress and state legislatures continue to consider ways to hold managed care accountable. Judges are reluctant to interfere with the deliberative process.

This conclusion does not mean that the judicial doctrine in health care cases is devoid of policy implications. Allowing or disallowing challenges to cost-containment programs certainly has widespread policy implications, though the effects are largely indirect. It is difficult to characterize the extent to which the courts actually shape health policy and delivery beyond the argument here that the judiciary has supported cost-containment programs, hence protecting the growth and development of managed care. Just because the courts have interpreted ERISA narrowly does not mean that they necessarily endorse the underlying policy choices. For the most part, courts have reinforced the underlying changes in health-care delivery as opposed to shaping those changes.

Judges are clearly aware of the conflicting policy objectives presented in managed care litigation. In a substantial number of cases, judges are quite explicit about the policy conflicts raised by the litigants. Indeed, some evidence suggests that how a case is framed, between cost and efficiency on one side and justice and fairness on the other, makes a difference in how cases are decided.[14] Nonetheless, judges have refrained from second-guessing public policy favoring managed care's approach to cost-containment even as they question the harshness of that result. Judge Young's distress in the *Andrews-Clarke* case is hardly a cry in the wilderness. Many judges have felt similar bitterness and outrage.

If it is accurate to say that we live in an age of litigation, it is a paradox of our litigious society that the courts have become reluctant partners in how litigation is used to shape public policy and influence how our health care is delivered. Although courts have been instrumental in facilitating the expansion of managed care, it is unlikely that the judiciary will retain its strict neutrality indefinitely. That judicial decisions have been favorable to the managed care industry so far does not mean that the courts' policy role will remain dormant forever. The historical examples of the railroads and mass-produced goods suggest otherwise, and the post-1996 ERISA preemption cases clearly evince judicial discomfort at continuing to block legitimate claims from being heard.

If state courts are allowed to hear more challenges to managed care's cost-containment programs, we are likely to see a less favorable judicial response to managed care. As long as the public perceives MCOs to be unfairly denying care, any trend toward state court litigation is likely to engender an angry jury reaction, at least at the beginning of the litigation cycle. Over time, that anger will dissipate, with stable rules emerging. At first, like the transition from physician to hospital liability, the transition from hospital to MCO liability will be bumpy. Once juror anger subsides, the industry will absorb the liability implications like the hospital industry did before.

Is There Too Much Law in Health Care?

Without question, the legal system intrudes into the health-care delivery system. But is there really too much law in health care? At this point, many readers may be tempted to say the answer is pretty obvious. "Of course there's too much law. Let's get the lawyers out of this and return control to physicians, where it belongs." Not so fast. Certainly, many legal scholars and economists argue strenuously that the legal system should simply defer to the market by limiting its involvement to reviewing and interpreting contractual agreements. They also argue that the legal system, especially the judiciary, lacks the investigative and analytical skills needed to make appropriate policy choices.

Even if those criticisms are justified, though, the legal system is likely to continue to play a key role in health-care delivery for the variety of reasons suggested in previous chapters. And it should. Legal oversight of the health-care system is needed to ensure that the managed care industry is accountable to the public. Health care is simply too important to leave to the whims and dictates of the market without independent oversight. The appropriate question to ask is how the legal system can be more effective in its role, not whether the legal system should have any role at all. The same debate is now underway with regard to regulating the Internet. To those who decry Internet regulation as an intrusion into the freedom the Internet offers, one scholar responds as follows:

This attitude is profoundly mistaken. It betrays an extraordinary ignorance about the history of the Internet, and this ignorance threatens to undermine the innovation that the Internet has made possible. Innovation has always depended on a certain kind of regulation; the greatest examples of innovation in our recent past evince this reliance. And unless we begin to see the relationship between this type of rule and the innovation it promotes, we are likely to kill the promise of the Internet.[15]

The same could be said about health care generally and about managed care specifically.

Deciding if there is too much law in health care depends on several factors. One is the proper role of the courts in social and political questions in principle. Another is how courts have ruled in specific health-care cases. A third important consideration is the availability of superior alternative policy-making entities. There is no "correct" level of intervention that can be used as a benchmark by which the issue of whether there is too much law in health care can be debated. As usual when discussing legal issues, the answer is: It depends. Too little legal intervention can be as dysfunctional as too much, though the interests affected will be quite different in either case. The more important question is whether judicial intervention has a beneficial or adverse effect on health-care delivery or medical practice.

That said, it is important to consider the limitations of an extensive legal presence in health care. Courts are not capable of monitoring an entire industry, as the problems encountered with antitrust litigation against AT&T, IBM, and Microsoft have demonstrated. The difficult line-drawing problems may well strain the courts' structural capacities (as the Supreme Court noted in *Pegram v. Herdrich*). Another concern is that courts solve problems retrospectively, while health policy should be prospective. Most important, the danger of too much law is a dependency on the courts to resolve ambiguity and uncertainty and to make the hard choices that are better left to the political process.

Even so, legal oversight of the health care industry is needed to ensure fairness of process. One explanation for the backlash against the managed care industry is the general public perception that MCOs have been unfair, if not arbitrary, in deciding when to deny or delay health-care benefits. Another concern is the industry's failure to explain its internal processes to patients. More generally, the failure to include the public in developing cost-containment initiatives has fueled public apprehension that managed care is indifferent to an individual patient's health-care needs.

Those who believe that there is too much law in health care must reflect on the fact that one of the legal system's roles is to monitor potential excesses of the marketplace. The managed care industry has done a poor job of responding to legitimate patient complaints about delayed and denied care. Continued failure to address these grievances invites intervention from the legal system (especially litigation) that will often be less precise than measures the industry might have taken voluntarily to alleviate potential problems.[16] Opponents of the legal system's intervention must also consider whether their proposed alternatives, specifically a health-care reform strategy based on contract law, just support the shift to industry dominance without addressing the legitimate grievances.

Those who believe that the amount of law in health care is either adequate or even insufficient must recognize that there is no guarantee that litigation or legislation will dramatically change what many see as managed care's prime deficiency—financial incentives to deny care. As a matter of public policy, Congress has refused to consider interfering with managed care's incentives, and the courts have resolutely deferred to the legislature in this decision. Legal intervention, especially through individual litigation, may blunt the harsh effects of improperly implemented financial incentives, but it will not change the structure or basic financial incentives of managed care. In any event, advocates of a judicial strategy to address health policy need to be concerned that the judicial decisions may not reach the desired policy result and may even support the challenged policy.

A strong argument in favor of more judicial intervention, is the managed care industry's lack of external accountability. At this point, the managed care industry has not demonstrated a willingness to hold itself accountable for its products, and there are few legal or political constraints on its activities. Therefore, judicial intervention to hold the industry accountable is entirely justified.

The case of *Maio v. Aetna Inc.*,[17] is indicative and instructive of why there is not too much law in health care. Aetna elected to defend a legal challenge to its managed care operations by asserting that public statements touting its primary commitment to quality of health care were "mere puffery." Translated from the technical language of the law, the essence of Aetna's defense was that reasonable consumers would understand that its avowed commitment to quality was a statement of opinion not intended to be relied upon or to convey anything factual about its managed care plans.[18] Regardless of the merits of Aetna's legal argument, a voluntary characterization of public and repeated commitments to quality medical care as "mere puffery" seems an unusual way to represent one of managed care's core functions. It is ironic that when quality of care is perhaps the central issue concerning public attitudes toward managed care, one of the industry's major players simply discounts its own stated commitment to high quality care.

Reacting to the *Maio* case, a prominent health law scholar has argued that ". . . such advertising provides a weak basis for a consumer class action. If such advertising works at all, it is most likely to attract healthy rather than unhealthy subscribers. . . . It is simply too much to expect competing health plans to pay special attention to quality when it is clearly against their commercial interests to do so."[19] As far as it goes, that may be accurate. But the dismissiveness of the false advertising claims betrays the effects of the false advertising on an individual patient. Consider, by analogy, the long-running Volvo automobile advertising campaign to portray the car's safety.[20] Imagine, if you will, an accident where a new Volvo simply crumbles when hit by another comparably sized car, revealing structural defects in the car's manufacturing or design process. Should Volvo simply be excused from its commitment to safety by saying "we didn't really mean it after all"? A jury would probably not be so forgiving.

Equally important, the *Maio* case is symptomatic of a larger failure to provide adequate information to the public.[21] Maintaining a market-based health care system requires that patients have adequate access to information that allows them to make an informed decision about the type and amount of health care to purchase. A fundamental flaw in the market approach in health care is the patient's inability to judge the quality of health care. Deliberately depicting a commitment to quality of care in terms that an MCO has no intention of upholding may be nothing more than puffery in the law and may not meet the legal definition false and deceptive advertising. But it certainly undermines the rationale for a self-regulated, market-driven system that proponents have offered. The managed care industry proclaims to the public and to political officials that it shares professional values in ways that differ from those of other sellers in several key dimensions. In contrast, the defense of "mere puffery" about commitment to quality strikes at the heart of the managed care enterprise and the social contract between the managed care industry and the public.

The *Maio* case and current industry practices also demonstrate the need for the managed care industry to involve patients and the public in the decision-making process so that the public begins to accept the need for cost controls generally, and to revive trust particularly. Touting a commitment to quality without openly acknowledging the inevitable quality–cost trade-off has contributed to public mistrust of the managed care industry. It behooves the industry to take responsibility for patients confused by the product they purchased as well as patients injured by poorly implemented cost-containment programs. MCOs should embrace a strong, expedient, and independent grievance processs to resolve challenges to delayed or denied care. They should also welcome a patient advisory board with meaningful oversight of cost-containment strategies, along with providing a patients' rights advocate.

From a public policy perspective, this episode ought to be instructive to Congress, state legislatures, and the courts. *Maio* exposes the absence of voluntary accountability and the need for closer political and regulatory scrutiny.

Congress can, and should, act to impose real accountability standards, including the right to legal recourse for improperly operating cost-containment policies. Congress and the states should require complete and accurate disclosure about managed care products and financial incentives. They should closely monitor member materials that may have a tendency to mislead, misrepresent, or obfuscate.

The managed care industry is likely to argue that the *Maio* case is a trivial example and not indicative of the industry's overall commitment to quality health care. Perhaps so. Yet Aetna's stance in that case was certainly consistent with a philosophy that puts patients a distant second to other considerations, and is not an isolated event. Virtually the same story was repeated over the issue of state mandated grievance panels. To deflect patients' rights legislation, the industry has issued public statements favoring voluntary grievance panels as an alternative to both litigation and state-mandated grievance processes. In court, however, the industry argues that ERISA preempts such state mandates. Undoubtedly, voluntary action is preferable to mandatory, and the industry has every right to use ERISA preemption as a defense. Still, there has been ample time to implement voluntary grievance panels, with only limited progress. It should not be surprising that states have acted to fill the void. It is also not surprising that industry wants to have it both ways. The incongruity between public statements and private decisions further exposes the accountability gap.[22] Casual and cavalier promises of quality of care undermine managed care's legitimate initiatives. Either the industry has a good product that it is willing to stand behind without reservation, or it should stop complaining about attempts to ensure public accountability. The choice is simple—it is past time for the industry to choose. Otherwise, as with public antipathy to the tobacco industry, the managed care backlash will return in a politically more virulent form, and the opportunity for the managed care industry to achieve its early promise of managing care and cost to improve quality and accessibility will be lost.

Is there too much law in health care? Sadly, no. Any movement the legal system makes toward greater managed care accountability would be welcome.

Final Thoughts on Law and Medicine

A nagging question remains: Overall, how should we assess the role the legal system has played to date in the transition to managed care? Has the legal system responded effectively to the challenges of the new health-care environment, or has the system abdicated its responsibilities to the market? Has the legal system performed constructively in shaping health-care policy or in influencing health-care delivery?

In my view, the legal system has failed to maintain overall institutional oversight of the health-care system. Neither litigation (largely because of ERISA preemption) nor the political process has responded adequately to impose accountability on MCOs for inappropriately delayed or denied care. The policy agenda has clearly been set and dominated by the managed care industry. Even before the U.S. Supreme Court's decision in *Pegram v. Herdrich,* litigation accomplished very little in changing health-care policy. State court rulings imposing liability in some instances and some erosion of ERISA preemption suggest the beginnings of accountability, but it is difficult to discern any major health-care policy shifts resulting from litigation. If anything, the industry has been emboldened to expand its reach by the judicial response to cost-containment initiatives.

What we must keep in mind is that I am telling a story whose ending has yet to be written. If courts follow the pattern found in the judicial response to earlier social and economic transformations, they will begin to impose accountability on the egregious operation of financial incentives. When that happens, the managed care industry will respond by developing systems to alleviate patient concerns.

The legal system is neither the cause of physicians' and patients' problems with the managed care system nor the salvation. Absent a public consensus on resolving the resource allocation dilemmas, Congress is unlikely to act. We should not expect the legal system (especially the judiciary) to solve social problems that it is not structurally designed to resolve. But we should expect that the courts will accept responsibility for maintaining their proper role in setting limits, ensuring fair processes, and in holding all health-care system participants accountable for their actions.

Legal philosophers can debate at length about conceptions of legal philosophy and the search for certainty in law. My approach is much more pragmatic. As one of my colleagues has noted in a different context:

> Ultimately, however, the need for a definitive assessment may prove as unnecessary as it is elusive. Certainty, or the search for it, is the life's blood of the scholar; ambiguity, and probability, are both the dominant realities of life and the currency of politics and the law.[23]

My students are often surprised at how much ambiguity there is in the law. Contrary to their initial expectations that the law would provide clear answers to situations they might face as future health-care executives, the reality is that the law is often ambiguous and constantly in flux.

Remember, it took decades for the courts to establish stable rules in response to both the railroads and mass-produced goods. It is not surprising that only a decade or so into the managed care revolution, there is much ambiguity and little stability. Clearly, the courts are reluctant participants, with very little to guide their decisions. While not a simple undertaking, the concept of fiduciary duty offers stakeholders a way to take control and provides courts with a path for resolving any remaining disputes. Over time, stable fiduciary law will emerge that balances individual patient needs with legitimate health plan cost-containment objectives.

Taken in its entirety, the evidence is compelling that the legal system can and should play an integral role in monitoring the failures of the health care market. At a minimum, it is quite possible that without the potential for litigation over delayed or denied care, the situation would be much worse for managed care patients. Even if the specifics of legal intervention remain open to dispute, the validity and need for legal oversight remain unassailable.

Physician dominance over the health-care delivery system has been in retreat since the mid-1970s. Managed care's emergence simply confirmed what was an inevitable decline in influence under pressure from government and from large employers. A similar decline in managed care's dominance is equally inevitable. Sooner or later, patients will demand greater physician autonomy, and the political system will respond by imposing greater accountability on the managed care industry. What we need to achieve is a balance between unbridled physician autonomy, leading to unsustainable cost increases, and insufficient physician autonomy, leading to too many instances of denied health care. I have argued that a refined version of fiduciary duty is one way for a better balance to be maintained between conflicting policy objectives.

Health care may not be treated as a public good in the United States, but its importance to individual lives and to the country's economic health means that the managed care industry does not operate like a typical private firm. The public has the right to expect that the industry will adopt measures reflecting the public's need for input into how the industry is structured and how patient care is delivered. As a society, we have entrusted a relatively small number of health-care administrators with life-and-death decisions. We have done so with too little attention to how health-care rationing decisions are made and with inadequate public accountability. Though made by the private sector, health-care resource-allocation decisions raise fundamental public concerns that demand public accountability. "Managed care accountability is not only necessary to make a system of private health care operate efficiently, accountability is necessary to create the social and political consensus required to entrust the function of medical rationing to private managed care executives."[24] The only question is whether the industry will develop voluntary standards with public input or whether the legal system will impose more stringent accountability measures.

A reader might object that this book has very little to say about how to fix the health-care system. That would be a legitimate comment—the book is not designed to develop reform proposals. Instead, it speaks to the legal system's role under the current health-care system and lessons that might be applicable to the next health-care system. At its best, the legal system provides a public forum for carefully articulating and balancing conflicting values and goals. Fairness and transparency are elemental judicial goals. The book may not provide a blueprint for health-care reform, but it offers a strategy for making the health-care system fairer and more responsive to patients and physicians— qualities that are essential to restore Americans' trust in their health care.

The historical interdependence between law and medicine illuminates the public's stake in how the legal system oversees medical care. To a degree most people may be surprised to learn, the legal system is an important influence in health-care delivery. The transformation into managed care was facilitated by active support from the legal system—inadvertently in the case of ERISA preemption, more overtly when courts refused to undermine managed care's financial incentives. Along the way, the individual patient has been forced to share available resources with the broader patient population without really understanding the nature of the resource allocation choices underlying the managed care revolution.

The limits on the amount of care provided, and even the constraints on physician autonomy, are not altogether unwelcome developments. Returning to the cost excesses of the fee-for-service system would be untenable. At the same time, if managed care is to survive and thrive, it must find acceptable compromises to allocate scarce resources in ways that recognize the fundamental value of individual care and that animate public trust in the health-care system. In the end, the public will not support cost containment, no matter how worthwhile, if it undermines patient care and well-being. One legitimate goal cannot be sacrificed to the other. The legal system's focus on fair process as an organizing principle is something that the managed care industry can profitably exploit to demonstrate its commitment to a better balance.

There is nothing inevitable about the antagonism between law and medicine. Law and medicine need not and cannot be strangers to one another. A more conciliatory and cooperative relationship is essential for the benefit of patients and the health-care system.

Notes

1. Mechanic (1998) at p. 678.
2. *Ibid.*, p. 663.

3. Daniels (1985).

4. Hyman (1999a).

5. See, for example, Hall (1997b); Daniels (1985); Daniels and Sabin (1997); Powers (1992); Agrawal (1998); Bloche (1999). The most interesting aspect of the debate is to observe the process of changing norms and ethics regarding physician rationing at the bedside. In the fee-for-service system, physician rationing at the bedside was considered to be unethical. Does the shift to managed care justify a change in doctors' ethics to justify bedside rationing? See Hall (1997b) and Agrawal (1998) for illuminating responses to that question.

6. Lesser and Ginsburg (2001).

7. See a more extensive discussion in Jacobson and Warner (1999).

8. Rosenberg (1991); Rosenberg (1995). Rosenberg (1991), a proponent of the constrained view, argues that the presumed political and social changes stemming from civil rights, abortion, and environmental litigation have been illusory. Instead, Rosenberg (1991, 1995) concludes that changes in public opinion and action by elected officials, rather than court decisions, are required to engender significant social change. Rosenberg's conclusions and model remain controversial. For example, McCann (1996) criticizes the approach for ignoring ". . . the many more subtle, variable ways that legal norms, institutions, actors and the like do matter in social life" (p. 472). For our purposes, Rosenberg's framework simply provides a useful starting point.

9. McCann (1983, 1996).

10. Horowitz (1977), p. 357; Melnick (1983, 1994). Rosenberg studied the effects of judicial decisions in civil rights, abortion, and environmental cases. Horowitz reached similar results in studying the effects of leading cases in police practices, education, juvenile justice, and the Model Cities program. Melnick studied environmental litigation (1983), welfare, education for handicapped persons, and the food stamp program (1994).

11. Schuck (1988); Capron (1990); Horowitz (1977); Melnick (1983, 1994).

12. For a similar analysis, see Hammer (2001).

13. Komesar (1994).

14. Jacobson, Selvin, and Pomfret (2001).

15. Lessig, (2001), p. 26.

16. For an examination of the relationship between litigation and the legislative process in formulating public health policy, see Jacobson and Warner (1999).

17. *Maio v. Aetna Inc.*, 1999 WL 800315 (E.D. Pa. 1999), aff'd, 221 F.3d 472 (3rd Cir. 2000).

18. Preston (1998).

19. Havighurst (2001) pp. 15–16.

20. I thank Jeffrey Wasserman for suggesting this analogy.

21. I am indebted to Gail Agrawal for this observation.

22. *Rush Presidential HMO, Inc. v. Moran*, 1999 U.S. Dist. LEXIS 9127 (N.D. Ill. 1999), cert. granted, 121 S. Ct. 2589 (2001).

23. Warner (1986).

24. Hammer (2001), p. 786.

REFERENCES

Abraham, K.S. 1981. Judge-made law and judge-made insurance: Honoring the reasonable expectations of the insured. *Virginia Law Review* 67:1151–1191.

Abraham, K.S. and P. Weiler. 1994a. Enterprise liability and the choice of the responsible enterprise. *American Journal of Law and Medicine* 20 (1 and 2):29–36.

Abraham, K.S. and P. Weiler. 1994b. Enterprise medical liability and the evolution of the American health care system. *Harvard Law Review* 108:381–436.

Ad Hoc Committee to Defend Health Care. 1997. For our patients, not for profits: A call to action. *Journal of the American Medical Association* 278:1733–1734.

Agrawal, G.B. 1998. Chicago hope meets the Chicago school. *Michigan Law Review* 96:1793–1824.

Anders, G. 1996. *Health against wealth: HMOs and the breakdown of medical trust.* Boston: Houghton Mifflin.

Anderson, G.F. 1992. Courts and health policy: strengths and limitations. *Health Affairs* 11:95–110.

Angell, M. 2001. A wrong turn on patients' rights. *The New York Times*, June 23, p. A13.

Annas, G.J. 1989a. Doctors and lawyers and wolves. *Jurimetrics Journal* 29:437–449.

Annas, G.J. 1989b. Health law at the turn of the century: From white dwarf to red giant. *Connecticut Law Review* 21:551–569.

Annas, G.J. 1995. Reframing the debate on health care reform by replacing our metaphors. *New England Journal of Medicine* 332(11):744–747.

Arrow, K.J. 1963. Uncertainty and the welfare economics of medical care. *American Economic Review* 53:941–973.

Atiyah, P.S. 1986. Medical malpractice and the contract/tort boundary. *Law and Contemporary Problems* 49:287–303.

Ayers, S.M. 1996. *Health care in the United States: The facts and the choices.* Chicago: American Library Association.

Black's Law Dictionary, Abridged Sixth Edition. 1991. St. Paul, Minn.: West Publishing Company.

Blackmun, H.A. 1987/1988. Remarks. *Law, Medicine, and Health Care* 14:175–77.

Blakely, S. 2001. Defined contribution health benefits: The next evolution? *EBRI Notes* Vol. 22, No. 8, August 2001.

Blendon, R.J. and Benson, J.M. 2001. Americans' views on health policy: A fifty-year historical perspective. *Health Affairs* 20(2):33–46.

Bloche, M.G. 1999. Clinical loyalties and the social purposes of medicine. *Journal of the American Medical Association* 281: 268–274.

Bloche, M.G. 2000. Fidelity and deceit at the bedside. *Journal of the American Medical Association* 283:1881–1884.

Bloche, M.G. One step ahead of the law: markets and medicine in the 1990s. In M.G. Bloche, ed., *The Privatization of health-care reform.* New York: Oxford University Press (in press).

Bloche, M.G. and P.D. Jacobson. 2000. The Supreme Court and bedside rationing. *Journal of the American Medical Association* 284:2776–2779.

Block, L.E. 1997. Evolution, growth, and status of managed care in the United States. *Public Health Reviews* 25:193–244.

Blum, J.D. 1996. The evolution of physician credentialing into managed care selective contracting. *American Journal of Law and Medicine* 22(2 and 3):173–203.

Blumenthal, D. 1994. The vital role of professionalism in health care reform. *Health Affairs* 13(1):252–256.

Blumstein, J.F. 1984. Court action, agency reaction: The Hill-Burton Act as a case study. *Iowa Law Review* 69:1227–1261.

Blumstein, J.F. 1994. Health care reform and competing visions of medical care: Antitrust and state provider cooperation legislation. *Cornell Law Review* 79:1459–1506.

Bogert, G.T. 1987. *Trusts* (6th ed.). St. Paul, Minn.: West Publishing Company.

Bovbjerg, R.J. 1975. The medical malpractice standard of care: HMOs and customary practice. *Duke Law Journal* 1375:1408–1409.

Brennan, T.A. 1998. The role of regulation in quality improvement. *Milbank Quarterly* 76:709–731.

Brewbaker, W.S. 1997. Medical malpractice and managed care organizations: The implied warranty of quality. *Law and Contemporary Problems* 60:117–157.

Butler, P. 2001. *Key characteristics of state managed care organization liability laws: Current status and experience.* Washington, D.C.: The Henry J. Kaiser Family Foundation.

Calabresi, G. 1982. A *Common law for the age of statutes.* Cambridge, Mass.: Harvard University Press.

Calamari, J.D. and J.M. Perillo. 1990. *Contracts* (2nd ed.). St. Paul, Minn.: West Publishing Company.

Califano, J.A., Jr. 1986. *America's health care revolution: Who lives? Who dies? Who pays?* New York: Random House.

Cantor, C.A. 1997. Fiduciary liability in emerging health care. *DePaul Business Law Journal* 9:189–220.

Cantor, N.F. 1998. *Imagining the law.* New York: New York University Press.

Capron, A.M. 1987. So quick bright things come to confusion. *American Journal of Law and Medicine* 13:169–187.

Capron, A.M. May/June 1990. The burden of decision. *Hastings Center Report* 36–41.

Chase-Lubitz, J.F. 1987. NOTE: The corporate practice of medicine doctrine: An anachronism in the modern health care industry. *Vanderbilt Law Review* 40:445–488.

Chernew, M.E.; and D.P. Scanlon. 1998. Health plan report cards and insurance choice. *Inquiry* 35(1):9–22.

Chirba-Martin, M.A.; and T.A. Brennan. 1994. The critical role of ERISA in state health reform. *Health Affairs* 17:142–156.

Church, G.J. 1997. Backlash against HMOs. *Time* 149(15):32–36.

Cole, H.M. 1989. From the office of the general counsel: A new *JAMA* column. *Journal of the American Medical Association* 262:1513.

Conison, J. 1994. ERISA and the language of preemption. *Washington University Law Quarterly* 72:619–669.

Cooter, R. and B.J. Freedman. 1991. The fiduciary relationship: Its economic character and legal consequences. *New York University Law Review* 66:1045–1075.

Costilo, L.B. 1985. Antitrust enforcement in health care: Ten years after the AMA suit. *New England Journal of Medicine* 313:901–904.

Council on Ethical and Judicial Affairs, American Medical Association. 1995. Ethical issues in managed care. *Journal of the American Medical Association* 273:330–335.

Croley, S.P.; and J.D. Hansen. 1993. Rescuing the revolution: The revived case for enterprise liability. *Michigan Law Review* 91:683–796.

Cruess, R.L., Cruess, S.R., and S.E. Johnston. 1999. Renewing professionalism: An opportunity for medicine. *Academic Medicine* 74:878–884.

Cruess, S.R. and R.L. Cruess. 1997. Professionalism must be taught. *British Medical Journal* 315:1674–1677.

Cunningham, J.F. 1996. ERISA: Some thoughts on unfulfilled promises. *Arkansas Law Review* 49:83–91.

Curran, W.J. 1981. Medical staff privileges in private hospitals: Can modern hospitals exclude uncooperative applicants? *New England Journal of Medicine* 304:589–591.

Curran, W.J., Hall, M.A., Bobinski, M.A. and D. Orentlicher. 1998. *Health care law and ethics* (5th ed.). New York: Aspen, Law and Business.

Curriden, M. 2001. Doctors, lawyers forge an alliance—Trend leads to larger verdicts for patients. *The Dallas Morning News*, August 6:A1.

Daniels N. 1985. *Just health care: Studies in philosophy and health policy.* New York: Cambridge University Press.

Daniels, N. and J.E. Sabin. 1997. Limits to health care: Fair procedures, democratic deliberation, and the legitimacy problem for insurers. *Philosophy and Public Affairs* 26(4):303–350.

Daniels, N. and J.E. Sabin. 1998a. The ethics of accountability in managed care reform. *Health Affairs* Sept/Oct: 50–64.

Daniels, N. and J.E. Sabin. 1998b. Last chance therapies and managed care: Pluralism, fair procedures, and legitimacy. *Hastings Center Report* 28(2):27–41.

Danzon, P.A. 1997. Tort liability: A minefield for managed care? *Journal of Legal Studies* 26:491–519.

Department of Justice and Federal Trade Commission. August, 1996. *Statements of antitrust enforcement policy in health care.* Washington, D.C.

DiBacco, T.V. 1987. *Made in the U.S.A.: The history of American business.* New York: Harper and Row.

Dickens, B.M. 1987. Patients' interests and clients' wishes: Physicians and lawyers in discord. *Law, Medicine, and Health Care* 15:110–117.

Dorros, T.A. and T.H. Stone. 1995. Implications of negligent selection and retention of physicians in an age of ERISA. *American Journal of Law and Medicine* 21:383–418.

Dreyfuss, R. 1998. Which doctor? *The New Republic* 218(25):22–25.

Eddy, D.M. 1996. Benefit language: Criteria that will improve quality while reducing costs. *Journal of the American Medical Association* 275:650–657.

Emanuel, E.J. and N.N. Dubler. 1995. Preserving the physician-patient relationship in the era of managed care. *Journal of the American Medical Association* 273:323–329.

Emanuel, E. and L. Emanuel. 1996. What is accountability in health care? *Annals of Internal Medicine* 124:229–239.

Enthoven, A. and R. Kronick. January 5, 1989. A consumer-choice health plan for the 1990s. Universal health insurance in a system designed to promote quality and economy (1). *New England Journal of Medicine* 320(1):29–37.

Enthoven, A. and R. Kronick. January 12, 1989. A consumer-choice health plan for the 1990s. Universal health insurance in a system designed to promote quality and economy (2). *New England Journal of Medicine* 320(2):94–101.

Epstein, R. 1989. The unintended revolution in product liability law. *Cardozo Law Review* 10:2193–2222.

Epstein, R. 1997. *Mortal peril: Our inalienable right to health care?* New York: Addison-Wesley.

Ferguson, J.H., Dubinsky, M. and P.J. Kirsch. 1993. Court-ordered reimbursement for unproven medical technology. *Journal of the American Medical Association* 269: 2116–2121.

Fisk, C.L. 1996. The last article about the language of ERISA preemption? A case study of the failure of textualism. *Harvard Journal on Legislation* 33:35–103.

Fox, D.M. 1987. Physicians versus lawyers: A conflict of cultures. In *AIDS and the law*. Dalton, H. and Burris, S., eds. New Haven: Yale University Press. 367–376.

France, M. Sept. 18, 2000. (Commentary) The hidden culprit: the U.S. legal system. *Business Week* p. 42.

Friedman, E. 1996. Capitation, integration, and managed care: Lessons from early experiments. *Journal of the American Medical Association* 275(12):957–962.

Friedman, L.M. 1985. *A history of American law* (2d ed.). New York: Simon and Schuster.

Freidson, E. 1986. *Professional powers: A study in the institutionalization of formal knowledge.* Chicago: University of Chicago Press.

Furrow, B.R. 1989. The changing role of the law in promoting quality in health care: From sanctioning outlaws to managing outcomes. *Houston Law Review* 26:147–190.

Furrow, B.R. 1997. Managed care organizations and patient injury: Rethinking liability. *Georgia Law Review* 31:419–509.

Furrow, B.R. 2001. The problem of medical misadventures: A review of E. Haavi Morreim's Holding health care accountable. *Journal of Law, Medicine & Ethics* 29: 381–393.

Gabel, J. 1997. Ten ways HMOs have changed during the 1990s. *Health Affairs* 16(3) 134–145.

Galligan, Jr., T.C. 1995. Contortions along the boundary between contracts and torts. *Tulane Law Review* 69:457–534.

Gibson, J.M. and R.L. Schwartz. 1980. Physicians and lawyers: Science, art, and conflict. *American Journal of Law and Medicine* 6:173–182.

Gilmore, G. 1974. *The death of contract.* Columbus: Ohio State University Press.

Ginsburg, P.B. and C.S. Lesser. 1999. The view from communities. *Journal of Health Politics, Policy and Law* 24: 1005–1013.

Gold, J.A. 1981. Wiser than the laws? The legal accountability of the medical profession. *American Journal of Law and Medicine* 7:145–181.

Goold, S.D. 2000. Conflicts of interest and obligation. In *20 common problems—Ethics in primary care*, J. Sugarman, ed. New York: McGraw-Hill. Chapter 8, pp. 93–102.

Gostin, L.O. 1993. What's wrong with the ERISA vacuum? Employers' freedom to limit health care coverage provided by risk retention plans. *Journal of the American Medical Association* 269:2527–2532.

Gostin, L.O. 2000. *Public health law: Power, duty, restraint.* Berkeley, Calif.: University of California Press.

Greaney, T.L. 1994. Managed competition, integrated delivery systems and antitrust. *Cornell Law Review* 79:1407–1545.

Greaney, T.L. 1997. Night landings on an aircraft carrier: Hospital mergers and antitrust law. *American Journal of Law and Medicine.* 23:191–220.

Hacker, J.S. and T.R. Marmor. 1999. The misleading language of managed care. *Journal of Health Politics, Policy and Law* 24:1033–1043.

Hackney, J.R. 1995. The intellectual origins of American strict products liability: A case study in American pragmatic instrumentalism. *American Journal of Legal History* 39:443–505.

Hadorn, D.C. 1992. Emerging parallels in the American health care and legal-judicial systems. *American Journal of Law and Medicine* 18:73–96.

Hall, M.A. 1988. Institutional control of physician behavior: legal barriers to health care cost containment. *University of Pennsylvania Law Review* 137:431–536.

Hall, M.A. 1989. The malpractice standard under health care cost containment. *Law, Medicine, and Health Care* 17(4):347–355.

Hall, M.A. 1993. Informed consent to rationing decisions. *Millbank Quarterly* 71:645–668.

Hall, M.A. 1997a. A Theory of Economic Informed Consent. *Georgia Law Review* 31:511–586.

Hall, M.A. 1997b. *Making medical spending decisions: The law, ethics, and economics of rationing mechanisms.* New York: Oxford University Press.

Hall, M.A. and G.F. Anderson. 1992. Health insurers' assessment of medical necessity. *University of Pennsylvania Law Review* 140:1637–1712.

Hall, M.A. and R.A. Berenson. 1998. Ethical practice in managed care: A dose of realism. *Annals of Internal Medicine* 128(5):395–401.

Hall, M.A., Smith, T.R., Naughton. M. and A. Ebbers. 1996. Judicial protection of managed care consumers: An empirical study. *Seton Hall Law Review* 26:1055–1069.

Hammer, P.J. 2001. Pegram v. Herdrich: On peritonitis, preemption, and the elusive goal of managed care accountability. *Journal of Health Politics, Policy and Law* 26:767–787.

Havighurst, C.C. 1986a. Changing the locus of decision making in the health care sector. *Journal of Health Politics, Policy, and Law* 11:697–735.

Havighurst, C.C. 1986b. Private reform of tort-law dogma: Market opportunities and legal obstacles. *Law and Contemporary Problems* 49(2):143–172.

Havighurst, C.C. 1995. *Health care choices: Private contracts as instruments of health care reform.* Washington, D.C.: The AEI Press.

Havighurst, C.C. 1997. Making health plans accountable for the quality of care. *Georgia Law Review* 31:587–648.

Havighurst, C.C. 2000a. American health care and the law—We need to talk! *Health Affairs* 19(4):84–106.

Havighurst, C.C. 2000b. Vicarious liability: Relocating responsibility for the quality of medical care. *American Journal of Law and Medicine* 26:7–29.

Havighurst, C.C. 2001. Consumers versus managed care: The new class actions. *Health Affairs* 20(4):8–27.

Havighurst, C.C. 2001b. Health Care as a (Big) Business: The Antitrust Response. *Journal of Health Politics, Policy and Law* 26:939–955.

Havighurst, C.C., Blumstein, J.F. and T.A. Brennan. 1998. *Health care law and policy: Readings, notes, and questions* (2nd ed.). New York: Foundation Press.

Hawke, D.F. 1988. *Nuts and bolts of the past: A history of American technology 1776–1860* New York: Harper and Row.

Hazard, G.C. Jr. 1997. "Practice" in law and other professions. *Arizona Law Review* 39:387–399.

The Health Care Study Group. 1994. Understanding the choices in health care reform. *Journal of Health Politics, Policy and Law* 19:499–541.

Helms, W.D., Gauthier, A.K. and D.M. Campion. 1992. Mending the flaws in the small-group market. *Health Affairs* 11(2):7–27.

Henderson, Jr., J.A.; and T. Eisenberg. 1990. The quiet revolution in products liability: An empirical study of legal change. *UCLA Law Review* 37:479–553.

Henderson, J.A. and J.A. Sciciliano. 1994. Universal health care and the continued reliance on custom in determining medical malpractice. *Cornell Law Review* 79: 1382–1404.

Hensler, D. 1999. Do we need an empirical research agenda on judicial independence? *Southern California Law Review* 72:707–721.

Holmes, O.W. 1881. *The Common Law*. Boston, Mass.: Little, Brown, and Company.

Honson, N. 1996. Note, Iowa tort history, 1839–1869: Subsidization of enterprise or equitable allocation of liability? *Iowa Law Review* 81:811–832.

Horowitz, D.L. 1977. *The courts and social policy*. Washington, DC: Brookings Institution.

Horwitz, M. 1977. *The transformation of American law, 1780–1860*. Cambridge, Mass.: Harvard University Press.

Hunt, J.L. 1988. Note, Private law and public policy: Negligence law and political change in nineteenth-century North Carolina. *North Carolina Law Review* 66:421–442.

Hunt, J.L. 1998. Ensuring the incalculable benefits of railroads: The origins of liability for negligence in Georgia. *Southern California Interdisciplinary Law Journal* 7: 375–425.

Hyman, D.A. 1999a. Accountable managed care: Should we be careful what we wish for? *University of Michigan Journal of Law Reform* 32:785–811.

Hyman, D.A. 1999b. Drive-through deliveries: Is 'consumer protection' just what the doctor ordered? *North Carolina Law Review* 78:5–99.

Hyman, D.A. 2000. Regulating managed care: What's wrong with a patient bill of rights? *Southern California Law Review* 73:221–275.

Jacobi, J.V. and N. Huberfeld. 2001. Quality, control, enterprise liability, and disinter-mediation in managed care. *Journal of Law, Medicine & Ethics* 29:305–322.

Jacobson, P.D. 1989. Medical malpractice and the tort system. *Journal of the American Medical Association* 262: 3320–3327.

Jacobson, P.D. 1991. Medical malpractice in California: Recent trends and future pros-pects. *Journal of Ambulatory Care Management* 14:60–67.

Jacobson, P.D. 1996. Gays in the military: Legal considerations. In *Out in force: Sexual orientation and the military*, G. Herek, J.B. Jobe, R.M. Carney, eds. Chicago: University of Chicago Press.

Jacobson, P.D. 1999. Legal challenges to managed care cost containment programs: An initial assessment. *Health Affairs* 18(4):69–85.

Jacobson, P.D. 2000. The Supreme Court's view of the managed care industry's liability for adverse patient outcomes. *Journal of the American Medical Association* 284(12): 1516 (letter).

Jacobson, P.D., Asch, S., Glassman, P.A., Model, K.E. and J.B. Hernandez. 1997. Defining and implementing medical necessity in Washington State and Oregon. *Inquiry* 34:143–154.

Jacobson, P.D. and M.T. Cahill. 2000. Redefining fiduciary responsibilities in the managed care context. *American Journal of Law and Medicine* 26(2 and 3):155–174.

Jacobson, P.D., Carter, G.L., Kominski, G. and D.L. Bean. 1996. *The operation of business health purchasing coalitions.* The RAND Corporation: Santa Monica, P.M. 554–1-HCFA.

Jacobson, P.D. and M.L. Kanna. 2001. Cost-effectiveness analysis in the courts: Recent trends and future prospects. *Journal of Health Politics, Policy and Law* 26:291–326.

Jacobson, P.D., Parker, L.E. and I.D. Coulter. 1998. Nurse practitioners and physician assistants as primary care providers in institutional settings. *Inquiry* 35:432–446.

Jacobson, P.D. and S.D. Pomfret. 1998. Form, function, and managed care torts: Achieving fairness and equity in ERISA jurisprudence. *Houston Law Review* 35: 985–1078.

Jacobson, P.D. and S.D. Pomfret. 1999. Establishing new legal doctrine in managed care: A model of judicial response to industrial change. *University of Michigan Journal of Law Reform* 32:813–61.

Jacobson, P.D. and S.D. Pomfret. 2000. ERISA litigation and physician autonomy. *Journal of the American Medical Association* 283:921–926.

Jacobson, P.D. and C.J. Rosenquist. 1988. The introduction of low osmolar contrast agents in radiology: Medical, economic, legal and public policy issues. *Journal of the American Medical Association.* 260:1586–1592.

Jacobson, P.D. and C.J. Rosenquist. 1996. The diffusion of low osmolar contrast agents: Technological change and defensive medicine. *Journal of Health Politics, Policy and Law* 21:243–266.

Jacobson, P.D. and E. Selvin. 2002. Health, inequality, and the courts. In L. Brown, L. Jacobs, and J. Morone, eds., *Inequality and the politics of health: How politics makes Americans sick.* Westview Press (in press).

Jacobson, P.D., E. Selvin, and S.D. Pomfret. The role of the courts in shaping health policy: An empirical analysis. *Journal of Law, Medicine, and Ethics* (in press).

Jacobson, P.D. and K.E. Warner. 1999. Litigation and public health policy: The case of tobacco control. *Journal of Health Politics, Policy and Law* 24:769–804.

Jordan, K.A. 1996. Traveler's insurance: New support for the argument to restrain ERISA preemption. *Yale Journal on Regulation* 13:255–336.

Jost, T.S. 1995. Oversight of quality medical care: Regulation, management or the market? *Arizona Law Review* 37:825–868.

Jost, T.S. 1997. Introduction—Regulation of the healthcare professions, in T.S. Jost, ed., *Regulation of the healthcare professions.* Chicago: Health Administration Press.

Kaczorowski, R.J. 1990. The common law background of nineteenth century tort law. *Ohio State Law Journal* 51:1127–1199.

Kakalik, J.S., Dunworth, T., Hill, L., McCaffrey, D., Oshiro. M., Pace, N.M. and M.E. Viana. 1996. *Evaluation of judicial case management under the Civil Justice Reform Act.* Santa Monica, Calif.: RAND.

Kapp, M.B. 1985. Medicine and law: A symbiotic relationship? *American Journal of Medicine* 78:903–907.

Kassirer, J.P. 2001. Financial conflict of interest: An unresolved ethical frontier. *American Journal of Law and Medicine.* 27:149–162.

Kearney, J.D., and T.W. Merrill. 1998. The great transformation of regulated industries law. *Columbia Law Review* 98:1323–1409.

Keeton, W.P., Owen, D.G. and J.E. Montgomery. 1980. *Products liability and safety: Cases and materials.* Mineola, NY: Foundation Press.

Kessler, F. 1943. Contracts of adhesion—Some thoughts about freedom of contract. *Columbia Law Review* 43:629–642.

Kintner, E.W. 1978. *A Primer on the law of deceptive practices: A guide for the businessman* (2d ed.). New York: Macmillan.

Klein, M. 2001. In technology, supply precedes demand. *New York Times,* 2 September, 2001, Sec. 3, p. 4.

Klein, S.A. 1999. Jury punishes Aetna with $120 million verdict. *American Medical News* 42(1):30–31.

Kleinke, J.D. 2001. *Oxymorons: The myth of a U.S. health care system.* San Francisco: Jossey-Bass.

Kluger, R. 1976. *Simple justice: The history of Brown v. Board of Education and black America's struggle for equality.* New York: Knopf.

Komesar, N.K. 1994. *Imperfect alternatives: Choosing institutions in law, economics, and public policy.* Chicago: University of Chicago Press.

Kominski, G.F. and G. Melnick. 2001. Managed care and the growth of competition. In Andersen, Rice, and Kominski (eds.), *Changing the U.S. health care system* (2nd ed.). San Francisco: Jossey-Bass.

Korobkin, R. 1999. The efficiency of managed care "patient protection" laws: Incomplete contracts, bounded rationality, and market failure. *Cornell Law Review* 85:1–88.

Kranzberg, M. 1997. History of the organization of work: Organization of work in the industrial age: The coming of mass production. *Britannica CD, Version 97.* Encyclopedia Britannica, Inc.

Krause, E.A. 1996. *Death of the guilds: Professions, states, and the advance of capitalism, 1930 to the present.* New Haven: Yale University Press.

Krause, M.I. 1999. Restoring the boundary: Tort law and the right to contract. *Cato Institute Policy Report No. 347.*

Kronman, A.T. 1993. *The lost lawyer: Failing ideals of the legal profession.* Cambridge, Mass.: Belknap Press of Harvard University.

Landa, A.S. 2001. Big insurers getting too big, too powerful, AMA study concludes. *Amednews.com* (3 December 2001).

Larson, M.S. 1977. *The rise of professionalism: A sociological analysis.* Berkeley: University of California Press.

Langbein, J.H. and B.A. Wolk. 1995. *Pension and employee benefit law* (2nd ed.). Westbury, NY: Foundation Press.

Leape, L.L. 1994. Error in medicine. *Journal of the American Medical Association* 272: 1851–1857.

Lee, P. and A.E. Benjamin. 1999. Health policy and the politics of health care. In *Introduction to health services*, S.J. Williams and P.R. Torrens, eds., (5th ed.). New York: Delmar Publishers, pp. 439–465.

Legnini, M.W., Rosenberg, L.E., Perry, M.J. and N.J. Robertson. 2000. Where does performance go from here? *Health Affairs* 19(3):173–177.

Lesser, C.S. and P.B. Ginsburg. February 2001. Back to the future? New cost and access challenges emerge: Initial findings from HSC's recent site visits. Center for Studying Health System Change. *Issue Brief No. 35.* Washington, DC.

Lessig, L. 1997. Erie-effects of volume 110: An essay on context in interpretive theory. *Harvard Law Review* 110:1785–1812.

Lessig, L. 2001. Innovation, regulation, and the internet. *The American Prospect* March 27–April 10, 26–29.

Levy, J.K. 1997. Because judges went to law school, not medical school: Restrictive covenants in the practices of law and medicine. *Journal of Health and Hospital Law* 30(2):89–102.

Liang, BA. 1998. Patient injury incentives in law. *Yale Law and Policy Review.* 17:1–93.

Louisell, D.W. and H. Williams. 1960. *The parenchyma of law: A dissection of legal principles affecting the doctor, his practice, and his role as a citizen, witness, or defendant.* Rochester, NY: Professional Medical Publications.

Luft, H.S. 1999. Why are physicians so upset about managed care? *Journal of Health Politics, Policy and Law* 24:957–966.

Mariner, W.K. 1996. Liability for managed care decisions: ERISA and the uneven playing field. *American Journal of Public Health* 86:863–869.

Mariner, W.K. 1998. Standards of care and standard form contracts: Distinguishing patient rights and consumer rights in managed care. *Journal of Contemporary Health Law and Policy* 15:1–55.

Mariner, W.K. 2000. What recourse?—Liability for managed-care decisions and the Employee Retirement Income Security Act. *New England Journal of Medicine* 343: 592–596.

Mariner, W.K. 2001. Slouching toward managed care liability: Reflections on doctrinal boundaries, paradigm shifts, and incremental reform. *Journal of Law, Medicine & Ethics* 29:253–277.

Melnick, R.S. 1983. *Regulation and the courts: The case of the Clean Air Act.* Washington, D.C.: Brookings Institution.

McCann, M.W. 1996. Causal versus constitutive explanations (or, On the difficulty of being so positive). *Law and Social Inquiry* 21:457–482.

McClean, T.R. and E.P. Richards. 2001. Managed care liability for breach of fiduciary duty after Pegram v. Herdrich: The end of ERISA preemption for state law liability for medical care decision making. *Florida Law Review* 53:147.

McLaughlin, C.G. and P.B Ginsburg. 1998. Competition, quality of care, and the role of the consumer. *The Milbank Quarterly* 76:737–743.

McLaughlin, C.G. and W.K. Zellers. 1992. The shortcomings of voluntarism in the small-group insurance market. *Health Affairs* 11(2):28–40.

McLaughlin, C.G., Zellers, W.K. and K.D. Frick. 1994. Small business winners and losers under health care reform. *Health Affairs* 13:221–233.

Mechanic, D. 1998. The functions and limitations of trust in the provision of medical care. *Journal of Health Politics, Policy and Law* 23(4):661–686.

Mehlman, M.J. 1990. Fiduciary contracting: Limitations on bargaining between patients and health care providers. *University of Pittsburgh Law Review* 51:365–417.

Melnick, R.S. 1994. *Between the lines: Interpreting welfare rights.* Washington, D.C.: Brookings Institution.

Meyer, J.A., Silow-Carroll, S., Tillman, I.A. and L.S. Rybowski. 1996. *Employer coalition initiatives in health care purchasing,* Vol. 1. Washington, D.C.: Economic and Social Research Institute.

Miller, R.H. and H.S. Luft. 1994. Managed care plan performance since 1980: A literature analysis. *Journal of the American Medical Association* 271:1512–1519.

Miller, R.H. and H.S. Luft. 1997. Does managed care lead to better or worse quality of care? *Health Affairs* 16(5):7–25.

Miller, T.E. 1997. Managed care regulation. *Journal of the American Medical Association* 278:1102–1109.

Millenson, M.L. 1997. *Demanding medical excellence: Doctors and accountability in the information age.* Chicago: University of Chicago Press.

Mohr, J.C. 1993. *Doctors and the law: Medical jurisprudence in nineteenth-century America.* Baltimore, Md.: The Johns Hopkins University Press.

Mohr, J.C. 2000. American medical malpractice litigation in historical perspective. *Journal of the American Medical Association* 283:1731–1737.

Mooney, R.J. 1995. The new conceptualism in contract law. *Oregon Law Review* 74: 1131–1206.

Morantz-Sanchez, R.M. 1999. Conduct unbecoming a woman: Medicine on trial in turn-of-the-century Brooklyn. New York: Oxford University Press.

Morreim, E.H. 1987. Cost containment and the standard of medical care. *California Law Review* 75:1719–1763.

Morreim, E.H. 1989. Stratified scarcity: Redefining the standard of care. *Law Medicine and Health Care* 17(4):356–367.

Morreim, E.H. 1994a. Redefining quality by reassigning responsibility. *American Journal of Law and Medicine* 20:79–104.

Morreim, E.H. 1994b. Of rescue and responsibility: Learning to live with limits. *Journal of Medicine and Philosophy* 19:455–470.

Morreim, E.H. 1995. Moral justice and legal justice in managed care: The ascent of contributive justice. *Journal of Law, Medicine and Ethics* 23:247–265.

Morreim, E.H. 1997. Medicine meets resource limits: Restructuring the legal standard of care. *University of Pittsburgh Law Review* 59:1–95.

Morreim, E.H. 1998a. Benefits decisions in ERISA plans: Diminishing deference to fiduciaries and an emerging problem for provider-sponsored organizations. *Tennessee Law Review* 65:511–553.

Morreim, E.H. 1998b. Cost containment: Challenging fidelity and justice. *Hastings Center Report* 18(6):20–25.

Morreim, E.H. 2000. Playing doctor: Corporate medical practice and medical malpractice. *University of Michigan Journal of Law Reform* 32:939–1040.

Morreim, E.H. 2001. *Holding health care accountable: Law and the new medical marketplace.* New York: Oxford University Press.

Naitove, B.J. 1982. Medicolegal education and the crisis in interprofessional relations. *Amercan Journal of Law and Medicine* 8:293–320.

Noble A.A. and T.A. Brennan. 2001. Managing Care in the New Era of "Systems-Think": The Implications for Mananged Care Organizational Liability and Patient Safety. *Journal of Law, Medicine & Ethics* 29:290–304.

Oberman, M. 2000. Mothers and doctors' orders: Unmasking the doctor's fiduciary role in maternal-fetal conflicts. *Northwestern Law Review* 94:451–500.

O'Neil, P. 1994. Protecting ERISA health care claimants: Practical assessment of a neglected issue in health care reform. *Ohio State Law Journal* 55:723–780.

Pacey, A. 1983. *The Culture of technology.* Cambridge, Mass.: MIT Press.

Pacey, A. 1990. *Technology in world civilization: A thousand-year history.* Oxford, UK: Basil Blackwell.

Pear, R. February 21, 1998. Clinton orders rights action in health care. *The New York Times,* A7.

Pear, R. 2001. Drive for more mental health coverage fails in congress. *The New York Times,* December 19, 2001, p. A-20.

Peele, P.B., Lave, J.R., Black, J.T., and J.H. Evans III. 2000. Employer-sponsored health insurance: Are employers good agents for their employees? *Milbank Quarterly* 78:5–21.

Peterson, M.A. 1997. Introduction—Health care into the next century. *Journal of Health Politics, Policy and Law* 22:291–313.

Peterson, M.A. and M. Selvin. 1991. Mass justice: The limited and unlimited power of courts. *Law and Contemporary Problems* 54:227–247.

Pittman, L.J. 1994. ERISA's preemption clause and the health care industry: An abdication of law-creating authority. *Florida Law Review* 46:355–442.

Pomfret SD. 1998. Emerging theories of liability for utilization review under ERISA health plans. *Tort and Insurance Law Journal* 34:131–166.

Powe, L.A.S. 2000. *The Warren Court in American politics*. Cambridge, Mass.: Belknap Press of Harvard University Press.

Powers, M. 1992. Efficiency, autonomy, and communal values in health care. *Yale Law and Policy Review* 10:316–61.

Preston, I.L. 1998. Puffery and other "loophole" claims: How the law's "don't ask, don't tell" policy condones fraudulent falsity in advertising. *Journal of Law and Commerce* 18: 49–114.

Priest, A.J.G. 1970. Possible adaptation of public utility concepts in the health care field. *Law and Contemporary Problems* 35:839–848.

Prosser, W.L. 1978. *Handbook of the law of torts* (4th ed.). Minn.: West Publishing Company.

Prosser, W.L. and W.P. Keeton. 1984. *Prosser and Keeton on the law of torts (5th ed.)*. St. Paul, Minn.: West Publishing Company.

Rabin, R. 1981. The historical development of the fault principle: A reinterpretation. *Georgia Law Review* 15:925–961.

Rabin, R.L. 1988. Tort law in transition: Tracing the patterns of sociolegal change. *Valparaiso University Law Review* 23:1–32.

Relman, A.S. 1985. Cost control, doctors' ethics, and patient care. *Issues in Science and Technology* 1(1):103–111.

Resnik, J. 2000. Trial as error, jurisdiction as injury: Transforming the meaning of Article III. *Harvard Law Review* 113:924–1037.

Robinson, J.C. 1999. The future of managed care organization. *Health Affairs* 18(2):7–24.

Robinson, J.C. 1999b. *The corporate practice of medicine*. Berkeley, CA: University of California Press.

Robinson, J.C. 2001. The end of managed care. *Journal of the American Medical Association* 285:2662–2628.

Rodwin, M.A. 1989. Physicians' conflict of interest: The limitations of disclosure. *New England Journal of Medicine* 321:1405–1408.

Rodwin, M.A. 1993. *Medicine, money and morals: Physicians' conflicts of interest*. New York: Oxford University Press.

Rodwin, M.A. 1995. Strains in the fiduciary metaphor: Divided physician loyalties and obligations in a changing health care system. *American Journal of Law and Medicine* 21(2–3):241–57.

Rosenbaum, S., Frankford, D.M., Moore, B. and P. Borzi. 1999. Who should determine when health care is medically necessary? *New England Journal of Medicine* 340: 229–232.

Rosenberg, G.N. 1991. *The hollow hope: Can courts bring about social change?* Chicago: University of Chicago Press.

Rosenberg, G.N. 1995. The real world of constitutional rights: The Supreme Court and the implementation of the abortion decisions. In *Contemplating courts*, ed. L. Epstein. Washington, D.C.: Congressional Quarterly.

Rosenblatt, R.E. 1993. The courts, health care reform, and the reconstruction of American social legislation. *Journal of Health Politics, Policy and Law* 18:439–476.

Rosenblatt, R., Law, S. and S. Rosenbaum. 1997. *Law and the American health care system.* Westbury, N.Y.: The Foundation Press, Inc.

Rossi, J. 1998. The common law "duty to serve" and protection of consumers in an age of competitive retail public utility restructuring. *Vanderbilt Law Review* 51: 1233–1321.

Rubin, P.H. 1999. Treatment decisions: Tort or contract. *Regulation* 22:25–30.

Sage, W.M. 1997a. Judge Posner's RFP: Antitrust law and managed care. *Health Affairs* 16(6):44–61.

Sage, W.M. 1997b. Enterprise liability and the emerging managed health care system. *Law and Contemporary Problems* 60:159–209.

Sage, W.M. 1998. Judicial opinions involving health insurance coverage: Trompe l'oeil or window on the world. *Indiana Law Review* 31:49–73.

Sage, W.M. 1999a. Physicians as advocates. *Houston Law Review* 35:1529–1630.

Sage, W.M. 1999b. Regulating through information: Disclosure laws and American health care. *Columbia Law Review* 99:1701–1829.

Sage, W.M. 2001. The Lawyerization of Medicine. *Journal of Health Politics, Policy and Law* 24:1179–1195.

Sage, W.M., Hastings, K.E. and R.A. Berenson. 1994. Enterprise liability for medical malpractice and health care quality improvement. *American Journal of Law and Medicine* 20(1–2):1–28.

Schneider, C. 1998. *The practice of autonomy: Patients, doctors, and medical decisions.* New York: Oxford University Press.

Schuck, P.H. 1988. The new ideology of tort law. *The Public Interest* 92:93–109.

Schwartz, G.T. 1981. Tort law and the economy in nineteenth-century America: A reinterpretation. *Yale Law Journal* 90:1717–1775.

Schwartz, G.T. 1983. New products, old products, evolving law, retroactive law. *New York University Law Review* 58:796–852.

Schwartz, G.T. 1989. The character of early American tort law. *UCLA Law Review* 36: 641–718.

Schwartz, J.R. and H.C. Horn, Jr. 1999. *Health care alliances and conversions: A handbook for nonprofit trustees.* San Francisco: Jossey-Bass Publishers.

Schwartz, W.B. and N.K. Komesar. 1978. Doctors, damages and deterrence. *New England Journal of Medicine* 298:1282–1289.

Sellers, C. 1991. *The market revolution: Jacksonian America, 1815–1846.* New York: Oxford University Press.

Selznick, P. 1987. The idea of a communitarian morality. *California Law Review* 75: 445–463.

Silver, T. 1992. One hundred years of harmful error: The historical jurisprudence of medical malpractice. *Wisconsin Law Review* 1992:1193–1241.

Skocpol, T. 1996. *Boomerang: Clinton's health security effort and the turn against government in U.S. politics.* New York: W.W. Norton and Company.

Smillie, W.G. 1976. *Public health: Its promise for the future.* New York: Arno Press.

Smith, D.B. 1999. *Health care divided: Race and healing a nation.* Ann Arbor, Mich: University of Michigan Press.

Southwick, A.F. 1988. *The Law of Health Care Administration.* Ann Arbor, Mich: Health Administration Press.

Sox, H.C. March, 1999. Current controversies in screening: Cholesterol, breast cancer, and prostate cancer. *Mount Sinai Journal of Medicine* 66(2):91–101.

Starr, P. 1982. *The social transformation of American medicine*. New York: Basic Books, Inc.

Stevens, R. 1989. *In sickness and in wealth: American hospitals in the twentieth century*. New York: Basic Books.

Stevens, R.A. 2001. Public roles for the medical profession in the United States: Beyond theories of decline and fall. *Milbank Quarterly* 79:327–353.

Stoecker, K.J. 1997. ERISA remedies after *Varity Corp. v. Howe*. *DePaul Business Law Journal* 9:237–258.

Stone, A.A. 1985. Law's influence on medicine and medical ethics. *New England Journal of Medicine* 312:309–312.

Stone, D. Managed care and the second great transformation. *Journal of Health Politics, Policy and Law* 24:1213–1217.

Stryker, L.P. 1932. *Courts and doctors*. New York: The Macmillan Co.

Sunstein, C.R. 1996. Health–health tradeoffs. *The University of Chicago Law Review* 63:1533–1571.

Thompson, D.F. 1993. Understanding financial conflicts of interest. *New England Journal of Medicine* 329:573–576.

Traynor, R.J. 1965. The ways and meanings of defective products and strict liability. *Tennessee Law Review* 32:363–376.

Tushnet, M. 2000. The politics of constitutional law. *Texas Law Review* 79:163–187.

Vladeck, B.C. 1999. Managed care's fifteen minutes of fame. *Journal of Health Politics, Policy and Law* 24: 1208–1211.

Wade, J.W. Fall 1989. Strict product liability: A look at its evolution. *The Brief* 19:8, 53, 56.

Warner, K.E. 1986. *Selling smoke: Cigarette advertising and public health*. Washington, D.C.: American Public Health Association.

Weiler, P.C., Hiatt, H.H., Newhouse, J.P., Johnson, W.G., Brennan, T.A. and L.L. Leape. 1993. *A measure of malpractice*. Cambridge, Mass.: Harvard University Press.

Weinstein, J.B. 1994. Ethical dilemmas in mass tort litigation. *Northwestern University Law Review* 88:470–568.

Weissert, C.S.; and W.G. Weissert. 1996. *Governing health: The politics of health policy*. Baltimore, Md.: Johns Hopkins University Press.

Wicks, E.K. and M.A. Hall. 2000. Purchasing cooperatives for small employers: Performance and prospects. *The Milbank Quarterly* 78: 511–546.

Wilson, J.Q. 1980. *The politics of regulation*. New York: Basic Books.

Winfield, P.H. 1926. The history of negligence in the law of torts. *Law Quarterly Review* 42:184–201.

Wing, K.R. 1999. *The law and the public's health*, 5th ed. Chicago: Health Administration Press.

Woolhandler, S. and D.U. Himmelstein. 1995. Extreme risk—the new corporate proposition for physicians. *New England Journal of Medicine* 333:1706–1708.

Wynia, M.K., Latham, S.R., Kao, A.C., Berg, J.W. and L.L. Emanuel. 1999. Medical professionalism in society. *New England Journal of Medicine* 341:1612–1616.

INDEX